WITNESS TO THE FAITH

RELIGION 8 FOR YOUNG CATHOLICS

SETON PRESS
FRONT ROYAL, VA

Nihil Obstat
Reverend Thomas Haake
Censor Deputatus

Imprimatur
+Most Reverend Robert W. Finn
Bishop of Kansas City-St. Joseph
July 16, 2010

The *Nihil Obstat* and *Imprimatur* are a declaration that a book or pamphlet is considered to be free from doctrinal or moral error. It is not implied that those who granted the *Nihil Obstat* and *Imprimatur* agree with the contents, opinions, o statements expressed therein.

Seton Home Study School
1350 Progress Drive
Front Royal, VA 22630
540-636-9990
540-636-1602 fax

For more information, visit us on the Web at www.setonhome.org.
Contact us by e-mail at info@setonhome.org.

ISBN: 978-1-60704-079-8

Cover: *Christ Gives to Peter the Keys of the Kingdom*

DEDICATED TO THE SACRED HEART OF JESUS

TABLE OF CONTENTS

INTRODUCTION

We have called this book *Witness to the Faith*. A true witness is a person whose life and faith are so completely one that when the challenge comes to stand up and testify for his faith, he does so, disregarding all risks, accepting all consequences. In this book, you will become a witness to the two great faiths of history, faith in God and faith in Man. These are mankind's two oldest faiths. The Catholic is blessed for he has knowledge of the true Faith.

It is a duty of every Catholic to try to learn the history of the Catholic Church. It is through the knowledge of the history of the Catholic Church that you can be a witness for the Faith. Most of us will never be called upon to sacrifice his or her life for the Faith. However, many of us will have the opportunity to defend the Faith by bearing witness to the truths of the Faith. Many of those truths are part of the history of the Church. The enemies of the Church attack her on all sides. They attack her doctrine, her saints, and her history. As Catholics, we must witness to her doctrine, so we study the catechism. Sometimes, we may need to defend those Catholics who have gone before us, so we study the lives of the saints. Finally, we may need to defend the reputation of the Church itself, so we study the history of the Church.

The history of the Catholic Church cannot be told in five hundred pages. The great Catholic historian, Warren Carroll, wrote a six-volume history of Christendom will run to more than four thousand pages when it is completed. In *Witness to the Faith,* there are many great saints whose names are not mentioned. There are many tremendous men and women whose stories are told only briefly. If this book succeeds in arousing your interest in the Church and these great Catholic men and women, we hope that your interest will be expanded by other books to fill in the details that are presented here only in summary.

In this history of the Catholic Church, we will lead you through sunny fields and dark forests. We will visit soaring cathedrals and extraordinary monasteries. We will walk through narrow gorges through which dark things slither into the shadows. We will meet men and women who devoted their lives to defending the Church and other men and women who dedicated their lives to destroying it. In our journey, we will meet also those remarkable men and women who have earned the highest honor, the name of Saint. If we have led you correctly, at the end of the journey you will make out three crosses, from two of which hang thieves. This is the meaning of the journey.

CHAPTER 1

THE EARLY CHURCH

Peter Receives the Keys, by Perugino

Early History of the Jewish People

During His public ministry Jesus Christ, the Founder of the Catholic Church, never left the Holy Land. He announced the glad tidings of salvation first to the people of Galilee, then, to the inhabitants of Judea. Finally, He preached to all those who lived within the area now known as Palestine. His Apostles, chosen by Him to continue the work of preaching the Gospel after His death, confined their initial efforts to the task of converting the Jews, God's chosen people. It was only after the Jews refused to accept their message that St. Paul turned to the Gentiles.

"Palestine" refers to the region between the Mediterranean Sea and the Jordan River. Its geographical position makes it a trading crossroads. Thus all the conquerors of ancient times coveted it. Consequently, its history was a one of constant trouble. The Assyrians, Chaldeans, Egyptians, Persians, Greeks, and Romans all waged wars involving the Jews. The Assyrians and the Chaldeans finally took the Jews into captivity. In 538 B.C., the Persians under Cyrus released them. He permitted them to return to their country and rebuild

Map of Palestine

their Temple. Initially, the rule of the Greeks was as kind as that of the Persians. However, in 164 B.C., the Greeks provoked the Jews by trying to force a number of pagan customs on them. The Jews rebelled under the leadership of the Machabees. Judea won its political independence and the Machabees governed her until the time of the Roman conquest.

The Romans always thought it wise to allow their subjects some freedom. For the Jews, they allowed the existence and authority of the Sanhedrin. The Sanhedrin was the Jewish supreme court of justice. It was presided over by the High Priest and consisted of seventy members from among the priests and the scribes. This was the tribunal that condemned Our Lord to death and delivered Him up to the Romans.

In Palestine at this time there were two important religious groups: the Pharisees and the Sadducees. The Pharisees were very strict in religion and extreme nationalists in politics. They were zealots in defending the Jewish traditions and insisted on the strict observance of

2

the Mosaic Law. They resented all foreign interference in the affairs of Palestine.

On the other hand, the Sadducees were lax in their religious views. They tried to minimize the spirit of Jewish nationalism and favored cooperation with Rome. For the most part they belonged to the more prominent priestly families and aristocracy. They were generally schemers grasping for the office of high priest and the chief functions of the Temple.

The Pharisees hated Jesus because He denounced their insincerity. The Sadducees considered Him an agitator who would arouse the Romans. Thus, the Sanhedrin condemned Him. Pontius Pilate, the Roman governor, at first showed a lack of interest in the matter. However, he yielded to the demands of the angry mob incited by the crafty scribes and Pharisees, and condemned Jesus to death.

Ecce Homo, **by Ciseri**

The Life and Death of Christ

Immediately after the fall of Adam and Eve, God promised to send a Redeemer. The prophets foretold the coming of the Redeemer. The Jews were given certain signs so that they could recognize Him. During His lifetime Christ fulfilled all the prophecies about His early youth, His ministry, and especially His Passion. However, because His kingdom was "not of this world" and because the conditions for entrance into that kingdom differed so greatly from those expected by the Jews, His own refused to accept Him. They condemned Him to death and delivered Him to the Romans to be crucified. Most Jews looked for a worldly Messiah, a Messiah who would restore the earthly kingdom of Israel, free them from the Romans, and make them the rulers of the earth.

During His life, Christ preached penance and the forgiveness of sins. He instituted the Sacraments and explained the necessity of their reception. He taught that entrance into His kingdom depended upon the practice of both the natural and the supernatural virtues.

The Resurrection and Pentecost

The success of the early Church is largely explained by two great events: Christ's Resurrection and the Descent of the Holy Spirit on Pentecost. Of the Resurrection, St. Paul wrote that if Christ had not risen from the dead, then Paul's preaching and the Catholic faith is in vain (I Cor. 15: 13). Truly, Christ's Resurrection is the basis of Catholicism. It is the most significant of all His miracles. It is the one that confirmed the Apostles' belief in Him.

The Descent of the Holy Spirit changed the Apostles from weak and worldly-minded men into strong, spiritual, courageous champions of His doctrine. When the Twelve went forth from the Upper Room, filled with the burning zeal of the Holy Spirit and inspired by the kind words of Our Blessed Mother, they faced the vast crowds gathered in the city. St. Peter, their leader, preached to the crowd. His speech was so moving that three thousand souls embraced Catholicism and asked to be baptized.

The Church Grows

Our Lord had promised His Apostles the power to work miracles in His name. One day Peter and John went to the Temple to pray. At the Temple gate lay a man who had been lame from birth. He was brought there every day to beg for alms. As Peter and John passed, he begged them to have pity on him. Peter stopped, turned to the beggar, and said that he had no silver or gold, but that what he did have he would give. He told the man that in the name of Jesus of Nazareth he should arise and walk. The beggar was cured and, leaping with joy, went with the Apostles into the Temple to praise God. News of this miracle spread throughout the city. Within a few days thousands more had joined the Christian community. People carried their sick into the streets so that Peter's shadow might fall upon them and cure them.

The Resurrection

5

St. Stephen, the First Martyr

As the number of Christians increased, they were bound with a great sense of love for one another. They established a common fund into which everyone donated and from which everyone received what was necessary for daily life. However, some foreign Jews, who were members of the Christian community, complained that they were not receiving their share of supplies from the common fund. To fix this, the Apostles appointed seven deacons. This relieved the Apostles of the worry of caring for the material welfare of the early Church. It allowed them to devote themselves to preaching and spiritual matters.

Among the seven deacons, one was especially notable for his learning and holiness. He was a Greek Jew named Stephen. Being

Martyrdom of St. Stephen

comfortable among the most learned of his countrymen, he labored zealously to convert them. His preaching in the synagogues was eloquent and eventually aroused the anger of the Pharisees. They brought him before the Sanhedrin, where they accused him of blasphemy and of being an enemy of the Temple and the Law. Despite his wonderful defense, the Sanhedrin condemned him to death. Taking him outside the city, they stoned him. His last words were a prayer for his murderers. The official witnesses to the execution laid their garments at the feet of a young man named Saul. Thus did Stephen become the first martyr of the Catholic Church.

The Church Grows Despite Persecution

St. Stephen's death was the signal for a bitter persecution of the followers of Christ. While the Apostles remained in and around Jerusalem for about twelve years or so, the faithful scattered through Judea, Samaria, and Syria. One day an angel appeared to Philip, one of the seven deacons, and told him to go to Samaria. Philip obeyed. On the road he met a man sitting in his chariot reading Isaias the Prophet. The man was the treasurer for the Queen of Ethiopia. Philip approached him and asked him if he understood what he was reading. He answered, "How can I unless some man show me?" He invited Philip to travel with him.

As they traveled, Philip explained Isaias' words and showed the Ethiopian how the prophecies were fulfilled in Christ. When they passed a place where there was some water the Ethiopian said, "See, here is water; what hinders me from being baptized?" Philip said if he believed he could be baptized. The Ethiopian answered, "I believe that Jesus Christ is the Son of God." Then Philip baptized him and the Ethiopian went away with great joy in his heart.

As a result of the many converts that Philip made in Samaria, Peter and John traveled there to administer the sacrament of Confirmation. Among the converts was a man called Simon Magus. When Simon saw the wonderful changes that were made in the converts when they received the Holy Spirit, he sought to buy the Apostles' "power." Peter rebuked him sternly for thinking that money could buy the gifts of God. The word **simony**, which is the sin of buying or selling of spiritual things, had its origin in this episode.

In 42 AD, the persecution was resumed with new vigor. Herod Agrippa, a grandson of Herod the Great, the murderer of the Holy Innocents, became king of Judea. In an attempt to gain popularity among the Jews, he launched a persecution against the Christians. He martyred the Apostle James the Greater. Peter was to be executed but an angel miraculously set him free from prison. Herod Agrippa died in 44 AD. His successor, Agrippa II, ended the persecution for a time.

Peter Brings the Gentiles into the Church

The early Christians, who were converted Jews, continued to follow many customs and practices of the Law of Moses. In the beginning the Church was a sort of Christian synagogue, with membership restricted to Jews. The conversion of Cornelius completely changed this.

Cornelius was a centurion in the Roman army. Although not a Jew, he was a good and decent man. One day an angel appeared to him with the happy news that his prayers and good works had found favor with God. The angel told him that he should send for St. Peter, who was living at Joppa in the house of a tanner. Cornelius promptly sent three messengers to the Apostle.

St. Peter also had a vision. He saw a great linen sheet coming down from heaven to earth. On the sheet were all kinds of animals, creeping things, and birds. A Voice told him to "kill and eat." Peter refused, saying that he never ate anything that was "common and unclean." The Voice spoke to him again telling him that he should not call common what God had cleansed. This happened three times, and then the vision was over. Peter was very puzzled and wondered what the vision meant. While he was thinking about it, he received word that Cornelius' men were at the door asking for him. Again St. Peter heard a heavenly Voice, "Behold, three men seek thee. Arise, therefore, get thee down, and go with them, doubting nothing, for I have sent them." Peter went down and Cornelius' servants gave him their master's message.

The following day they all left for Caesarea. When they arrived, they found Cornelius waiting for them, together with his kinsmen and close friends. Cornelius explained how he had been instructed by an angel to send for Peter. St. Peter told the centurion that it was God's will that he receive the Gentiles into the Church. As Peter was speaking the Holy Spirit came upon Cornelius and his family. Then Peter baptized Cornelius, his friends, and family.

THE CHURCH AMONG THE GENTILES

The Conversion of St. Paul

At Tarsus (in modern day Turkey) a Jewish family had a baby boy whom they named Saul. When he was a young man Saul went to Jerusalem to study the Jewish Law. By trade he was a tentmaker, and even during his missionary activities he supported himself by this craft. His ambition, however, was to become an expert in the Law of Moses.

Tradition tells us that Saul was small in stature and not blessed with the best of health. In spite of this, he had tremendous energy, possessed great mental powers, and had a zealous nature. He had taken part in the martyrdom of St. Stephen. Saul had listened to St. Stephen's preaching but being a loyal Pharisee and zealous to preserve the religion of his fathers, it is not surprising that he came to hate all that Stephen represented. Thus, he decided to destroy the Christian "sect."

When the Christians fled from Jerusalem after Stephen's death, Saul decided that they should be pursued. He obtained a commission to go to Damascus to arrest any Christians he could find there and return them to Jerusalem. On the road to Damascus, a flash of light knocked him from his horse. As he lay on the ground, Christ Himself appeared to him. Our Savior's reproach, "Saul, Saul,

The Conversion of St. Paul

why dost thou persecute Me," effected the most complete change ever wrought in any person. He answered, "Who art thou, Lord." The Voice replied, "I am Jesus whom thou dost persecute." Trembling and astonished, Saul asked, "Lord, what wilt Thou have me do?" The Voice answered, "Arise and go into the city, and there it shall be told thee what thou must do." When Saul arose from the ground, he discovered that he was blind.

His companions led him into Damascus, where he remained for three days. In Damascus there was a disciple named Ananias whom the Lord told to go seek Saul. Ananias went to the house where Saul was lodged. He told Saul that Our Lord had sent him to restore Saul's sight and fill him with the Holy Spirit. Immediately Saul's sight was restored. Saul arose and asked Ananias to baptize him. The talent and the energy that had been devoted to the persecution of the Christians were now dedicated to the cause of Jesus Christ.

For a while, the future Apostle of the Gentiles preached in the synagogue of Damascus. However, he soon went to Arabia. It was in this solitude that Christ prepared St. Paul for his great mission. Shortly after returning to Damascus, he left the city to escape the persecution of the Jews. He then visited Jerusalem, where Barnabas introduced him to the Christians, many of whom had been distrustful of him. Upon his return to Tarsus he preached the Gospel in Cilicia and Syria. Around the year 42 or 43, Barnabas called him to Antioch to assist in the conversion of the Gentiles.

When the Christians scattered during the persecution of Herod Agrippa, several of them went to Antioch. There, they succeeded in bringing a number of Gentiles into the Church. The community grew so large that Barnabas was sent from Jerusalem to

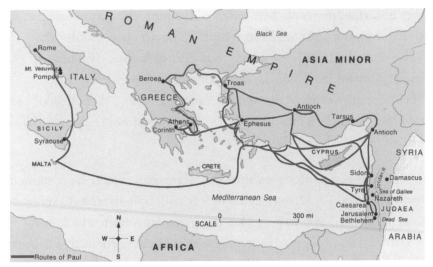

St. Paul's Missionary Journeys

assist in the work. Before long Barnabas felt unable to cope with the situation and asked his friend Paul to come to help him. It was at Antioch that the followers of Jesus were first called Christians. The name "Christian" was given to Christ's followers by the pagans in order to distinguish them from the Jews.

St. Paul's First Missionary Journey

After Herod Agrippa's death, the Church experienced a period of peace. With Antioch as their base, Paul and Barnabas undertook their first great missionary campaign that lasted from about 45 to 49 AD. Departing Antioch, they first preached on the island of Cyprus. Then they passed into Asia Minor (modern Turkey). They made their way to Iconium and to Lystra, where Paul was stoned, dragged outside the town, and left for dead. However, he quickly recovered. After a long stay in various other cities of Asia Minor, Paul returned to Antioch where he resolved to turn from his fellow Jews to the Gentiles. The Jews who resisted St. Paul's efforts became his bitter enemies. They were the cause of the major portion of the trouble he encountered on his journeys.

When the Jewish-Christians of Jerusalem learned of the great influx of Gentiles into the Church through the efforts of Paul and Barnabas, they grew concerned. These Jewish Christians felt that converts should follow the Mosaic rituals and the Jewish law. Paul and Barnabas argued with them. The argument became so heated that the parties agreed to go to Jerusalem and place the question before the Apostles. The heads of the Church convened, with Peter, James the Less, and John taking the primary places. At this first council of the Church, Peter agreed with Paul and Barnabas that the Christians should be freed from the ritual and ceremonial obligations of the Jewish law.

St. Paul's Second Missionary Journey

Following the Council of Jerusalem, Paul left Antioch, in the summer of the year 50, on a second missionary journey. He revisited the countries where he had preached on his first journey. At Lystra he found a reliable helper in the person of Timothy. Paul planned to preach in Asia Minor but the "Spirit of Jesus" directed him to change his course and enter Europe.

Upon Paul's arrival in Troas, St. Luke, who was to become his biographer and constant companion, joined him. Paul had a vision instructing him to travel to Macedonia. So he set sail from Troas. He landed in Macedonia and journeyed to Philippi, Macedonia's main city. He preached at Philippi, but as the result of a riot, he and his companions were scourged and imprisoned. The next day the city's judges, who were very disturbed when they learned that they had scourged Roman citizens, released them. Next, Paul and his companions traveled to Thessalonica,

St. Paul preaches in Athens

where they converted a large number. However, an uprising took place here as well, and they fled to Berea.

Still harassed by the Jews, Paul left his companions at Berea, and fled, first to the coast, and then by sea to Greece. At Athens he delivered his famous speech before the Areopagus, the Great Council of the city. The wise and learned men of Athens listened with skeptical smiles. "Ye men of Athens," he began, "I perceive that in all things you are religious men. For passing by and seeing your idols, I found an altar also, on which was written: To the unknown God. What therefore you worship, without knowing it, that I preach to you." Then he explained the doctrines of Catholicism. Sadly, only a few Athenians converted.

During the autumn of 51 AD, Paul moved on to Corinth. His three companions met him and they founded a small community. They remained there until 53 AD. During this time he stayed at the home of a Jewish couple named Aquila and Priscilla. Like Paul himself, they were tentmakers, and in their humble home he wrote his two letters to the Thessalonians. Angered at Paul's success, the Jews again seized him. They dragged him before the proconsul Gallio, but he refused to hear to their complaints. In the spring of 53, St. Paul left Corinth, accompanied by Aquila and Priscilla.

After a short stay at Ephesus, Paul returned to Jerusalem to fulfill a vow he had made. His second missionary journey is marked by notable results. From the communities in Macedonia and in Greece the new Faith soon spread to the farthest limits of the pagan world.

St. Paul's Third Missionary Journey

After a brief stay at Antioch, St. Paul set out on his third missionary journey. His main purpose was to strengthen and consolidate his previous gains, rather than to make new conversions. In the spring of 54, he arrived at Ephesus where he remained until the autumn of 56 AD. In Ephesus he wrote his First Epistle to the Corinthians. Ephesus was the home of the pagan temple of Diana and a pilgrimage site for pagans from all over the ancient world. The silversmiths in Ephesus made a great amount of money from the sale of idols, particularly miniature images of the goddess Diana and her temple. With the spread of Christianity, the silversmiths saw a decrease in business. They rioted and created such disorder throughout the city that St. Paul had to leave.

Early in 57, St. Paul revisited Europe. He went first to Macedonia, where he wrote his Second Epistle to the Corinthians. From there he went on to Corinth, to judge for himself the effects of his letter. At Corinth he also wrote his great Epistle to the Romans. This letter was meant principally to pave the way for a visit to the city of Rome. Paul had contemplated this visit for a long time, but before going to Rome, he wished to deliver the money he had collected for the poor in Jerusalem.

Paul arrived in Jerusalem around Pentecost of the year 58 AD. A few days later he was threatened with death. The Roman tribune Lysias rescued him, but in an attempt to force a confession of guilt, ordered him to be scourged. Lysias then sent Paul in chains to Caesarea, where the Jews made various accusations against him before Felix, the governor of Judea. Felix found no cause for condemning Paul, but kept him a prisoner for two years hoping that Paul or his friends would purchase his freedom with a bribe.

In the year 60, Festus succeeded Felix as governor. Paul decided to appeal to Caesar, and Festus agreed to send Paul to Caesar. Foiled in their plans to injure Paul, the Jews took revenge against James the Less, the Bishop of Jerusalem. The high priest Ananias summoned James before the Sanhedrin who sentenced him to death.

The Work of Other Apostles

The other Apostles also obeyed Our Lord's charge and carried the Gospel to distant pagan lands. St. John the Apostle was Bishop of Ephesus. He was the only Apostle to escape martyrdom, although he was thrown into a cauldron of boiling oil but miraculously escaped. During the persecution of the Emperor Domitian, the Romans banished St. John to the Island of Patmos. There he wrote the Book of the Apocalypse, or the Book of Revelations. He also wrote the fourth Gospel and three Epistles. He died at Ephesus around 100 AD.

St. James the Less remained at Jerusalem, where he was bishop. A very devout man, he practiced great penances. He wrote an

St. John miraculously escaped martyrdom

Epistle to the Jewish Christians who were in his charge. Shortly after St. Paul left in chains for Rome, St. James suffered martyrdom.

St. Matthew first preached to the Jews and wrote his Gospel for them in their language. Then he went abroad to preach to the Gentiles in Persia and Parthia (modern-day Iran). Tradition holds

17

that he suffered martyrdom in Ethiopia. St. Thomas is known as the Apostle of India. He was martyred in India and buried in Edessa. St. Jude, the brother of St. James the Less, wrote an Epistle to the Jewish converts in Palestine. St. Jude was sent by St. Thomas to the King of Edessa and was martyred in Beirut.

Tradition says that St. Andrew was crucified on an X-shaped cross in Scythia. St. Bartholomew was flayed alive in Armenia. St. Simon was likely martyred in Babylon. St. Philip preached in Samaria and was martyred in Hieropolis. The Evangelist St. Mark accompanied St. Paul on one of his journeys, but afterwards remained with St. Peter, from whom he learned the facts that he recorded in his Gospel. He established the Church of Alexandria in Egypt. St. Luke wrote a Gospel and the Acts of the Apostles. He was the faithful friend and companion of St. Paul. After St. Paul's death, he labored in Greece. We shall study more about the deaths of St. Peter and St. Paul in the next chapter.

Review Exercises

1. What events explain the early Church's success?
2. Who was St. Philip the Deacon?
3. What did he do?
4. What is simony?
5. Briefly explain how the Gentiles were received into the Church.
6. Where was the first Church council held?
7. What dispute was settled at the Council?
8. Briefly describe St. Paul's activities in Athens.
9. Describe the conditions in Ephesus when Paul arrived.
10. Which Apostle was not martyred?

CHAPTER 2

THE CHURCH IS PERSECUTED BY THE ROMANS

The Crucifixion of St. Peter

The hostility of the Jews to the early Christians was minor compared to the violent hostility of the mighty Roman Empire. The Roman persecutions began in 64 AD, and lasted off and on for more than 250 years. Under some of the emperors the persecutions were widespread and very brutal. Under others, the persecution was local. The degree of its cruelty depended upon the attitude of the provincial governor or some local official. There were also times when the Church openly thrived.

Why was it that this great Empire, the mightiest the world has ever seen, feared the power of Jesus Christ and hated His followers? The answer is found in the words of our Savior, "My Kingdom is not of this world." We are not made for this world and have not here "a lasting dwelling-place." We are strangers, pilgrims on our way home. While we must render to Caesar the things that are Caesar's, we belong first of all to God, and must not give to Caesar the things that are God's. The Kingdom of God is the Catholic Church.

The Romans were not interested in any life after death. They put all their trust in this life and sought for happiness in worldly power, possessions, and pleasures. They depended on the State, in the person of the Emperor, to obtain for them the fullest measure of all these things. They recognized no authority above the State, and no power above the Emperor. For them the State was divine, and they worshipped the Emperor as a god.

The Church taught its members to obey the State as long as its laws did not go against the Law of God. They did not believe as the pagans did, that the State could do no wrong. The State was to be respected, and its laws obeyed but only so long as they did not interfere with the right of the citizen to do what was necessary to save his soul. As a consequence, the Romans could not see how Christians could be good citizens. They regarded Christians as traitors to the Empire. The Romans claimed to be tolerant of all religions. However, they were only tolerant if these religions did not interfere with loyalty to the State. They mocked the claim of the Christians that the religion of Christ was the only true religion, and that all others were false.

The Martyrdoms of Saints Peter and Paul

The Christian community at Rome began to attract the attention of the Roman authorities as early as the year 64 AD. In the beginning the Christians were simply regarded as Jews. However, before long even the casual observer could notice a difference.

The Romans had always given the Jews a hard time. Therefore, the Jews welcomed the chance to transfer some of the charges made against them to the Christians. Soon the Christians were accused of the most atrocious and shameful crimes. Thus popular prejudice was created against them.

In 64, an incident occurred which Emperor Nero resolved to exploit. On July 18, some storehouses in Rome near the Circus Maximus caught fire. The flames spread rapidly to the center of the city. For six days the fire raged, destroying much of Rome. Suddenly, the rumor circulated that Nero himself started the fire. To divert suspicion he blamed the Christians. Several were arrested for arson. Then, in an effort to quiet the people, new arrests were made to supply the rabble with victims and public games. Christians were branded as "enemies of the human race" and were accused of practicing magic and perpetrating the most abominable crimes.

Both the pagan historian Tacitus and Pope St. Clement have preserved for us the horrible details of Nero's persecution. The death toll was very high, although no other names have come down to us but those of St. Peter and St. Paul. When the persecution broke out, St. Paul was arrested and imprisoned in Rome. St. Paul had already foreseen the end of his career and his life. In a letter to his "beloved son" Timothy, he wrote: "The time of my dissolution is at hand. I have fought a good fight, I have finished my course, I have kept the faith." (II Tim. 4:6-7). Being a Roman citizen, Paul was beheaded. He was buried on the Ostian Way. Outside the walls of the city of Rome in a beautiful basilica erected by the Emperor Constantine on the Ostian Way the body of St. Paul, the Apostle of the Gentiles, awaits the final resurrection.

St. Peter was martyred on the Vatican Hill. He was crucified upside down because he considered himself unworthy to die the same way as Our Lord. Today in Rome inside St. Peter's Basilica, a pilgrim may visit the tomb of the Galilean fisherman whom Christ made the head of His Church, the first pope and Bishop of Rome.

The Basilica of St. Paul Outside the Walls in Rome

The Church Grows Despite Persecutions

Nero's persecution ended with that tyrant's death in 68 AD. During the reign of his two successors, Vespasian (69–79 AD) and Titus (79-81 AD), the Catholics were not disturbed. In 66 AD, the Jews at Jerusalem rebelled against Rome. A Roman army besieged the city. Vespasian was called to Rome to become emperor, but his son, Titus, continued the siege. Finally the Jews were unable to defend the city.

When the Roman army marched into the city in 70 AD, it massacred the people, destroyed the Temple, and razed the city to the ground. When Jerusalem fell, the Jewish Christians at last realized that the old religion was truly at an end. It had served its purpose. Through the ages it had kept alive the knowledge of the one true God, and had prepared men for the coming of the Messiah. Now its work was finished.

Following the death of Titus, his brother Domitian (81–96 AD) became emperor. He re-issued Nero's harsh edicts against the Christians. Following Domitian's assassination, the Roman Senate named Marcus Nerva (96-98) emperor. Pope Clement was martyred during the reign of Marcus Nerva.

In 97, Pope Evaristus (97-105) succeeded Clement and guided the infant Church for eight years. St. John the Apostle still lived. The Faith spread rapidly. Just as her Divine Master had predicted, the Rock of Peter stood firm, even when angry waves were crashing hard against her. According to tradition, the first twenty-four popes form an unbroken line of martyrs.

The next great persecution occurred under the Emperor Trajan (98-117). The most well known martyr to die during the reign of Trajan was St. Ignatius of Antioch. St. Ignatius was the bishop of Antioch for nearly fifty years. St. Ignatius was a very old man when he was arrested and taken to Rome for execution. As he journeyed towards Rome, he worried that the Catholics in Rome, because of his age, would plead with the Roman authorities to try to save him. However, he longed to shed his blood for Christ. In the Roman Colosseum, the holy bishop obtained his wish. He was martyred by beind devoured by lions.

During the reign of Emperor Antoninus Pius (138-161) another great saint suffered martyrdom. In 155, at certain public festivals, the cry was suddenly heard: "Death to the atheists! Arrest Polycarp!" St. Polycarp was the bishop of Smyrna. For almost thirty years he had been the disciple and companion of the Apostle St. John. The mob dragged him before the proconsul, but he refused to insult God. "Eighty and six years I have served Him," he said, "and He never did me anything but good." The proconsul condemned him to be burned at the stake. As his murderers were about to fasten his hands to the stake by spikes, he begged them merely to tie him. The frail old bishop declared that God would give him strength to remain unmoved in the middle of the flames. The fire burned slowly and true to his word St. Polycarp remained unmoving. To end his suffering, one of the soldiers killed Polycarp with a sword thrust.

The next great persecutor was Marcus Aurelius (161-180). He is often referred to as the "philosopher on the throne." He wrote a small book about philosophy called *Meditations*. Marcus Aurelius professed the philosophy of the Stoics, who prided themselves on their learning. His writings contain many noble ideas that show that he was a deep thinker. Yet, he had nothing but contempt for Christianity because it was a religion that admired suffering and humility. He admired strength and power. He issued a decree ordering that persons of noble birth who became Christians were to be banished. Those of lower birth were threatened with death.

In 177, during the preparations for a public festival at Lyons, the people suddenly began to vent their anger against the Christians. Several Christians were arrested. Many more were hunted down and driven from their homes. Frightened by the awful tortures inflicted on their companions, some Christians weakened and denied their faith. Others lied and confessed that they had been guilty of horrible crimes.

The judges who tried these Christians felt that, since they had admitted their guilt, the whole sect should be persecuted as the enemies of society. The Christians, led by their ninety-year-old bishop, St. Pothinus, displayed heroic courage. The Roman officials and the mob brutally mistreated the saintly bishop who died after two days in jail. Many Christians who had apostatized returned to the Faith. St. Blandina, a young slave girl, showed remarkable courage. She was the last to suffer martyrdom when she was thrown to wild animals.

In the part of Rome called Trastevere, a beautiful church rises over the tomb of a noble Roman lady who suffered martyrdom under Marcus Aurelius. Her name was Cecilia. She was forced to keep the fact that she was a Christian a secret even from her own family. When her parents arranged a marriage for her to a young Roman noble named Valerian, she told him her secret. At his request she took him to the pope. As a result Valerian became a Catholic. Somehow the Romans discovered she was a Christian and condemned her to be suffocated by steam in her bathroom. However, she was miraculously preserved. Then they killed her with a sword. She is the patroness of church music and is usually pictured with a musical instrument in her hands.

Emperor Septimius Severus (193-211) was at first favorably disposed toward the Christians. However, as their numbers grew, he became alarmed for the state religion and the safety of the Empire which he felt was closely connected with that religion. As we have seen, all "good" Romans believed that they owed the gods for the founding of their Empire and its prosperity. They felt that the gods would continue to favor them only if the pagan religion remained the state religion. Consequently, people who showed disdain for the state religion were regarded not only as nonbelievers, but also as disloyal and dangerous to the Empire.

The Basilica of St. Cecilia

In an attempt to prevent the spread of the Christian religion, the new Emperor began by prohibiting all conversions to the faith. He prohibited Baptism, hoping to put an end to Christianity. It was forbidden to become a Christian or to induce others to become a Christian. New converts were to be hunted down everywhere. This explains why the majority of the martyrs of this period were **neophytes** or catechumens.

This persecution was worst in Egypt and in Africa. St. Perpetua, St. Felicitas, and their companions suffered martyrdom at Carthage, in North Africa. While in prison, St. Perpetua, a young wife and mother, wrote the story of her suffering from the time of her arrest to the time of her martyrdom. Others completed the story of her death. This little band of Christians was first scourged and then thrown to wild animals. St. Perpetua and St. Felicitas are both honored in the canon of the Mass.

During the reign of Maximinus Thrax (235-238), in some parts of the Empire the persecution was very severe, in other parts it was rather mild. This brutal soldier became emperor by having his predecessor assassinated. Then he had himself proclaimed emperor by the army. Although he understood very little about Christianity, as a soldier he knew that the best way to weaken an army was to kill its leaders, so he felt that the surest way to weaken the Church, and perhaps destroy it, would be to kill its leaders. Therefore, at first, he commanded that only the Church leaders be killed. He ordered Pope Pontian (230-235) to be banished to Sardinia. He executed Pontian's successor, Pope Anterus (235-236), because the pope collected the **acts of the martyrs** from the court records and hid them in his church. This monster's reign ended in a scene of bloodshed like the one that began it. One day as he slept in his tent his guards rushed in and killed him.

While Septimius Severus and Maximinus tried to prevent the spread of Christianity, Emperor Decius (249-251) set out to get rid of it. His first step was a general persecution of Christians as a measure of "public safety." Commissions were established in every city to question everyone. All were given the choice of either denying the Faith or being killed. Each person had to prove that he was not a Christian or that he no longer intended to remain one. Decius' purpose was not really to kill the Christians. There were so many that killing them all would have financially ruined the Empire. He wanted them to apostatize and practice the Roman religion. So much pressure was brought to bear that many lapsed into paganism, especially among the rich. Among those martyred were Pope St. Fabian (236-250) in Rome and St. Denis of Paris.

After the persecution ended, the apostates, like prodigal sons, wished to come back into the Church. This caused a great controversy. A Roman priest named Novatian said that the sin of apostasy could not be forgiven. Pope St. Cornelius (251-253) condemned this idea. The Church received the apostates back, although they received severe punishments and many of them had to do penance for the rest of their lives.

After a pause of seven years, Emperor Valerian (253-260) resumed the persecutions. The new emperor saw the futility of trying to destroy the Faith by forcing its members into apostasy. Therefore he decided to kill the Church by attacking its very foundations as a society. Accordingly in 257, he issued an edict directed against the heads of the Christian communities, the bishops and priests. They were given the choice of apostasy or exile. He forbade the Christians under pain of death to pray at the cemeteries or places of worship banned by the government.

In 258, Valerian issued a second edict, more severe than the first. He replaced exile with the death penalty. Among the numerous victims of this persecution were Pope St. Stephen I (254-257) and Pope St. Sixtus II (257-258). Also martyred were the deacon St. Lawrence and St. Cyprian of Carthage. The Romans arrested Pope Sixtus II during Mass. They led him away to behead him along with six of his deacons. A seventh deacon, Lawrence, was reserved for greater sufferings than those of his master. Although they arrested Lawrence, they did not kill him immediately because he was known to be in charge of the Church's treasury. The Romans hoped that they could force him to tell them where the Church's money was so that they could steal it.

When St. Lawrence was ordered to deliver up the treasures of the Church, he asked for three days in which to collect them. On the appointed day he presented to the authorities a large crowd of poor people, whom he declared to be the real riches of the Church. Enraged, the authorities ordered St. Lawrence to be tortured and killed. Soldiers threw him on an iron grating and cooked him. In the midst of his sufferings he told his tormentors: "I am roasted enough on this side; turn me over."

The Martyrdom of St. Lawrence

Valerian's persecution came to an abrupt end when the Persians captured him and made him a slave. His son Gallienus (260-268) ended the persecution.

Persecution under Diocletian

In 284, a soldier named Diocletian became emperor. He was a man with a strong will. He was determined to reform the government and to bring back the glory of the past. Almost immediately, he realized that the task of ruling the Empire was becoming too difficult for one man, especially as new enemies, the Germans, were beginning to threaten its western boundaries. Thus

he chose Maximian, who had been his friend in the army, to help
him. He gave Maximian the title of "Augustus" and the rule of the
western provinces. When the Persians threatened in the East, he
appointed two "Caesars" to act as assistants. One was his son-in-
law Galerius, who acted as his representative in the East. The other
Caesar was Constantius Chlorus who aided Maximian in the West.

Diocletian lived in Nicomedia (in Asia Minor) in the
East. He made Nicomedia his capital and took Asia Minor as his
share of the Empire. Maximian ruled from Milan. He moved
the government from Rome to Milan and governed Italy, Spain,
and the province of Africa. Thus the city of Rome ceased to be
the administrative center of the Empire. Galerius ruled from
Sirmium (in modern Serbia) and ruled the Balkan Peninsula and
the Danubian provinces. Constantius Chlorus ruled from Trier (in
modern Germany). He ruled over Gaul and Britain.

Despite the fact that two of the rulers had the title of "Augustus"
and the other two had that of "Caesar," each one of them did what they
wanted in the parts that they ruled. Thus there were persecutions in
the East, while Rome and Gaul in the West enjoyed a period of peace.
However, even the Christians in the West must have felt uneasy when
the religious policy of the government was so changeable.

The main job that Galerius had was to protect the borders
of the Empire. To do this he needed a strong and dedicated military.
He believed he could make the military stronger by compelling all
his soldiers to attend the official pagan worship services. Bravely,
the Christian soldiers refused to comply with this order. It was
the beginning of a new persecution. Almost all the reports of the
martyrdom of Christian soldiers date to this period. Among the martyrs
of this time are St. Maurice and the Theban Legion. Also martyred was

St. Sebastian, a high-ranking member of the elite Praetorian Guard, who was shot to death with arrows. St. George, St. Theodore of Amasea, and St. Menas were also martyred during this period. Enraged by the resistance he encountered from the Christians in the army, Galerius urged Diocletian to issue a general edict of persecution. Diocletian agreed.

In 303, Diocletian issued an edict against the Christians. He ordered the destruction of all Christian sacred books and places of worship. Christians were commanded to renounce their faith publicly under pain of the loss of civil rights for the nobility and of slavery for the common people. An unbloody persecution of this kind failed to satisfy Galerius. When two fires erupted in the imperial palace, he blamed the Christians for the blaze. The result was a local persecution in Nicomedia. There, the Christians were burned to death in their cathedral. About this same time people rioted in Syria and Armenia. Once again the Christians were blamed.

Diocletian then issued a second edict commanding that all the clergy be imprisoned. Almost immediately he issued a third edict giving them the option of sacrificing to the gods or being tortured. Finally, a fourth edict appeared, pronouncing the death penalty against any Catholic who refused to sacrifice to the gods. Diocletian's persecution was perhaps the bloodiest of all those inflicted upon the Church. The prisons overflowed and every means was used to track down Catholics. Statues were erected in public places, and everyone was required to worship them. Thousands of Catholics sealed their fate with their blood. The most outstanding martyrs of this time were Saints Cosmas and Damian, Felix, Lucy, Catherine of Alexandria, and Margaret.

In 305, at Galerius' urging, Diocletian and Maximian resigned. The two Caesars at once assumed the title of Augustus.

Galerius ruled in the East and Constantius Chlorus ruled in the West. Galerius was still determined to kill all the Christians he could. In order to put his plan into action he chose a man he believed he could trust to carry out his plans. This man was his nephew, Maximinus Daia. Galerius appointed him governor of Egypt and Syria.

An edict issued in 306 resulted in a persecution as systematic as that of Emperor Decius. In every city the head of each family was summoned and given the choice of sacrificing to the gods or being condemned to death. The Catholics remained firm in their Faith. As a result, the prisons were filled to overflowing. No room was left for fresh chain gangs in the mines. At the quarries and mines throughout the Empire, long trains of Christians arrived every day. They were subjected to every kind of hardship and abuse.

However, the persecutor was the first to tire of it all. Stricken with a dreadful and protracted disease, Galerius sought to obtain a cure from the God of the Christians. In 311, he issued a decree in which he granted them the right to hold meetings, provided they did not disturb the public peace.

Galerius finally died and Maximinus Daia succeeded him as master of the East. He resumed the persecution of Christians, but used different methods. He realized that the entire strength of a religion depended upon the quality of its priesthood. Therefore he applied all his efforts against the bishops and priests. At the same time he tried to instill new life into official pagan worship by reorganizing its administration, modeling his changes upon the Catholic hierarchy. At the head of the local pagan priests he put a provincial high priest. He also started a campaign of lies about Our

Lord. These lies were taught to the children in the schools and made the topic of public debate.

The persecutions finally slowed. A disastrous military expedition in Armenia diverted Daia's attention from the persecution. In the meantime Constantius Chlorus died. The West came to be ruled by the man who would become the great protector of the Catholic Faith: Emperor Constantine.

The Catacombs

Often, especially at Rome, the bodies of the martyrs were buried in catacombs. These consisted of long, narrow underground passages, intersecting one another, with spaces hollowed out in the sidewalls. The bodies were placed in these recesses, which were then sealed with a marble slab or a thin partition of masonry. Some of the passages led into small rooms or opened upon large crypts. At times there were as many as five passages or galleries one above another and connected by staircases. The uppermost gallery usually was located about twenty feet below the ground. The lowest was at a depth of eighty feet.

The earliest and most famous catacomb is the Cemetery of St. Callistus. The Christian community in Rome acquired it during the reign of Septimius Severus. Many inscriptions in the catacombs help to identify a martyr or others buried there. In addition to the inscriptions that are carved on the tombs, much can be learned about the Faith of the early Christians from the paintings on the catacomb walls. The early Christians believed all the truths that the Catholic Church teaches today. They believed in the Divinity of Jesus Christ and the Divine Institution of the Papacy. They believed in the Real Presence in the Eucharist and the existence of Purgatory. They also recognized Mary's special role as the Mother of God. They realized the power and value of the intercession of the saints and the value of prayers for the dead. The hopes of the early Christians were also the same as our own: forgiveness of sins, resurrection of the body, and eternal life.

Paintings and drawings of Our Lord in the catacombs most often depict Him as the Good Shepherd. He is shown carrying the lost sheep on His shoulders. In the days of so many martyrs it is not surprising that the early Christians painted many images that dealt with death and the resurrection. Pictures showing scenes from the Bible were also very popular. There are many of the drawing of Noe and the Ark, Jonas and the whale, Daniel in the lions' den, and the raising of Lazarus.

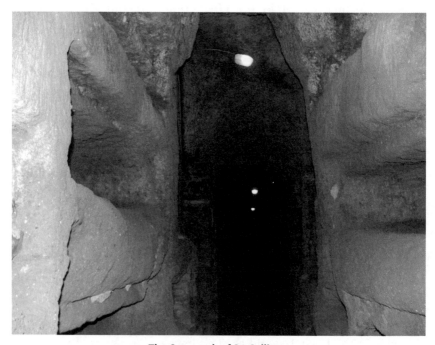

The Catacomb of St. Callistus

"The Institution of the Eucharist" from the catacombs

A tradition that we have kept from the catacombs is the altar stone. The early Church said Mass on altars under which lay the bodies of the martyrs. From this practice comes the custom of having stones on our altars in which have been placed the relics of the saints, one of which must be the relic of a martyr.

Review Exercises

1. How did St. Peter die?
2. How did St. Paul die?
3. Why did Marcus Aurelius hate Christianity?
4. Describe the martyrdom of St. Cecilia.
5. Who is an apostate? How did the Church deal with apostates in the early ages?
6. Who was St. Lawrence? How did he die?
7. Name five Emperors who persecuted the Church.
8. How is our Lord represented in the catacombs?
9. What is the origin of the altar stone?
10. What does the altar stone contain?

CHAPTER 3

THE VICTORY OF THE CHURCH OVER PAGAN ROME

Our Lord Gives the Keys to St. Peter

The Decay of Roman Paganism

At the time St. Paul was making his missionary journeys, Rome was at the height of her power. The Romans had conquered all the lands that bordered the Mediterranean Sea, and had established an Empire that was the envy of all other nations. Drunk with success, the Roman emperor time and again proclaimed himself a god. The people continued to regard him as a god so long as he gave them bread and games. The most popular sports were chariot racing and gladiatorial combats.

Most of the inhabitants of this vast Empire were pagans and worshiped many gods. However, paganism itself was in a state of decay. The pagans were growing tired of their own religion with all its superstitious practices. Some began to seek spiritual comfort in the various occults and mysterious sects. Others drowned the voice of their conscience in various immoral practices. A few looked for peace of mind in the stern teachings of the Stoics.

Widespread disrespect for religion always creates immorality in both private and public life. This fact was never more evident than in pagan Rome. Lifelong marriages were the exception among the Romans. There was little regard for the virtue of purity. Even when the home was brightened by the presence of children, their education was entrusted to slaves, whose very influence was corrupting. Slaves were obliged to serve the whims of their masters, who exercised the right of life and death over them. The theater, literature, and the arts, instead of lifting up the morals of men, encouraged the practice of vice. The Roman Empire was sorely in need of a religion that would repair the holes in its moral structure. Catholicism filled that need.

Christianity in Rome

There are several opinions as to how and when Christianity was introduced in Rome. It may be that some of the Roman converts who heard Peter preach in Jerusalem at Pentecost brought the new religion to the capital. In any event, in the Acts of the Apostles we read that there were "strangers of Rome" present at the first speech delivered by St. Peter. Roman soldiers, serving in Palestine, may also have helped spread knowledge of the new religion on their return to Rome. It is also possible that St. Peter first visited Rome during the reign of Claudius between 41 and 44 AD. He would have remained there until 48, when an imperial edict banished all Jews from the city. One thing certain is that, when St. Paul wrote his Epistle to the Romans, the Roman Church was already organized.

The Church of Rome consisted mainly of Gentiles with a minority of Jews. Under the guidance and direction of St. Paul, who arrived there in chains in 61 AD, the community increased so much that in 64 AD, the Roman historian Tacitus called attention to the fact. Tacitus wrote that the Christians already comprised an "immense multitude."

By the end of the first century Catholicism had spread to many lands. The first places to receive the glad tidings of the Gospel were Samaria, Syria, and Cilicia. Then, as a result of the zealous labors of St. Paul, the countries bordering on the eastern shores of the Mediterranean, Asia Minor, Macedonia, and Greece, also received the Gospel. Through the work of Titus, Catholicism forged its way to Illyria and Dalmatia on the eastern coast of the Adriatic Sea. In the West, it gained a foothold in the city of Rome. It then spread to the commercial seaport of Marseilles and from there to the Roman colony of Narbonne in southern Gaul (modern France).

Life of the Early Christians

Information regarding the early Christian Church must be sought in the writings of the **Apostolic Fathers**. This title is applied to several authors who wrote at the end of the first and the beginning of the second century. Some of these authors personally knew the Apostles or their immediate successors. Others lived so close to the time of the Apostles that we are certain to find in their words a faithful echo of the Apostles' teaching.

From the Apostolic Fathers we learn that membership in the Catholic Church meant a complete break with pagan customs. The first Christians were not only forbidden to attend the theater and the public games, but were also strictly commanded to shun the many idolatrous practices woven into the very fiber of everyday pagan life. The Christians continued to fulfill their various civic duties. They obeyed the laws, paid their taxes, prayed for the emperor, and fought his wars. However, they could only marry fellow Christians. The virtuous nature of their private and public lives was a source of admiration to the pagans. The Christians practiced virtues almost unknown to the pagans, mostly notably justice and chastity. They recognized the dignity of every human being, even the rights of slaves. They instilled in their children love and honor for parents and respect for women. However, they aroused suspicions because of their absence from public life, especially the theatre and the public games.

The public religious life of the early Christians was modeled on the synagogue. Christians read the Scriptures at their religious meetings, in which the Holy Eucharist had a special place. The Consecration consisted of a prayer in memory of the Passion of Christ and the words of Consecration as the priest at Mass recites them today. Until the end of the first century, the Eucharistic service was held in the evening in connection with a dinner known as the Agape, or the Love-feast. Later, it became the custom to have the Eucharistic service in the morning.

Early Catholics received Holy Communion under both species: bread and wine. Deacons carried the Blessed Sacrament to those unable to attend because of age or illness. Early Catholics were permitted to keep the Blessed Sacrament in their homes, and carry It with them on journeys. The early Church made Sunday the day for religious celebration rather than Saturday, the Jewish Sabbath. This decision was made for two reasons. First, it honored the miracle of the Resurrection, which took place on Sunday. Second, it clarified to the

Jewish converts and to the Roman pagans that the Jewish law did not bind Catholics.

To become a Christian, one must be born again of water and the Holy Spirit, which means that one must be baptized. In the early Church, the convert was baptized as soon as he said he believed in Christ. Later the Church required a period of preparation that lasted for two or three years. During this period of preparation the converts were called "catechumens," which means "instructed." They spent their time praying and learning about the Truths of the Faith. They were allowed to participate at the Mass, but only up to the Offertory.

When the catechumen was ready for baptism, he went into the baptismal font. There the bishop immersed him in the water three times. Afterwards he was immediately confirmed, a custom which is still followed in the Eastern Rite Churches. The early Church baptized converts any day it was convenient. Later, Holy Saturday and the Saturday before Pentecost became the appointed days for baptizing the catechumens. The tradition of the Church regarding the practice of infant baptism is clear from the very beginning. Both Origen and St. Augustine, whom we will later study, declare that the Church received from the Apostles the tradition of infant baptism.

Any Christian who committed a grievous sin was required to dress in a rough garment and take his place with the catechumens for a period of penance. After he had done his penance, the bishop publicly absolved him.

Establishment of the Hierarchy

After Our Lord instituted the Holy Eucharist at the Last Supper, He turned to His Apostles and said to them: "Do this in commemoration of Me." After His Resurrection He gave the

Apostles the power to forgive sins. All the Apostles were bishops invested with the fullness of the power of Holy Orders. They had the power to administer all the Sacraments and to consecrate other bishops and priests like themselves. We know from Scripture that the Apostles passed the fullness of this power to a few chosen disciples, like Titus and Timothy, in order to insure the Apostolic succession.

The Roman Primacy

In discussing the primacy of the Bishop of Rome, we must distinguish between **primacy of honor** and **primacy of jurisdiction**. Primacy of honor would have given one Apostle superiority over the others in terms of the respect and honor due to him as their senior. He would merely be the first among equals. He could advise and guide but not command.

Primacy of jurisdiction deals with the power to command based on authority which Christ conferred on Peter. It demands obedience of all the faithful. Primacy of jurisdiction made him the head of the Church with supreme authority over all the other Apostles. It is clear from the Bible that Our Lord promised not only primacy of honor but also primacy of jurisdiction in His Church to St. Peter, when He said: "Thou art Peter, and upon this rock I will build my church, and the gates of hell shall not prevail against it" (Matt. 16:18). After His Resurrection, Our Lord conferred the primacy of jurisdiction upon Peter as the visible supreme head of the Church, when He said to him: "Feed my lambs… feed my sheep" (John 21:16-21).

From the very start, the Church in Rome, the See of St. Peter, had first place among all the Church particularly Jerusalem and Antioch. St. Paul's Epistle to the Romans sets forth the most important

Peter is Given the Keys, by Rubens

truths relating to the Church and its Founder, Jesus Christ. The fact that he sent this important Epistle, not to the Ephesians or the Hebrews, but to the Romans, who, at the time, were a very small community, argues strongly that he considered the Roman Church to be the head of all Christian Churches and the center of Christian unity. Later, Paul journeyed to Rome and ended his life in that city.

Moreover, even while St. John the Apostle still lived, the Bishop of Rome became involved in a quarrel that had arisen at

Corinth. Pope St. Clement (88-97) wrote to the Catholics in Corinth and told them that they must stop fighting among themselves. The Christians of Corinth did not regard the action of St. Clement as an intrusion. They received his letter and so sincerely appreciated his efforts to establish peace in their community that seventy years later they still continued to read his letter at Mass.

St. Ignatius of Antioch, a disciple of the Apostles, also regarded the Bishop of Rome as the head of all Christians. So did St. Irenaeus, bishop of Lyons. He was a disciple of St. Polycarp who was a disciple of St. John. Also, many of the early bishops went to Rome to obtain the condemnation of heresies that had arisen in their community. Even some of the heretics themselves sought approval from the pope. They believed that his acceptance of their views would mean a complete victory for them.

Early Defenders of the Faith: The Apologists

During the second century, Catholic writers emerged who began to defend the doctrines of the Church against the attacks of the pagans. They explained Catholic teachings and showed that the arguments of the Church's opponents were false and unreasonable. These writers are known as the **Apologists**.

St. Justin Martyr

The greatest of the early apologists was St. Justin Martyr. He was born in Palestine about 100 AD. His parents were Greek pagans. He spent many years searching for truth at the different schools of philosophy, without obtaining rest for his soul. Finally, he found peace of mind in the Christian religion. During the reign of Antoninus Pius, he journeyed to Rome where he founded a famous school. In his "Dialogue with Trypho," he defends the truth of the Christian religion against the claims of the Jews. In his two "Apologies," which he addressed to the Roman pagans, he protests against their prejudice. He notes that they are persecuting Christians merely because they are Christians, not because of anything they have done wrong.

St. Irenaeus

Another Apologist was St. Irenaeus, the Bishop of Lyons. He was a disciple of St. Polycarp. The Church faced not only attacks from the pagans, but even more dangerous were the errors and heresies that were started by the Christians themselves. Some of the Christians, mostly learned men, had been studying Eastern religions. They ended up confusing Christianity with these false religions. They tried to explain Christianity according to ideas that had nothing to do with Divine Revelation. St. Irenaeus wrote against these men and their ideas. He also wrote the oldest catechism in existence. In it St. Irenaeus very clearly stated the fundamental truths of Christianity. St. Irenaeus died in 202.

Origen

The most prolific of the early apologists was Origen. He is known as the Father of Christian Theology. Origen was born in Egypt around 185. At the age of eighteen he was selected to be the head of the famous Catechetical School of Alexandria. During the Decian persecution the Romans imprisoned and tortured him. This caused his death in 254.

Origen's writings address such varied topics as apologetics, the spiritual life, Holy Scripture, and theology. His most important work was the "Hexapla" (six fold Bible). The Hexapla contained in parallel columns six different translations of the Old Testament, a method which favored comparative study. St. Jerome made use of the Hexapla as the basis of his own work on Holy Scripture. Almost three centuries after his death, his writings were condemned because they were found to contain a number of heretical doctrines. Among his errors, Origen could not see how an all-merciful God could condemn anyone to eternal damnation.

Tertullian

Tertullian was born at Carthage in 160. His conversion to Christianity took place when he was about thirty-five years old. Energetic in mind, independent in character, and a rigid logician, he was a born apologist. His style is confrontational, colorful, crisp, and rich. A trained lawyer with an enormous vocabulary, he was the father of Latin theology.

The *Apologeticus* is the most remarkable of all his controversial writings. It proves the innocence of the Christians and the unfairness of the laws of Emperor Trajan. Tertullian also attacked the heretics. In 200, he wrote his *Prescription Against Heretics*. This was a general refutation of all erroneous doctrinal ideas. He also urged the faithful to abide by the authority of tradition and of the Church.

Tertullian was above all a moralist, harsh and severe. He was concerned especially with the conduct of Christians in their association with pagans. He tended to be too severe and became rather fanatical. He wrote that all amusements were sinful. He forbade Christians from being tradesmen, teachers, soldiers, or office-holders. He ultimately wrote that the Church could not absolve Christians who had fallen into mortal sin. By the time of his death his views had become heretical.

St. Cyprian of Carthage

The last of the great apologists of this period was St. Cyprian (210?-258), the Bishop of Carthage. St. Cyprian was born of a very wealthy family of Carthage, where, after having received a thorough education, he became a teacher of rhetoric. About 246, he converted to Catholicism. From his conversion onwards, he sought to follow Our Lord's advice to the rich young man. He used his wealth to aid the poor and distressed and to advance the cause of the Church. Three years later he became Bishop of Carthage. The best known of St. Cyprian's writings is his "On the Unity of the Catholic Church." In another work, he likens the Church to the seamless robe of Christ: "Outside the Church there is no salvation. He cannot have God as his Father who has not the Church for his Mother." He died a martyr's death in 258.

Emperor Constantine

In 305, Diocletian and Maximian abdicated. The Emperor Galerius succeeded Diocletian in the East. In the West Constantius Chlorus took the place of Maximian. One year later Constantius Chlorus died. His son Constantine came to the throne. Maxentius, the son of Maximian, made himself ruler of Italy and Africa. In 312, Maxentius and Constantine went to war against each other. Constantine quickly crossed the Alps, and gave battle at the Milvian Bridge, on the banks of the Tiber River. Maxentius perished in the Tiber along with thousands of his soldiers. Victorious, Constantine entered Rome, on October 29, 312.

After his victory Constantine erected a triumphal arch that still stands among the ruins of the city of the Caesars. Upon the arch he engraved the words "instinctu divinitatis," which credited his triumph to the inspiration of God. Constantine subsequently swore under oath to his biographer Eusebius, who wrote the first history of the Church, what had happened. As he approached Rome he saw a cross of light in the heavens, around which were displayed the words: "In this sign thou shalt conquer." That night, Christ appeared to him in a dream, bearing the emblem that Constantine had seen in the heavens. Our Lord commanded him to make it his military standard. The Emperor sent for goldsmiths and commanded them to copy the pattern in gold and precious stones. The following day Constantine's pagan soldiers won their battle while fighting under the Sign of the Cross.

The Arch of Constantine

The Edict of Milan

Constantine soon proved that he would champion the cause of Christianity. In the East, Emperor Galerius had died, after having granted Christians the right to practice their religion. The new emperor, Licinius, had defeated the successor of Galerius, Maximian Daia. Constantine traveled from Rome to Milan, where he met Licinius. In 313, they proclaimed the Edict of Milan, which established principles of religious tolerance for both Christians and pagans. They also decided that all Church property that had been taken was to be returned to its rightful owners.

It is clear from the actual wording of the Edict of Milan that Constantine's only concern was for the Christians. In fact, they are the only ones mentioned by name. Moreover, it is explicitly stated that the tolerance given to other religions is only a result of that granted to Christianity. He also gave the Church the right to receive gifts and bequests and forbade public business and servile work on Sunday. Lastly, he abolished crucifixion as a form of punishment.

Since he had to work with Licinius, Constantine tried to adhere as strictly as possible to the spirit of the Edict of Milan by treating Christians and pagans equally. However in 323, when Licinius started persecuting Catholics, Constantine declared war upon him. Constantine twice defeated him. The first time, Constantine spared his life and merely imprisoned him. However, the second time he had him executed because he was found guilty of committing treason with the enemies of the Empire. At last the ruler of the great Roman Empire was a friend and protector of the Church. The persecutions were over. An era of peace and expansion was about to begin.

Constantine's Final Years

After consolidating his power, Constantine decided that he should rule the empire from a city located in the middle of it. Thus, he founded the city of Constantinople (modern day Istanbul). This change had important consequences in the future. It meant the seat of ancient culture and civilization was removed from Rome. Otherwise they might have been destroyed and lost forever when the barbarians overran Italy. Secondly, since the political power was far away from the Church's spiritual power, it allowed the Church to grow without too much interference from the State. In the East, the Church became almost a slave to the Empire and drifted further and further away from the influence of the pope. Later we shall see the tragic consequences of this.

Constantine died in 337. He did not receive Baptism until he was on his deathbed. His three sons divided his Empire among themselves. However, they fought with one another until finally one of them, Constantius, became the sole ruler. He did everything possible to eliminate paganism. He made the act of sacrificing to pagan gods punishable by death. He ordered all pagan temples be destroyed or converted to other purposes. However, he made the mistake of allowing pagan philosophers to teach in the schools and other institutions of learning. These men did everything they could to injure the Christian religion and to instill pagan ideas in the minds of their pupils.

Review Exercises

1. Relate some of the ideas as to how and when Christianity was introduced in Rome.
2. Who are the Apostolic Fathers?
3. Why did the early Church make Sunday the day for religious celebration?
4. Distinguish between primacy of honor and primacy of jurisdiction.
5. What evidence do we have that the Pope is the Head of the Church? (Give 3 examples)
6. What is an Apologist?
7. St. Irenaeus was bishop of what city?
8. What was the "Hexapla?"
9. What serious theological error did Tertullian finally make?
10. What is the Edict of Milan?

CHAPTER 4

THE TRIUMPH OF THE CHURCH OVER HERESY AND PAGANISM

The Triumph of the Church over Heresy and Paganism, **by Rubens**

Causes of the Rapid Spread of Catholicism

In listing the main causes for the rapid spread of the Catholic Faith in a corrupt and pagan world, the first place must be given to the divine assistance which Our Lord promised to His Church when He said that He would be with the Church until the end of the world. The continued success of the Faith is due to the fact that the Founder of the Catholic Church is God. He will never permit His work to crumble or be destroyed.

The second cause of the Faith's rapid spread was the zeal of its missionaries and the saintly lives of its first converts. Led by St.

Paul, the early bishops of the Church worked tirelessly in preaching the new religion and winning new members. Many among them sealed their faith with their blood, thus testifying by the supreme act of heroism that the religion that they preached was of God. Moreover, the first Christians led exemplary lives. They were a constant source of admiration to the pagans, who could not help but remark: "See how these Christians love one another."

The third cause of the rapid spread was the very nature of the religion itself. Christianity in its essential teachings was a religion that appealed to rich and poor, to master and slave, to ruler and subject. It maintained a definite set of beliefs. It championed virtues which appealed to the masses. It proposed a moral code loftier than any ever held.

The fourth cause for the Faith's rapid spread was the condition of the pagan world at the time. It was a time of moral reform. Men were awaking to the need for better and purer living. To those who felt this need, Christianity offered the highest moral ideals. It was also a time of great religious interest. Old cults were being revived, and new ones were finding acceptance on all sides. Catholicism, with its one God and its promise of redemption and a blessed immortality based upon Divine Revelation, met the awakening religious needs as no other faith did. Its principles of Christian brotherhood, equality of all people in the sight of God, and concept of a new social order, appealed very strongly to the large numbers of the poorer classes.

The fifth cause of its rapid spread were the many advantages the Faith derived from the organization of the Roman Empire. The excellent Roman roads made the travel easy for the early missionaries. They had easy access to distant lands. The fact that the Empire was a cohesive unit, at the peak of its power, also added to the initial success of the new religion. The language issue was also critical. Wherever missionaries went, they were sure to be understood by races that had come under Roman rule and influence.

A final cause for the rapid spread of Christianity was its own superb organization. Within this vast army of followers of Christ, each individual community was a definite unit. Each community had at its head a bishop, who was assisted by priests and deacons. The great Christian centers, such as Antioch, Caesarea, Alexandria, Ephesus, and Carthage, were closely linked with Rome, the hub of the Church. The Bishop of Rome was acknowledged throughout the known civilized world as the successor of St. Peter. Questions of faith, morals, and even discipline were referred to him. All regarded his decision in these matters as final.

Obstacles to the Spread of Christianity

The main obstacle to the spread of Christianity, and the one which certainly would have overwhelmed it, had it not been founded by God, was the incredible persecution by the Roman Empire. The strength of the Empire could not be overcome by any merely human force. There were no enemies it could not crush. The power it wielded was almost unlimited. Had the Catholic Church been a mere human institution, it would have perished very early. The profession of Christianity was a crime that in almost every instance was punishable by death. It required almost supernatural heroism to join a society that the government was so dedicated to destroying. For three hundred years the Empire attacked the new religion with persecutions that seemed to become more and more bloody and cruel. Tens of thousands were killed in an attempt to destroy the new Church.

The second obstacle to Christianity's spread was its attitude to other religions. At the time, paganism was the state religion. Yet here was a religion that would abolish all forms of paganism and replace them with the worship of one God. It was because Christians were intolerant of other creeds that they were hated and despised. They were called enemies of the Empire, irreligious, immoral, and atheists. They were blamed for all the calamities that befell the world.

The third obstacle to the spread of the Faith, at least among the Roman nobility, was the way that Our Lord had died. Under

Roman law, crucifixion was the penalty given to slaves and those convicted of terrible crimes. In the eyes of a Roman noble, Our Lord had not only been despised by His own people, but was also put to death by the Romans for rebelling against Roman rule. For a noble Roman, this was a very serious obstacle to overcome.

The fourth obstacle to Christianity's spread was the protection it afforded slaves. Proud Romans must initially have resented being told that their slaves were, like themselves, creatures of God, endowed with spiritual faculties and possessing immortal souls. Catholicism did appeal to the slave; but from this point of view at least, it did not win the good will of the master.

The fifth obstacle to the spread of Christianity was the Christians' refusal to pay divine honors to the person of the emperor. On this point they would not yield. They rightly contended that divine honors were due to God alone. By refusing to adore the emperor, the Christians laid themselves open to the accusation of high treason against the head of the state.

A final obstacle to the spread of the Faith were the lies told about it by the pagans. Since Christians held their meetings at night and in secret, it was easy to claim they were doing bad things. They were charged with being immoral as well as other wild accusations especially involving the Eucharist.

The Church Explains Her Fundamental Doctrines

The first announcement of the coming of the Kingdom of God was made in simple terms. The Church proclaimed that God had become Man to save men and women and to restore the blessings that had been lost by Original Sin. Jesus Christ, the Incarnate Word, had established a Church in which He would dwell until the end of the world. That Church would teach people the Truth and make them holy. The Holy Spirit would dwell in that Church. The Holy Spirit would bring its members together in love for the Father. The Holy Spirit working in the Church would help them to understand the full meaning of Christ's teachings.

As time passed, and the persecutions ceased, men were able to think more deeply about the Faith. They rightly began to consider the theological reasons for the doctrines that they believed. The Church encouraged these theologians, just as she had encouraged the Apologists decades before. The Church taught then, as now, that the Truth had nothing to fear from analysis and discussion. The Church felt that the better people understood their faith, the greater the power it would have in the world.

The Christian Martyrs' Final Prayer

Two of the basic doctrines of Christianity are the Trinity and the Incarnation. The Blessed Trinity is the existence of the Father,

Son, and Holy Spirit: three Persons in one God. The Mystery of the Incarnation means that the Second Person of this Trinity, while maintaining His Divinity, became a human Man, Who suffered and died for us. The Catholics of the first three centuries paid divine honors to Christ. Thousands were martyred for Him.

The Arian Heresy

In 318, a Libyan priest named Arius began to preach a false doctrine about the Son of God. Arius denied that the Son is God in the same way that the Father is God. According to Arius, the Son is not eternal nor of the same substance as the Father, but is a mere creature. At this point the Church had not officially defined this teaching. Arius was quite skilled in the art of debate and was a very learned and eloquent man. He made effective use of these gifts in concealing the true meaning of his words. Many were fascinated by his winning and earnest manner. Sadly, many lapsed into heresy with him. Although his bishop condemned him and excommunicated him and his followers, his heresy quickly spread. Soon there were Arians all over the world.

The Council of Nicaea

In 325, Emperor Constantine, the de facto protector of the Church, got involved in the Arian matter. To settle the dispute, he suggested a general council. With the consent of Pope Sylvester I (314-335), he summoned all the bishops of the Church to Nicaea in Asia Minor. Old age prevented Pope Sylvester from attending, so his delegate, Bishop Hosius of Cordova, Spain, presided over the Council. Initially, the number of bishops present was 250, but, before the Council had held its last session, this number had grown to 318.

Pope Sylvester I baptizes Constantine

The Council of Nicaea was a general council. It defined the true doctrine concerning the Son and His relation to the Father. It created the profession of Faith which we know as the Nicene Creed, and which is recited at Mass. The Nicene Creed proclaims Jesus Christ as True God, God from God, Light from Light, True God from True God, begotten, not made, of the same substance as the Father, by Whom all things were made.

As a result of the decrees of the Council, Arius and his followers were exiled. Later, Arius was allowed to return. During his lifetime, and for many years after, Arianism continued to be a source of trouble to the Church. Some emperors favored the Arians for political reasons. Other emperors, faithful to the Church, opposed the Arians and tried to drive them from the Empire. However, even in exile, the Arians continued to spread their heresy. Sadly, many of the barbarian tribes converted to Arian Christianity.

St. Athanasius

The blame for the later, temporary triumph of Arianism must be placed upon Emperor Constantine. He allowed Arius to return to Alexandria. However, at this moment in history Our Lord called forth a giant of the Faith. A formidable opponent of Arianism entered the battle: Athanasius, the new bishop of Alexandria. From this moment on, the history of Arianism is largely the history of St. Athanasius.

Arius had deceived Emperor Constantine into thinking that he was no longer a heretic. Thus, the Emperor ordered Athanasius to restore Arius to his former position in the Church. While Arius might have fooled the Emperor, he did not fool St. Athanasius. He absolutely refused to allow Arius to re-enter Alexandria. As a result of his refusal, St. Athanasius was banished by the Emperor to Trier in 335. The following year, Arius, after some time at Alexandria, was triumphantly escorted into the city of Constantinople. There, he died suddenly. The people saw in his death God's just punishment.

By this time, St. Athanasius had become the most well known person in the Roman world. The Arians, unable to break his will and win him to their side, spread lies about him. He was accused of murdering Bishop Arsenius and cutting off his dead hand for magical purposes. He was accused of trying to stop food ships from sailing to Constantinople from Alexandria. He easily disposed of these lies at a synod convened by Constantine's order at Tyre. Bishop Arsenius appeared alive—and with both hands.

In 337, Athanasius returned to Alexandria, where the people enthusiastically welcomed him home. Immediately the Arians protested against his resuming his post. They forcibly installed someone else as bishop. Suddenly, the situation changed completely. Constans, Constantine's eldest son and ruler of the western portion of the Empire, took a Catholic stand. He referred the matter to the papacy. Pope Julius I (337-352) called a council at Rome. In 341, the fifty bishops present unanimously acquitted Athanasius of all the charges against him. A council held two years later at Sofia in Bulgaria upheld both the Roman council and the Nicene Creed.

Two of Constantine's three sons were Catholics. However, the third, Constantius, was an Arian. In 350, Constantius became ruler of the Empire. For a time it seemed as though Arianism might again be about to triumph. In 355, Constantius convoked a council at Milan for the clear purpose of admitting the Arians into the Church. When the bishops protested that an emperor had no right to convene a Church council, the Emperor lost patience. He declared that his will was canon law and that the bishops either had to obey him or be exiled. He even went so far as to draw his sword and brandish it before the bishops. Terrorized, the majority yielded. Only a few noble characters stood firm.

The strongest protest came from Pope Liberius (352-366). "You have three days to make up your mind," threatened the Emperor. "Three days will not change my decision," replied the

Pontiff, "exile me to any place you please." The Emperor banished him to Berea in Thrace. Orders were given to arrest St. Athanasius. Five thousand soldiers were sent to carry out the arrest order. They encircled both the saint and his people during Mass, but, as they entered the church, Athanasius mysteriously disappeared. Thanks to the good will of the monks, he remained in hiding in the desert. However, an Arian was immediately installed as Bishop of Alexandria. Athanasius hid in the desert where he continued in his capacity as bishop until Constantius died in 361.

Julian the Apostate succeeded Constantius. Julian allowed the Catholic bishops who had been exiled by the Arians to return to their dioceses. However, as we shall later study, his reasons for allowing their return were not to support the Church, but rather to injure her. With the aid of these bishops, Athanasius began to labor to restore unity to the Church. This brought the Emperor's displeasure down on him. Once more the saint was sent into exile. "This little cloud will soon pass," said St. Athanasius patiently. He was right, for Julian died in battle shortly thereafter. His successor, Jovian, called the saint to Antioch so that Athanasius could instruct him in the Catholic Faith.

Upon Jovian's death, the Eastern Empire was given to Valens, a rabid Arian. Valens did everything possible to restore Arianism to power. He persecuted the Catholics and issued a special decree banishing Athanasius. However, this time the people rose to the defense of the saint and threatened to bring him back by force. Thus, in 367, Athanasius at last came home to stay. He spent the remaining six years of his life in the midst of his flock. His last years were dedicated to repairing the damage done during the earlier years of violence, dissent, and exile. He returned to his writing and preaching undisturbed. On May 2, 373, having consecrated his successor, he died quietly in his own house.

The Pagan Reaction under Emperor Julian the Apostate

When Julian became Emperor his first act was to recall the bishops exiled by Constantius. However, his motive was not to restore peace to the Church, but to create more divisions and confusion. Julian hated Christianity. Enemies of his family who claimed to be Christians had killed his father and his brothers. Therefore, upon his accession to the throne, he immediately tried to stamp out Christianity and to rebuild the dismantled pagan temples. He even established a pagan religion with a hierarchy modeled on the Catholic Church. The high priest of each province was made a sort of bishop under the sovereign protection of a "pope," who was Julian himself. Julian also sought to create apostates. He offered positions and honors to those who would deny their faith. He proclaimed that paganism was again the official religion of the Empire. He compelled judges to sacrifice to the gods. However, his efforts were of no avail. Paganism had lost its appeal. The only converts were some soldiers and a few people who reverted to paganism for personal advantage.

In 362, Julian went to war against the Persians. He made his headquarters at Antioch. While he was there he tried to disprove Christ's prophecy by rebuilding the Temple at Jerusalem. By divine intervention, the attempt proved a complete failure. Globes of fire repeatedly burst forth from the earth near the construction site slowing all progress. Julian was killed in 363, in battle with the Persian cavalry. A story, probably legendary, has him crying out, "Galilean, Thou hast conquered." Following his death, Jovian was hastily elected to succeed Julian. Paganism was relegated to the status of a barely tolerated religion. Christianity again became the creed of the Emperor and the majority of his subjects.

The Three Cappadocians

In his attempt to cause trouble for the Church, Julian had recalled both Arians and Catholics from exile. After his death, Arianism again loomed as a danger on the horizon. Valentinian, a Catholic, succeeded Emperor Jovian. Unfortunately, he took as his associate in the East his brother Valens, a confirmed Arian. Valens issued an edict, banishing all the bishops who had recently returned from exile. However, God raised up three new champions to defend the Faith. These were St. Basil of Caesarea, his brother St. Gregory of Nyssa, and their friend St. Gregory of Nazianzus. Since they were from Cappadocia (Asia Minor), they are known as the Three Cappadocians.

St. Basil was born at Caesarea in Cappadocia in 329. He attended the schools of Athens along with Julian the Apostate and St. Gregory of Nyssa. After a pilgrimage to the monks of Palestine and Syria, he returned to his native land and organized a small religious community. In 364, the archbishop of Caesarea ordained him a priest. Six years later, he became the archbishop of Caesarea. His chief doctrinal writings are a treatise against the Arians and another on the Holy Spirit. He also composed a splendid theological account of the six days of creation.

St. Basil was an energetic and well-balanced man, endowed with good common sense. His friend, Gregory of Nazianzus (330–390), on the other hand, was a sensitive and impressionable soul, not well suited for the public life. For a time he lived with St. Basil at his religious community. However, he was forced to sacrifice his life of solitude to assist the aged bishop of Nazianzus in administering his diocese. Consecrated Bishop of Sasima in Cappadocia by St. Basil in 372, Gregory refused to take his post. Instead he withdrew to a solitary retreat. Finally yielding to the requests of the Catholics of Constantinople, he again took up the duties of an active life and became their bishop. Later he resigned and became bishop of Nazianzus. By the

Basil and Emperor Valens

end of 383, his health made him too weak to cope with the duties of a
bishop. He resigned as bishop and again withdrew into a life of solitude.
After five peaceful years, he died January 25, 389.

St. Gregory of Nyssa had none of the advantages of higher
education which his older brother, St. Basil, enjoyed. Nevertheless,

The Three Cappadoccians

he became a great philosopher and teacher. He married, but when his wife died, he became a priest. St. Basil appointed him Bishop of Nyssa. However, in 374 Emperor Valens deposed him, and for a time he labored in Armenia. He played a prominent role in the Council of Constantinople. He wrote a lengthy treatise against the Arians. He also wrote a catechism explaining the basic teachings of the Faith, the Trinity, the Incarnation, the Redemption, and the Sacraments. He died in 395. With St. Gregory of Nyssa, the story of the Arian heresy was nearing its close. The Council of Constantinople would write the word "Finish" in 381.

Council of Constantinople

In 381, a council convened at Constantinople that was attended by 150 bishops from the Eastern Empire. The Council began by saying that it completely agreed with the teachings of the Council of Nicaea. Then, in order to deal with the errors of the times, it wrote a Creed to supplement the Nicene Creed. Unfortunately, the words used in the new Creed to describe the manner in which the Holy Spirit proceeds from the Father and the Son gave rise to varying interpretations. The Catholics of the West adopted the phrase: "Who proceeds from the Father *and* the Son." The Catholics of the East preferred the phrase: "Who proceeds from the Father *through* the Son." Correctly understood, both phrases are true. Nevertheless, these initial differences gave rise to disputes regarding the word "Filioque" (Latin for "and the Son"). Although Arianism would continue to infect the barbarian tribes, the Council marked the beginning of the end of Arianism in the Roman Empire.

The Death of Paganism

While Arianism was disappearing in the East, paganism began disappearing in the West. Until this time paganism was still somewhat associated with the government, even though Constantine's successors had relegated it to the status of a tolerated cult. Gratian (375-383) was the first emperor to sever the official bond linking paganism to the imperial power. Under the direction of St. Ambrose (340-397), Bishop of Milan, Gratian began working to wipe out paganism. He removed the pagan statue of Victory from the senate despite the objections of the senators. He abolished all the privileges of the pagan priesthood.

Unfortunately, Gratian was assassinated in 383 by followers of his rival, Maximus. St. Ambrose convinced Maximus to allow

Valentinian II, Gratian's brother, to rule over Italy and Africa. Once again paganism was forced to retreat. The final blow was dealt by one of Valentinian's successors, Emperor Theodosius the Great. Early in his reign, Theodosius issued orders forbidding any Christian from becoming a pagan and criminalizing various pagan acts. In 390, Theodosius declared Catholicism to be the faith of both the Eastern and Western Empires. The following year, he issued another decree fining anyone who entered pagan temples. Then he forbade the private worship of the pagan gods in homes. By 423, Emperor Theodosius II was able to declare that there were almost no pagans left in his domains.

St. Ambrose

Review Exercises

1. List six causes for the rapid spread of the Catholic Faith.
2. List six reasons why the Faith might not have spread.
3. What was the Arian Heresy?
4. What did the Council of Nicaea proclaim?
5. Who called the Council of Milan, and why?
6. Name the Three Cappadocians.
7. Which Emperor issued the decrees that finally brought an end to paganism?

CHAPTER 5

THE CHURCH BEGINS TO BUILD A CATHOLIC SOCIETY: CHRISTENDOM

St. Ambrose and Emperor Theodosius by Rubens

The Edict of Milan granted the Church protection from persecution. As the fourth century progressed, the Church received greater protection and support from the Empire. At last the Church was able to begin to establish and build a truly Catholic society: Christendom. During the fourth century the Holy Spirit blessed the Church with some of her greatest saints: St. John Chrysostom, St. Ambrose, St. Jerome, and St. Augustine. These men and others would lay the foundation for a Christian society that would last for over 1,000 years.

St. John Chrysostom

St. John Chrysostom (the golden-tongued) was so named because of his great eloquence. He was born in 344 at Antioch to a noble and wealthy family. Sacrificing a promising secular career, he devoted himself exclusively to prayer and the study of the Bible under the guidance of the saintly bishop of his native city. He was ordained a deacon in 381, and a priest before long. Shortly after his ordination he wrote his beautiful treatise "On the Priesthood." During the next ten years St. John Chrysostom preached the famous homilies on the Scriptures, which earned him the nickname "Chrysostom."

When the patriarch of Constantinople died in 397, Chrysostom was chosen to succeed him. There, he proved as popular as at Antioch, until he began to reform the laxity of his clergy and the morality of the imperial court. The climax came when he offended the proud Empress Eudoxia by a homily on worldliness. She believed she heard references to herself in his words.

St. John Chrysostom preaching to Empress Eudoxia

Immediately the Empress enlisted the services of the proud Theophilus. He was the Bishop of Alexandria and the sworn enemy of Chrysostom. She hoped he could oust the holy bishop from his See. Theophilus called the Synod of the Oak in Chalcedon where many false charges were raised against St. John. St. John, who refused to attend, was deposed and exiled. He had not gone far when Eudoxia, who had been frightened by an earthquake, pleaded for him to return to the city.

Two months after his return, he again found himself at odds with the Empress. This time Eudoxia had erected a silver statue of herself within the cathedral grounds. St. John publicly protested against such a desecration. Once again, the Patriarch was sentenced to exile, despite the protests of his people.

An inquiry was instituted. Pope Innocent I declared the decree of deposition formulated against St. John at the Synod of the Oak to be null and void. The pope also sent a letter of reprimand to Theophilus. However, St. John Chrysostom was not recalled from exile. His enemies, fearing his influence in the capital, resolved to afflict him with even more severe punishments. Accordingly, in the summer of 407, the Emperor issued an order banishing him to the northeast coast of the Black Sea. He never reached his destination. He died on the way, September 14, 407.

St. Ambrose

St. Ambrose, the great Bishop of Milan, is another outstanding example of the kind of men the West gave to the Church. St. Ambrose was born at Trier in 340. His father was prefect of Gaul. Gaul was a vast territory comprising modern France, Belgium, and parts of Holland and Germany. At the age of 30,

Ambrose was appointed governor of northern Italy. All the people soon recognized his excellent administrative qualities.

The Bishop of Milan was an Arian. When he died, a bitter quarrel erupted between the Catholics and the Arians concerning the choice of his successor. Ambrose, wishing to restore peace, spoke to the people. When he finished, a child in the crowd called out, "Let Ambrose be our bishop." At once the whole host, both Arians and Catholics, took up the cry. The people unanimously voted to make him bishop. He protested to them in vain that he was only a catechumen. He had not yet been baptized. Hence, he was ill suited for this high position in the Church. Nevertheless,

St. Ambrose

70

the citizens of Milan were insistent. Within eight days he received all the necessary Sacraments. He was baptized, ordained a priest, and consecrated bishop.

At once the new Bishop made every attempt to overcome the disadvantages of his tardy and unplanned vocation. He began by diligently reading the Scriptures and studying the Church Fathers. Throughout his life, however, he always remained the administrator. He was always more concerned with his duties as a pastor of souls than with trying to acquire literary and oratorical fame.

After being the main architect of the overthrow of the pagan religion with the Emperor, Ambrose began the task of establishing a Christian government. In such a government, the state would be subject to the Church in all matters pertaining to religious doctrine and public morality. Even the Emperor would be subject to the bishop in these matters.

In 390, a rebellion broke out at Thessalonica. The rebels murdered their unpopular governor and several other important people. The murders infuriated Emperor Theodosius who ordered drastic reprisals. He sent imperial soldiers to the city where they massacred almost all the people in the city as they huddled together in the town center. St. Ambrose immediately demanded that the Emperor make a public penance for the massacre. Theodosius humbly submitted to the Bishop's demands.

All of St. Ambrose's writings reveal the strength and beauty of his character. His hymns made a strong impression on St. Augustine and he was to a great extent responsible for Augustine's conversion. The Bishop of Milan also wrote short spiritual treatises. His most important work is "Duties of Sacred Ministers." In it, in conversational language, he lays down rules for the life of his clergy.

St. Jerome

St. Jerome was born in 342 to wealthy Christian parents in Dalmatia. He was the most learned of all the Western Fathers. He knew Latin, Greek, and Hebrew, and had a working knowledge of Chaldaic and Aramaic. At the request of Pope Damasus, St. Jerome undertook the task of creating a new and better Latin translation of the Bible. His knowledge of Hebrew enabled him to understand the meaning of every syllable of the Scriptures that had been written in that language, and to decide which of the Greek and Latin translations was best. After almost twenty years he completed his work. In the Middle Ages his translation was termed the "Vulgate." The Council of Trent (1545) ordained that this translation was the authentic Latin translation.

Since the sixth century, St. Jerome's Vulgate has been the official Latin text of the Bible. Its influence on the development of the Latin language was great. St. Jerome expressed himself in Latin like no one else. His writing style in the Vulgate was so simple and

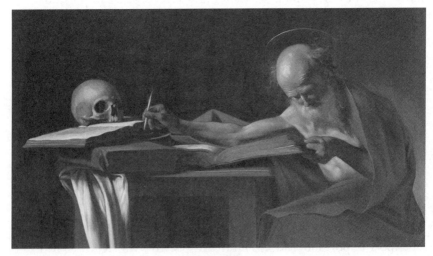

St. Jerome

clear that his Bible became a book that everyone could read, so it was widely read. Consequently, it had a great influence on everyday speaking and writing.

In 386, St. Jerome moved to the Holy Land. He settled in Bethlehem. There, with the aid of a noble woman, he built three convents for women and a monastery for men. Jerome lived in a cave only large enough to house himself and his library. He died in 420.

St. Augustine

Aurelius Augustinus was born November 13, 354, in northern Africa. His father was a pagan, but his mother, Monica, was a Christian. Although she did not have her child baptized, she did instruct him zealously in all the truths of the Catholic faith. All her life she prayed for him and his conversion.

As a young man Augustine went to Carthage where he completed his studies. In Carthage he lived a life of pleasure and strayed far from the virtuous ways that his pious mother had taught him. He taught rhetoric in Carthage and Rome, and finally obtained a job teaching rhetoric in Milan. It seemed that Divine Providence guided Augustine's steps to this city, where he met the man destined to convert and baptize him: St. Ambrose.

The sermons of St. Ambrose made such an impression on the worldly young man that he resolved to make a deep study of the Christian religion. Then he heard Christ's call to him personally. In July, 386, he heard a voice crying out to him: "Take and read." He opened his Bible at random and read a passage. The passage caused him to reevaluate his life. On Easter, 387, St. Ambrose baptized Augustine. The Church had gained one of its greatest champions.

St. Augustine

Augustine's saintly mother Monica died during their return journey to Africa. She was content and fulfilled at last. The next year Augustine went with a number of friends into monastic seclusion. While on a visit to Hippo in 391, he was designated by the voice of the people to become the assistant bishop with Valerius, the old and venerable bishop of that city. Five years later he succeeded Valerius as Bishop of Hippo. For the next thirty-five years he was the most outstanding figure not only in the African Church, but in all Christendom.

Through his writings, Augustine became known throughout the Christian world. He wrote essays dealing with the fall of Adam and Eve, the necessity of Baptism, man's free will, and the nature of divine grace. In addition to these writings, he also wrote two other extraordinary books. One of them was his autobiography, the *Confessions*. In it he tells his life story from his childhood onward. He demonstrates how divine grace led him from error to Truth and from sin to a holy life. It is one of the greatest spiritual books of all time.

At certain moments in history, when the world is passing through great crises, and everything seems to be changing, great thinkers write important books. These men write with the idea of showing how the present came from the past, and try to lead the way into the future. St. Augustine wrote such a book. It is called *The City of God*. Augustine wrote *The City of God* as a response to the sack of "eternal Rome" by Alaric the Goth.

In the *City of God,* Augustine tries to show how the City of God, which is the congregation of all believers, is in conflict with the Kingdom of Satan, and how this conflict will last until the end of the world. St. Augustine asserts that the City of God will ultimately triumph. The Church will be the glorious way of bringing not only spiritual salvation to men and women, but temporal happiness as well.

This great Doctor of the Church died August 18, 430, while Genseric and his Vandal army were besieging Hippo.

Nestorius and the Council of Ephesus

On Christmas Day, 428, the brash new patriarch of Constantinople, Nestorius, preached a sermon in which he said that no human being could be the Mother of God. Immediately there was turmoil in the church. Among his listeners was a lawyer who spoke out against Nestorius defending Our Blessed Lady. Nestorius went on to deliver a series of sermons in which he developed his theme. Essentially he came to say that Christ's humanity was only "a garment," which God puts on. Mary conceived and bore that fleshly garment.

The mightiest opponent against Nestorius was St. Cyril, the Patriarch of Alexandria. In 429, St. Cyril entered the fray in behalf of Our Lady. He wrote a letter to his monks clearly stating that Mary was the Mother of God. He sent an additional report to Pope St. Celestine I (422-432) detailing the history of the controversy. The pope also received letters from Nestorius explaining his position.

In August 430, Pope Celestine called a meeting in Rome to review the material he had received. The pope declared Nestorius' views on the Blessed Mother to be heretical. The pope demanded that he recant immediately upon pain of excommunication. The pope praised the work of St. Cyril and appointed him his representative in the East for carrying out his instructions. However, Nestorius refused to change his views. At this point Emperor Theodosius II proposed that an ecumenical council be called to resolve the dispute. Pope Celestine approved the Council in May, 431.

St. Cyril convened the Council of Ephesus in the Pope's name on June 22, 431. The Council quickly condemned the doctrine of Nestorius. The Council removed him as patriarch of Constantinople and banished him to Egypt, where he died in 451. His followers were likewise banished. They scattered into Armenia, Persia, and India, where remnants of this heresy still remain.

The Hermits and the Beginning of Monasticism

During the fourth century, as the Church grew, there were some holy men who wanted to give themselves more completely to God than was possible under the conditions of normal daily life. They did not want to marry or possess any worldly possessions. In the middle of the third century, a number of these holy men left the cities where they lived. They went out into the desert to spend their lives in prayer and mortification. The most well known of these men were St. Anthony of Egypt and St. Paul of Thebes, who were known as the first hermits.

St. Paul, who died in 340, lived a life of prayer and mortification for almost one hundred years in the desert, not far from the Red Sea. St. Anthony is considered the father of early monasticism. He placed himself at the head of a number of men wishing to lead an **ascetic** life. Thus, the first groups of hermits came into existence.

St. Anthony was an Egyptian by birth, the son of noble and wealthy parents. For twenty years he lived in absolute seclusion on the east bank of the Nile River. Eventually people seeking his advice and prayers discovered his retreat.

The first monks who placed themselves under his direction did not live in complete seclusion. Rather, they met at certain times for Mass, prayer, and spiritual conferences. They settled in the upper Egyptian desert.

About this time St. Basil, one of the three Capadocians, traveled to Egypt to investigate the conditions of monastic life. He lived in a wilderness in Asia Minor until the time he became a bishop in 370. He later composed two Rules that to this day continue to guide the monasteries.

St. Athanasius introduced Eastern monasticism into the West during his first exile at Trier in 335. While in Rome he told of the austerities practiced by the monks in the East. These accounts aroused a spirit of pious emulation among the Christians of that city. St. Jerome and St. Ambrose also supported monasticism in the West.

St. Martin of Tours

The man responsible for the spread of monasticism in Gaul was St. Martin of Tours. He was born in 316 to pagan parents in present-day Hungary. At the age of ten he became a catechumen. As a young man he enlisted in the army. While stationed at Amiens, one winter day he encountered at the city gate a half-clad beggar. The beggar was suffering from hunger and cold. Without a moment's hesitation Martin cut his tunic in two with his sword and placed one half around the poor man's shoulders. The following night Our Lord appeared to Martin in a dream. Christ wore Martin's half cloak. Angels surrounded Him. Our Lord addressed these words to Martin: "Martin, still a catechumen, wrapped Me in this garment."

St. Martin of Tours

In 339, Martin received baptism. After living as a hermit on a wild and uncultivated island in the Mediterranean Sea, he set out to visit St. Hilary of Poitiers. He founded the first monastery in Gaul about five miles from Poitiers, at Ligugé. In 371, Martin was elected bishop of Tours. The holy bishop also founded a monastery just outside Tours called Marmoutier.

Development of the Church Hierarchy

The Papacy

In the battles waged against the heretics of the fourth and fifth centuries, the popes proved themselves the champions and best guardians of the Faith. The emperors called the ecumenical councils of this period because they were better able to bring the bishops of the world together. However the popes always presided at these councils through their legates. Additionally the popes ratified the decrees enacted by the councils. Moreover, decrees had force of law and were binding on the faithful only if they received papal approval. Pope Sylvester I (314–335) ratified the decisions of the First Council of Nicaea (325). His successor, Julius I (337-352), championed the cause of St. Athanasius. Through his legates Julius presided over the Council of Sofia, in Bulgaria. The Council of Sofia expressly declared, "Rome is the See of Peter, to which all the bishops of every province must refer." Finally, at the beginning of the fifth century, Pope Innocent I (402-417) condemned the Pelagian heresy. Pope Zosimus (417-418), at a council held in Rome, condemned Pelagius himself.

The Bishops and Priests

From the beginning of the Church the popes always claimed the right to appoint bishops. However, for a time, they tolerated the election of bishops by the clergy and people of the diocese. Until the Council of Nicaea in 325, laymen could vote in the election of a bishop. Laymen could either propose a candidate to the clergy or approve the choice that the clergy had made. However, by the end of the fourth century, the election of bishops was removed from the people's power. At that point, the clergy of the diocese would act with the neighboring bishops and the archbishop to elect a new bishop.

In every political division of the Empire, there was one bishop whose position was superior to the others. He was called the "**Metropolitan.**" In the East a number of provinces with their Metropolitans were placed under the authority of a "Patriarch." There were **Patriarchs** in Alexandria, Antioch, Constantinople, and Jerusalem. In the West the Pope was the only Patriarch.

In the early Church, each Christian community had its own bishop, who cared for the needs of the people. The communities were small, consisting of the city and its surrounding neighborhood. Thus, the people could easily find the bishop when they needed his services. As the number of the Catholics increased, especially in the fourth century, the bishops appointed deacons to assist them. Among the deacon's duties were helping the poor, assisting the bishop at Mass, and bringing Holy Communion to the sick and imprisoned.

As the Faith spread into rural districts, the bishops ordained priests who could offer Mass and forgive sins, but who did not have the full power of a bishop. Initially, these priests lived with the bishop. They were not assigned to any special district, but went where the bishop sent them.

At first, married men were allowed to become priests. However, even in the earliest days, they were not allowed to marry after they had been ordained. There were large numbers of laymen who had decided to sacrifice the joys of a wife and family and instead experience the joy of a life dedicated to God. They remained unmarried. Since these men were usually the most zealous members of the Christian community, it was only natural that the bishops should choose them for priests instead of men who were married. Gradually this became the general rule. By the end of the third century the law in several dioceses in the West was that only unmarried men could become priests.

Great changes were about to take place in the civilized world. The final chapter was being written in the history of the Roman Empire. Like a great tidal wave, the barbarian invasion was gathering forces in the North. Soon it would rush south changing the face of the earth. The power of the Caesars would not be able to withstand it. However, our Savior built His Church on a rock, and not on the shifting sands of human institutions. His Kingdom is not of this world. "And the rain fell, and the floods came, and the winds blew, and they beat upon that house, and it fell not, for it was founded on a rock."

Review Exercises

1. St. John Chrysostom was Patriarch of what city?
2. What do we call St. Jerome's translation of the Bible?
3. Where was St. Augustine born?
4. Who baptized St. Augustine?
5. Where was St. Augustine bishop?
6. What did St. Augustine call his autobiography?
7. What was the great crisis that caused Augustine to write *The City of God*?
8. Who were the first two hermits?
9. What is a Metropolitan? What is a Patriarch?
10. How many Patriarchs were there in the West?

CHAPTER 6

THE CHURCH BEGINS CONVERTING THE BARBARIAN TRIBES

Pope Leo the Great Meets Attila, by Raphael

The Migrations of Barbarian Tribes

Both Christians and pagans firmly believed that the Roman Empire would last forever. It seemed to rest on such a solid foundation. It had weathered every storm. Its armies had always ultimately been victorious. To think that it might some day crumble was to imagine the impossible. Yet this structure, built by man, was destined to break up and slowly disintegrate. The divinely created fabric, the Church, would rise even more gloriously from its ruins.

For a long time the Germanic, or Gothic, tribes had been seeking to establish themselves in the Empire. To achieve their purpose, many used lawful means such as settling in its provinces as colonists, or enlisting in the Roman armies. However, these peaceful incursions were followed by a sudden eruption, caused by the advance of the Huns, an Asiatic tribe, who finally penetrated into Europe. The Huns first attacked the Eastern Germans, or **Ostrogoths**. The Huns continued their westward advance that forced the Western Germans, or Visigoths, to seek the protection of Valens, the Emperor of the East. In 376, Valens allowed the Visigoths into the Empire. The barbarian invasions had begun.

Unfortunately Valens, before allowing the Goths into the Empire, insisted that they become Arians. Consequently, the Goths brought the Arian heresy along with them in all their invasions. In 410, Alaric, the leader of the Western Goths, captured the city of Rome. His brother Ataulf migrated with his people into southern Gaul. Ataulf established himself so firmly there that Wallia, his successor, obtained title to the land from Emperor Honorius. Such was the origin of the Visigoth kingdom in Toulouse through which Arianism took root in the West. It spread rapidly to all neighboring districts.

In 406, pressed by the Huns, the Germans, living along the banks of the Rhine, overflowed the narrow limits of their province and

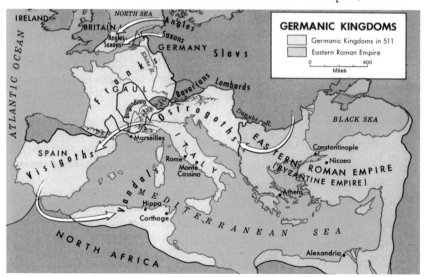

The Barbarian Migrations

83

swarmed into Gaul. Meanwhile the tribe called the Franks established themselves on the banks of the Rhine and the Meuse. Another tribe, the Burgundians, settled in the Rhone River valley. The tribe known as the Vandals moved into Africa, where they laid waste to all the Roman provinces. Due to their contacts with the Visigoths of Toulouse, Arianism contaminated both the Burgundians and the **Vandals**.

It was not long before the Vandals began persecuting the Church in North Africa. The cause was twofold. The Catholic episcopate and aristocracy represented the Roman Empire which the Vandals hated. Additionally, the Vandals were fanatical Arians. The Vandals, under their leaders Genseric and Hunneric, took the Church's property and gave it to their own Arian clergy.

Pope St. Leo the Great

In 451, the Huns themselves poured into the Empire. After crossing the Rhine River, the Huns, led by Attila, swept down upon northeastern France. The inhabitants of Paris resolved to flee. However, a saintly maiden, Genevieve, assured them that Christ would protect their city. He did. Attila turned his back upon Paris. He directed his steps toward Troyes, where this time the holy Bishop Lupus inspired the inhabitants with confidence. Continuing his march, Attila appeared at the gates of Orleans, but St. Anianus, the bishop of the city, had enlisted the help of the Roman General Aetius. Aetius and his army defeated the Huns at the battle of the Catalaunian Fields. Meeting with failure in Gaul, despite sacking numerous cities, Attila turned his eyes towards Italy.

As word of the Huns' approach reached him, Pope St. Leo (440-461) determined to stop Attila before he attacked Rome. Pope St. Leo went out to meet Attila in the Po valley. Leo was able to convince Attila to spare the city. Attila was persuaded to leave Italy and live in peace with Rome.

By this time, the Church was the only power that dared to oppose the barbarian invaders and try to check their unbridled appetite for conquest. Faithful to her trust, the Church, which had been instituted for all peoples, set out to win the rude and proud barbarians to the religion of her divine Founder. The task was an extremely difficult one. These new races had little or no education. Also, they were either strongly attached to their own pagan gods or tainted with Arianism.

Such was the situation that confronted the Church when Theodoric, the king of the Ostrogoths, assassinated the ruler of Italy and took the title of "King of Italy." Although Theodoric was very tolerant in his policies, he was an Arian. When he became ruler of the Empire, Arianism was the religion of all the barbarians except the Franks. The Franks were pagans.

The Conversion of the Franks

When the Germanic tribe called the Franks entered Roman Gaul in 485, they were entirely pagan. The Franks occupied the land that is modern Belgium, Holland, and northeastern France. The rest of France was divided between the Arian Visigoths, in the south and west, and the Arian Burgundians in the east.

In 493, Clovis, the great warrior-king of the Franks, married a seventeen-year-old Burgundian princess named Clotilda. Though Clotilda's parents had been Arians, she was a devout Catholic. From the beginning, Clotilda urged her husband to become a Catholic. She prayed for him unceasingly. When their first child was born, she obtained his permission to baptize the baby. However, when the child died shortly after his baptism, Clovis blamed the Christian

God for the child's death. It seemed that the death of his baby son had hardened his heart and driven him more deeply into paganism. However, "Clotilda" means "renowned in battle" and she was also a warrior. She refused to give up her fight for the soul of her husband. Their second son was baptized as well, and lived.

During the time they spent together, Clotilda told Clovis that, if ever in battle he saw himself facing defeat, he should call upon Jesus Christ to save him. Such a day came. Clovis found himself facing defeat at the hands of his enemies. He remembered his wife's words and called upon our Savior for aid. Immediately the tide of battle turned and the Frankish forces were victorious. Clovis returned to tell Clotida that he was ready to take instruction as a Catholic.

Clotilda summoned St. Remi, the holy bishop of Reims, to instruct her husband. Although a man of war, the heart of Clovis was open to the Faith. It is said that when the agonies of Our Lord's Crucifixion were first described to Clovis, a righteous anger overtook him. He grasped his weapons and cried: "If I had only been there with my Franks!" St. Remi baptized Clovis along with three thousand of his nobles and warriors on Christmas Day, 496. The cause of Catholicism had scored an important victory in Gaul.

Gradually, the entire Frankish nation converted to Catholicism. Like their great leader they were always ready to defend Our Lord and His Church against her enemies. They would not tolerate Arianism in their land. Later the Franks conquered the whole of northern Gaul as far south as the Loire River. They called their kingdom Francia. Paris was its capital. As she was the first of the barbarian tribes to convert to the Faith, France became known as the "Eldest Daughter of the Church."

The Baptism of Clovis

Theodoric and the Ostrogoths

In Italy, the barbarians remained stubborn Arians. King Theodoric was a clever politician. He tried to blend the Gothic and Roman elements in the Empire. He also sought to live at peace with Pope Gelasius I (492-496) and Pope Anastasius II (496-498). However, when the new Emperor at Constantinople, Justin, a Catholic, began a campaign against all heretics including the Arians, Theodoric interpreted this as an attack upon himself. Believing the papacy to be involved in the campaign, he summoned Pope John I (523-526). He told the Pope to go at once to see Justin and convince him to withdraw the anti-Arian legislation.

Emperor Justin received Pope John as if he were Peter himself. Justin even requested the Pope to crown him a second time. This made Theodoric furious. Upon the Pope's return, Theodoric threw him into prison, where he died from his ill treatment in 526. Theodoric died the same year, but first took the precaution of appointing John's successor, Felix III (526-530).

For a while the papacy succumbed to the dominion of the Gothic kings. However the days of the Gothic dynasty were numbered. Justinian, Justin's successor, reconquered Italy and Rome.

Justinian

During his reign, the Emperor Justinian (527-565) had such an impact on history that his times are called "the age of Justinian." He was intelligent and well educated. He was also an excellent administrator and a hard worker. Through the famous Justinian Code he accomplished an immortal legislative reform. He infused the rigor and severity of the ancient Roman law with the spirit of Christianity. He introduced into the Roman law an element previously unknown, namely, consideration for social justice, public morality, and human welfare. It was also during his reign that Byzantine art reached its climax with the construction of the famous Church of Hagia Sophia (Holy Wisdom) in Constantinople.

Pope St. Gregory the Great

Gregory I was born in 540 to an ancient Roman patrician family. He began his public career and by the age of thirty, Emperor Justinian II made him Prefect of the City of Rome. Upon the death of his father, Gregory renounced his secular career and became a monk. He spent his entire fortune founding seven monasteries.

After Gregory's ordination in 578, Pope Benedict I made him papal nuncio (ambassador), to the Imperial court in Constantinople. In 585, Gregory returned to Rome and his monastery. The sight of

some young Anglo-Saxon slaves in the slave-market inspired him
with the idea of evangelizing the British Isles. His presence in Rome,
however, seemed indispensable. Gregory had barely left on his mission
to Britain, when Pope Pelagius III called him back to Rome. When
Pelagius died in 590, both the clergy and people of Rome literally
forced Gregory to accept the papacy by their unanimous acclamation.

Emperor Justinian was barely dead, when a migration of
barbarians again threatened Imperial rule in Italy. This time it was
the Lombards who were responsible for the calamities. The Emperor
in Constantinople was utterly powerless to defend Italy against the
invaders. The Lombards overran almost the whole of Italy.

When St. Gregory (590-604) became Pope in 590, the Church
already owned vast amounts of land in Italy, Sicily, Corsica, Sardinia,
and more distant provinces. These church lands were called the
Patrimony of St. Peter. The pope was determined to repair the damage

Hagia Sophia

done by the barbarians to the Church lands. All the while he had to deal with the Lombards. So often did he buy off the Lombard hordes, that he used to call himself the "paymaster of the Lombards."

Meanwhile, at Rome, close to the city's main churches, Pope Gregory established homes for the poor, places of rest for pilgrims, and orphanages. He signed several treaties with the Lombard king. He defended Italy and Rome by raising military forces for the defense of Italy and repairing the walls of the city. He passed laws to help slaves and laid the foundations for the temporal power of the papacy. He finally succeeded in converting Adaloald, the Lombard king, who was baptized in 603. However, Adaloald was only thirteen years old when he came to the throne and was deposed

Pope St. Gregory the Great

ten years later without having brought his people into the Church. Theodelinda, Adaloald's Catholic mother and the wife of the two preceding kings, had tried in vain to convert her husbands. Sadly, not all barbarian chieftains were Clovis, nor all princesses Clotida. Nevertheless, Theodelinda did found the famous monastery of Bobbio, and erected a basilica dedicated to St. John the Baptist at Monza, near Milan. Agilulf, Adaloald's father, placed on its altar the iron crown, upon which was engraved his name, together with the title "King of all Italy." This crown was later used in the coronation ceremonies of

Charlemagne and Napoleon. It is supposed to have one of the nails used to crucify of Our Lord as its inside circle.

Pope St. Gregory was concerned about the welfare of the Church in every part of Christendom. Despite his temporal problems, he never lost sight of the fact that he was head of the Church, and that his main job was to teach all nations. He opposed the Arians in Spain, where they had become very powerful after the Visigoth invasion. Before his death he was able to see the Visigoths converted to the true Faith. He stamped out paganism in Corsica and Sardinia. He laid the foundations for the conversion of the Lombards. He vigorously defended the rights of the papacy against John the Faster, Patriarch of Constantinople, who granted himself the title of "Universal Patriarch." Gregory set an example of Christian humility by referring to himself as the "Servant of the Servants of God," a title which his successors have retained to the present day. Gregory's zeal for the beauty of divine worship has made his name a household word. Even today, we speak of the music of the Church as Gregorian Chant.

Throughout his pontificate, Pope St. Gregory suffered from ill health. During his last years, he ruled the Church from his sick bed. He died March 12, 604.

The Founding of the Benedictine Order

St. Benedict was born about 480 at Nursia, in Italy. His parents belonged to the nobility, so they sent him to Rome for his education. Terrified at the sight of the sins and vices of his companions, he fled into the solitude of a cave. His sole purpose was to live there alone under the eye of God. However, soon disciples gathered around him. This growth encouraged him to establish in the neighborhood of his cave twelve small monasteries, each housing twelve monks.

In 528, Benedict moved his establishment to Monte Cassino, about halfway between Rome and Naples. Here, with his own hands, he built two chapels. Soon numbers of men flocked to him, hoping to lead a monastic life under his direction. This was the beginning of the Benedictine order, which was destined to play such a crucial role in the history of Europe and the Church.

The sons of the noblest Italian families as well as the most devout among the converted barbarians of Italy came to St. Benedict at Monte Cassino. From Monte Cassino he sent them forth as missionaries and teachers into all of Europe. Wherever these monks went they established new monasteries, which became centers of holiness and culture. By the middle of the seventh century the labors of the Benedictine monks had nearly restored the civilization of Europe that had been so greatly upset by the barbarian invasions.

In the solitude of his retreat, St. Benedict composed a Rule, which was the result of long experience and is stamped with the genius of a Roman organizer. It aims, firstly, to make the individual member of the community holy. However, since he is to become holy by living in a community, it creates rules and regulations based on Christian charity to enable the individual members to live together happily in peace and in

Monte Cassino

unity. The Rule stresses the virtues of obedience, patience, and charity. The monk is to become perfect, as his Heavenly Father is perfect. The tools he is to use for this purpose are prayer and labor.

The Rule of St. Benedict gives the abbot absolute authority over all the monks. They, under the abbot's direction, engage in the praises of God. Perfect obedience to the abbot, uniformity of a common life, and the perpetual bond linking the monk to his monastery were the guaranties that his Rule would last. Finally, in all its details, there is a spirit of moderation that makes it possible for all to follow the Rule.

Although a strict vow of poverty barred the monks from returning to worldly things, it did not mean that the monks were not concerned with the affairs of the world outside their monastery. Each monastery worked diligently to help the people in the surrounding communities. The monks taught farmers how to grow food and generally contributed to the economic welfare of the areas in which they lived. They opened schools, and the monasteries became centers of learning. The great universities of the Middle Ages were originally monastery schools.

Perhaps of all the work that the Benedictine monks did, nothing has been of greater value to civilization than the work they

Statue of St. Benedict at Monte Cassino

did in the Scriptorium. This was a room in the monastery where certain monks wrote down the history of the times to be preserved for future generations. Even today historians visit Monte Cassino to consult its archives. In addition to this, the monks made careful and beautiful copies of the Scriptures. They copied them exactly and illuminated, that is, decorated the pages with beautiful designs.

St. Benedict died in 547 at Monte Cassino surrounded by his monks. He left behind him an institution that has been of tremendous service to the Church in every age down to the present. His rule has been the model for every other monastic rule since.

The Beginning of Christianity in Ireland

The conversion of Ireland to Catholicism began in the fifth century. In 431, Pope St. Celestine I (422-432) sent Palladius to Ireland as her first bishop. Two years earlier, the Pope had sent St. Germain of Auxerre and St. Lupus of Troyes to Britain to deal with a heresy there. Probably when they returned to Gaul and met with the Pope, they not only reported on the results of their mission, but also talked about the neighboring island of Ireland. They likely recommended that its struggling Catholic communities should receive encouragement and assistance. As a result of this counsel the Pope sent Palladius to Ireland.

The new bishop, sailing from southern Britain, probably landed on the Irish coast near present-day Dublin. He then proceeded to the interior of the island. According to Irish tradition, he made some conversions and established a few churches. However, he died shortly after arriving. The man who was to be the Apostle of the Irish nation took his place at the head of the mission: St. Patrick. It is the clear and unvarying testimony of the Irish records that St. Patrick arrived as a missionary in Ireland in 432.

St. Patrick: The Apostle of Ireland

St. Patrick was born in Kilpatrick, Scotland, about 399, to a family of Roman nobility. Due to the weakness of the Roman power in Britain, Irish raiders would strike into Britain, plundering it. They would carry off slaves and property. In one of these raids, pirates captured the sixteen-year-old Patrick and took him to Ireland. There he was sold as a slave to an Irish chieftain. He worked tending his master's flocks on the Irish hillsides. In his autobiography, *Confessions*, he writes that during his captivity, while tending the flocks, he prayed many times during the day. On the hillsides a remarkable change occurred in the young slave's soul. He underwent an extraordinary conversion experience.

In the ways of Providence, the years of Patrick's captivity actually became a preparation for his future apostolate. He acquired a perfect knowledge of the Irish language. He also became familiar with all the details of the pagan Druid religion from whose bondage he would one day free the Irish people.

Six years passed in prayer and study. Then one night, as Patrick slept, he heard an angelic voice that whispered that he should return to his own country. He made the perilous journey westward about two hundred miles to a place on the coast which he had never before seen and where he knew no one. There a ship lay ready to sail. Patrick asked to be taken on board. The captain at first refused but changed his mind and admitted the fugitive slave as a passenger.

The ship arrived to find western Gaul being cruelly devastated by barbarian hordes. The conditions were so bad that Patrick and his companions wandered through uninhabited country for a month, nearly dying of hunger. They also had the bad luck to be captured by a roving band, in whose hands they remained for two months.

Patrick's movements during the next few years are obscure. It is likely that he visited southern Gaul, Italy, and the abbey on the Mediterranean island of Lerins. Lerins Abbey was just then acquiring widespread renown for learning and piety. At Lerins he saw something of monastic life. Eventually he arrived in Britain where his family greeted him as a long-lost son. They begged him to settle with them permanently but his heart was now set on devoting himself to the service of God. He realized that it was God's will that he should return to the land of his slavery and spend his life preaching the Catholic Faith to its pagan inhabitants.

At this time, there was a close connection between the Church in Britain and in Gaul. Thus it was to Gaul that Patrick traveled to prepare for his missionary career. To succeed he would need to engage in serious theological study, secure the guidance of prudent and holy men, and win approval and support from the appropriate authorities. According to Irish records, he attached himself to the Church of Auxerre, under that city's bishop St. Germain. A few years later St. Germain ordained Patrick to the priesthood.

Patrick's desire to become a missionary in Ireland soon became well known. However, a few difficulties lay in his path. Those in authority felt that he lacked the necessary education. They also had a general impression that he was not the man for so demanding an enterprise. Nevertheless, he clearly made a positive impression on St. Germain.

In 429, the Holy See commissioned St. Germain to go to Britain to fight a heresy which had arisen there. St. Germain chose Patrick to accompany him. During this missionary campaign to Britain, a missionary journey to Ireland was discussed. Patrick was mentioned as a suitable person to lead it. However, later, in Gaul, when the matter arose for final decision, Patrick was rejected. Pope Celestine chose Palladius whom he consecrated as bishop for Ireland. Soon afterward, however, Patrick also received permission to travel as a missionary to Ireland. He was already on his way when news of Palladius' death arrived. This caused the Church authorities to change their plans. They chose Patrick to succeed the deceased prelate. He was consecrated bishop before he resumed his journey to Ireland.

According to Irish tradition, St. Patrick's first converts were the people of eastern Ulster province, among whom he had spent his youth as a slave. He made his way to Tara, where the high-king Loigaire had his chief fortress. Although the high-king remained a pagan, he did allow the saint to preach wherever he wished. Of course, outside the area that was under Loigaire's personal control such permission was of little value unless Patrick secured the good will of the lesser kings. The older rulers generally remained stubborn in their paganism, but the young princes showed a readiness to hear the Gospel message. This,

St. Patrick preaches to Loigaire

again, would be of little value unless the free men of the country accepted the new religion. The political structure of Ireland was democratic in spirit although monarchical in form. Preaching to the people was therefore necessary. Over time, the saint preached in the provinces of Connacht and Munster.

In 439, three bishops arrived in southern Ireland to succeed Palladius. They communicated periodically with Patrick in the North. In 457, they met with him to create the initial rules governing the Irish church. One of these canons decreed, "If any difficult questions arise in this island, they are to be referred to the Apostolic See."

In 444, St. Patrick established the spiritual capital of Ireland at Armagh. He likely chose this site because of its nearness to the ancient capital of the Ulster kings. The city has remained the ecclesiastical capital of the country ever since. Today the Anglican cathedral stands upon the spot where Patrick built his stone church. Construction of the Catholic cathedral in Armagh began during the latter half of the 1800s. The present Catholic cathedral replaced the medieval cathedral which the Protestant Church of Ireland took during the Protestant Revolt. Armagh is one of the few cities in the world which is home to two cathedrals of the same name: St. Patrick.

St. Patrick refers more than once in his *Confessions* to the amazing success of his missionary endeavors. His converts numbered in the thousands. The ordination of clergy is mentioned no less than three times. For the most part, they must have been of native Irish stock. Before St. Patrick died, he made some of these men bishops.

From the *Confessions* it is evident that St. Patrick venerated the monastic life. He thought it a true triumph of divine grace when the young men and women of his flock became monks and nuns. He regarded these as the fairest fruits of his missionary labors.

St. Patrick's Catholic Cathedral in Armagh

Irish tradition fixes St. Patrick's death in 493. He was buried quietly at Saul, probably in the first church that he had founded. The major role that St. Patrick played in Irish history has always been recognized. During his sixty-year apostolate, he organized whatever Christianity already existed in Ireland. He converted a large portion of pagan Ireland. He brought the country into the brotherhood of Christian nations. When he died, the Catholic faith was the religion of the country. Soon St. Patrick would become the hero of the Irish race. His name continues to be cherished with a fidelity and enthusiasm for which there is no parallel.

From St. Patrick's death to the end of the sixth century, bands of barbarians overran both Gaul and Britain. The Church in Ireland could expect little help from the Church in these countries. The Church in Ireland, still in its infancy, had to rely upon its own resources. It is an amazing tribute to the manner in which St. Patrick accomplished his work, that the Church continued to grow and flourish.

Irish Monasticism

At this time monasticism was becoming increasingly popular everywhere in the West. Nowhere did the monastic ideal find more enthusiastic admirers than in Ireland. In some mysterious way it made an irresistible appeal to the Irish nature. After 500 AD, the Church in Britain began to enjoy an era of peace. Close relations resumed between that country and Ireland. As a result, monasteries began to multiply.

The man most responsible for bringing about the great explosion of Irish monasticism was St. Finian. St. Finian had been educated by one of St. Patrick's disciples. St. Finian's disciples were known as the "twelve apostles of Ireland." They all became celebrated abbots and founders of monasteries. Before the end of the sixth century, a large number of monasteries dotted the face of the country.

Since the Catholic clergy and monks replaced the native learned class of druids as the nation's philosophers and theologians, it was taken for granted from the beginning that they should devote themselves to serious study. By 600, the monastic schools had combined the ancient native learning inherited from the Celtic past with the new Latin learning that came with Christianity. Having accepted, absorbed, and fostered native culture, these schools exerted a profound influence in Ireland. Having also adopted classical culture, which the Church preserved for Europe, the Irish clergy were able to proceed to the Continent where they played a major part in repairing the intellectual and spiritual losses caused by the barbarian invasions.

The finest leaders in Ireland devoted a tremendous amount of energy and passion to religion and learning. Not only were there many monasteries and religious institutions but they were filled. As a result, a very large proportion of the population practiced lofty and even heroic virtue. Consequently Ireland in the seventh century merited the proud title, "Island of Saints and Scholars."

St. Columbanus

The Irish monasteries were not large buildings. They consisted of small huts and chapels surrounded by earthworks. Thus, although the monks lived in a community, their existence was something like that of the hermits. It may have been this desire for solitude that led some of the Irish monks to separate themselves from their country and embark upon long pilgrimages. The Vikings found traces of the Irish monks when they discovered Iceland. Evidence exists showing that some monks, notably St. Brendan, may have journeyed as far west as North America.

St. Columbanus was a monk from the Bangor monastery in Ulster. With twelve fellow monks, he sailed for the Kingdom of the Franks in 585. They then traveled eastward into the land of the Burgundians. The king of the Burgundians helped them in building a monastery at Luxeuil around 590.

Luxeuil Monastery

Luxeuil became the center of the monastic movement in Western Europe. From Luxeuil, missionaries went into Switzerland and Germany. They even traveled into northern Italy to convert the Lombards. Although St. Columbanus' rule was very strict and more severe than St. Benedict's, it attracted the barbarian converts. As a result they entered the monasteries in great numbers.

The Conversion of Britain

There had been Christians in Britain as early as the second century. British martyrs died during the persecution of Diocletian. However, the invasions of the Saxons in the fifth century and the Angles in the seventh century drove the native Britons into Cornwall and Wales, and Christianity with them. The bishops and priests were driven out, and their churches were either destroyed or converted into pagan temples. The Anglo-Saxons occupied the country where they gradually established seven kingdoms. In the south, they created Kent, Sussex, and Wessex. In the east they formed the kingdoms of East Anglia and Essex. In the north they fashioned the kingdom of Northumbria. The kingdom of Mercia was located in the center of the island. In these kingdoms they implanted the bloodthirsty religion of Odin.

While still a simple monk, Pope St. Gregory the Great had conceived the plan of evangelizing the Angles. As pastor of the Universal Church, he put this plan into action. The story is told that one day Pope St. Gregory saw some Angle slaves in a Roman slave market. Their noble bearing and natural dignity so impressed him that he exclaimed, "These are not Angles, but Angels." Pope Gregory entrusted the task of spreading the Faith in Britain to forty monks from his own monastery. They were placed under the direction of St. Augustine of Canterbury. These missionaries left Rome in the autumn of 596. In 597, Augustine and his companions landed on the English coast and began their missionary work.

The work of the missionaries was made a little easier because King Ethelbert of Kent had married the Frankish princess Bertha, a devout Catholic. Bertha persuaded her husband to meet the missionaries. He received them warmly and gave them permission to preach throughout his kingdom. Within a short time the king and several thousand of his people embraced Christianity.

Great success crowned St. Augustine's missionary labors. In 601, Pope Gregory appointed him "Bishop of the English." The pope sent him the pallium as a mark of his supremacy over the churches of

Canterbury Cathedral, England

England. Augustine established his **See** at Canterbury. Very soon the kingdom of Essex followed the example of Kent. The capital of this kingdom was London, and the first bishop was Melletius. When St. Augustine died in 605, the Faith had taken deep root in England.

St. Columba

St. Columba, the Apostle of Scotland, was born in Donegal in 521. He received his education at the great monastery of Clonard. When he was forty-two years old, he went to northern Britain to preach to the Scots. The King of the Scots gave him a little island off the western coast. There he founded a monastery that for centuries was one of the most famous in Europe. It was the monastery of Iona. When St. Columba died in 579, northern Scotland had been won to the Faith.

Review Exercises

1. Who forced the Gothic tribes to become Arians?
2. Why did the Vandals persecute the Church?
3. Who stopped the Huns from attacking Rome?
4. Why is France called the Eldest Daughter of the Church?
5. What three virtues does the Rule of St. Benedict stress?
6. Where is the spiritual capital of Ireland?
7. Who was St. Finian?
8. What was the name of the monastery St. Columbanus founded?
9. Who was the first English King to convert to Catholicism?
10. Where did St. Augustine establish the See for the primary English bishop?

CHAPTER 7

The Church Converts Europe and Faces its Greatest Challenge:
The Church in the Seventh Century

St. Wilbrord Preaches the Gospel to the Frisians

During the seventh century, the Church experienced some of its greatest triumphs. The Church continued to grow in Ireland and Britain. The Church would spread its message to the German peoples who would come to embrace it. In France, the descendants of Clovis and Clotilda would continue to grow in love for Christ and His Church. It seemed that all of Europe was turning ever more towards the Catholic Faith. However, in the desert of Arabia, the greatest threat that the Church has ever known was about to sweep forth.

The Church Grows in Britain

Of the seven Anglo-Saxon kingdoms, only Kent and Essex initially embraced Catholicism. However, after St. Augustine's death, the Roman monks won more victories. Two more kings embraced the true Faith. St. Paulinus, the first Bishop of York, converted and baptized King Edwin of Northumbria. St. Felix of Dunwich and King Sigebert brought the Faith to East Anglia. Unfortunately, the pagan king of Mercia, Penda, defeated these two Christian kings in battle. Sadly, paganism was once more dominant.

At this pivotal moment, however, the Irish saved the day. Oswald, Edwin's nephew, who had been in exile in Ireland, re-conquered Northumbria with an Irish army. Right away he requested missionaries from St. Columba's great abbey of Iona to spread the Faith in the newly conquered region. These monks made the base of their missionary labors the island of Lindisfarne, where they built a monastery. Oswald later defeated Penda and implanted Christianity in Mercia.

From the very beginning a serious danger threatened these newly founded British churches. The danger arose from a dispute between the "Romans" and the Irish regarding the date for the celebration of Easter. The "Romans," that is, those who followed the Roman custom, celebrated Easter one week later than the Irish. This created division and confusion everywhere. The move towards unity began at Lindisfarne.

Wilfrid was a monk at Lindisfarne. He followed the Irish practice regarding Easter. However, he wanted to understand both sides of the issue and he traveled to Canterbury and Rome, so that he could study the question first hand. Upon his return to Lindisfarne, he introduced the Rule of St. Benedict and the Roman tradition

Ruins of Whitby Abbey

regarding Easter. In 664, a meeting, or synod, was called at Whitby
Abbey to discuss the issue. At the meeting the leaders of the two
sides made their arguments. Thanks to Wilfrid's eloquence, the
Roman cause carried the day.

Pope Vitalian (657-672) sent a new group of Benedictine
monks to Britain to help unify the two sides. The group was lead by
the Greek monk St. Theodore of Tarsus. At the age of sixty-seven
the Pope consecrated him Archbishop of Canterbury. During his
twenty-two years as Archbishop (668-690) he sowed the seeds of
learning among the English. He established a famous monastery
school at Canterbury. St. Aldhelm, who received his early training
there, became bishop of Malmesbury in Wessex. Another of
Theodore's companions, Benedict Biscop, founded the monasteries of
Wearmouth and Jarrow. St. Bede, the Father of English history, was
educated at Jarrow. From these English schools went forth the leaders
of the Carolingian reform on the Continent, among them the great
Alcuin of York.

The Church in Germany

In addition to the conversion of Britain, Irish monks also undertook the conversion of all the tribes located along the Rhine River. Four barbarian nations had established themselves there: the Bavarians, the Alemanni, the Thuringians, and the Saxons. Arriving primarily for the purpose of preaching the Gospel in Gaul, where he founded the monastery of Luxeuil, the Irish monk St. Columbanus settled at Bregenz on the shores of Lake Constance. From there his influence and that of his missionaries spread throughout present-day Germany and Austria.

Eustasius, St. Columbanus' successor as abbot of Luxeuil, preached the Gospel to the Bavarians. However, it was not until the end of the century that St. Rupert of Worms was able to make large-scale conversions. He preached throughout the land, baptized Duke Theodo, and erected the monastic church of Salzburg. In the meantime St. Emmeram established the Church at Ratisbon, and St. Corbinian that of Freising in the Tyrol (Austria). The majority of the leading towns in this country owe their origin to the establishment of monastic churches which the Duke richly endowed.

St. Gall, another disciple of St. Columbanus, preached Catholicism to the Alemanni. St. Gall also established a monastery in Switzerland that bears his name. From this center of piety and learning, scholarly and holy missionaries went forth spreading the Faith to other regions.

The Irish monk St. Kilian brought the Faith to the Thuringians. He preached the Gospel to the inhabitants of the provinces located along the banks of the Main River. He also founded the Church at Wurzburg. On July 8, 689, an evil duke and his wife, whom the saint had denounced for their immoral lifestyle, had St. Kilian and two of his companions murdered. St. Kilian is the patron saint of the diocese of Wurzburg in Germany.

St. Willibrord

In 668, St. Wilfrid was expelled from his See of York. He left Britain to go to Rome to plead his case before the pope. However, contrary winds drove his ship on to the coast of Frisia (northwestern Netherlands). The Frisian ruler Aldfrid honorably received him and permitted him to preach the Gospel. Upon his return to England, he spoke of Frisia to his monks at Ripon monastery. Twelve years later he sent his disciple St. Willibrord to the Frisians.

Echternach Basilica, burial place of St. Willibord

Upon his arrival, St. Willibrord placed himself under the protection of the Frankish leader, Pepin, who had recently conquered southern Frisia. St. Willibrord established his base at Utrecht, where he built a cathedral and began recruiting a native clergy. In order to protect himself and his monks he fortified his monastery at Echternach against possible uprisings by the Frisians. Then he began preaching the Gospel to the native peoples. Finally, upon the advice of Pepin, he went to Rome to be consecrated a bishop at the hands of Pope Sergius (687-701). With the Pope's consent he created a new ecclesiastical province. For the next forty years, until 739, he preached the Gospel throughout Frankish Frisia. By the time of his death he had succeeded in eliminating all traces of pagan worship.

The Rise of Islam

Arabia had resisted all attempts at conversion. It continued to cling to paganism. There was in the Arabian town of Mecca a famous sanctuary called *The Kaaba*. The Kaaba was the center of a bizarre religion, which consisted partly of Jewish traditions and partly of idolatrous practices. The Kaaba was a small, cubical stone building. Near the building there was a spring. Followers of the religion venerated the spring because they believed that the Angel Gabriel had used its waters to quench the thirst of Hagar and Ishmael when they were lost in the desert. The temple contained 360 different idols. Each of the various Arabian tribes had its own idol.

In 571, the family to whom the guardianship of the Kaaba was entrusted had a son, whom they named Mohammed. Orphaned as a child, he earned his livelihood as a camel driver and shepherd. He likely would have lived and died in poverty and obscurity had he not attracted the attention of a rich older widow. She first employed him as a trader then married him. Mohammed was twenty-five years of age at the time. His sudden rise to fame and wealth gave him the opportunity he desired to cultivate an inborn taste for quiet meditation. He relates that he had a vision from the Angel Gabriel. From that moment Mohammed believed himself called to overthrow idolatry and to restore the true worship of God.

As his program included the destruction of the idols in the Kaaba, he drew down upon himself the hatred of its guardians. Thus, on July 16, 622, Mecca's rulers forced him to flee that city and depart to Medina. This is the date of the "hegira" (flight), and marks the beginning of the Moslem era. In Medina his power and the number of his followers grew. Mohammed was soon able to have his revenge. He returned and seized Mecca and purified the Kaaba. When he died in the year 632, he had won the whole of Arabia to his cause.

The tenets of his religion, Islam, are contained in the *Koran*. The *Koran* is a book composed of so-called revelations that the angel Gabriel gave to Mohammed. The Moslem creed is utterly stark and simple: there is no other God but Allah, and Mohammed is his prophet. Merely to pronounce this creed makes a man a Moslem. Thereafter the penalty for apostasy is death. Beyond this life there is another. After death, men cross a narrow bridge. The wicked are hurled from this bridge into Hell, but the good are admitted into a paradise. Any faithful Moslem who dies in battle is guaranteed a place in paradise. Although Mohammed proclaimed that all Moslems were brothers, forbidding them to fight one another, unbelievers were always fair game. Unbelievers could be attacked mercilessly and converted or subjected to Moslem rule.

The moral teachings of the *Koran* are based on the false doctrine of **fatalism**, which discards human freedom and the foundations of morality. All worship is reduced to formal acts. Moslems observe certain hours for prayer (five times a day). They are required to give alms, fast every day during the entire month of the Ramadan, and abstain from wine, pork, and games of chance. Sadly, the *Koran* treats women rather poorly.

The Spread of Islam

One reason for Islam's rapid spread was that it promised its heroes treasure of all kinds on this earth, and material joys in the world to come. Consequently, immediately after Mohammed's death, his followers started a "holy war." In the East, the Arabs conquered Persia and Turkestan, and pushed into India. In the West, they seized the city of Jerusalem in 637. They overpowered Syria, Palestine, and Egypt. Still pressing forward, the Moslems finally succeeded in dominating the whole of northern Africa. Fifty years after the death of Mohammed, they had extended their conquests as far as the Atlantic Ocean. In all these countries the conquerors violently persecuted the Christians.

After these important conquests, they crossed the narrow strip of water that separates Spain from North Africa. In Spain the Moslem horde clashed with the Visigoths there. The country, divided against itself, offered little resistance to the invaders. The Moslems

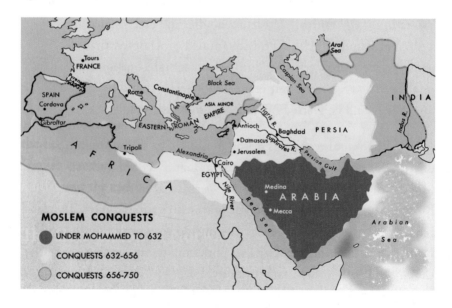

MOSLEM CONQUESTS

UNDER MOHAMMED TO 632

CONQUESTS 632-656

CONQUESTS 656-750

crossed the Straits of Gibraltar, and with the help of the traitor Count Julian, defeated King Roderic at the pivotal Battle of the Guadalete River, in 711. In the space of a few months the Moslems had conquered virtually the entire peninsula. Toledo, the capital of Visigothic Spain, surrendered to the invaders in the space of one afternoon in the autumn of 711. By 714, the great Gothic kingdom that had endured for three centuries was no more.

It had taken the Moslems three years to conquer the entire Iberian Peninsula. This was a task that Hannibal could not accomplish, and would be beyond the powers of Napoleon. The Roman legions had taken the greater part of a century to conquer the land. Of the Gothic kingdom, only a small remnant remained, huddled in a cave in the north of Spain. However, from that cave the Spanish would launch the greatest comeback in the history of the world.

The Church in France

The Merovingians were the first Frankish dynasty in Gaul. Founded around the beginning of the sixth century, the dynasty lasted until 751. Before the Merovingian era the clergy and people of a city selected and nominated their bishop. During the Merovingian period, kings began to recommend candidates. This procedure soon amounted to imposing the individual of their choice upon the electors.

A bishop had considerable influence. He was usually a great landowner. He obtained his property largely from donations made by kings and their families, prelates and clerics, and the wealthier citizens. In those days of deep faith, people gave to a church or monastery just as people donate today. They were a means of supporting the holy patrons of these institutions who in turn prayed for the donors and their spiritual well being.

There is no denying that the practice of the king choosing the bishop occasionally gave rise to serious abuses. However, as a general rule, the Merovingian kings tried to select the best-suited and most virtuous candidates to be bishops. Moreover, the Church through her councils did everything she could to curb the greed of unscrupulous clerics. The bishops could only use Church money for specific purposes. The bishop's income supported his clergy, built and maintained diocesan churches, and provided for the needs of the poor. As regards the poor, the Church paid all the expenses for their food, clothing, and shelter. In the course of time the Church built a hospital in every episcopal city to provide for the poor. The bishop also offered protection to the weak and to orphans. He acted as their guardian, so that even local rulers could not bring suit against them without informing him. He appointed his archdeacon to defend them in the civil courts. He also took a special interest in prisoners, and frequently provided them with food or interceded with the courts on their behalf.

Finally, the bishop, as the representative of the Church, while not explicitly condemning slavery, a move that would have caused a social revolution, fought strenuously to suppress its abuses. He excommunicated any master who killed his slave without the permission of the courts. He proclaimed the lawfulness of the marriages of slaves, an action that was an important step in the direction of morality. Lastly, he ensured that Christian slaves did not fall into the hands of pagans.

When the Gospel penetrated into outlying country districts, it became necessary to establish religious centers, which were called "rural parishes." The priests in charge of these parishes were called the "priests of the people." The bishop established some of these parishes directly and put an archpriest at their head. The wealthy established other parishes on their own estates where they served as private oratories for the use of their families. By an inevitable development, the practice of placing oneself under the patronage of the powerful became more and more widespread during the sixth and seventh centuries. The need for protection induced priests, even parish priests, to seek the favor of the local ruler. Bishops and abbots sought the protection of the king. This caused secular rulers to have more influence in Church affairs. Over time, the great and powerful began to usurp the administration of Church property as well as the supervision of the work of the clergy.

Review Exercises

1. What is Lindisfarne?
2. What did the synod at Whitby decide?
3. Where did St. Gall establish his monastery?
4. Who was the apostle to the Thuringians?
5. Who was the apostle to the Frisians?
6. Who founded Islam?
7. What false doctrine is the basis for the moral teachings of the *Koran*?
8. What is the "hegira?"
9. What is the significance of the Battle of the Guadalete River?
10. What were some of the things the bishops of this period did to help slaves?

CHAPTER 8

To Defend the Church from the Infidel Without and the Heretic Within:

The Creation of the Holy Roman Empire

The Coronation of Charlemagne

The Moslem hordes had rolled across Iberia and conquered the Visigoths in a matter of months. The Visigoths had not fought a war in over a hundred years so they were, perhaps, not the strongest opponents to face the Moslems. Once Visigothic Spain fell to the Moslems, the next logical target was Frankish Gaul. The Franks were still, at heart, a barbarian people. In their veins flowed the blood of Clovis and Clotida, warriors to the last. The promise of Clovis was going to be fulfilled: "If only I had been there with my Franks!"

St. Boniface, Apostle of Germany (672-754)

St. Boniface

The Anglo-Saxon monk Winfrid had begun the apostolate to the Germans east of the Rhine River. He received his commission from Rome, when he journeyed there in 719. "Go," said Pope Gregory II to him, "from this moment on you shall be called Boniface (that is, he who does good)." Crossing the Rhine at Mainz, he traveled to Bavaria, Hesse, and Thuringia. In all these places he made numerous conversions.

After this first journey, Boniface returned to Rome. Pope Gregory II rewarded his labors by consecrating him the first bishop of Hesse and Thuringia. At the same time the Pope vested him with authority to reform, in the name of the Holy See, the clergy and the faithful of these regions. Armed with his commission, Boniface set out to score more victories.

In Hesse he dealt paganism a fatal blow when, with his own hands, he felled the sacred oak tree of the pagan god Odin. As he started to chop down the tree, he called upon Odin to strike him down. When Odin failed to strike him down, the pagans converted to Catholicism.

Soon native clergy swelled the ranks of his Anglo-Saxon companions. He and his assistants founded monasteries for men and convents for women throughout the land. Later he established several great abbeys, like Hildesheim and Fulda, which developed into seminaries as well as centers of prayer and preaching.

In 732, Pope Gregory III named Boniface metropolitan of all Germany. The pope charged him to consecrate bishops for those areas of Germany where the faith was most quickly growing. From that moment on, and especially after his third journey to Rome (737-738), he devoted all his time and energy to the reform and organization of the hierarchy.

At that time Bavaria consisted of not only its present area, but also Upper Austria as well. Boniface divided this vast land into four Sees. He defined the boundaries and selected bishops for each one. Then, with the assistance of these bishops, he called the first German synod. This synod was concerned with improving the morals and discipline of the clergy. Later, Eichstadt Abbey, where one of Boniface's relatives was

Cathedral at Fulda

abbot, also became a bishopric. This See was to serve as an outpost for future missionary journeys to the Slavs along the River Elbe.

The Victory over the Moors

The material aid of Frankish ruler Charles Martel, secured by Pope Gregory II, contributed greatly to St. Boniface's success. Boniface himself wrote that without the protection of the Frankish king, he could not govern his people, defend his priests, or forbid the practice of pagan rites in Germany. However, the great Frankish monarch did more than lend assistance to the Apostle of Germany. To the south of his kingdom he succeeded in completely stopping an invasion of the Arabs from Spain.

In 719, the Moslems crossed the Pyrenees and took possession of three cities in southern Gaul. Outside the walls of Toulouse the Moslem armies were halted and completely crushed. Yet the Arabs would not acknowledge defeat. They invaded Gaul a second time. They seized the city of Bordeaux. They were preparing to advance on Tours, where the treasures of St. Martin's shrine were an irresistible attraction.

In 732, at Poitiers, just outside Tours, in one of history's most decisive and critical battles, Charles Martel defeated the Moslem army. Contrary to Frankish custom he placed his heavy cavalry on the defensive. It was bitterly cold, but the Moslems were dressed for the Spanish summer. The Frankish warriors were wrapped in wolf skins. They stood before the Moslems like a wall of ice. The Moslem light cavalry, which was very fast, hurled itself time and again against this wall. They could not break through the firm ranks of the Franks.

A few years later, the Arabs returned. This time they followed the Rhone River valley and threatened the city of Lyons. Charles again hurled them back. However, it would take two generations before his successors completely expelled them from Gaul.

The importance of the Battle of Tours-Poitiers cannot be overstated. Had Charles Martel lost, France could have become a Moslem country. Moreover, as their every action showed, the Moslem army would not have stopped at France. It would have spread into Germany, Italy, and the rest of Europe, as it would try years later. As the Moslems had no sea power, Britain and Ireland may have been safe, but completely isolated. As a result of Martel's fierce opposition, which ended Moslem advances and set the stage for centuries of war to come, Islam moved no farther into Europe.

Statue of Charles Martel at Versailles, France

Charles Martel died on October 22, 741. He was buried at Saint Denis Abbey, later Basilica, in Paris. Wisely he had divided his kingdom among his adult sons a year earlier. He gave Germany to his son Carloman and France to his son Pepin. Both Pepin and Carloman were true and loyal sons of the Church. St. Willibrord baptized Pepin who received his education at the famous abbey of St. Denis. Carloman ruled until 747, when he entered a monastery where he spent the last seven years of his life.

The Reform of the Church in Gaul

St. Boniface was the first to see the danger that threatened the Church in Gaul. He wrote to Pope Zachary warning that too many of the Frankish bishops were unworthy clerics. Invested by the Holy See with full powers, and fortified by the protection of King Pepin, St. Boniface began to reform the Church in Gaul. He started by calling several councils. He was determined to craft a well-organized hierarchy modeled on the one which had proven so successful in Germany. St. Boniface also wrote disciplinary rules to improve the clergy. In addition to improving the priests and bishops, the councils also worked to abolish a number of superstitious practices that had been inherited from the pagans. The principal synod to achieve these results was convened in 742. It is known in

Statue of St. Boniface outside of Mainz Cathedral

history as the First German Synod. A Second German Synod convened three years later.

To cap this most important work, Boniface convoked a national council of the entire Frankish Empire in 745. Very soon virtuous and educated men occupied the various Sees in Gaul. St. Boniface had completely revived the Church in Gaul.

In 748, the Pope placed the final seal of approval on St. Boniface's work. In that year the Pope made the saint Archbishop of Mainz. Mainz became the metropolitan See of all Germany, just as Canterbury was in England.

Despite all these accolades and triumphs, the soul of St. Boniface was still the soul of a missionary. He decided to go to Frisia to complete the work of preaching the Gospel that St. Willibrord had started. A year later, on June 5, 755, he was slain along with fifty-two companions by an infuriated mob of Frisian pagans at Dokkum. His body was carried to Fulda where the saint was laid to rest in the abbey church. Today, Fulda's magnificent cathedral is a great pilgrimage site. Buried in the crypt lies the monk who had done much good.

The Beginning of the Holy Roman Empire

In return for the aid that Pepin had given to St. Boniface, Pope Zachary acknowledged him as King of the Franks. Zachary crowned him at St. Denis in Paris. Pepin promised to aid the Pope against the Lombards, who were acting up again.

Pepin requested Aistulf, the Lombard king, "out of respect for the Apostles Peter and Paul," not to march against Rome. When Aistulf would not listen, Pepin crossed the Alps, defeated Aistulf, and besieged his armies at Pavia, the Lombard capital. The Lombard king promised to pay for all the damages that the Lombards had done, but broke his promise. Again, the Pope had to call for aid. Pepin, always ready to come to the defense of the Church, re-crossed the Alps and once more defeated the pigheaded Aistulf. Pepin then gave Pope Stephen II twenty-two towns that he had reconquered from the Lombards. These towns came to be called the donation of Pepin.

Pope Stephen II died in April 757. His brother and successor Pope St. Paul I, was a prudent and holy man. During his ten-year pontificate he maintained the close papal alliance with King Pepin. [Note: There has been confusion with the numbering of popes named Stephen since March 752. In that month a pope was elected who took the name Stephen II (752-757), after a predecessor of the same name had died just three days after his election as pope, but before he could be consecrated. For purposes of this history the authors have followed the official numbering of popes named Stephen.]

During his pontificate, Paul I had made a good and trusted priest named Christopher the papal chancellor. Upon Pope St. Paul's death, Christopher took charge of the preparations for the election of Paul's successor. Meanwhile, a group of Roman nobles led by Duke Toto of Nepi had gathered an army in Rome. Christopher was able to obtain Toto's promise that he would not interfere in the papal election. However, Toto's oath proved worthless. With his army at his back, he forced his way into the Lateran Palace. Once inside, he proclaimed one of his brothers, a layman named Constantine, pope.

Duke Toto then compelled the elder Bishop Theodore, whom he had captured, to pass Constantine through all the clerical orders in a single day. On July 5, Constantine became "pope." The antipope governed the Church for thirteen months. During that time he wrote several times to Pepin. He did not receive a reply.

Meanwhile, though Christopher had fled from the villainous Toto and his army, he had not surrendered. Christopher enlisted the aid of the Lombards. In July, 768, the Lombards, ever eager to attack Rome, crushed Toto and his army. Christopher imprisoned antipope Constantine. On August 1, Christopher held a valid election which chose as pope a Sicilian priest, who took the name Stephen III.

A council held at the Lateran recognized Stephen as the true Pope. The council decreed that from then on, cardinal priests or cardinal deacons alone would be eligible for the office of pope. Moreover, laymen would be excluded from the electoral body. Adrian I (772-795) succeeded Stephen III when he died in 772.

Not surprisingly, the Lombards, who had been instrumental in defeating Toto and Constantine, wanted some of the papal land for their effort. Pope Adrian appealed to Charles, Pepin's son, the new Frankish king. History would know him as Charles the Great, or Charlemagne. Charlemagne defeated the Lombards, seized their capital at Pavia, and annexed their country to his empire.

From this moment on, Charlemagne showed his feelings for the Church. During the siege of Pavia, he traveled to Rome, arriving on Holy Saturday, 774. He conducted himself as a pious pilgrim. He dismounted from his horse and advanced on foot to St. Peter's Basilica. There, he climbed the steps of the church on his knees. At a meeting with the Pope in the Basilica, he confirmed the donation of Pepin, and even enlarged it. After the fall of Pavia, Charlemagne returned to Pope Adrian several towns that the Lombards had taken from him.

In 781, on the occasion of another visit by Charles to the Eternal City, the pope received additional lands. In the same manner he gained possession of the Lombard territories in Tuscany. Thus were the Papal States created. They would exist until the nineteenth century.

Charlemagne and the Saxons

Everywhere Charlemagne proved himself to be the champion of the Church. Through the conquest of Saxony he added considerably to the results achieved by St. Boniface. Saxony was the citadel of the pagan god Odin. The Saxons fiercely hated the Franks because the Franks had deserted the cause of paganism. This accounts for the Frankish missionaries' lack of success in Saxony. Charlemagne resolved to conquer Saxony, and win it to the Church.

Charlemagne's first campaign against the Saxons was very successful. His forces took the fortress of Eresburg. They destroyed

Paderborn Cathedral

the *Irmerlsul*, a giant tree that the Saxons thought was the pillar upon which the whole world rested. In 777, at a great assembly at Paderborn, a large number of Saxons converted to Catholicism.

Charlemagne then divided the kingdom of Saxony between the dioceses of Mainz, Cologne, and Wurzburg. The Abbey of Fulda became the center of an apostolate which was first entrusted to Sturm, the beloved disciple of St. Boniface, and later to Willibald. However, before long, the Saxons broke their word of honor which they had given to the Frankish king. They rose against the Franks and massacred Frankish priests and soldiers. They even set fire to the monastery of Fulda.

In 782, the Saxon revolt became more alarming when the Saxons defeated a Frankish army. Although normally a good and wise king, Charlemagne's actions following the defeat were appalling and excessive. He ordered the execution of 4,500 Saxon prisoners. Finally, after a war of three years, the Saxons surrendered. Widukind, their leader, received Baptism.

The baptism of Widukind was the signal for new attempts to spread the Faith. Willibald founded several new Sees. Conversions to the Faith were numerous. Saxon hostages, raised and educated by the Franks, demonstrated such ability and piety that most of the bishops of the country came from their ranks. From its beginning in 659,

Corbie Abbey in Northern France received a great number of Saxons as monks. Corbie, started by monks from Luxeuil Abbey, became the center of missionary labors throughout the North. From its halls went forth such men as St. Ansgar, the apostle of Denmark and Sweden. Finally, the work of organizing the

Corbie Abbey

Saxon nation paved the way for the future of medieval Germany, in which the Saxons were to play a critical role.

Charlemagne and the Moors

The pledge that the Holy Roman Emperor made to the Church was that he would defend her from the heretic within and the infidel without. Charlemagne took this promise very seriously. He was, after all, the grandson of Charles Martel. Thus, he waged war to drive the Moors out of France. He also fought them in Spain.

In 778, Charlemagne crossed the Pyrenees mountains from France into Spain at the head of an immense army. At Saragossa, Spain, the Moslem army defeated him. As his army retreated back across the mountains, the Moslems attacked the rear guard of his army. The Moors completely crushed the rear guard in the narrow mountain pass of Roncesvalles. Many French soldiers, including the gallant knight Roland, immortalized by the epic French poem, *The Song of Roland*, perished.

Charlemagne then created the kingdom of Aquitania to protect the frontiers of Gaul from the Moslems. The kingdom would act as a buffer zone between Gaul and Moslem Spain. He entrusted this bulwark to Duke William. William attacked and seized the Spanish cities of Barcelona, Tarragona, and Tortosa, which the Moors controlled. William converted these cities into a barricade against the Moorish invaders.

Thus Charlemagne and the Franks fulfilled their mission as the sword and shield of Christendom. The memory of these struggles was celebrated in famous French epic poems. These kept alive the spirit which would later embolden so many brave French knights to join the Crusades.

The Coronation of Charlemagne

Charlemagne's services to the Church deserved recognition and reward. Pope Leo III (795-816) was determined to strengthen his relationship with the Frankish king, whom he also needed to check the Roman aristocracy. Leo III's authority had been contested by the nephews of his predecessor, Adrian I. Things had become so bad that a band of armed conspirators had even attacked and severely wounded the Pope during a public procession.

The pope fled from Rome and went at once to Charlemagne, who was then at Paderborn. Immediately upon his election to the pontificate, Leo III had sent him the banner of Rome, and issued orders that the Roman people should swear allegiance to him. Charlemagne received the Pontiff with the greatest respect. He had Leo escorted back to Rome by a bodyguard of Frankish nobles and bishops.

The following year an investigation was opened, and Charlemagne himself arrived at the gates of Rome. Some days were spent examining the charges made against Leo by his enemies. However, the Pope completely cleared himself in the presence of the king.

The following day was Christmas Eve. Charlemagne came to St. Peter's Basilica. As he knelt before the high altar, Pope Leo placed a jeweled crown upon his head. The people shouted: "To Charles, most pious, most august, crowned by God, great and pacific emperor of the Romans, long life and victory!"

Leo III's coronation of Charlemagne made him the defender of all Christendom, and the Pope's associate in the task of governing the great Catholic family. The emperor was to protect and manage those things temporal. The pope guarded over spiritual matters. This new idea of imperial authority is embodied in the Lateran mosaics, in which Leo and Charlemagne are shown kneeling at the feet of St. Peter. To the Pope, Peter gives the pallium, the sign of the spiritual authority. To the emperor, he gives the banner, the sign of temporal power.

The Church and the Holy Roman Empire

Sadly, the idea of a great Catholic empire, which was created by St. Augustine in *The City of God* and appeared briefly during the reign of Leo III, would not ultimately succeed. It only worked when the Emperor was a man of great strength, courage, and holiness, and the Pope was a man of great holiness and vision. The plan was sound in theory but somewhat impractical in practice. It failed to recognize that the Pope, while the supreme head of the Church and infallible in matters of faith and morals, was still a man with human failings. Another difficulty lay in the fact that the popes of this era were both spiritual and temporal rulers, whereas the emperors were temporal rulers only. It often happened that the two powers, designed to work in harmony, became engaged in conflict.

While many of the Emperors, especially those of the Hapsburg dynasty, would be great defenders and loyal supporters of the Church, some Emperors tried to control the Church. Some attempted to exert more influence over the election of the Pope than was appropriate. Others meddled in affairs over which they did not have jurisdiction.

On the other hand, sometimes the pope failed to remember that his chief office was that of Vicar of Christ on earth. Some popes showed more concern for their temporal power than for the Church and the souls of the Faithful. Too often over the next centuries politics got in the way of prayer.

It was not long before Charlemagne himself went outside the lawful bounds of his jurisdiction. Although well intentioned, he began to meddle in the spiritual affairs of the Church. The bishops came to be regarded as government officials, and church synods regarded as state councils. The Emperor, concerned about the sacredness of the Mass, issued rules about the sacred liturgy and church music. Seeing some clerics not living holy lives, he reminded them of their obligation to lead by example. He issued a law forbidding them to carry weapons.

Charlemagne: Patron of Learning

Charlemagne came to the throne amid almost universal ignorance. Thankfully, the Benedictine monks had preserved many of the works of the great Greek and Latin writers. However, the condition of the times and the disorder caused by the barbarian invasions had greatly interfered with the spread of learning. Charlemagne decided to restore learning to the people and infuse new life to the arts.

In his travels through Italy, Charlemagne had been very impressed by the wealth of learning displayed by the clergy there. Desiring to possess an equally cultured clergy in his own country, he asked several learned scholars to return with him to his palace at Aachen. With the aid of these men, he established the palace school at Aachen, as well as many other episcopal and monastic schools throughout the land. The head of the palace school, and the most outstanding of these scholars, was an Anglo-Saxon Benedictine, named Alcuin.

Alcuin was born at York in England, in 735. He studied under the direction of Egbert, one of St. Bede's disciples. When he

Aachen Cathedral

came to Aachen, Alcuin brought with him the methods in use in the monastic schools of Britain. He possessed in a high degree the qualities needed to carry out the different functions of his office. He was first and last a teacher. He wrote clear and concise papers on grammar and the basics of composition and literature. From the palace school and the other schools that Charlemagne established came forth an army of bishops and abbots. They made it their purpose in life to advance the cause of learning.

Alcuin directed the Palace School for fifteen years. He worked with the Emperor to create schools everywhere and to revive learning. Though he retired to a monastery in 796, he continued to be Charlemagne's adviser until his death in 804.

As far as the duties of running his kingdom would permit, Charlemagne was a student. He spoke Latin fluently and knew some Greek. The book he loved best was St. Augustine's *The City of God*. He studied it constantly. He dreamed of building his empire in accordance with its theory.

The Death and Legacy of Charles the Great

When Charlemagne was seventy years old he realized that he was nearing the end of his life. At Aachen, before a vast assembly of clergy, nobles, and people, he solemnly declared that his son Louis was to be his successor. Charlemagne died in 814. One of the most influential figures in history, he has justly been called the founder of the modern world. In the Providence of God he brought together the old and the new, the Romans and the barbarians, the Church and the State. He welded them together into the beginnings of the Europe that we know today.

Review Exercises

1. Which Pope named Boniface metropolitan of Germany?
2. What is the significance of the Battle of Tours?
3. Where is St. Boniface buried?
4. Who reformed the Church in France?
5. What is the Donation of Pepin?
6. Why was the election of Constantine as pope invalid?
7. Who crowned Charlemagne?
8. Who was Alcuin of York?

CHAPTER 9

THE GREAT SCHISM

Throughout history, Catholic armies have carried sacred images into battle.

Seeds of a Schism: Iconoclasm ("Icon-breaking")

In the East, as well as the West, there was an impressive veneration of images. For example, armies carried sacred images before them into battle. However, the veneration of images had met with some resistance, especially in the East. Outside the Church, Jews and Moslems regarded this Christian devotion as idolatry. Even inside the Church, some of the faithful regarded it with suspicion.

Abuses in devotions involving images existed. However, most were no more than the typical fervent Catholic piety that had been practiced since the time of the catacombs, and continues today. The people represented by the statues and pictures that Catholics venerate really exist: Our Lord and Lady, the saints and angels. It is

Mother of Perpetual Help

that person being venerated, not the statue or icon. Most of the alleged abuses were based upon either misunderstandings or falsehoods.

In 726, there was a terrifying volcanic eruption in the Aegean Sea. For some reason this eruption caused the Eastern Emperor at Constantinople, Leo III, the Isaurian (717-741), to believe that he and his people had done something to displease God. He concluded that the reason for God's anger was idolatry and issued a decree, ordering the destruction of all images in the churches (iconoclasm). It was bitterly opposed by both the clergy and the laity all over the Eastern Empire. Leo then ordered the destruction of a famous icon of Christ which stood over the entrance to the Imperial palace. The destruction of the icon caused an uprising, which Leo quickly and bloodily suppressed. In 727, the Greeks rose in revolt against Leo because of the decree. Again, Leo violently suppressed the people.

Encouraged by these victories, Emperor Leo III ordered the ninety-year-old Patriarch of Constantinople to sign the edict. When he refused, Leo replaced him with a certain Anastasius. Anastasius was willing to go along with Leo. He agreed to a decree which banned all images of Christ, the Blessed Mother, saints, or angels in churches or elsewhere.

In the autumn of 727, Pope St. Gregory II (715-731) held a synod in Rome to discuss the issues raised by Leo's iconoclasm. The synod completely defended the proper veneration of images. Then, the Pope sent a letter to Leo setting forth the Church's teachings. The pope told Leo that "it would have been better for you to have been a heretic than a destroyer of images." The pope also refused to recognize the appointment of Anastasius as the Patriarch.

St. Gregory II died in February 731. His successor, Gregory III (731-741), continued to defend the use of images as aids in Christian worship. He, too, called a synod at Rome which ninety-three bishops attended. The synod excommunicated all who professed iconoclasm. Leo replied to the Pope and the synod by sending his navy to Italy to punish the Pope. However, storms wrecked his ships in the Adriatic Sea.

In another effort to hurt the Pope, Leo put all the churches in his empire under the authority of the Patriarch of Constantinople. Sadly, from this point forward, the Eastern Emperor and the popes would rarely cooperate on any major issues. The seeds had been planted for the final formal break of the Greek Orthodox Church from Rome in 1054.

The sinking of his navy and the opposition from his subjects somewhat lessened Leo's enthusiasm for his program. He resolved to carry on his work but without persecutions. Following Leo's death, his son, Constantine V (741-775), adopted the same policy as his father. In 754, after purging the hierarchy of opposition, he convoked a council at Hieria (in modern-day Turkey). There, all the bishops, with slavish obedience, signed an edict banning images.

In the churches the sacred images were destroyed. They were replaced by landscape paintings or pictures of birds or paintings of huge golden crosses in a deep blue field. The emperor told the bishops and monks that if they refused to go along with his program, he would make them suffer. The bishops yielded, but the monks offered heroic resistance. This made Constantine furious. He started a bitter persecution in which many were martyred. Nevertheless, the protests continued.

Meanwhile, in the West, Pope Stephen III (768-772) again condemned iconoclasm at a council held in Rome in 769. In the East, in 767, a council held at Jerusalem, representing the three patriarchates of Antioch, Jerusalem, and Alexandria, did as well.

Leo IV succeeded his father Constantine V. Despite the fact that the new emperor surrounded himself with monks, he remained an iconoclast. His wife, Empress Irene, was a confirmed opponent of that heresy. When, after Leo died, she became regent, she determined to restore the veneration of images.

When Irene became regent, a large number of the bishops at the imperial court and much of the army supported iconoclasm. One of Irene's first acts was to replace the iconoclast Patriarch with one who supported her position. She also won over to her cause a number of bishops who had been enticed into joining the opposing forces either through fear or flattery. Soon she was able to propose to Pope Adrian I the convocation of an ecumenical council to refute the errors of the synod of Hieria.

The council opened at Constantinople with two legates representing the Holy See. However, a riot of the military hampered its work, so Irene disbanded the troops and moved the council to Nicaea in 787. The council then defined exactly the veneration which is due to images. It is a veneration of honor. It is not the adoration which is due to God alone.

The Filioque Controversy

The Filioque controversy furnished additional material for another dogmatic grievance between the Greek Church and the Latin. *Filioque* is a Latin word, meaning "and the Son," found in the Creed. The passage refers to the Holy Spirit and reads: "Who

The Holy Spirit proceeds from the Father and the Son.

proceeds from the Father and the Son." The procession of the Holy Spirit from the Father and the Son was clearly taught by the Greek and Latin Fathers of the fourth century, although it was not contained in the Nicene Creed. The Spanish added it to the Creed in the fifth century to clarify difficulties they were having. The Greeks heard the word in the Creed from the Latin monks of Bethlehem. The Greeks accused the monks of heresy and threatened them with expulsion. The monks promptly appealed their case to the pope and the emperor. This storm reached its climax under Photius, Patriarch of Constantinople.

Divisions between East and West Worsen: The Photian Schism

The First Revolt of Photius

In 847, Empress Theodora, acting as regent, appointed St. Ignatius to be Patriarch of Constantinople. Ignatius was a monk and strong opponent of the iconoclasts. When the regency passed from Empress Theodora to her brother Bardas, matters reached a turning point. Bardas tried to corrupt the morals of the young emperor, his nephew, Michael III. Ignatius warned Bardas about his behavior, but to no avail. In January 858, the Saint publicly refused Bardas Holy Communion. He paid dearly for this act of courage. Bardas exiled him. A synod of bishops then met in Constantinople to nominate a new patriarch. The man Bardas and Michael wanted was a nobleman named Photius.

Photius was probably, from a literary, theological, and scientific standpoint, the most learned man of his time. However, he was also very worldly, crafty, ambitious, and dishonest. Although only a layman, the synod at Constantinople did not let that stop them from nominating Photius. They quickly ran him through all the holy orders and consecrated him Patriarch of Constantinople on Christmas Day 858. In a sign of things to come, he was consecrated by an excommunicated bishop from Sicily.

About a year and a half after his elevation to the See of Constantinople, Photius sent a letter to Pope St. Nicholas I, the Great (858-867). The letter craftily distorted the facts of his election and consecration. The letter delicately referred to Ignatius' arrest and removal from office as "when my predecessor left his charge." However, in Pope St. Nicholas, Photius had a worthy adversary. The pope fired back a letter asking Photius and Emperor Michael just how exactly Ignatius had "left his charge." The pope also demanded to know why he had not been notified sooner. He also noted in the letter that Photius had risen from layman to Patriarch in a remarkably short period of time.

Determined to learn the facts for himself, Pope Nicholas sent two bishops to Constantinople to investigate the matter. The record is unclear, but the two bishops were either tricked or bribed by the crafty Photius. They confirmed Photius in his See. A council was quickly convoked, consisting of 318 bishops, who, in obedience to an order from the emperor, declared Photius to be the lawful patriarch.

In 863, Pope Nicholas, having finally learned the truth of the events

Pope St. Nicholas I

in the East, called a synod in Rome. He declared that Photius was not a lawful bishop. He also stated that St. Ignatius was the rightful Patriarch of Constantinople and told Photius he was excommunicated if he did not accept St. Ignatius as such. The synod also suspended all clergy ordained by Photius from their priestly functions.

The situation worsened when the Bulgarians decided to unite with the Latin Church. In 867, Photius sent letters to the Eastern patriarchs and the Bulgarians. The letters attempted to provoke the Bulgarians to break from the Church by causing them to refuse to recognize the authority of the pope. This type of separation is called a **schism**. The letters pointed out the theological, canonical, and liturgical differences between the Greeks and the Latins. That same year Photius called a council at Constantinople. The council deposed Pope Nicholas I for interfering with the Church of Constantinople.

Meanwhile, the rule of the Eastern Empire was about to fall into the hands of one of history's most sinister figures. Since the ascension of Photius, the real ruler of the Empire had not been Emperor Michael, but his uncle Bardas. Over the years a man named Basil the Macedonian had become friendly with Michael and gained his confidence. He slowly turned Michael against Bardas. In April 867, Basil murdered Bardas in front of Michael. A month later Michael made Basil co-emperor.

In September, Basil murdered Michael, becoming sole emperor. The following day he locked Photius in a monastery and recalled Ignatius as Patriarch. Likely, he simply wanted the devious Photius out of the way. Basil entered into friendly relations with Pope Adrian II, Nicholas' successor. A council was held at Constantinople in 869, which reinstated Ignatius and reduced Photius to the lay state.

The Second Revolt of Photius

When St. Ignatius died in 877, Photius regained the favor of the evil Emperor Basil. Once again Photius ascended the patriarchal throne. (although it appears he was not re-ordained). Pope John VIII (872-882), desiring unity with the East, was willing to recognize Photius as Patriarch of Constantinople on certain conditions. Photius had to apologize publicly for his past behavior, restore Bulgaria to the Roman Church, and make no laymen bishops. Lastly, the Pope asked that Photius work with the supporters of Ignatius to bring peace to the Eastern Church.

Photius, in his pride, refused. Apparently an apology of any kind was totally unacceptable to him. He convoked a council at Constantinople. During the council, through various nefarious means, he had the papal legates annul the decrees of the general council of 869-870. John VIII, when he learned of Photius' duplicity, excommunicated him in 881.

However, Photius still had Emperor Basil's support, so he refused to give up his office. In this second conflict with Rome, he adopted new tactics. Instead of directly attacking the Roman primacy, which was too firmly established to suffer from his opposition, and instead of stressing differences in customs and traditions, he centered all his assaults on the Filioque question. Photius argued that it was the belief of the Greek Church that the Holy Spirit proceeds from the Father only. Thus, the old wound stayed open.

Finally, in 886, the new emperor, Leo VI, Photius' enemy, had him arrested and tried for treason. Photius was again deprived of his office and banished to a monastery in Armenia. He died around 893. It is the position of the Greek Orthodox Church that Photius was not guilty of the charges brought against him by the Pope. In fact, the Eastern Orthodox churches consider him a saint.

The Final Break: The Schism of Michael Cerularius

The next 150 years were a period of relative harmony between the popes and the Greek Church. However, in 1043, Patriarch Michael Cerularius repeated the old charges that Photius had made against the Roman Church. It was the secret ambition of this proud patriarch to make the Eastern Church completely independent of Rome and to make himself Emperor of Constantinople.

Pope St. Leo IX (1049-1054) ordered Cerularius to be obedient to papal authority. The pope sent Cardinal Humbert to Constantinople with orders to depose the patriarch if he persisted in

Interior of *Hagia Sophia*, which is currently a mosque

his revolt. Sadly, Humbert and Cerularius were unable to come to an agreement. Humbert solemnly excommunicated Cerularius in the Church of Hagia Sophia. Cerularius retorted by excommunicating the Pope. This was the final break between the Greek Church and Rome. Although attempts have been made, most recently by Pope Paul VI and John Paul II, there has been no reunion to this day.

Review Exercises

1. What is the heresy called iconoclasm?
2. What evils resulted from iconoclasm?
3. What is a schism?
4. How did the Greek Schism come about?
5. What heresy did Photius promote concerning the Holy Spirit?
6. Who was Michael Cerularius?

CHAPTER 10

THE GOSPEL GOES NORTH AND EAST

St. Adalbert baptizes St. Stephen of Hungary

St. Ansgar, the Apostle of the North

Charlemagne's conquest of Saxony opened the gateway to the North. The Danes, Normans, and Swedes of Scandinavia had resisted all efforts to bring them into Western civilization. On the contrary, they frequently pillaged the coasts of England and France. Sailing up the rivers, they raided and looted churches and monasteries.

In the midst of this scene of general terror, Ansgar, a Frankish monk, determined to win these Viking marauders to Christ. He began preaching the Faith in Denmark in 826. In 831, he returned to Germany and was appointed Archbishop of Hamburg. This was a new See which had the right to send missionaries into all the northern lands and to consecrate bishops for them. Ansgar was consecrated in November of 831. He went to Rome where Pope Gregory IV named him papal legate for the northern lands. For a time Ansgar devoted himself to the needs of his own diocese, which was still missionary territory with only a few churches. He founded a monastery and a school in Hamburg. The school was intended to serve the Danish mission, but accomplished little.

Ansgar also preached the Gospel in Sweden, where he established his fellow-countryman Gosbert as bishop. However, the missionaries did not receive the Frankish protection upon which they had relied. Consequently, their work met with a disastrous setback. In 845, the Vikings unexpectedly sacked Hamburg, destroying all the church's treasures and books and leaving the entire diocese unrestorable. The Swedes killed Bishop Gosbert. Ansgar, undismayed, continued his efforts. He died in Bremen in 865.

At the time of Ansgar's death, Catholicism had a small presence in the Northlands. The Vikings were a constant threat to Europe. However, he had planted the seeds. His successors eventually reaped the full benefit of his labors. A century later, three Sees were created in Danish territory. However, the work of conversion was not completed until about the end of the tenth century.

The Conversion of Norway

The man most responsible for bringing Norway into the Church was Olaf Tryggvasen. Before his conversion he had been a Viking adventurer. While traveling in the Scilly Islands, he met a hermit who converted him to Catholicism. When he learned that the people of Norway were unhappy with their king, he returned to Norway and proclaimed himself king. He soon won the affection of his people.

Due to Olaf's great popularity, most of his subjects followed his example and became Catholics. He invited missionaries from Germany and England to evangelize his people. The missionaries established a number of bishoprics and many schools throughout his kingdom. He changed the laws of his nation to bring them into harmony with Catholic teaching.

Olaf was also involved in the conversion of the people of Iceland and Greenland. He persuaded Leif Ericson, who had become a Christian, to introduce Christianity into Greenland in the year 1000. Fifty years later, there were ten thousand Christians on the island and Greenland received its first bishop.

Saints Cyril and Methodius, the Apostles of the Slavs

The Slavs originally lived in the eastern portion of Europe. However, constant harassment by the hordes from Asia finally drove them to settle in Central Europe. There were three branches of Slavs: the southern branch, including the Serbs and the Croatians; the western branch, consisting of the Moravians, Bohemians, and Poles; and the eastern or Russian branch.

The Moravians had settled in lower Austria and on the southern slopes of the Carpathian Mountains. They came into contact with the Franks during the reign of Louis the Pious and accepted Frankish rule. German missionaries from Salzburg initially brought the Faith to them. However, the Slavs loathed these German missionaries because they preached to them in a foreign language, brought new customs and laws with them, and were preceded or followed by bands of looting soldiers. Duke Ratislas, the Moravian leader, wished to rid himself of these German missionaries, so he asked Eastern Emperor Michael III to send him missionaries. Michael sent Saints Cyril and Methodius. They played the same part in the conversion of the Slavs as St. Boniface had in that of the Germans.

Sts. Cyril and Methodius

Cyril and Methodius were brothers. They were born at Thessalonica, on the very border of the Slavonic dependencies of the Empire. They had a perfect command of the Slavic language as well as a thorough understanding of Slavic customs. They were of noble birth and well educated. However, instead of aspiring to posts of honor, they embraced the monastic life.

The Moravians enthusiastically welcomed the brothers. Since they used the Slavonic language in their preaching and when they said Mass, they caused no ill will. However, their success soon aroused the jealousy of the German missionaries and a serious conflict arose between them. The Germans objected to the use of the Slavonic language in the Mass. They argued that the Church allowed only Hebrew, Greek, and Latin to be used in the Mass.

In 868, the brothers journeyed to Rome to present their case to the Holy Father and obtain his approval of their mission. Pope Adrian II (867-872) settled the dispute in favor of the two brothers. He placed the Slavic liturgical books on the altar of the basilica of St. Mary Major, and had the Slavonic liturgy celebrated in the four Roman basilicas. He then made Methodius archbishop and papal legate to the Slavic nations.

As the brothers were preparing to return to Moravia, Cyril fell sick and died. Methodius returned alone, only to find that Moravia had again fallen under the control of the Germans. Duke Ratislaw's own nephew, Swatopluk, had betrayed him to the Germans. German Bishop Hermanrich of Passau arrested St. Methodius. "You are teaching in our territory!" cried Hermanrich. "I would have avoided it, had I known that it was yours," calmly replied Methodius, "but it belongs to Saint Peter."

The German bishops of Passau, Salzburg, and Freising then convoked a council that put St. Methodius on trial. They imprisoned him for two years. In 872, Pope John VIII obtained his release. The pope allowed him to continue preaching in Slavonic, but forbade him to use the Slavonic liturgy. This step would have serious consequences. Methodius, always an obedient son of the Church, believed that the Pope did not understand the situation in Moravia. Therefore, he decided to wait to carry out the Pope's orders until he had a chance to explain himself to the Pope.

However, in 880, before Methodius had a chance to meet with the Pope, Swatopluk denounced him to the Holy See.

Swatopluk preferred the Mass in Latin as he considered it more traditional and more refined. Methodius again journeyed to Rome. Once again Pope John VIII approved the use of the Slavonic liturgy. However, he did require that the Gospel first be read in Latin at every Mass. The Germans' continued harassment of Methodius caused John VIII to reprimand them the next year. St. Methodius died in 885, after having translated a large portion of the Bible into the Slavonic language.

The Conversion of the Poles

At the period when the history of Poland begins, the Germans were the most powerful nation of Europe. To keep the peace with the Germans, Duke Mieszko, the Polish ruler (962-992), accepted the German Emperor as his overlord. In 963, Mieszko and his people embraced Catholicism.

The person most responsible for the spread of the Faith in those early years was Duke Mieszko's wife. In 965, the duke had married a Catholic Bohemian princess named Dubravka. She had received a splendid Catholic education at the royal court. When she came to Poland, she brought a priest named Jordan with her from Bohemia. In 968, Pope John XIII (956-972) made Fr. Jordan the first bishop

Poznan Cathedral

of Poland with his See at Poznan. From Germany and Bohemia numerous missionaries entered the country to baptize the people. Immigrants and monks came from all the Western countries, and convents and monasteries began to be built.

Shortly before his death in 992, Duke Mieszko donated Poland to the Pope. This placed it under the Pope's special protection and created a special relationship between Poland and the Holy See that still exists. Perhaps the Duke hoped that one day Poland would give something more unique to the Papacy than merely land.

During the reign of Boleslav Chrobry, later known as "Chrobry the Brave," (992-1025), Duke Mieszko's eldest son, the Faith continued its rapid increase. He outlawed paganism and did everything he could to bring about the spread of Christianity. He also worked for Polish independence from German control. At the outset of his reign, Poland was still under the control of the German Emperor Otto III (983-1002). In 1000, St. Adalbert, the second bishop of Prague, was martyred by the pagans of Prussia, where he had gone as a missionary. Boleslav bought the saint's body from the Prussians and placed it in a tomb in the Church of the Blessed Virgin Mary at Gniezno, in Poland. This act pleased Otto III. St. Adalbert had been Otto's confessor when he came to the throne. The saint had deepened and strengthened Otto's faith.

In the spring of 1000, Otto made a pilgrimage to Gniezno to pray at the St. Adalbert's shrine. With papal permission, while he was in Poland he established four new Polish dioceses under a metropolitan at Gniezno. This placed them outside German control. He also granted Poland political independence.

The last major pagan uprising in Poland was during the reign of King Casimir I (1039-1058). Casimir successfully put down

The Tomb of St. Adalbert

the pagan revolt. From then on Poland was a thoroughly Catholic country.

Casimir's son, Boleslav II (1058-1081) began his reign as a model Catholic king, supporting the Church and reform. However, he later turned against the Church. St. Stanislaus, the Bishop of Krakow, unsuccessfully tried to make him see the error of his ways. The saintly bishop finally excommunicated him. Enraged, the king came to the cathedral where he found the holy bishop praying at the altar. Boleslav drew his sword and slew him. When the people learned of this despicable act, they revolted against the king, who fled for his life. He sought refuge in a monastery, where he died a short time later.

The Murder of St. Stanislaus

151

The Conversion of Russia

Over the years Viking raiders and traders had established trading posts along Russia's larger rivers. Over time, these posts had become towns. From these towns the Vikings had built a country.

In 945, Olga, the wife of a Russian Viking chieftain, became Russian ruler of the Grand Duchy of Kiev (Russia) when her husband was killed in battle. In 957, while visiting Constantinople, Olga was drawn to Catholicism and baptized. However, she could not convert her son, who died a pagan. When her son died, he was succeeded by his three sons.

In 977, Vladimir (977-1015), one of Olga's three grandsons, became the sole ruler of Russia when he had his brother murdered. (The other brother had died in battle the previous year.) Vladimir was completely, and seemingly permanently, pagan.

In 987 Vladimir married Anna, the sister of the Greek Emperor Basil II. In order to marry her he had to be baptized, so he was baptized on the day of his marriage. The baptism was clearly part of a military and political deal that had been made. Vladimir had saved Basil's throne when he had come to Basil's rescue with several thousand Viking raiders. His reward was marriage to the Imperial Princess Anna.

There is nothing to suggest that Vladimir's conversion was sincere. However, the history of the Church is the story of the Holy Spirit working in the minds and hearts of men and women. The channels of grace are hidden, though the effects can be spectacular.

Once Vladimir had been baptized, the incredibly focused nature of his character, which had been aimed at acquiring power, was now focused on discovering what a follower of Christ would do, and doing it. He began to read the Bible. He built Catholic schools in Russia. He destroyed the pagan shrines and built Catholic churches in their place. He became a saint.

Much of the help Vladimir received came from Constantinople, which was still in communion with Rome. Vladimir was also in contact with the Papacy. In 990, Pope John XV sent bishops to Russia to establish dioceses. Until his death in 1015, Vladimir continued close relations with the Papacy and the Catholic kingdoms of Europe. His three daughters became the queens of France, Poland, and Sweden.

The Southern Slavs and Bulgarians Accept the Faith

The Croatians were the first Slavonic nation to be converted completely. The Gospel was first preached to them in the seventh century, and by the beginning of the ninth, they were all Catholics. The Slovenes had settled on the border of the Diocese of Salzburg and received the knowledge of the Faith through its bishops.

The Eastern Roman Emperor Heraclius (610-641) forcibly imposed the Faith on the Serbs. However, they did not really abandon their pagan practices until the ninth century, when the Greeks once more subdued them.

The main actor in the conversion of Bulgaria was their great King Boris. Boris had been baptized in 864. As was the practice of the time, he ordered that all his subjects receive baptism. Two years later he sent an embassy to Rome asking Pope St. Nicholas I to send him a bishop and some priests. He had some questions for the Pope about the obligations the Catholic Faith imposed upon his people. The pope responded to the questions and sent along two bishops as well.

Under Boris, the Faith continued to spread with the establishment of schools and monasteries. Books were translated into Slavonic under his patronage. With the conversion of his country well underway, Boris did something few kings have ever done. In 889, he abdicated his throne and entered a monastery. His oldest son Vladimir succeeded him. However, Vladimir began to move the country back to paganism. Boris came roaring out of his monastery like an old lion from his lair. He replaced Vladimir with his younger son who kept Bulgaria on the true path. Then Boris returned to his monastery, where he spent the last fourteen years of his life in prayer. He died in 907.

It appeared that Bulgaria had become Catholic; however, it was not to be. The revolt of Photius, which broke out a few years later, plunged this young Catholic community into schism. When the Greek Church broke away, Bulgaria went with them. The old lion was gone.

Hungary Becomes Catholic

The conversion of Hungary began when the great Hungarian military leader Geza converted to Catholicism. His wife was an Eastern Rite Catholic, but Geza encouraged missionaries from Germany to evangelize Hungary. The great Bishop of Prague, St. Adalbert, in his missionary journeys arrived in Hungary around 996. St. Adalbert baptized Geza's son, who later became King St. Stephen (997-1038). In 997, Stephen became King of Hungary, a country he ruled for the next forty years.

Once he became King of Hungary and suppressed a pagan uprising, Stephen donated his kingdom to the Pope. In return, Pope Sylvester II and Emperor Otto III gave Stephen a royal crown and

Main altar at St. Stephen's Cathedral in Budapest, Hungary

permission to establish dioceses and consecrate bishops in Hungary. Stephen established the first diocese in Hungary at Esztergom. The Church in Hungary grew and flourished during Stephen's reign. Towards the end of his reign, Stephen appointed St. Gerard, a Venetian monk, as bishop of southeastern Hungary. St. Gerard recognized that there was a lack of native Hungarian clergy. He launched a successful campaign to create a native clergy by educating Hungarian boys in cathedral schools and selecting the most promising for ordination.

Towards the end of his life, King Stephen had intended to abdicate and retire to a life of holy contemplation. He planned to hand the kingdom over to his son Emeric, who had shown every sign of being a good king and a true son of the Church. No sooner had Stephen made this announcement, than Emeric was wounded in a hunting accident and died in 1031. Future events suggest that the Hungarian nobles may have murdered him.

Esztergom Basilica

Stephen mourned for a very long time over the loss of his son. The king's grief took a great toll on his health. He eventually recovered, but never regained his original vitality. With no living children, he struggled to find someone among his relatives capable of competently ruling the country and maintaining the Catholic Faith. He did not trust his cousin, Duke Vazul, whom he suspected to be following pagan customs. The duke took part in a conspiracy to murder Stephen, but the assassination attempt failed and Stephen had Vazul executed. Although he knew the Hungarians would resent a foreign ruler, he finally chose his nephew, who was not Hungarian but Venetian, as his heir. King Stephen died August 15, 1038, at Szekesfehervar, where he was buried.

The last traces of paganism disappeared from the kingdom during the reign of St. Ladislas (1077-1095).

Basilica of Szekesfehervar

Review Exercises

1. Briefly describe St. Ansgar's labors among the Scandinavians.
2. How did Olaf Tryggvasen help in the conversion of Greenland?
3. Who were Sts. Cyril and Methodius?
4. How did the Polish Church become independent of Germany?
5. Who was St. Stanislaus of Krakow?
6. Through whose influence did Russia embrace the Faith?
7. Briefly describe the role of King Boris in the conversion of Bulgaria.
8. How did the conversion of Hungary begin?
9. What was the first diocese in Hungary?

CHAPTER 11

THE PAPACY UNDER ATTACK:
THE CHURCH IN THE LATTER PART
OF THE FIRST MILLENNIUM

The Battle of Ostia

The Saracens Attack Italy

Departing from the northern coast of Africa, the Saracens, Moslems from North Africa, landed in Sicily. There, in 831, they captured the cities of Messina and Palermo. With the fall of Sicily the entire Italian coast, including Rome, was at their mercy. In 846, during the reign of Pope Sergius II (844-847), they advanced to the very gates of Rome. They plundered the churches of St. Peter and St. Paul, which were located outside the city walls.

Hearing of these sacrileges, the Franks launched a campaign against the Saracens. For a time the Franks expelled the invaders from Italy. Before long, however, the peninsula was completely isolated from all imperial aid. Internal squabbles also weakened Italy and divided her into greedy, quarrelsome principalities.

Italy had to look for help, as it had at the time of the barbarian invasions, from the papacy. Pope St. Leo IV (847-855), the successor of Sergius II, took charge. He repaired the walls of Rome. To prevent St. Peter's from another attack, he enclosed the Vatican within a high wall.

In 849, at the naval Battle of Ostia, fought under the very eyes of Pope St. Leo, who had blessed the ships, Papal and Italian forces destroyed the Saracen fleet. As this victory came after the Moslem sack of Rome, it reversed the tide of the war and raised Christian morale.

The Rise of Feudalism

The Christian empire created by Charlemagne was short-lived. Only a great man could have kept his empire together and his successors were not great men. Under the rule of his son and successor, Louis the Pious, his empire began to fall apart. In 843, his grandsons divided the Empire into three kingdoms: Germany, Francia, and Lorraine.

Louis the Pious

Soon a troublesome aristocracy replaced the Empire. This deprived the Church of a valuable ally. There were rulers in France, Germany, Burgundy, and Italy. All claimed some distant relationship with Charlemagne. By the tenth century, the title of emperor had little meaning.

In 843, with the break up of the Empire, feudalism was born. An age began during which force too often prevailed over law. A dark age was dawning for the Church. The Papacy would suffer attacks not only from the Saracens, but also from those sworn to protect her.

The Viking Raids

Even before Charlemagne died, the alarm had spread through northern Europe that the Vikings were coming. These Scandinavian raiders attacked every city and town on the seacoast. In their shallow draft boats they traveled up all the rivers of Europe. The Vikings overwhelmed Ireland, England, Iceland, and Greenland. They captured Sicily and southern Italy. They landed at the mouth of the Tiber and sacked the churches of Rome. With the break-up of Charlemagne's Empire, there was no strong central power that could deal with them.

These predatory Viking raids caused the people to realize that the central power, the king, was not strong enough to keep the peace internally or to deal with outside attacks. They had to defend themselves. Thus, the people organized themselves around strong men with military experience. These men built sturdy fortresses which later became castles. In times of danger the people sought refuge in these fortresses.

In order to protect themselves, local landowners banded together under a regional ruler who could call them together in a time of danger, such as a Viking raid. In return for his protection, the regional ruler, a duke or a count, demanded that all the land, the only real source of wealth, be given to him. His "vassals," those who promised him allegiance, could use the land if they would fight in his military during times of danger. Over time dukes and counts became more powerful than the king.

Theoretically, dukes recognized the king as their lord. The dukes promised to aid the king during a foreign war. There was a special ceremony where the duke promised allegiance to the king. The duke knelt before the king and made an oath pledging "fealty." The duke placed his hands within the hands of the king. The king gave him a twig or piece of dirt as a sign that he was conferring the duke's land, the manor, upon him. By this act of investiture the manor lord became the king's vassal. In return, the vassal paid the king a sum of money. This hierarchal system of protection was Feudalism.

The Church under Feudalism

Feudalism, because it was based upon personal allegiance, was, in a sense, not friendly to strong central authority, whether the Church or the State. The most highly organized institution in Christendom, the Church, was bound to suffer the most from the Feudal system. The system worked well, and was necessary on the local level to protect the peasants and small farmers in an increasingly bloody age. Nevertheless, for the Church it posed some major concerns.

Problems began to come up almost at once. Just as kings claimed the right to invest secular lords, they also claimed the right to give the bishop his power and authority by handing him the crosier, the symbol of his authority. They expected the bishop to take the oath of fealty and to present them with a sum of money. This would make the bishop the king's vassal. The bishop would be under the king's authority, not only in civil matters, but in the spiritual direction of his diocese.

The payment of the money upon the bishop's appointment was another terrible problem. For the most part, kings were not interested in who was appointed bishop as long as he had enough money. Too often the office went to the highest bidder rather than the best man.

The Decline of the Holy Roman Empire

When the sons of Louis the Pious divided the Empire in 843, Louis II became ruler of Italy. He continued to exercise the right granted to his father in 824 of ratifying the papal elections. As long as he lived, there was harmony between the emperor and the Holy See. However, when Louis II died, a fight for the imperial crown began between Louis the German and Charles the Bald. Pope John VIII thought that Charles would aid him against the Saracens, who continued to pillage southern Italy and threaten Rome, so he crowned Charles emperor on December 25, 875.

Although Charles was a valiant ruler and devoted to the Church, he only had a small army. However, he was still

Charlemagne

the grandson of Charlemagne. He determined to march to Italy to aid the Pope. He had barely crossed the Alps when he learned that his own kingdom of France was under attack by Carloman of Bavaria. Charles prepared to return home. He never made it. He fell ill and died in 877 while re-crossing the Alps.

Four years later, Pope John VIII made another attempt to restore the Empire in the person of Charles the Fat. The pope crowned Charles Holy Roman Emperor in February 881. As emperor, Charles was ineffective at best and cowardly at worst. Internal factions and external enemies tore at the Empire. The French finally tired of the cowardly and slothful Charles. The imperial assembly called the **Diet** met at Tribur in 887, and deposed him. Charles died the following year.

Like vultures around a carcass, contenders for the crown of Holy Roman Emperor began to circle. The problem of who was the best candidate was a hard one. The two strongest candidates were the Italian Guy of Spoleto and the German Arnulf, Duke of Carinthia. The pope hesitated to support either man. However, the Italian, Guy of Spoleto, being closer, was able to put more pressure on the Pontiff. Pope Stephen V reluctantly crowned him emperor in February 891.

When Stephen died, the Spoleto family continued pressuring his successor, Pope Formosus (891-896). They induced him to crown Guy's son, Lambert, co-emperor in April 892. Determined to control the Papacy, the Spoleto family made more and more demands on the Pope and threatened the independence of the Holy See.

With nowhere else to turn, Formosus asked Duke Arnulf for help. Arnulf agreed to help him and Formosus crowned him Emperor in Rome. If either man thought that this meant that the Spoleto family were going to give up, they were sadly mistaken.

At Guy's death, his widow, the ruthless Ageltrude, and her son Lambert took up the battle against Arnulf. Arnulf, having suffered a paralyzing stroke, saw all his hopes crumble, together with those of Pope Formosus. At the advanced age of eighty, Formosus died of grief in 896. What followed was the greatest sacrilege to occur in the history of the Church until the Protestant Revolt.

The Trial of Pope Formosus

With an army at her back, Ageltrude and her son took the city of Rome. By her order, the decayed body of Pope Formosus was removed from its tomb in St. Peter's where it had lain for nine months. She ordered the body to be clothed in the papal vestments, including the hair shirt that the Pope had worn in life. Then, the corpse was put on trial.

At the end of the "trial," the new Pope, the timid Stephen VI (896-897), pronounced the corpse guilty. Formosus was deposed and his acts were declared null and void. Then the body was handed over to the mob, which threw it into the Tiber River.

The Trial of Pope Formusus

Pope Stephen VI, who had become a tool of the Spoleto family, became the victim of reprisals. In 897, he was arrested and thrown into a dungeon. There some unknown person strangled him. (Sadly at this period of history it is likely that several popes were murdered. The great Catholic historian Warren Carroll in his *The Building of Christendom* feels that in addition to Stephen VI, John VIII (882), Adrian III (885), and Leo V (903) were also murdered. There may have been more, as several other popes of the time had strangely short reigns.)

For more than thirty years a heated battle raged around the dead Pope Formosus. The conflict focused chiefly on the validity of the ordinations he made. Initial reaction was in his favor.

Pope Romanus succeeded Stephen VI. However, he reigned for only four months.

Theodore, an energetic man, succeeded Romanus as pope, but reigned for only twenty days. However, during those three weeks he had the courage to repair the outrages inflicted on Pope Formosus. Theodore solemnly reburied the Pope's remains in the Vatican Basilica and proclaimed the validity of the former Pope's ordinations. Theodore was clearly a good and brave man. One wonders if he died a natural death, given the times in which he lived.

The next pope, John IX (898-900), also rehabilitated Formosus and convoked three councils to that effect. The next two popes, Benedict IV (900-903) and Leo V (903-904), were only passing figures.

The next man to be elected pope was Sergius III. He had been antipope during the reigns of Theodore and John IX. Once Sergius became pope, he reopened the trial of Pope Formosus.

Sergius had participated in the "Synod of the Corpse." He had come to Rome at the head of an army, and may have had Pope Leo V killed. Sergius decided that those ordained by Formosus had to submit to reordination. Sergius III was the first of the protégés of the infamous Theophylactus family.

The Domination of the Papacy by the Theophylactus Family

For years, the empire started by Charlemagne had been the sole protector of the papacy. When that empire crumbled, little kingdoms governed by dukes and counts who divided up the land sprang up in its place. These dukes and counts soon began fighting with each other for power. For a while, one or other of these petty rulers controlled the papacy. (It is a witness to the truth of the doctrine of papal infallibility, that during these years, when dishonorable men served as pope, none of them ever taught error.)

In Italy, the scheming Theodora, the wife of Theophylactus, was one of the first of these minor rulers to meddle in papal affairs. In 915, the nobles of the city of Rome elected Theophylactus, the Count of Tusculum, to rule Rome as consul. However, the family saw this as only the stepping stone to bigger things. They were always interested in increasing their wealth and power. By various sinful and dishonest means, Theodora gained influence over several important people. With their influence she increased her family's power and riches. Her daughter Marozia, following in her mother's footsteps, also considerably increased the power of the family. For more than fifty years the Theophylactus family dominated Rome. They imposed the candidates of their choice on the papacy.

Pope Sergius III (904-911) owed his office to Theodora's influence. Pope John X (914-928) was indebted to Marozia for his election. However, as so often happens when a man puts on the fisherman's ring, the Holy Spirit begins to work in the heart of that man. John quite unexpectedly overcame the handicap of his unworthy election. In course of time, he did many fine things.

One of Pope John's finest acts was to defeat the Saracens who were a constant threat to the Patrimony of St. Peter. Periodically, these Islamic raiders would sweep into Roman territory and pillage it. John X succeeded in defeating them by forming a powerful alliance. It consisted of the feudal rulers of central and southern Italy and the Byzantine Emperor. The pope himself led the allied armies into battle. In 916, they surrounded the Saracens in their fortress at Garigliano, and totally wiped them out.

One of Pope John X's last acts was to try to shake off the yoke of the unholy princess who ruled Rome. At the death of Berengarius, whom he had crowned emperor, the Pope attempted to appoint as his successor Hugh, the duke of Provence. However, Marozia would not allow it. When her husband died, she had married the powerful Duke of Tuscany. Fearful that the creation of a new emperor might diminish her power in Rome, she incited a revolt. The insurgents invaded the Lateran Palace where they seized and murdered the Pope's brother.

The Lateran Basilica and Palace

They threw John himself into prison, where they smothered him to death with a pillow.

Marozia now had full control of the papacy. She gave it in turn to Leo VI (928) and Stephen VII (929-931). Finally, she gave it to her own son, who called himself John XI (931-935).

Marozia always had higher ambitions. Although she was a princess and a duchess she wanted to be Empress. Thus, after the death of her husband the Duke of Tuscany, she decided to marry Hugh, the Duke of Provence, the former candidate for emperor. Marozia felt certain that her son, Pope John XI, would crown his own mother and his stepfather. However, she failed to reckon with the other members of her family.

Marozia had another son, Alberic, whom Hugh had the misfortune to insult on the day he married Marozia. Alberic raised a small band of soldiers and attacked his mother and her new husband. Hugh was forced to flee. Alberic put Marozia in prison where she met with a mysterious death. Rome was only changing hands; however, Alberic showed himself somewhat more worthy of his office than had his awful mother.

Following the death of his mother, Alberic ruled the city of Rome. Popes Leo VII (936-939), Stephen VIII (939-942), Marinus II (942-946), and Agapetus II (946-955) all served at his pleasure. Despite the way he came to power, Alberic did do some good. He was able to re-establish order in Rome. He also worked with St. Odo of Cluny to reform several Roman monasteries.

Unfortunately, Alberic was also his mother's son. He named his own son, Octavian, successor to Pope Agapetus II while Agapetus still lived. Alberic died in 954. Pope Agapetus II died the following year. Octavian inherited both his father's office as ruler of Rome, as well as the Papacy. He took the name John XII (955-964).

THE CHURCH AND THE GERMAN KINGS

Otto I, the Great

In the midst of these trying times, another great power loomed on the horizon. Otto I (936-973), of the House of Saxony, resolved to revitalize Charlemagne's empire and thus add to the prestige of

Germany. As a first step, Otto had himself crowned at Aachen. Next, he secured his power at home. He crushed the power of some rebellious dukes, securing his internal power base. He determined to defend his borders from external threats. Otto's most important victory was over the Hungarians, which

Otto the Great

forever ended their invasions. In addition, Otto successfully defended his kingdom against the Vikings and the Slavs from the North.

In 961, Pope John XII (955-964) appealed to Otto for aid. The Roman aristocracy and Berengarius, the Lombard king, threatened the

Pope's authority. Otto left for Rome. At Pavia, the Lombard capital, he assumed the crown of Italy and triumphantly entered the city of Rome. In gratitude for his services, John XII crowned him emperor on February 2, 962. This is the origin of the title "Holy Roman Emperor of the German Nation," which, far from protecting the Church and Italy, more often oppressed both.

Otto made a grant to the papacy of about three-fourths of the kingdom of Italy. He also swore to protect these possessions. For his part, Pope John XII unwisely took an oath of fidelity to the emperor. Moreover, he promised that his successors would do likewise before the ceremony of their ordination. Pope John also renewed the imperial rights over Rome and the papal elections, which had been granted by Pope St. Leo III to Charlemagne.

Pope John XII soon realized that Otto was not the solution to his problems, but was going to be a greater problem. Therefore, the Pope swiftly opened negotiations with Adalbert, the son of Berengarius, the former king of Italy. However, Otto reappeared in Rome to battle the opposing faction and completely routed it.

As a result of the defeat, Pope John XII fled Rome. Otto held a pseudo-council, which declared the Pope unworthy of his office and elected Otto's secretary, a layman, in his place. Otto had the new candidate ordained a deacon and a priest on the same day. Otto had him consecrated pope as Leo VIII, and given the title of viceroy.

However, the Romans would not allow themselves to be oppressed like this. They revolted, but Otto quickly suppressed them. The emperor had scarcely left the city, when John XII re-entered it. The unfortunate Pontiff died a few days later, but the Romans continued in their resistance by electing a new pope, Benedict V. Otto was furious. He hastened once again to Rome, and imposed his candidate, Leo VIII

(964-965). Benedict V, a good and holy man, resigned to avoid further harm to the Papacy.

After Leo VIII's death, Otto proposed Theophylactus for the Papacy. Theophylactus was the son of Marozia's sister. By this move, Otto hoped to win the most powerful member of the opposing party over to his side. However, his plans were completely frustrated.

Theophylactus, as Pope John XIII (965-972), adopted a hard-line with regard to the turbulent Roman nobles who once again revolted. The pope was arrested and imprisoned in Castel Sant'Angelo, the Roman fortress on the banks of the Tiber. Otto again put down the rebellion. This time he remained in Rome for six years. He had his thirteen-year-old son, Otto II, crowned as co-emperor. The rule of Otto I seemed firmly established in Italy, when he died, May 7, 973.

Castel Sant'Angelo

Otto II

The main thought in the minds of the Romans was to rid themselves of the hateful yoke of the German oppressor, so once again they revolted. Pope Benedict VI (973-974), John XIII's successor, was strangled. Boniface Franco, who took the name of Boniface VII, became pope. As his father had done before him, Emperor Otto II (973-983) put down the Roman revolt.

The intruding Boniface VII fled to Constantinople. The Bishop of Sutri was made pope with the emperor's consent. He took the name Benedict VII (974-983). During his pontificate he displayed great zeal for the reform of the Church. After Benedict's death, Otto II nominated his own chancellor, who took the name John XIV (983-984).

Towards the end of his reign, Otto II made an attempt to conquer southern Italy. However, the Saracens defeated him. He died shortly afterwards.

Otto III

The new emperor, Otto III (983-1002), was barely sixteen years old and not practical. He conceived the plan of organizing a Catholic empire with Rome as its capital. His first move in this direction was to appoint to the papacy the imperial chaplain. This man was a priest named Bruno, a grandson of Otto the Great. Bruno took the name Gregory V (996-999), the first German pope.

The emperor had scarcely left Rome, when the Italian faction rose in rebellion. They proclaimed the archbishop of Piacenza as pope. Upon receipt of the news, Otto III returned to Italy, deposed the pretender, and executed the rebels. After Gregory V's death, Otto

III designated as his successor another of his protégés the Frenchman Gerbert d'Aurillac, who took the name Sylvester II (999-1003).

St. Henry II

After the death of Pope Sylvester II in 1003, the Roman faction again gained the upper hand. The Roman faction was able to influence the election of Popes John XVII (1003), John XVIII (1003-

The *St. Henry* window from St. Patrick's Cathedral (NYC) depicts Emperor Henry in battle against the Slavonians, who had rebelled against ecclesiastical authorities. The rebels killed priests, drove out bishops and laid waste to Poland. Henry, badly outnumbered, invoked God's help. He was aided in his victory by St. Lawrence and St. Adrian.

1009), and Sergius IV (1009-1012). However, the Roman power was destined to be short-lived. At this point a new player emerged on the scene: the Tesculum family. The Tesculums, to further their own interests, began to take a deep interest in the German regime.

Henry of Bavaria succeeded Otto III in 1002. The new emperor had received his early education at the monastery of Hildesheim. Later St. Wolfgang, the bishop of Ratisbon, taught Henry. A solid Catholic, Henry II was thoroughly familiar with the needs of the Church. He at once resolved to give the Church his full protection. Moreover, he said that he would become involved in the affairs of Italy only as a protector and only for the greater good of the Church.

In 1012, Henry became involved in the papal election. Upon finding two candidates for the papacy, Henry declared himself in favor of the Tusculum candidate, who became Benedict VIII (1012-1024). Benedict's election began an era of peace and harmony between the Tusculum Pope and the German Emperor. Their relationship became even closer when on February 14, 1014, Pope Benedict VIII invested both St. Henry II and his wife St. Cunigundis with the imperial purple in St. Peter's Basilica. Following the imperial coronation a decree was promulgated. It stated that all future papal elections were to be conducted according to the sacred canons. It was also at this time that the "Filioque" was added to the Nicene or Mass Creed in Rome.

Henry III

Henry II was the last Saxon emperor. His successor was Conrad II, the first member of the Franconian dynasty. This dynasty would produce some of the Church's bitterest enemies. Emperor

Henry III succeeded Conrad. These rulers, by violence and intrigue, placed several unworthy candidates upon the throne of St. Peter.

In 1045, Gregory VI became pope. He tried to re-establish peace and calm in Rome and the Papacy. With the assistance of two great reformers, St. Peter Damian and St. Odilo, the abbot of Cluny, he tried to restore the Holy See to its proper dignity. As a first step, he tried to make an agreement with Henry III (1039-1056). However, Henry was determined to appoint Germans to the Holy See. Thus, Henry forced Pope Gregory to resign in 1046. Upon a visit to Rome, the emperor imposed upon the clergy and people a candidate of his choice, the bishop of Bamberg, who took the name Clement II (1046-47). The new Pope invested both Henry III and his wife Agnes with the imperial purple. Four Germans in a row now served as pope: Clement II, Damasus II (1047-48), St. Leo IX (1049-54), and Victor II (1055-1057).

Review Exercises

1. What was Feudalism?
2. How did Feudalism affect the Church?
3. Who crowned Guy of Spoleto Emperor?
4. What is the origin of the title "Holy Roman Emperor of the German Nation?"
5. Who was the first German Pope?
6. Who was the last German Pope?
7. Why do you think Henry II was friendlier to the Church than many of the German Emperors of this period?

CHAPTER 12

The Church Is Cleansed by New Fountains of Holiness

Pope Gregory VII condemns lay investiture.

The Monastic Reform of Cluny

As the tenth century dawned, darkness had enveloped the Church. The Papacy was under the control of cold and ruthless men. It seemed that the Church and Christendom were on the very brink of destruction. Yet Our Lord had made a promise to St. Peter.

The monasteries did not escape the darkness that fell over the Church in the ninth and tenth centuries. Under the feudal system their abbots too often were the vassals of kings and dukes. The monks began leading worldly lives as the strict discipline of former days was relaxed. However, the old spirit of holiness and discipline was never entirely lost. Scattered throughout Christendom were monks and abbots who labored and prayed for the return of the spirit of holiness. Many monasteries still adhered to the ideals of St. Benedict and faithfully observed his Rule. At the dawn of the tenth century in France, a light began to gleam in the darkness.

The first reaction to the evils engulfing the Church came from the Abbey of Cluny in Burgundy. Duke William of Aquitaine had founded Cluny in 910. Cluny succeeded not only in strengthening its own organization as a unit, but also in completely freeing itself from the secular power, and even from the power of bishops. It created a reform among its own members that

Cluny Monastery

would spread to the Church at large and become a powerful aid to the Papacy. The monks of Cluny, and those who followed their example over the next two hundred years, would complete the building of Christendom.

The success of the Cluniac reform was due in no small part to the holy men who came to the abbey. The abbots of Cluny were especially holy men. They worked to bring other monasteries under their influence. St. Odo, St. Odilo, and St. Hugh were all abbots of Cluny. They traveled extensively, visiting and reforming monasteries everywhere.

The Reform under the Predecessors of Pope Gregory VII

During the trying days of feudalism, many abuses crept into the Church. One of the most serious of these was simony, the buying and selling of holy offices. Pope Clement II (1046-1047) began the process of reform by decreeing that he would excommunicate anyone guilty of simony. Pope St. Leo IX (1048-1054) also condemned simony. He traveled the length and breadth of Christendom to see to it that papal decrees were enforced. Pope St. Leo also sought the aid of the secular powers. He called upon King Henry I of France, Emperor Henry III of Germany, and King St. Edward the Confessor of England. Under his successor, Pope Victor II (1055-1057), numerous synods were held to enforce regulations aimed at reform.

Several famous preachers also lent a helping hand. The most outstanding of these was St. Peter Damian. He traveled throughout Italy, Germany, and France, urging a loftier standard of spirituality among the clergy. He made numerous studies of the monasteries and reported back to the Holy See.

To make these reforms permanent, lay investiture, which was the real source of all these evils, had to be abolished. The reformers realized that the only remedy for this evil was to subordinate the temporal power to the spiritual in spiritual matters. Pope Gregory VII would institute this reform.

The Allies and Enemies of the Holy See

In 1059, Pope Nicholas II (1059-1061) issued an edict that finally settled the manner of electing the Pope. Emperor Henry IV and his successors retained only the right to approve the election. This was clear proof that the papacy was starting to free itself from German power. However, the Germans were not so easily routed.

At the death of Nicholas II the Germans insisted on electing the Bishop of Parma, who took the name of Honorius II. This election took place despite the fact that the Romans had already elected the Bishop of Lucca, who took the name of Alexander II (1061-1073). In the face of these difficulties, the papacy began to look for powerful allies in a final effort to throw off the German yoke.

One of these allies was the Normans. During the pontificate of Pope St. Leo IX (1048-1054), they had offered their services to the Greeks of Sicily in an attempt to expel the Saracens. Acting on a promise that they would receive Sicily as payment, they drove the Saracens from the country. However, the Greeks broke their promise and attempted to cheat the Normans of their reward. The Normans, not a forgiving people, immediately attacked the Greek possessions in southern Italy.

The allied forces of the Eastern Empire, the Holy Roman Empire, and the papacy failed to expel the Normans. The Normans, under the war leader Robert Guiscard, defeated Pope Leo IX and took him prisoner. The Normans, desiring to legalize their conquests, paid homage to the Holy See. The pope agreed with their request that he become their feudal lord. In return they swore that they would be faithful vassals and furnish him with troops to fight his enemies.

The Election of Pope St. Gregory VII

At the death of Pope Alexander II, the people of Rome nominated the archdeacon Hildebrand for the Papacy. In order to comply with Pope Nicholas II's edict, the cardinals confirmed the people's choice. In honor of his friend and teacher, Pope Gregory VI, Hildebrand chose the name Gregory VII (1073-1085).

Maria del Priorato, formerly the monastery of St. Mary of the Aventine

The new Bishop of Rome was born in Tuscany in 1020. He grew up and was educated at the Roman monastery of St. Mary of the Aventine, which was under the jurisdiction of the abbot of Cluny. From early childhood his heart burned with a great love for Rome and for the Church. When he finished his studies in Rome, he went to Cluny where he spent a number of years in prayer and study under the abbot St. Odilo. Hildebrand received minor orders from Pope Gregory VI, who had been one of his teachers in Rome. He left Cluny and became secretary to the Pope. As papal secretary, Gregory was in a position to see first hand the problems that were facing the Church.

When Gregory VI died, Hildebrand returned to Cluny. While on his way to Rome, Pope Leo IX (1049-1054) stopped at Cluny and asked Hildebrand to accompany him to Rome. The Emperor had nominated Leo IX to be Pope; however, Leo needed to be elected by the people and the clergy of Rome. Acting on Hildebrand's advice, Leo entered Rome as a pilgrim. He only put on the papal vestments after he had been legally elected by the people and the clergy.

Pope Leo realized, like Pope Gregory before him, that Hildebrand was a very special man. Pope Leo ordained Hildebrand a deacon and made him a Cardinal. From this moment forward, Hildebrand became one of the most important people in the Church. The four popes who succeeded Leo all relied upon Hildebrand for advice and support.

In 1059, Pope Nicholas II had issued his decree governing papal elections. It freed the Pope from the power of the German Emperors and the Italian nobles. According to this decree, papal elections were to be held at Rome. The candidate, if possible, was to be a member of the Roman clergy. The Cardinals should nominate him and only the Cardinals could vote in the election. The lone action that the Emperor and the Roman people and clergy were allowed to take was to consent to the election.

At every papal election since Leo IX died, the people and the clergy had demanded Hildebrand be elected to the throne of St. Peter. Finally they had their way. In 1073, Hildebrand, the monk from Cluny, became Pope Gregory VII.

Pope Gregory was a true son of Cluny. He was completely filled with the spirit of reform. He began working at once to abolish the three great evils that existed in the Church: simony, the marriage of the clergy, and lay investiture. He was determined to free the Church completely from lay influence. Thus, while urging harmony between the Church and the empire, he stressed the superior character of the sacred, over the royal power. Royal power, he pointed out, is purely human in origin and exercised merely with regard to human beings. As head of the Church, the Pope is the judge of kings and emperors. However, the humble Gregory did not seek to make himself a universal king. He merely intended to suppress the abuses and scandals that resulted from secular interference with the Church.

Gregory believed lay investiture was the greatest evil facing the Church. It was the root of simony and the other abuses in the Church. He began at once to rid the hierarchy of this scourge. In 1075, he called a synod in Rome. He decreed that if anyone received a bishopric or an abbacy from a layman, that person would not be regarded as a bishop or an abbot. Similarly, if an emperor, a duke, or a count invests a person with a bishopric or any other church office, that ruler was excommunicated.

Pope Gregory's Conflict with Emperor Henry IV

No ruler was more strongly affected by this decree than Emperor Henry IV of Germany. Nowhere did prelates appear richer than in Germany. Nowhere were prelates more under the control of the king, who used them to keep undisciplined vassals under control. Nevertheless, in the beginning, Henry IV resigned himself to accept the decree against lay investiture.

Henry was only twenty-two years old when Gregory became pope in May 1073. Henry had been raised at an Imperial court filled with discord of all kinds. In March 1065, the immature fourteen-year old became Emperor. Corrupted by the scheming barons around him, lacking a positive parental influence, or a strong religious one, he emerged a despot when he took the throne. Very soon neighboring princes tried to shake off his bondage. In Saxony, they talked of electing the Duke of Swabia in his place. This shaky situation explains why Henry IV at first accepted the decree against lay investiture. He hoped Gregory VII would aid him. With this end in view, Henry sent him letters filled with expressions of loyalty.

However, the Emperor quickly changed his tactics after he defeated his enemies. Moreover, he knew that he could count on the support of a portion of the German clergy. In the autumn of 1075, in direct violation of the papal decree, he himself invested three bishops in Italy. He gave the See of Bamberg to one of his favorites, too. He also imposed his own candidate upon the clergy and people of Cologne in spite of their protests.

Gregory tried in vain to make Henry IV listen to reason. On December 8, 1075, Pope Gregory sent Henry the last letter he was ever to address to him. It began: "Gregory, servant of the servants of God, to King Henry, health and apostolic benediction if he yields to the Apostolic See that obedience which is due from a Christian king." The letter was full of kindness and consideration. However, it did rebuke Henry for consorting with men who had been excommunicated and appointing them to official positions.

Pope Gregory also sent ambassadors to meet with Henry. They told him that if he did not change his policies and reform his life he might be excommunicated and the Pope would no longer recognize him as Emperor. Henry refused to heed the Pope's warnings. Instead, in January 1076, he convoked a meeting of German bishops at Worms and proceeded to depose the Pope. The decree of deposition was sent to Gregory with the insulting statement: "Henry, king, not by usurpation, but by the holy will of God, to Hildebrand, now no longer the pope, but a false monk…. Condemned by all our bishops and by us, vacate the place which you have usurped." Gregory replied by excommunicating Henry. He also released Henry's subjects from their oath of allegiance. Also excommunicated were any bishops who had joined in the actions of the Diet of Worms unless they had acted under duress.

In Germany, Gregory's action caused many newly reformed bishops and members of the clergy to abandon Henry. Many of Henry's lay vassals began to desert him. In October 1076, the bishops and princes of the Empire met at Tribur and ordered Henry to make peace with the Pope or be deposed. The Diet of Tribur also decreed that a council should meet in February to decide whether Henry was even fit to be emperor. The council was to meet in Augsburg and be presided over by Gregory VII in person. Meanwhile, Henry was not to exercise royal power.

In worldly terms, Henry knew that he was lost if the Pope arrived to judge him publicly. His only hope was that the Pope would forgive him and renew his support for him as Emperor. Whether Henry was motivated solely by political concerns, or whether the prayers of Pope Gregory had touched his heart (Henry was only twenty-five years old, not a hardened sinner), what he did next showed remarkable courage. In the dead of winter, with his wife and young son, Henry crossed the Alps amid the greatest hardships. Oftentimes he had to crawl through the snow on his hands and knees. Finally, the small party arrived at the castle of Canossa.

Meanwhile, Pope Gregory had heard that Henry was raising an army, so he had taken refuge in the impregnable castle of Canossa. On January 25, the Emperor appeared before the ramparts of the castle and asked for absolution. The pope refused. He declared he would give his decision at Augsburg. Henry took off his shoes and dressed as a penitent.

For three days he knelt bare foot in the snow outside the gates of the castle asking the Pope to forgive him. On the evening of the third day, Pope Gregory agreed to hear the Emperor's confession on the condition that Henry abide by Gregory's decision on his right to rule and that the papal legates would have safe conduct in Germany. Henry agreed and the following day the Pope heard his confession.

The Triumph and Fall of Henry IV

To regain possession of his throne, Henry IV had to await the decree of his reconciliation. This was to be issued in the presence of a large

Henry at Canossa

assembly in Germany by the Pope himself. However, the Emperor violated his promises. His opponents met at the Diet of Forchheim where they deposed him and elected Rudolf of Swabia as his successor. Civil war broke out in Germany in April in 1077 and lasted until 1080 without any clear victor.

The pope remained patient until Henry demanded that Gregory either recognize him as emperor or be replaced with an antipope. In March 1080, at a synod in Rome, the Pope excommunicated and deposed Henry. Gregory also recognized Rudolf as Germany's new ruler. Henry retaliated in June by setting up Bishop Guibert of Ravenna, whom Gregory had excommunicated two years before, as antipope Clement III.

The events that followed favored Henry. Rudolf fell at the battle of Merseburg. In spring 1081, Henry set out for Italy. After a series of battles and sieges, he gained possession of Rome in March 1084. Henry had himself crowned emperor in the Lateran Basilica by the antipope Clement III.

Meanwhile, as Henry was about to take Rome, Gregory took refuge in Castel Sant'Angelo. Henry was besieging the castle and was about to take Gregory prisoner, when the Pope's Norman vassal, Robert Guiscard, came to his rescue with a powerful army. Robert, the greatest general of the day, forced the Germans to retreat.

However, the Normans, when assaulting a city, were impossible to control. Over the course of three terrible days the Normans pillaged the city and set it on fire. The flames burned an entire section of Rome to the ground. The Roman people blamed the Pope. Gregory VII was no longer safe in the midst of a people exasperated by the many misfortunes that had befallen him. He followed the Normans, when they withdrew from Italy, and spent the last months of his life at Monte Cassino and at Salerno. It was here that he died in 1085. His last words, which constitute a fitting epitaph for one of the greatest popes, were: "I have loved justice and hated iniquity, therefore I die in exile." Pope Paul V canonized him in 1606.

Henry IV was to pay for his treatment of Pope Gregory. Henry's sons Conrad and Henry both turned against him. Finally, he was forced to abdicate and died in exile.

The End of the Investiture Controversy

Henry V, like his father, was an obedient son of the Church so long as the imperial crown did not rest firmly on his head. However, once he became the undisputed master of the Empire in 1109, he appeared in Italy, presumably to be crowned at Rome, but in reality intending to impose his views on Pope Pascal II (1099-1118). Pascal II and his successors, Gelasius II (1118-1119) and Calixtus II (1119-1124), all defended the rights of the Church against the Emperor.

The Concordat of Worms in 1122 finally settled the long struggle between Pope and Emperor. In this agreement both parties made major concessions. Since a bishop possessed both an episcopal See and a fief, it was agreed to confer upon him two investitures. First, the bishop would be elected by the canons of the cathedral. Then the religious investiture with the crosier and the ring would occur and be conferred by a prelate delegated by the pope. Finally, the emperor conferred the feudal investiture with the scepter and the sword.

The Investiture Quarrel in England

Sadly, the investiture quarrel was not confined to Germany. In England the same fight was waged between William II Rufus, the son of William the Conqueror, and St. Anselm. When William II died his successor Henry I continued to struggle with St. Anselm. The final outcome was a papal decision. The pope declared that in the future bishops should be freely elected, then be invested with the crosier and the ring. After that ceremony they should pay homage to the king.

St. Thomas a Becket (1118-1170)

Hostilities were again renewed in the reign of Henry II. Henry demanded that clerics charged with certain crimes should be handed over for trial to the secular courts. He argued that Church courts were not strict enough in these matters. Therefore, it was crucial that the civil arm intervene.

To carry out his plans, Henry II felt he could rely on the aid of England's primate and his friend and former chancellor, Thomas a Becket. However, as sometimes happens, when Thomas was consecrated bishop, a change had taken place in his soul. Suddenly he gave up his worldly ways and embraced a life of rigid austerity. Instead of supporting Henry, he became his greatest opponent.

St. Thomas a Becket

Henry retaliated by placing Thomas on trial. Thomas forbade the English bishops to take any part in his trial and appealed his case to Rome. He himself appeared before the tribunal, vested in his episcopal robes. Henry's court found him guilty of treason, and condemned him. Taking advantage of a storm that broke out the following night, Thomas escaped and reached the Flemish coast.

Enraged, Henry swore that he would be avenged on the traitor. He expelled all Thomas' relatives from England, and seized the lands of Pontigny abbey, which had sheltered the bishop. Thomas retorted by excommunicating all the King's supporters, and surrounding himself with powerful allies. Pope Alexander III (1159-1181) actively supported Thomas. King Louis VII of France, who saw Henry II as a dangerous rival, also supported the Primate. Yielding to the pleas of the French king, Thomas and Henry agreed to meet. Henry gave in and allowed Thomas to return to England.

However, peace between the two did not last long. In June 1170, the Archbishop of York and the bishops of London and Salisbury crowned Henry's son in York. This was a breach of Canterbury's privilege of coronation. In November 1170, Becket excommunicated the bishops of London and Salisbury and suspended the Bishop of Durham and the Archbishop of York. Soon word of this reached Henry. He burst into a violent passion and exclaimed, "Will no one rid me of this meddlesome priest?" Four knights heard the King and rode at once to Canterbury, where they murdered Thomas a Becket in his cathedral. Pope Alexander III demanded public reparations for the crime, and Henry did public penance for his part in the murder. Pope Alexander III canonized Thomas a Becket in 1174.

New Monastic Orders

St. Bruno

The twelfth century witnessed a revival of the monastic life and the establishment of several new monastic orders. The two most outstanding monks of the century were St. Bruno and St. Bernard. St. Bruno founded the Order of the Carthusians. He was born at Cologne and studied at Paris. He later became headmaster of the Cathedral School at Reims, where he had as one of his pupils the future Pope Urban II. Later he taught for a while in Paris.

St. Bruno

However, for many years Bruno had the secret desire to lead an ascetical life in some solitary place. Therefore, he went to Molesmes, where he lived under the direction of St. Robert, the future founder of the Order of Citeaux. Later he settled in a wild and desolate valley, called La Chartreuse, located a few miles from Grenoble, France. A number of disciples followed him. They built a monastery. Their time was divided between prayer and manual labor, to which they also added the reading and copying of manuscripts. In the opening years of the thirteenth century the Order included an affiliated Order for women. At the time of the French Revolution the Order had one hundred seventy monasteries and thirty convents.

St. Robert of Citeaux

The greatest of all monastic revivals originated at Citeaux. The founder of the new Order, the Cistercians, was St. Robert. He had entered a Benedictine monastery at the age of fifteen. Upon becoming abbot, he set out to reform his community. However, when he failed to achieve success, he withdrew to Molesmes, where a few hermits elected him their superior. Here, too, he encountered serious difficulties that he was unable to resolve, so he established himself with about twenty faithful monks in the solitude of Citeaux in Burgundy. Neither St. Robert nor his two successors intended to found a new Order. However, the arrival of an extraordinary novice was the signal for a remarkable transformation in monastic ideas. That novice was named Bernard.

St. Bernard of Clairvaux

St. Bernard

St. Bernard was born in 1090. As a young man, he was a reserved and very timid student. The memory of his mother, whom he lost early in life, moved him to break away from all worldly ties. Thus, in the autumn of 1111, he retired from the world. Amazingly, Bernard possessed such a strong character and engaging personality that he had no difficulty in inducing thirty of his friends and family to join him in solitude. The following spring, all of them became monks at Citeaux. Bernard led a most austere life and started a monastic ideal far superior to any ever considered by St. Benedict. His holiness, coupled with his eloquence and his miracles, prompted many others to follow in his footsteps. St. Bernard died in 1153. He was canonized in 1174, and later given the title of Doctor of the Church.

St. Norbert

St. Norbert was born in 1082 in Xanten, Germany. He spent the early years of his religious life at the court of German Emperor

Henry V where he lived a very worldly existence. Converted to a life of austerity after being miraculously saved from lightning, he made an attempt to reform the secular clergy of Germany and France. However, he was soon forced to admit that the task was hopeless. He then journeyed to Reims and, in the valley of Premontre, about twenty-five miles northwest of that city, in the very heart of a forest, founded an abbey.

St. Norbert's new religious community was composed of canons who were to do the work of parish priests, particularly in the country districts, while living under a strict rule as monks. They also combined the active with the contemplative life and fulfilled the duties of monks as well as of parish priests. Pope Honorius II approved the new community in 1126. The new institution spread with astonishing rapidity, not only in France, but also in other countries. Less than thirty years after its foundation, the order had one hundred abbeys. A century later the order had one thousand monasteries and five hundred convents. These monks are known as the Norbertines.

Review Exercises

1. Name the three saints who were abbots of Cluny.
2. Why did Hildebrand choose the name Gregory VII?
3. What did Pope Gregory VII believe was the greatest evil facing the Church?
4. Describe the actions of Emperor Henry at Canossa.
5. Why was Pope Gregory VII forced to flee Rome?
6. Who said: "I have loved justice and hated iniquity, therefore I die in exile."
7. Who founded the Order of the Carthusians?
8. Who founded the Cistercian Order?

CHAPTER 13

THE CRUSADES

The Crusaders give thanks for the capture of Jerusalem.

Christian Chivalry

During the feudal period, kings and princes depended on the mounted soldier, the knight. Those who wanted the protection of the duke or the count were required to give him military service in return. The knight was required to provide his own armor and horse, and be ready to follow his lord into battle when called.

During this time rivalry was very intense among the nobles, and as we have seen, there were frequent revolts against the kings, and the Emperor. Ferocious battles were often fought. While the Church could not put an end to warfare, any more than she could put an end to sin, she was determined to make it less barbarous.

Through the monks and priests the Church preached the "Truce of God," which forbade fighting on Fridays, Saturdays, and

Sundays, and during Advent and Lent. She convinced the knights that it was cowardly to attack those who were weak and defenseless. The Church taught the knights that if there is any cause for fighting, it is to protect the weak and defenseless, or for the cause of justice, or in the defense of the Faith. The true knight battles for truth and justice, and is always a man of honor. The name "chivalry" has been given to the ideals and principles according to which the true knight should live.

To promote the ideals of chivalry, the Church created a special religious ceremony in which the knight dedicated himself to these ideals. After his training in the arts of warfare had been completed, the young man spent the whole night in the church. Placed before him, as he knelt and prayed at the foot of the altar, was

Knights often fought ferocious battles.

the armor that he was to receive the next day. With the coming of
the new day he went to Confession and received Holy Communion.
A priest blessed his sword and dedicated it to the service of widows,
orphans, and the Church.

Causes of the Crusades

The Crusades were missions carried out by Western Europe
in the eleventh, twelfth, and thirteenth centuries to deliver Jerusalem
and the tomb of Our Lord from Moslem control. In these missions
all nationalities were banded together into one vast army. It has been
said that the Crusades were "the external wars of Christendom." In
the eleventh century, two important events impelled Catholic Europe
to try to win back the Holy Land.

The first event was the destruction of the Church of the
Holy Sepulcher. In 1009, the Moslem leader, Al-Hakim, ordered
the complete destruction of the church. The attack on the church
was part of a general campaign against places of Christian worship
in Egypt and Palestine. The Church of the Holy Sepulcher was
destroyed down to the ground and the foundations also destroyed.
The reaction of Catholic Europe was shock and dismay. Al-Hakim
had thrown a stone into the pond that would ripple for centuries.

The second great cataclysm to befall the Christian West
was the fall of Jerusalem. Jerusalem had been in the possession of
the Arabs for more than four centuries. However, the city had not
suffered too much under their rule. The Arabs looked upon it as a
holy city. They respected its monuments and allowed pilgrims to
make their devotions at its shrines. A change for the worse took
place at the end of the tenth century. In 1073, the Turks, who
had conquered all of Asia Minor, seized Jerusalem. The situation

was completely transformed. Being tyrannical fanatics, the Turks persecuted Catholic pilgrims.

Pope Gregory VII had formed a plan to deliver the Holy Land from these tyrants, but his conflicts with Henry IV had forced him to lay it aside. Pope Urban II (1088-1099) put the plan into execution. In 1095, he convoked a council at Clermont to discuss the reform of the French clergy. On the last day of the council, before a huge crowd, he described the sufferings of the pilgrims who visited Palestine. He closed with a stirring appeal in favor of an expedition to regain possession of the Holy Land. The pope's discourse was received with great enthusiasm, and the cry went up from the lips of all those present, "God wills it! God wills it!" The recruits adopted a cross of red cloth worn on the right shoulder, and another worn on the chest as their insignia. This

Statue of Pope Urban II in Clermont

accounts for the name Crusades, the word *Crusade* being derived from the Latin "crux," meaning "cross," in French "croisade."

Pope Urban II journeyed throughout France preaching the Crusade. Priests and monks followed his example. One especially effective preacher was Peter the Hermit, who had lived in the Holy Land and had personally suffered at the hands of the Turks. Peter went from city to city inflaming the people and arousing their fervor.

In preaching the Crusades, the movement toward a better and holier life, which had begun at Cluny and had been carried to the clergy by Gregory VII, reached the people. All of Europe saw in the movement an opportunity to devote themselves and their possessions to the cause of Christ. Bethlehem, Nazareth, and Jerusalem to them meant the Person of Jesus Christ. These were the lands upon which Our Lord had walked and lived. They felt they had more right to them than those who did not believe He was the Son of God. Moreover, the lands had been taken from the Christians by brute force.

The First Crusade

Since the First Crusade was led by the barons, it is known as the "knights' crusade." Many of the men who fought in the First Crusade were Franks. The promise that Clovis had made so many years ago was sounding through the ages: "If only I had been there with my Franks." This time the Franks would be there. The leaders of the First Crusade were Godfrey of Bouillon, Raymond of Toulouse, Tancred, and Bohemond. The Christian armies took the town of Nicaea and defeated the Turks at the Battle of Dorylaeum in 1097. After a dreary march through the desert, during which they suffered various misfortunes and calamities and were constantly

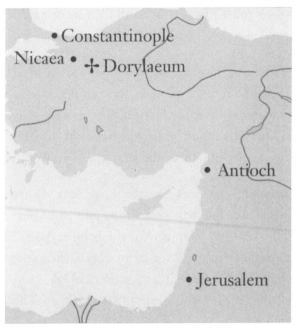

Map of the First Crusade

harassed by the enemy, they finally arrived at the gates of Antioch in Syria.

After an eight-month siege they gained possession of Antioch and defeated a Turkish army that arrived to besiege them. The route to Jerusalem now lay open before them. At the end of their strength, and dying of thirst, they attempted the heroic project of storming this stronghold. An attack made on Friday, July 15, 1099, at three o'clock in the afternoon, in memory of the death of Christ, was unexpectedly crowned with success.

The Crusaders then decided to found the Latin Kingdom of Jerusalem. They offered the crown to Godfrey of Bouillon, the most popular and the most unselfish of the leaders of the Crusade. He refused to wear a crown of gold in the city where Christ wore a crown of thorns. He accepted only the title of Defender of the Holy Sepulcher. Of all of the Crusades, the first was the most successful.

The Military Orders

During the Crusades a new kind of religious order emerged: the warrior monk. These orders consisted of fighting men and their purpose was to fight against the Turks, to offer protection to pilgrims, and to care for the sick and the wounded. Usually there were three classes of members: knights, serving brothers, and chaplains. Only the chaplains were priests. The three most important military orders were the Knights of St. John of Jerusalem, the Knights Templars, and the Teutonic Knights.

The Knights of St. John were sometimes called Knights Hospitallers from the hospital in Jerusalem, where they were first housed and where they received pilgrims and cared for the sick. In the thirteenth century they moved their headquarters to the island of Rhodes, and then to the island of Malta.

St. Bernard, who did much to spread the order, organized the Knights Templars at the Council of Troyes in 1128. With his blessing they became a favored charity and grew wealthy. They derived the name Knights Templars from their original home on the Temple mount in Jerusalem near a captured mosque. They referred to the mosque as Solomon's Temple. It was from this location that they took their official name, "Poor Knights of Christ and the Temple of Solomon," or Templars.

The Teutonic Knights appeared during the Third Crusade. They were organized by Germans and remained German in membership. This order was later on transplanted into Europe, to engage in warfare with the pagan Slavs of Prussia.

Since they were monks, these knights took the vows of poverty, chastity, and obedience. Since they were also soldiers, they wore armor under a cloak. The Hospitallers wore a black cloak with a white cross, and Templars wore a white cloak with a red cross. Their rule obliged them to acts of bravery and heroism. After the majority of the Crusaders had returned home, these military orders were transformed into a sort of permanent army. Because of its knowledge of the country and of the ways of the enemy, this army proved to be a very valuable asset.

The Second and Third Crusades

In 1144, the Moslems captured the ancient Christian town of Edessa. Once again Jerusalem was threatened. The uproar caused by the capture of Edessa led to the Second Crusade. St. Bernard preached this Crusade, and his appeal was received as ardently as that of Urban II. The French King Louis VII and the German Emperor Conrad III headed the Crusade together. Their forces, though not as numerous as those of the First Crusade, were better disciplined and were recruited almost entirely from the military. However, the Crusade was almost a complete failure. The only success occurred when some Flemish, Norman, English,

St. Bernard preaches the Second Crusade.

and Scottish Crusaders sailing to the Holy Land stopped and helped the Portuguese capture Lisbon in 1147.

The climax of these events occurred in 1187 when the Moslems, commanded by their formidable leader Saladin, crushed the Christian army and seized Jerusalem. Upon receipt of this news, Emperor Frederick Barbarossa, King Philip II of France, and King Richard the Lionhearted of England began a new Crusade. Sadly, the German army broke up after the accidental death of the aged Frederick, who drowned while crossing a river in Asia Minor. The French and the English set out for Palestine by way of the sea. From now on the sea route was the one followed in all the Crusades. Richard, on his way, conquered the island of Cyprus. The Crusaders also took the Palestinian seaport of Acre after a siege of two years.

Despite some successes the Crusaders were not able to take the city of Jerusalem. However, Richard was able to reach an agreement with Saladin. On September 2, 1192, Richard and Saladin signed a treaty. Jerusalem would remain under Moslem control but unarmed Christian pilgrims were allowed to visit the city in peace. This failure to take the city would lead to the Fourth Crusade six years later.

The Fourth Crusade

Pope Innocent III, who will be discussed in greater detail in the next chapter, had always wished to launch a great Crusade to free Palestine and all the Christian lands of the East. Thus, at the very first opportunity, he instructed several preachers to announce a new Crusade. The Crusade was the only enterprise during his reign in which he failed to achieve his purpose. The French, aided by the commercially minded Venetians, succeeded merely in capturing

Constantinople in April 1204. They then subjected the city to a hideous carnage, and erected a Latin Empire in the place of the Eastern Empire. When Innocent learned of the sack of the city, he excommunicated all those involved. This Latin Empire crumbled in 1261, without achieving anything for the cause of Christianity. The sack of Constantinople would have effects down to the present day. Whatever hope of a reunion between the Greek Orthodox Church and the Catholic Church was crushed April 13, 1204.

The Final Crusades:
The Crusades of King St. Louis of France

In 1244, King St. Louis IX of France began preparing to launch a Crusade. In July 1244, Jerusalem, which had come into the possession of the Catholics, once again fell to the Moslems. The news of the fall of Jerusalem reached France when King Louis was almost mortally ill. He vowed that, should he recover, he would head a Crusade.

At the end of 1244, Pope Innocent IV (1243-1254) called for a Crusade. However, only France answered the call. King Louis set sail from France, spent the winter on the island of Cyprus, landed in Egypt, and marched on Cairo. After the hard-earned victory of Mansura, in which the French gave ample proof of both courage and imprudence, Louis was forced to make a disastrous retreat in 1250. He was taken prisoner and had to pay a high ransom for his release. The saintly King, who would not be discouraged, remained four more years in Syria rebuilding the fortifications of Acre, Jaffa, Caesarea, and Sidon. Though it was his greatest desire, he was not able to assemble an army strong enough to assault Jerusalem. When his mother's death required that he return to France, he still held the hope of some day going back to Palestine.

Over the years, more disastrous news arrived periodically from the Holy Land. In early 1268, Sultan Baybars of Egypt gained possession of several places in Palestine, including Antioch, which he looted and destroyed. Thus it happened that King St. Louis, now old and sickly, again resolved to lead a Crusade. His first Crusade he had led with his brothers. This Crusade he led with his sons.

Louis and his sons set sail July I, 1270, and landed at Carthage. His plan was to seize Tunis and make this city the

King St. Louis leaves on the Crusade

base of his operations against Egypt. Sadly, the plan was completely frustrated by an outbreak of the plague in the army. The King himself caught the disease and died on August 25. The Crusade, which had scarcely begun, was thus brought to an abrupt end.

Pope Gregory X tried in vain to undertake another Crusade. For six years the Crusaders everywhere were unsuccessful. Left to its own fate, the East fell prey to the power of the Moslems who seized the last Christian centers, Tripoli and Acre, in 1291. Thus, as far as their chief goal was concerned, the Crusades failed. The Holy Land was not delivered out of the hands of the Turks, nor were the Greeks united with the Church. This is not to say that the Crusades were overall a failure. From a military point of view, the Crusades were successful in keeping the Turks from attacking Europe.

Moreover, the Crusaders accomplished a great deal of good in other ways. Since they were fighting in a spiritual cause, the ideals of the knights were uplifted and their lives ennobled. Also, the West became better acquainted with the East. Many of the finer things of Greek culture were brought back to Italy, Germany, and France. The products of the East, like spices and silks, were introduced into the West and commerce developed. Explorers set out to discover better trade routes, and as a result of this, in 1492, America was discovered.

Review Exercises

1. How did the Church influence warfare in this period?
2. What is chivalry?
3. Why were the Crusades undertaken?
4. What was the most important result of the First Crusade?
5. Which Pope preached the First Crusade?
6. Which Pope preached the Fourth Crusade?
7. Why were the religious orders founded at this time called Military Orders?
8. Name the most important of these orders.
9. Why did Louis IX's last crusade fail?
10. What were the overall results of the Crusades?

CHAPTER 14

THE AGE OF POPE INNOCENT III

Tomb of Pope Innocent III, in the Lateran Basilica

The Guelphs and Ghibellines

By the middle of the twelfth century, the papacy was supreme in both spiritual and temporal matters. This aroused the envy of the emperor. The conflict became open warfare when Frederick Barbarossa became Emperor (1152-1190). It lasted for over a hundred years. The war the emperors and the popes finally ended with the complete collapse of the Hohenstaufen dynasty of kings and emperors. During this time, the Hohenstaufens contested the authority of the papacy and attempted to meddle in its affairs. In this mighty struggle some people sided with the Pope and others with the Emperor. The Ghibellines, who were the emperor's supporters, were not heretics. The Guelphs, who were the pope's adherents, were not saints. No one questioned the authority of the Pope in spiritual affairs. The issue was how much authority the Pope had in temporal matters, and how much authority the Emperor had in Church affairs.

The names "Guelph" and "Ghibelline" came from Germany. They can be traced to the rivalry between the House of Welf (Bavaria) and the House of Hohenstaufen, whose ancestral castle was located at Waiblingen in Swabia. When Otto of Bavaria and Philip of Swabia began fighting for the imperial crown in Germany and Italy in the closing years of the twelfth century, the names of the rival parties were introduced into Italy. Guelfo and Ghibellino are the Italian forms of Welf and Waiblingen.

The Investiture Struggle had been between pope and emperor over bishops and abbots. The conflict with the Hohenstaufens was between the pope and emperor over each other's authority. All the elements of a quarrel were present. The popes had crowned the emperors, and the coronation of the emperors had seemed required before he could assume his imperial titles. On the other hand, the emperors had nominated some of the popes. Moreover, nearly all the popes up to the time of Urban II, even Gregory VII, had waited for imperial approval before being consecrated Pope.

Frederick Barbarossa had been ruling Germany for only two years when Nicholas Breakspear, the only English Pope, was elected to the papacy as Pope Adrian IV (1154-1159). They first clashed at the time of the Emperor's visit to Rome to receive the imperial crown. Frederick refused to hold the Pope's stirrup, as the Emperor Lothaire had done before him, for fear of appearing to be the Pope's vassal. However, in the end he yielded because Adrian threatened not to crown him if he refused. The chief object of the conflict between the two was the city of Rome. When the pope declared that he was its sole master, Frederick replied: "If it is not under my command, I am emperor in name only." An uneasy peace existed between the two until 1158 when Barbarossa made a second journey into Italy. He again claimed supremacy over all cities, including the city of Rome. Open conflict between the two powers loomed.

Open Conflict under Pope Alexander III

Pope Adrian IV died in 1159, and the Sacred College elected Cardinal Roland Bandinelli, who took the name of Alexander III (1159-1181). A minority set up an antipope named "Victor V." The validity of Alexander's election was above dispute. The kings of England, France, Spain, and Ireland all accepted his election. Only Barbarossa supported the antipope. His action resulted in open war between the Papacy and the Empire. Alexander III had to flee Rome. He took refuge at Sens, where Louis VII of France gave him shelter.

Sens Cathedral

Barbarossa made a third journey into Italy. He captured and completely destroyed Milan. The death of antipope Victor in 1164 brought no change in the state of affairs, for another antipope calling himself "Pascal III" was elected. At the Diet of Wurzburg in 1165, the German princes and bishops declared their support for Barbarossa's antipope.

In November 1165, Alexander III re-entered Rome and was acclaimed as its liberator. Unfortunately, for the popes of that time Frederick Barbarossa was the greatest general of his age. Once again Frederick journeyed into Italy. He seized Rome and had himself crowned by the antipope in St. Peter's. Alexander III, disguised as a pilgrim, fled.

Just then an epidemic broke out in Barbarossa's army, forcing him also to leave Rome. The Emperor came a fifth time into Italy, but was completely defeated at the Battle of Legnano in 1176. Frederick then began negotiations with Pope Alexander, which resulted in the Peace of Venice in 1177. The Emperor prostrated himself before the Pope under the archway of St. Mark's Cathedral in Venice. He humbly pleaded for forgiveness and accepted Alexander as the true pope.

The Third Lateran Council in 1179 confirmed the Peace of Venice. To prevent the chance of another schism, the decree

The Battle of Legnano

Nicholas II had issued in 1059 on papal elections was amended. From now on, a two-thirds majority in the College of Cardinals was required for the valid election of a pope.

The Election of Pope Innocent III

When Pope Celestine III died in 1198, he was succeeded by Lothario Conti of Rome, who took the name Innocent III (1198-1216). The new Pope was only thirty-seven years old. However, he was already well known for his theological writings and as an adviser to the previous Pope. He had a detailed knowledge of the Church's organization and government. When he became Pope he had very definite plans for the future relations between the Papacy and the empire.

Innocent III and Italy

The first task that confronted the new Pope was putting the affairs of Rome and Italy in order. Rome was controlled by very ambitious nobles, who were loyal to the emperor. Innocent replaced them with nobles loyal to him. Almost all the provinces of the Church were in the hands of German rulers set up by Henry IV. Innocent III effected quick and radical changes in this state of affairs. He championed the cause of the people against their German oppressors, and gave the latter the choice either to swear allegiance to him or to be deposed from their offices.

Pope Innocent III was equally successful in southern Italy. There, Queen Constance, who ruled southern Italy, declared herself to be a faithful vassal of the Pope. She completely banished the Germans from her kingdom in 1198. Shortly afterward she died, leaving her four-year-old son (the future Frederick II) in the care of

Innocent III. He immediately appointed two cardinals to take charge of the kingdom. In this manner the entire peninsula was returned to the Italians and entrusted to the care of the papacy.

Innocent III and the German Empire

Meanwhile the member of the Hohenstaufen dynasty, Philip of Swabia, and Otto of Brunswick, of the House of Saxony, were fighting for the throne of Germany. Both men appealed their case to the Pope. Innocent chose Otto. The pope felt that Philip belonged to a family that had always persecuted the Church, and, given the crown, would turn against the Church. However, Innocent had barely crowned Otto, when he began to show that he was as bad as any Hohenstaufen. He set out to conquer the entire Italian peninsula. Innocent III argued with him, and finally excommunicated him. Thereupon, the German princes chose the Pope's ward, Frederick II, as emperor. King Philip Augustus of France, who had come to the support of Frederick II at the Pope's invitation, finally crushed Otto in battle. By 1216 Frederick II was the undisputed head of the Empire.

Innocent III and England

In 1208, Innocent placed England under an interdict. (An interdict closed all the churches and suspended all public religious services.) King John insisted on appointing his own choice as Archbishop of Canterbury despite the fact that the Pope had appointed Cardinal Stephen Langton, an eminent theologian. Not only did Innocent place the country under interdict, but also excommunicated the king, deposed him, and offered England to the King of France. To save his kingdom, King John submitted to the Holy Father. He offered England to the Pope as a fief, agreed to pay an annual tribute, and acknowledged himself the Holy Father's vassal. Two years later, in

1215, the English barons rose up against the unpopular King John. At Runnymede the barons forced him to sign the great charter of English liberty, the Magna Carta.

Innocent III and France

In August 1193, King Philip Augustus married a Danish princess named Ingeborg. However, he quickly developed a strange dislike of her and wanted to dissolve the marriage. A council of bishops and barons, presided over by the king's uncle, the Archbishop of Reims, convened and annulled the marriage. When Ingeborg appealed her case to Rome, Philip locked her in a convent. The legates sent by Pope Celestine III to investigate the case were locked up in the monastery at Clairvaux. In open defiance of the Pope, Philip Augustus then married a Bavarian countess named Agnes.

King Philip Augustus

As soon as Innocent III became pope, he sent a letter to the king, defending Ingeborg and the validity of the marriage. Philip Augustus refused to listen. So, in 1200, the Pope placed the entire French kingdom under interdict. The enraged king tried to prevent the papal order from being carried out. However, the unhappiness and anger of his Catholic subjects soon forced him to yield to the Pope. Once he had made a complete submission to the Pope, the Pope lifted the interdict. The King's change of heart, however, was only a facade. Later he again imprisoned Ingeborg. He did not finally yield until 1213. The Church decided that his first marriage was valid.

The Albigensian Heresy

The Albigensian heresy was the last gasp of Manichaeism. In Italy and southern France, the members of the sect referred to themselves as the *Cathari* (the Pure), because they laid claim to a purity unknown to other men. They were also called Albigensians, because Albi was the main center of their operations.

The basic teaching of the Cathari was a belief in two opposing principles. One principle was good and one was evil. The good principle created the invisible and spiritual universe. The evil principle created the material world. Since the material world was evil, they rejected the humanity of Christ and the goodness of marriage and children. They taught that the body, the material part of a person, must be brought under control by fasting and

St. Dominic blesses Simon de Montfort

mortification, and even by suicide if necessary if the forces of evil proved too great.

This was one of the most terrible heresies to attack the Church. It descended upon France like a dark night that came down with the weight of lead and the coldness of ice upon the mind and the heart. It ate at all the bright and elevated faculties of the human soul. It was a deadly madness that choked the joy out of living and made existence appear like a bad dream. By 1165, the Cathars were so numerous and so strongly supported by many of the nobles that they were openly preaching their heresy. The bishops dared not move against them. The Cathars were helped by Philip Augustus' refusal to pay attention to the situation even when Pope Innocent III pointed it out to him.

When all other means failed to stop this heresy, in 1208, Pope Innocent III proclaimed a Crusade against it. Philip Augustus was fighting with England so he refused to head the Crusade. However, an army of about 200,000 Crusaders, recruited chiefly from the ranks of the nobility of northern France, answered the Pope's call. They chose a French-English nobleman, Simon de Montfort, as their leader. The Crusade dragged on amidst scenes of unspeakable cruelty for almost twenty years. France's southern provinces were completely devastated. The stalwart Simon de Montfort died during the siege of Toulouse in 1215. However, the heresy was finally suppressed. In 1229 the Council of Toulouse condemned it from the doctrinal point of view.

The Suppression of Heresy: The Inquisition

In the Middle Ages, when the Catholic Faith was the only recognized religion in Europe, and the Church and the state were joint powers; heresy was regarded as a crime against society and punished as such. The heretic in Christendom was as dangerous to public order as a terrorist is today. Up to the middle of the twelfth century the Church usually imposed only spiritual penalties, like excommunication and interdict. During the second half of the twelfth century, some rulers, realizing that heresy was undermining both the spiritual and the secular order, began to insist that the Church use physical coercion. According to an agreement made between Pope Lucius III (1181-85) and Frederick Barbarossa in 1184, heretics were to be sought out (*inquisitio*), tried before a Church court, and excommunicated. This task was entrusted to reliable bishops. Then the heretic was given to the civil power for suitable punishment. Unless a heretic withdrew his or her errors, the civil authority punished them.

However, the action of the bishops was limited to their own dioceses, whereas heresy often spread over large areas. The papacy soon realized that the work of suppressing heresy would have to be entrusted to papal legates who had a more universal authority. These legates were normally selected from the ranks of religious who belonged to the mendicant orders, Dominican or Franciscan friars. All Inquisitors were well educated and had university decrees.

The Inquisition adopted the following procedure. As soon as it was decided to conduct an investigation in a heresy-ridden district, the inquisitor promulgated two edicts. The Edict of Faith was addressed to the faithful and commanded them to denounce all heretics under pain of excommunication. The Edict of Grace was addressed to the heretics themselves. It summoned them to appear before the inquisitor. They were promised forgiveness if they recanted their errors within a period of fifteen to thirty days. When this time had elapsed, the person charged with heresy was denounced as a suspect, and kept under close observation or imprisoned to await trial. He could remain stubborn or repent. If he repented, the inquisitor heard his confession and gave him a suitable canonical penance. If the heretic persisted in his heresy, he could be further induced to recant by the fear of death, and imprisonment, although usually, by friendly persuasion. Though torture was used it was infrequent and did not cause any permanent injury. At the end of the procedure, the inquisitor pronounced the sentence in a public and solemn assembly.

The Inquisition imposed various kinds of penalties. Some were canonical penances, such as pilgrimages to the Holy Land, rather than physical punishment. Other punishments affected the material wealth of the condemned person, like a fine. Finally, other punishments were inflicted upon the person himself, such as imprisonment or death at the stake. However, even H. C. Lea, the Protestant historian of the Inquisition, and a bitter enemy of the Church, admits that probably not more than three or four percent of those convicted of heresy died at the stake. Recent research even more enhances the reputation of the Inquisition as one of the fairest forums for justice the world has ever seen.

The Rise of the Mendicant Orders

As so often happens in the Church, at the times of her deepest need, the Holy Spirit calls upon men and women to change adversity into glory and dark into light. So too, at this moment in history, Our Lord was preparing to call two men to His service. These men would change the history of the Church and the world. Their names were Dominic and Francis.

St. Dominic was born in Caleruega, Spain, in 1170. One day he heard a Cistercian monk preaching to the people. Although the monk was a holy and learned man, the people, many of them heretics, were not moved. Dominic told the monk that if the people were to be won to back to the Faith, that he must speak as one of them. From this moment onward, St. Dominic devoted himself to the task of popular preaching.

Dominic gathered a few zealous priests together and they decided to live a common life under the Rule of St. Augustine. To counter the severity of the Cathars, they took the vow of absolute poverty to prove that it is possible to live a very spiritual life without denying the Church. Dominic said, "Zeal must be met by zeal, humility by humility, false sanctity by real sanctity, preaching

Pope Honorius approved the order in 1216.

falsehood by preaching truth." From this little group grew an order whose main purpose was preaching the Gospel. Its members were called "Preaching Friars." Pope Honorius III approved the new order in 1216.

St. Dominic believed that unless a preacher had sound training in philosophy and theology, he could not preach successfully to the people and answer the questions that they were asking. Consequently, he sent the members of his order to Paris to study. When they were properly prepared, he sent them out, in pairs, throughout Europe. Their preaching was crowned with great success. By their learning and eloquence they stemmed the tide of heresy. Some of them became the most brilliant professors at the University of Paris. When St. Dominic died in 1221, his order numbered sixty religious houses.

St. Francis of Assisi

St. Francis was born in Assisi in 1182 to a wealthy family. As a young man he entered into the carefree life of the city's youth. He loved music and poetry and having fun. He was a good young man, just not particularly religious.

Outside the walls of Assisi there was a little church dedicated to St. Damian. One day, while he was praying in the ruins of the little church, he heard Our Lord saying to him: "Francis, go and rebuild My house." He took these words literally and spent his entire fortune in rebuilding the little church. His action aroused the displeasure of his father, who tried to reason with him, but in vain. Finally, in the presence of the bishop, his father disowned him. Francis' answer was to strip himself of his fine clothes as a sign that he was through with the world. He went around as a common beggar collecting alms for the repair of neglected churches.

Within a few years Francis had gathered together a few disciples and imposed upon them the observance of strict poverty, penance, and preaching two by two. Thus began the Franciscan Order. They made up their minds to live by manual labor and by begging. They called themselves "Fratres Minores," (little brothers), abbreviated as O. F. M. (Ordo Fratrum Minorum), to indicate that they belonged to the common people to whom they preached. Since they preached more by example than by word of mouth, their influence was remarkable.

In order that he might have the right to preach the Gospel publicly, Francis was ordained a deacon. However, he considered himself unworthy to be promoted to the priesthood. Innocent III conditionally approved the order in 1210. Pope Honorius III gave final approval to the order in 1223.

St. Francis also started a community of women, under the direction of his spiritual daughter, St. Clare of Assisi. This order was called the Poor Clares or the Second Order of St. Francis. Later a Third Order was founded for lay members who continued to live in the world. This order furnished many pious Catholics, who could not sever their family ties, with a chance to live a semi-religious life and share in the spiritual rewards of the Franciscan Order.

Toward the end of his life, Francis turned over the work of administering the order to others and devoted himself more

St. Francis receives the Stigmata

to prayer. He loved to go to alone to Mount Alvernia to pray. On the feast of the Exaltation of the Holy Cross in 1224, he saw a vision of an angel attached to a cross and shining in glory. St. Francis was overcome with love and gratitude to our crucified Savior. When the vision passed, he discovered in his hands, his feet, and his side, the wounds of the Stigmata. He died in 1226. Two years later Pope Gregory IX canonized him.

The Fall of the Hohenstaufen Dynasty

Frederick II had made several promises to his guardian, Pope Innocent III. He promised to keep the Kingdom of Sicily and the German Empire separate. He promised to protect the papacy and the cities of Lombardy from serious danger. He also promised to lead a Crusade. Despite his promises, he had his son Henry, already King of Sicily, elected and crowned King of Germany. He constantly delayed leaving on Crusade. Pope Honorius III, Innocent III's successor, was a saintly old man and did not oppose Frederick. However, with the election of Pope Gregory IX (1227-1241), there was a dramatic change. Gregory IX had the same energetic and firm character as his uncle Innocent III. Gregory demanded that Frederick keep his promise and depart on the Crusade.

Frederick reluctantly left on September 8, 1227, but returned three days later, feigning illness. Gregory then excommunicated him for not leading what would have been the sixth Crusade. In response, Frederick made a brilliant move. In June 1228, he set out for the East, hoping to regain the prestige that he had lost. He left even though the Pope had forbidden him to lead a crusade while he was excommunicated. Upon his arrival in Palestine he found the Prince of Damascus engaged in open conflict with the Sultan of Egypt. He promptly allied himself with

Emperor Frederick makes a deal with the Moslems.

the Sultan and agreed to protect him against further invasions from the Christian West. In exchange, the Sultan agreed to give Jerusalem to the Christians for ten years after which it would revert back to the Moslems. When Frederick returned from the Holy Land, he and Gregory IX reconciled in 1230.

Frederick's fight with the Papacy resumed during the reign of Innocent IV (1243-1254). Innocent pleaded again and again with Frederick to give up his claims in northern Italy but to no avail. In 1245, the Pope convoked a council at Lyons. At this council he revealed Frederick's true character and bad conduct. The council found the Emperor guilty of various crimes including collusion with the Saracens and waging a sacrilegious war against the papacy. It excommunicated Frederick and deposed him as Emperor. Germany was invited to elect a new ruler. For the last five years of his life Frederick was a ruthless enemy of the Church, fighting her constantly. He died of a sudden illness in December 1250. Frederick's three sons all died tragic deaths. The Hohenstaufen family was at an end.

The Rise of the Hapsburg Dynasty

On March 27, 1271 Blessed Pope Gregory X (1271-1276) became pope. This vigorous Pope felt that it was time to fill the vacancy in the office of Emperor that had been vacant since the departure of the Hohenstaufens. With no dominant noble family in Germany, it was possible for the Pope to choose a family who would support the Papacy. He made one of the greatest choices in the history of the Church. He chose Rudolf of Hapsburg. For the next six hundred years, the Hapsburg family would be the sword and shield of Christendom. They would defend the Church from the infidel without and the heretic within. The Hapsburg family would provide Christendom with some of its greatest leaders.

Review Exercises

1. Who were the Guelphs and Ghibellines?
2. Which Emperor was placed in the care of Innocent III?
3. Why did Innocent III place England under interdict?
4. Why did Innocent III place France under interdict?
5. Why was the Albigensian heresy so terrible?
6. What was the Edict of Faith? What was The Edict of Grace?
7. Who founded the Order of Preachers?
8. If a priest has the abbreviation OFM after his name, to which order does he belong?
9. Why was Frederick II excommunicated the first time?
10. Whom did Pope Gregory X choose to be the Holy Roman Emperor after the fall of the Hohenstaufens?

CHAPTER 15

THE CHURCH AND MEDIEVAL SOCIETY

Albert the Great teaching

The Papacy

During these centuries of deep faith the pope was the supreme authority. It was the pope who invested the emperor with his powers, who commanded his subjects to show him allegiance, and who settled all major disputes. As a result, civil rulers answered to the pope both as private persons and as public officials. When kings violated the moral order, they were subject to canon law like other members of the Church, and could be excommunicated. The pope punished Philip Augustus in this way for the sin of adultery. The popes punished the German emperors for taking Church property. Boleslaus of Poland and Henry II of England were disciplined for the murders of St. Stanislaus and St. Thomas a Becket.

Boleslaus was disciplined for murdering St. Stanislaus.

Against the political crimes of kings and princes the popes sometimes used the interdict, which closed all the churches and halted all public religious services in a country. This caused the people to become frustrated and forced their rulers to seek absolution. The pope could also release a ruler's subjects from their oath of allegiance, and could even depose the king. Pope Gregory VII did this in the case of Henry IV in 1080. Innocent II did it with King John of England in 1212. Innocent IV did it against Frederick II in 1245.

The pope's income came mainly from the revenues of the Papal States. Peter's Pence was another source of income. Several countries, notably England, furnished it. William the Conqueror promised it to Gregory VII, and King John fixed it at a definite sum. The other vassals of the Holy See paid the Pence according to their means.

The Bishops and Cardinals

The Council of Lyons in 1274 laid down definite rules about the role of Cardinals in papal elections. On the tenth day after the pope's death they were to assemble and remain absolutely locked away from the rest of the world in "conclave" (from the Latin *cum clave*, locked in with a key). Cardinals also acted as advisors to the pope on questions of faith and morals. Cardinals also advised the pope on other important decisions, such as canonizations, approval of religious orders, and founding universities and episcopal sees. They also helped him govern the Papal States. Their meetings with the pope were called consistories.

The way that bishops were elected was the main issue in the investiture quarrel, which ended in a total victory for the papacy. During the Middle Ages, papal influence in the appointment of bishops was felt more and more in the dioceses. Frequently the nomination of the bishop depended entirely upon the pope. The right to transfer a bishop from one See to another, and to accept a bishop's resignation, also belonged to the Holy Father. Finally, the popes began to exercise the right to make certain church appointments directly.

Ecclesiastical Justice

Church courts had authority over both personal and property cases. A cleric discovered committing a crime could be arrested by the civil government, but had to be turned over at once to the Church court. The Church turned over to the civil courts any cleric who made himself unworthy of his office either by attempting to marry or by practicing usury. In property cases the Church had authority in cases involving the Sacraments, vows, and Church discipline. The Church courts also tried cases of sacrilege, blasphemy, witchcraft, simony, and crimes committed in sacred places.

Medieval Piety

The people of this time loved and lived their Catholic faith. The clergy worked to promote the people's natural love for God chiefly through preaching and by what was known as "mystery plays." At different times throughout the year, especially at Christmas and Easter, the principal mysteries of the Faith, for example, the Incarnation and Our Lord's Passion, were represented in church. The actors in these mystery plays were priests or clerics dressed in slightly altered priestly vestments. The dialogue merely paraphrased the Scripture text. In the twelfth and thirteenth centuries, the mystery had the appearance of a modern play. The presentation was transferred from the church to the nearby public square. It set forth not only the Passion of Christ, but also the lives of the saints.

After the tenth century the liturgy remained fixed. However, several new feasts were introduced: the Transfiguration, the Immaculate Conception, and Corpus Christi. The feast of Corpus Christi was established in Liege, Belgium, in 1246, as a result of revelations made to St. Juliana. A few years later, Pope Urban IV made the celebration of this feast mandatory throughout the world.

The feast of Corpus Christi is revealed to St. Juliana

In 1215, the Fourth Lateran Council had to order that everyone receive Holy Communion at least once a year. Sadly, this decree shows that neglect must have crept into the devotion that is due to the Blessed Sacrament. This Council also said that in the Roman Rite, Holy Communion was to be received only under the appearance of bread.

The Lateran Council also required at least annual confession. Public penance, however, became less and less frequent. It was imposed only on persons who attacked a bishop. The penances imposed were much more severe than they are today. They included prayers, alms, fasts, pilgrimages, and even taking part in a Crusade. The practice of granting indulgences also increased. They were often given to a Crusader or to a person who equipped a Crusader. Pope Innocent III granted a plenary indulgence to all who assisted in building a bridge over the Rhone River. Innocent IV granted one to those who helped construct Cologne Cathedral.

Some of the most beautiful prayers to the Blessed Mother date from the Middle Ages. The "Hail, Holy Queen," for example, originated at Le Puy and was made popular by the Cistercians. The most popular of all devotions to Our Lady was the Rosary. In the Middle Ages a vassal made a practice of offering his lord a wreath of roses as a token of his obedience. Thus, the mystics, who were the knights and servants of Mary, offered her wreaths and crowns of roses, from which comes the name "rosary." The faithful also took delight in imitating the monks. Unable to wear the monk's full habit, they wore a small scapular, which gave them the right to share in some of the merits of the monks.

Philosophy in the Twelfth Century

Until the twelfth century, theologians had remained content simply to restate the arguments of the Fathers. In most cases they just copied them word for word. The general feeling was that this was the safest method of procedure. The Church Fathers had triumphed over error. The works of the Fathers ranked second only to the writings of the Apostles. The sensible thing, apparently, was to follow scrupulously in their footsteps. Thus one avoided straying from the path of truth. The first person to break with this method was St. Anselm, the Archbishop of Canterbury.

St. Anselm inspired theologians with new confidence in the power of human reason. Without setting aside the ancient proofs based on authority, he sought other arguments from **philosophy**, which is the study of truth. He developed many new viewpoints in his *Monologium*, a meditation on the divine Essence. In his *Proslogion*, he unfolds a new proof for the existence of God based on the idea of perfection.

Scholasticism

The new attempt to base the ancient proofs from authority in arguments based on reason was called Scholasticism, that is, "Science of the Schools" (schola, school). Philosophy and the natural sciences became the handmaids of theology. Churchmen realized that truth is one. They realized that the findings of science cannot disagree with the data of revelation found in Scripture. Scholasticism aimed to bring out the harmony existing between faith and reason and to prove that our faith is reasonable. Its success is the outstanding achievement of the Middle Ages.

The thirteenth century was the golden age of medieval theology. Three factors made this possible. The first was the creation of centers of theological culture, the universities, of which the University of Paris became the most important. The second was the arrival of new teachers and of the mendicant orders in these universities. The final cause was the revival Aristotle's teachings by these orders.

The Universities

The great universities of the Middle Ages were Salerno for medicine, Bologna for law, and Paris for theology. Gradually the University of Paris became directly subject to the pope. The popes then began to look upon Paris as the official school of theology. They came to rely upon its judgment to condemn heretics. Under the leadership of many outstanding professors, it soon became the greatest university of the Middle Ages.

The mendicant orders supplied the universities with famous teachers. St. Dominic was the first to establish an order having study and teaching among its chief duties. St. Albert the Great and St. Thomas Aquinas were the most famous Dominican professors.

St. Bonaventure was the most outstanding Franciscan professor.

St. Bonaventure, the Seraphic Doctor, received his master of theology degree in 1257. He regarded philosophy as the handmaid of theology. In his work, *The Threefold Way*, he describes the three ways that lead to God: meditation, prayer, and contemplation.

St. Albert the Great was born in 1206. While studying at Padua, he was attracted to the Dominican Order. Between 1245 and 1248 he wrote a book, which made all the teachings of Aristotle available to Western students. This work received the official approval of Pope Alexander IV in 1256. At Paris, one of Albert's students was Thomas Aquinas. The student soon surpassed the master, and the task of adapting the writings of Aristotle to the teachings of Catholic theology was brought to a happy completion. Albert the Great died at Cologne, November 15, 1280. Pope Pius

S:Bonaventura·

S. Thomas v. Aquin.

XI canonized him and proclaimed him a Doctor of the Church in 1932.

St. Thomas Aquinas was born in 1225. He studied first at Monte Cassino and later at Naples. Despite the protests of his family, he became a Dominican. He studied under Albert the Great at Cologne, and received his doctorate from the University of Paris. In 1261, the Pope called Thomas to Rome, together with the Flemish preacher, William of Moerbeke. Pope Urban IV commissioned William to translate Aristotle directly from the Greek, and St. Thomas to comment upon Aristotle based on the new translation.

St. Thomas began his greatest work, the *Summa Theologica*, in Bologna about 1271. It is the most important contribution ever made to Catholic theology and philosophy. It is a summary of both Catholic theology and philosophy. It deals with the existence of God and God's attributes. It discusses the return of man to God through Christ by means of the Sacraments. It deals with the creation and government of the universe, the origin and nature of man, human destiny, virtues, vices, and laws.

In 1274, Pope St. Gregory X summoned St. Thomas to attend the Council of Lyons. On the way he fell ill. He was taken to a Cistercian monastery and cared for by the monks. St. Thomas received the Holy Eucharist and died March 7, 1274. When he breathed his last, one of the brightest lights in the Catholic Church was extinguished. He was only forty-nine years old, but his work was done. Thomas Aquinas was canonized in 1324, on the fiftieth anniversary of his death. Pope Leo XIII declared him the patron saint of all Catholic schools and scholars. He is called the Angelic Doctor, as much for his clarity and precision in expounding the truth as for his purity and holiness of life.

Schools for the Common People

During this time, the Church did not neglect the education of the common people. While the cathedral schools, the monastic schools, and the universities were devoted to higher learning, there were other schools where both boys and girls could receive an elementary education. Some of these were parish schools and the towns conducted others. There were also "chantry" schools. Someone would donate money to build a chapel or a special altar in the cathedral or a parish church where Mass would be said for the repose of his soul. This was called a chantry. The priest, in charge of it, in addition to saying Mass, would often have a school to provide a free education for the poor.

The historian Paulsen writes, "It seems safe to assume that at the end of the Middle Ages the entire population of the towns, with the exception of the lowest classes, was able to read and to write." He bases his statement on the fact that printing developed so rapidly. Ordinary people must have been able to read; otherwise, there would have been no demand for books.

Medieval Architecture: Romanesque

It was not until the eleventh century that there was a revival of art and the Romanesque style of architecture came into use. The main feature of this style was the use of round arches and very thick walls. The walls had to be heavy and thick to support the roof, which, instead of being flat and wooden, was now arched and built of stone like the rest of the building.

The first thing one notices about a church built in the Romanesque style is the vault that covers the **nave**. This vault is the key to the style of the edifice. Since it is difficult to build a large semicircular vault if the nave is narrow, and because even a narrow vault causes terrific lateral pressure that tends to push

Speyer Cathedral

the walls apart, the walls are very thick. So that the walls may preserve their full strength, they are built without large windows. This accounts for the semidarkness usually found in the nave. To increase the resistance to the pressure of the vault, it is sustained at regular intervals by binding arches. These arches rest on columns or pillars set in the walls. On the opposite side of these, and on the outside of the church, were buttresses. These were massive pieces of masonry supports. However, all these precautions did not seem sufficient to the Romanesque architects. When the church had aisles, these buttresses were transformed into what has been termed flying buttresses, which strengthened the resistance to the pressure of the vault of the great nave. Thus, the vault created a complete change in the proportions, lighting, and appearance of the church edifice. The idea that is conveyed by the Romanesque style of architecture is a firm and stalwart faith. The most beautiful examples of this style are to be found at the German cathedrals of Speyer, Worms, and Mainz.

Mainz Cathedral

Medieval Architecture: Gothic

The main features of Gothic architecture are thinner and higher walls, upon which rest pointed arches instead of round arches. Gothic architecture also has larger windows. With Gothic architecture the entire edifice gains strength and slenderness. The pillars are transformed into slender columns, and the vault rises to heights previously unknown. In Beauvais Cathedral the vault is 137 feet. It is 124 feet at Amiens, and 109 feet at Notre Dame in Paris. Unlike the semidarkness of the Romanesque churches, the Gothic church is awash in light. The ground plan differs from that of the Romanesque only in detail. It is in the form of a Latin cross with very short arms, each of which is terminated by a doorway or vestibule.

Romanesque architecture is essentially monastic in character, whereas Gothic is first and last an episcopal creation. The great

Chartres Cathedral

Cologne Cathedral

Gothic monuments of the Middle Ages are the cathedrals of Reims, Paris, Amiens, Chartres, and Cologne. They are at once the admiration and despair of modern architects. The facades of some of these cathedrals teem with statues. The gorgeous stained-glass windows through which streams the light of the sun are silent witnesses to the artistic genius of the Middle Ages.

Review Exercises

1. What is a consistory?
2. What was the origin of the Feast of Corpus Christi?
3. Who was the father of Scholasticism?
4. Name the three great medieval universities.
5. What was St. Thomas Aquinas' greatest work?

CHAPTER 16

THE POPES AWAY FROM ROME: THE WESTERN SCHISM

St. Catherine of Siena leads Pope Gregory XI back to Rome.

Conflict between France and Rome

After the death of Pope Nicholas IV (1288-1292), the Holy See was vacant for two years. The cardinals finally elected the saintly hermit, Peter Murrone. He took the name Celestine V. Not at all versed in the ways of Italian diplomacy, Pope Celestine soon became aware that he was not fit to be pope. He freely resigned after five

236

months. The conclave that convened in Naples elected Cardinal Benedict Gaetani, who took the name Boniface VIII (1294-1303).

Boniface VIII was just over sixty years old when he became pope. He was a man of exceptional ability and strong opinions. Almost at once, he found himself in conflict with France. France was gradually replacing Germany as the leading nation in Europe.

The King of France, Philip the Fair (1285-1314), managed his kingdom's money poorly and was almost always at war. As a result, he always needed money. To fix a financial situation that was becoming more and more serious, Philip resorted to every possible means. He seized money from bankers. He imposed very high taxes on the serfs, the middle class, the noblemen, and especially on the clergy, since they were less able to defend themselves. Despite this, the Church did not refuse to pay these taxes. In fact, in 1294, the Church in France agreed to pay double taxes for two years. However, according to the traditional teaching, reaffirmed by the Lateran Council in 1215, the clergy could not be taxed without the pope's consent. This was a wise rule, because it protected the Church from excessive taxes.

In 1296, Philip the Fair called the bishops of France to Paris, to seek new money from the clergy. The bishops complained bitterly. Clergy and monks alike appealed to Rome. Boniface VIII came to their rescue with the bull (papal letter) *Clericis Laicos*. In it, he threatened to excommunicate any ruler who tried to tax the clergy without papal approval, as well as any cleric who paid such taxes to any layman. Philip felt that the bull was aimed at him. He responded by forbidding any money to be exported from his kingdom. This effectively cut off one of the Pope's chief sources of revenue. In another bull, Pope Boniface explained it was not his intention to forbid the

Philip the Fair

clergy from paying taxes to Philip, but only that it be done with papal permission. As a matter of fact, when the bishops of France met in Paris the next year and asked the Holy Father for permission to levy a tax, Boniface consented.

However, Philip the Fair not only taxed the clergy, he also meddled in the appointment of bishops. Boniface admonished him. He reminded Philip of the principle that the pope was supreme over kings. He then called bishops to a synod in Rome for the purpose of "correcting the king and promoting good government in France." In reply, Philip convoked a national assembly in opposition to the Roman synod. Boniface retorted with the most famous of all medieval bulls: *Unam Sanctam*. In this bull he strongly insisted on the subjection of the temporal authority to the spiritual authority. Boniface clearly stated that if Philip did not yield, he would be excommunicated.

Then Philip the Fair in his pride declared war on the Holy See. Assisting him in this sinful action was one of his chief advisers, William of Nogaret, and one of the Pope's greatest enemies, Sciarra Colonna. In 1303, Nogaret, Colonna, and a band of thugs surprised the aged Pontiff in his palace at Anagni. Pope Boniface was seventy years old and in bad health. Colonna and his henchmen verbally abused the old Pope. When they realized that Boniface was not wilting under their verbal abuse, and was even ready to die a martyr's death, Colonna struck the Pope in the face with his mailed fist. The pope remained in the power of these thugs for three days before the citizens of Anagni finally rescued him. Soon four hundred Roman knights arrived and escorted the Pope to Rome. He died a few weeks later from the injuries he had received.

Blessed Benedict XI (1303-1304) tried to settle all these troubles in a peaceful manner. He excommunicated those who had directly assaulted Pope Boniface. However, he absolved Philip from excommunication, though Philip showed no signs of repentance. Apparently, Benedict felt he was not in a strong enough position to discipline Philip directly. Benedict died after a reign of only one year. He was most likely murdered by Colonna and his agents.

The Holy See was vacant for eleven months after Benedict's death. Finally, the Sacred College elected the Archbishop of Bordeaux, who took the name of Clement V (1305-1314). The

Colonna strikes Pope Boniface VIII.

The Palace of the Popes at Avignon.

new Pope was the first of a line of French popes who moved the papal seat from Rome to Avignon in France. For the next seventy years the Papacy was under the influence of the French kings. Historians have likened these seventy years to the Babylonian Captivity of the Jews. The popes lived at Avignon for about as long as the Jews were captives in Babylon.

The End of the Knights Templar

Clement V was a kind and generous man. However, King Philip exploited these noble qualities. After living at Bordeaux and Poitiers, Clement moved to Avignon. Philip quickly took advantage of the situation. He obtained from his guest the annulment of the acts of Boniface VIII. Clement then assisted the greedy King in the prosecution of the Knights Templars. Philip brought the most atrocious charges against these valiant Knights, whose vast wealth had aroused his greed. In a sad moment for the Papacy, Clement suppressed the Knights in 1311. Fifty-four of the innocent Knights were burned at the stake.

Pope John XXII and Louis of Bavaria

Clement V and Philip the Fair both died in 1314. The Holy See stayed vacant for more than two years because of rivalries between the Italian and the French cardinals. Finally, the Sacred College elected another French Cardinal who chose to be called John XXII (1316-1334). The new Pope was quickly drawn into a conflict with Germany. After the death of Emperor Henry VII, there were two claimants to the imperial crown: Louis of Bavaria and Frederick of Austria. John XXII upheld the right of the papacy to settle all doubtful imperial elections. He declared that neither of the two rivals should call himself "King" until he had settled the dispute.

Louis of Bavaria chose to ignore the Pope. He decided to settle the matter not by dialogue with Rome, but by force of arms. Following his victory at the Battle of Muhldorf in 1322, he declared himself emperor. John XXII again reminded him that it was the Pope's right to approve or reject the imperial candidate. Louis refused to listen to the Pope so John excommunicated him. The pope's act was the signal for a renewal of the conflict between the papacy and the Empire.

Louis at once made a triumphal journey through northern Italy, at that time in the hands of the Ghibelline lords. At Milan he was crowned king of Italy. Shortly after he entered Rome without encountering any resistance. After two excommunicated bishops had conferred royal consecration upon him, he received the crown from the hands of Sciarra Colonna. Pope John was then brought to trial, convicted, and deposed. A commission then elected a new "pope" who took the name of "Nicholas V." Very soon, however, the Roman people rebelled against Louis. Milan closed its doors against him. He had no choice but to return to Germany. Antipope "Nicholas V," seeing that his cause was hopeless, begged John XXII for mercy.

Benedict XII (1334-1342), John XXII's successor, tried to reconcile with Louis. However, talks proved fruitless. Louis widened the breach between himself and the papacy when he forced his son to enter into an improper marriage. Benedict's successor, Clement VI (1342-1352), excommunicated Louis. The German princes finally abandoned Louis and elected Charles of Bohemia, a friend of the Pope's, as emperor. The death of Louis in 1347 brought the conflict to an abrupt end.

The Return of the Popes to Rome

The time seemed ripe for the pope to return to Italy. Conditions in France made it less and less fit as a place for the Pope to live. In 1360, an epidemic at Avignon killed 1,700 people, of whom nine were cardinals. Toward the end of his reign, Innocent VI (1352-1362) made plans to return to Rome. Urban V (1362-1370) carried out this plan despite the protests of the French king and the French cardinals. His action was timely. The long years spent in Avignon had exasperated the laity.

St. Bridget of Sweden

Sadly, Urban V stayed in Rome for only two years. The Romans implored him to remain. St. Bridget of Sweden warned him that if he returned to France, his death would quickly follow. Peter of Aragon insisted that if the pope departed from Rome, he would plunge the Church into a state of schism. Peter warned that the stay of the popes at Avignon, if prolonged, would create such a spirit of antagonism between the French and the Italians, that each nation would elect its own pope. Urban refused to heed their pleas and warnings. He returned to Avignon, where he died three months later.

If the popes were to return to Rome permanently, it seemed that it would require a saint with the power and determination of a St. Paul. In a small room in Siena, the Holy Spirit was preparing such a saint.

St. Catherine of Siena

St. Catherine was born in Siena on March 25, 1347. As a young woman she persuaded her parents to allow her to become a Third Order Dominican. She set aside one room in her home where she led the strictest kind of religious life, maintaining almost constant silence. She united herself with God in prayer and received many wonderful spiritual favors. She had the power to read people's hearts and converted many hardened sinners. After her father died in 1368, she cared for her sick mother. From that time until her own death, she cared for the poor and the sick.

From the start of his pontificate, Gregory XI (1370-1378) planned to return to Rome. However, a war with the city of Florence prevented his immediate return. The pope resolved to deal with the situation and placed Florence under interdict. St. Catherine devoted herself to restoring peace between the Pope and Florence. She went to the leaders of Florence, pleading with them to stop the war. They told her what they wanted in order to agree to peace.

Then Catherine set out for Avignon to persuade Gregory XI to return to Rome. At first the Pope was not inclined to listen to her. However, at the time of his election to the Papacy, Gregory had made a secret vow to return to Rome. He had never fulfilled this vow because he was not brave enough to face the opposition of the French king and the French cardinals. Catherine told the Pope that she knew about his vow. Since the vow was unknown to anyone in the world but himself, Gregory realized that Catherine was God's messenger. He agreed to leave Avignon and return to Rome. Wherever he stopped on his journey, he found Catherine waiting for him. She was at Marseilles when he boarded the ship for Genoa. She was in Genoa when he landed and she accompanied him into Rome.

St. Catherine of Siena

Gregory had authorized Catherine to act on his behalf in peace talks with Florence. Sadly, Gregory died before peace was made. Under Gregory's successor, Urban VI, the trouble was finally settled and Catherine returned to Siena.

Origin of the Schism

On the day after Gregory XI's death, the citizens of Rome clamored for a Roman, or at least an Italian, pope. The main concern of the cardinals at this vital moment was the question of nationalities. To elect a French pope was to condemn the Holy Father to exile at Avignon indefinitely. In the evening of April 7, 1378, the cardinals gathered to elect a new Pope. The morning of next day the conclave elected Bartolomeo Prignano, the Archbishop of Bari. He was an Italian, but not a Roman.

Cardinal Orsini went outside to announce the election to the mob of Romans that had gathered for the conclave. However, he could not be heard above the crowd noise, so he gave up. By late afternoon, a rumor had spread through the crowd that a pope had been elected. However, no one knew who it was, or, more importantly, what his nationality was.

In the evening Cardinal Orsini went out again to speak. However, the crowd was even louder and more worked up than before. He still could not be heard. The mob, which had been growing increasingly agitated from waiting all day without news, finally broke into the conclave. The cardinals, fearing for their lives, said that they had elected a Roman, the aged Cardinal Tebaldeschi. The frightened cardinals forcibly invested him with the papal insignia while Tebaldeschi cried out over and over that he was not the Pope. Finally, the crowd began to listen to Tebaldeschi. They had an Italian pope, but it was not he.

By April 9, the word of Prignano's election had spread through the city to the satisfaction of the Roman people. The pope-elect then met with the Cardinals. He asked if they had freely and canonically elected him. They confirmed in writing that they had. They ask him if he accepted election. He said that he did and would take the name of Urban VI (1378-1389).

At once, the Cardinals began seeking their accustomed favors from the new Pope. However, they were quickly disappointed. While Urban VI was a genuine reformer, he was also strikingly lacking in prudence and tact. He began to scold the cardinals for their worldly ways and to insult them. Very angry, thirteen of them went to the

St. Vincent Ferrer

Kingdom of Naples. They elected a Frenchman, Cardinal Robert of Geneva, as "pope." He called himself "Clement VII."

The disloyal cardinals then sent messengers to the different European courts to justify their action. King Charles V of France and the whole French nation declared themselves in favor of the antipope. Castile, Portugal, and Scotland also supported the antipope. England, Flanders, and the Empire acknowledged Pope Urban. Saints, too, were divided in their allegiance. St. Catherine of Siena and St. Bridget supported Pope Urban. St. Vincent Ferrer supported the French antipope. Thus distracted, the Catholic world was divided into two camps.

It is vital to remember that in an age before television and the Internet, it was difficult, and sometimes impossible, to learn all the facts of a case. Some of those who supported the antipope did so with the best of intentions, but out of ignorance. Others who supported the antipope did so knowing that he was not validly elected.

St. Catherine and the Schism

When the schism broke out, it seemed that all of St. Catherine's labors were for nothing. However, she did not lose courage. She did everything that she could to support Urban VI. She became his constant adviser and many times saved him from making mistakes. She tried to bring peace and order into the city of Rome, whose inhabitants were hard to control. She wrote letters to important people throughout Europe, in the hope that she could convince them to support the lawful Pope. Such labors were more than her frail constitution could stand. She contracted a painful illness and died at the age of thirty-three.

Futile Attempts to Restore Unity

Antipope "Clement VII," soon realized that he could establish the lawfulness of his claim only if he became the Pope of Rome. He also realized that his only option to become pope in Rome was through force. Thus, he determined to attack Rome. His expeditions into Italy were not only disastrous, but also very costly. The clergy began to complain bitterly. People were growing tired of the schism. So, when open attack failed, it was resolved to settle the difficulty in another way.

In 1394, the University of Paris found that public opinion favored the voluntary withdrawal of both claimants to the Papacy. Antipope "Clement VII" refused. However, his successor, the disloyal Cardinal Pedro de Luna, who called himself "Benedict XIII," was a wilier sort of character. He said he was in favor of negotiations. He asked that he be allowed to meet with the Pope of Rome. However, this plan also failed.

Meanwhile, the schism threatened to go on indefinitely. Boniface IX (1389-1404), Innocent VII (1404-1406), and Gregory

XII (1406-1415) succeeded Pope Urban VI as true popes. At the very outset of his reign Gregory XII repeatedly said that he would meet with antipope "Benedict." However, the plan proved fruitless, as antipope "Benedict" refused any resolution.

With the failure of this most recent plan to have both the Pope and antipope voluntarily resign, it was suggested that the way to end the schism would be by means of an ecumenical council. To this end, the Council of Pisa met in 1409. It deposed both the Pope and the antipope and elected a third claimant. However, an ecumenical council cannot be held without papal approval. Pope Gregory XII did not recognize the authority and competency of the Council of Pisa. Therefore he did not accept its decision. Thus, the cardinals who had met to bring about union, succeeded only in creating more division. There were now three claimants to the Chair of St. Peter instead of two, three colleges of cardinals, and in some dioceses three rival bishops. The following year, the Pisa antipope died and was succeeded by antipope "John XXIII." To make matters worse, two new heresies broke out in England and Bohemia.

Wyclif and Hus

John Wyclif started the heresy in England. Wyclif was born in Yorkshire in 1324. He studied at Oxford and was ordained to the priesthood. His heresy basically held that some souls were predestined to go to Heaven and others to Hell. Those souls destined to Heaven may indulge in any sort of sinful action, because sin cannot harm them. Those predestined to eternal damnation pray in vain, because God has already determined not to heed their prayers. Wyclif rejected most of the Sacraments and denied the Real Presence in the Eucharist.

In 1377, the bishop of London summoned Wyclif before a Church tribunal to answer for his heresy. However, he had powerful friends in the nobility who shielded him. They protected him even when Pope Gregory XI demanded he be jailed. However, when one of his disciples began to stir up rebellions against the wealthy landowners throughout England, the nobles abandoned him. Wyclif was tried and convicted before a church tribunal. He was forbidden from teaching and forced to retire to a monastery.

The marriage of King Richard II of England to Princess Anne of Bohemia created a close relation between the two countries. Before long, English students studying at the University of Prague, in Bohemia, introduced Wyclif's harmful teachings there. John Hus, a professor at the University of Prague, placed himself at the head of the heretical movement in Bohemia. Hus promoted all of John Wyclif's heresies, except his denial of the Real Presence. Eventually, the Church condemned all of Hus' writings. In 1411, the Pope excommunicated Hus and put any place that gave him refuge under interdict.

The Council of Constance: End of the Schism

Thus, by 1414, two formidable evils threatened Christendom: the Western Schism and the Hussite heresy. Unable to cope with the failing situation at Pisa, antipope "John XXIII" appealed to Emperor Sigismund as the protector of the Holy See. As head of the Holy Roman Empire, Sigismund longed to end the schism. In 1414, he convoked the Council of Constance. He notified Pope Gregory XII and antipope "Benedict."

"John XXIII" had agreed to the council, because he was certain it would ratify his election as pope. However, when he arrived at Constance, he discovered that public opinion was against him. He fled from the city in disguise. The council immediately agreed to depose him for having made the schism worse by his sudden departure.

The crucial fact in all of Church history and canon law is that an ecumenical council cannot be held without papal approval. At this point, Pope Gregory XII, the true Pope, had the least public support. One contender had fled because he thought he would not be elected. One contender remained inflexible, fought to be "Pope" and, until his death in 1422, persisted in calling himself the head of the Church. Only the true Pope was willing to sacrifice. Pope Gregory was willing to resign, but he had one condition. His representatives would convoke the council and authorize all its future acts. In other words, he would call the council and give it his approval. On July 4, 1415, the representatives of the true Pope convoked the Council giving it legitimacy. The council then accepted Pope Gregory's resignation.

The council next deposed "Benedict XIII." The way was now clear. On November 11, 1417, Cardinal Otto Colonna was elected pope and took the name of Martin V (1417-1431). The great Western Schism was at an end.

The Council of Constance also dealt with John Hus. The council condemned thirty heresies taken from his works. Despite this he refused to recant his errors. He was condemned as an obstinate heretic, handed over to the secular arm, and burned at the stake. The bloody wars that devastated Bohemia and parts of Germany for nearly two decades after his death bear witness to the strength of the Hussite party in those countries.

John Hus defends his doctrines before the Council of Constance.

Review Exercises

1. What was the root of the conflict between Pope Boniface VIII and King Philip of France?
2. Why do historians call the time spent by the popes at Avignon the Babylonian Captivity?
3. Which pope suppressed the Knights Templar?
4. To which order did St. Catherine of Siena belong?
5. Which pope did St. Catherine finally persuade to return to Rome?
6. Why was the Council of Pisa in 1409 unlawful?
7. What did Pope Gregory XII require before he would resign?
8. What was John Wyclif's heresy?
9. Why was John Hus burned at the stake?

CHAPTER 17

THE CHURCH AND THE RENAISSANCE

Marriage of Mary of Joseph, by Giotto

The Literary Renaissance

The eleven popes from Eugenius IV (1431-1447) to Leo X (1513-1521) are known as the Renaissance popes. They all aided the intellectual movement begun in Italy. The purpose of this movement was the re-birth (renaissance) of the classical authors of ancient Greece and Rome. These popes also supported great painting, sculpture, and architecture.

Pope Nicholas V (1447-1455) was a great student of ancient literature. He was also well educated in theology, philosophy, law, and medicine. His goal was to make Rome the great center of all art and science. To this end, he founded the Vatican Library. He collected all the books he could buy. In his day, there were five thousand books in the Vatican Library.

The leader of the Literary Renaissance in Italy was Dante Alighieri (1265-1321). He is considered the greatest of all Christian poets. Through his writings he gave definite form to the Italian language. His greatest book is the *Divine Comedy*. In it he takes an imaginary journey through Hell, Purgatory, and Heaven. On the journey, he introduces the reader to the souls of various historical figures. He tells of the fate of pagan and Christian kings, of bishops, cardinals, priests, monks, and nuns. His purpose is to show how the actions of men and women appear to God.

The Rise of Humanism

However, the literary Renaissance soon sunk into paganism. The fourteenth and fifteenth centuries saw the arrival of a new philosophy that dragged public morals into the mud. What the popes had done for the greater glory of God, others turned towards the glory of Man. Men began to realize that a great deal of worldly happiness could be had if they only knew how to obtain it. They began to become interested in themselves as human beings. Where before they had studied and learned about God, now they began to study and learn about Man.

This new learning was called "Humanism." It was interested in men and women and the things that could make them happy in this world and make their daily lives more beautiful. The Humanists believed that the study of the classical literature of Greece and Rome would bring about a much-desired change. It would transform men and women into perfect human beings. At first the Humanists were interested only in the literary style of the ancient authors. However, pagan ideas slowly began to take root in their minds. Soon, they began to start living like the ancient pagans about whom they were reading.

The Political Renaissance

The Renaissance was more than just a classical revival in art and literature. There was also a political aspect that weakened the Church. The Renaissance popes rightly felt that they had to keep the Church free from the control of kings and princes. However, they wrongly felt that the way to do this was to strengthen their temporal power by the same means that the secular rulers used. These popes began to feel that it was crucial to have temporal power, not only to protect the Church from secular rulers, but also to control the College of Cardinals.

One great evil that the popes used to gain power was nepotism. Papal nepotism was the practice of putting papal relatives into important positions in the Church in order to protect the papacy from its political enemies. The popes made their nephews (nipote in Italian) Cardinals. They gave their brothers key posts in the government of the Papal States. Generally, they enriched their own families. Of the thirteen popes who reigned from 1431 to 1534, all but three were related by blood to one of their predecessors or successors. Nepotism lowered the reputation of the papacy with the laity. This caused the popes to lose influence in spiritual matters.

Pope Sixtus IV (1471-1484) began his reign by making unholy men cardinals. His successor, Innocent VIII (1484-1492), did nothing to improve the type of men who held the highest offices in the Church. As a result, these unholy Cardinals next elected the Pope who would cause the Church her greatest scandal: Alexander VI (1492-1503), the Borgia pope. His worldliness and immoral private life made his reign one of the darkest pages in the history of the Church.

Girolamo Savonarola

Against the public and private immorality of the age, one eloquent voice cried out. It belonged to Girolamo Savonarola (1452-1498), a Dominican friar from Florence. Savonarola was a very stern and holy man, who achieved remarkable success as a preacher. His sermons reconverted the entire city of Florence, which had given itself over to the vices of the new culture. However, one person was not happy with his preaching: Pope Alexander.

Greatly disturbed by the sermons of the fiery Dominican, Pope Alexander VI attempted to silence him. Savonarola at first obeyed the order to be silent. However, after obtaining permission to resume his preaching, he fiercely denounced the corruption in the Church. He also urged that an ecumenical council be called. He was again

Statue of Savonarola in Florence

forbidden to preach, but this time refused to obey. As a result he was excommunicated, but continued to denounce the Pope.

For all his justified criticisms, Savonarola was now in revolt against the Pope's authority, and therefore a schismatic. Soon his popularity waned. Alexander VI ordered the city of Florence to surrender Savonarola, or at least to stop him from preaching. The friar retorted that he would abide only by the decision of a general council. The city of Florence arrested him, tried him, and convicted him of heresy (of which he was not guilty, though schismatic). He was burned at the stake.

The Early Artistic Renaissance in Italy

There were two successive attempts in Italy to revive popular interest in the arts. Great artists launched each of these periods. Art historians often referred to these periods as the Early and Late Renaissance. Giotto, Masaccio, and Beato Angelico began the early Renaissance.

The first great artist and the man who almost single-handedly started the Italian Renaissance was Giotto (1267-1337). Giotto was the first to make a decisive break with the Gothic style in which people appear in only two dimensions. He started painting as we know it today where canvas appears to have three dimensions. He also introduced the technique of drawing accurately from life. Giotto's masterwork is the fresco cycle which decorates the Scrovegni Chapel in Padua, commonly called the Arena Chapel. In 1305, after many years, Giotto completed his frescoes. His fresco cycle depicts the life of the Blessed Mother and the life of Christ. It is regarded as one of the supreme masterpieces of the Early Renaissance.

Masaccio (1401-1428) was the first great painter of the fourteenth century period of the Italian Renaissance. In Florence, Masaccio could study the works of Giotto. His frescoes introduce a realism previously unseen in figure painting. Sadly, he died quite young so he never achieved his full potential.

Masaccio worked in Florence side by side with Lippi, Botticelli, and Ghirlandaio. Filippo Lippi displayed great ease in his work along with a remarkable variety of expressions. He is most famous for his superb Madonnas and his frescoes in the Prato cathedral of the lives of John the Baptist and St. Stephen. His pupil, Botticelli, is known for his amazing Madonnas and his work in the Sistine Chapel. Ghirlandaio is noted for his calm simplicity, the beauty of his faces, and the clarity of his lines. Ghirlandaio painted

The Annunciation, by Beato Angelico

many brilliant masterpieces including some great frescoes in the church of Santa Maria Novella in Florence.

The third great artist of the early Renaissance was the Dominican friar, John of Fiesole. John is better known as Beato Angelico (1395-1455) because he painted like an angel. His frescoes are famous for their bright colors, gold and blue backgrounds, and tints of rose and blue. The calm expressions, supernatural beauty, and pure simplicity of his figures draw our attention and admiration. In 1436, Angelico moved to the monastery of San Marco in Florence. This was an important move as it put him in the center of artistic activity. Pope John Paul II beatified Angelico in 1982. In 1984, the Pope declared him the patron of Catholic artists.

The Early Renaissance in Northern Europe

The four outstanding masters of the Northern Renaissance were Jan van Eyck, Roger van der Weyden, Hans Memling, and Quentin Massys. Van Eyck's most important work is the great painting *The Adoration of the Mystic Lamb*. Roger van der Weyden is a more severe artist. His portrayal of the dramatic is intense, especially in his profoundly human and compassionating figures of Christ. His masterpiece is *The Descent from the Cross*. In this work the rigidity and lividness of the mangled body of Our Lord produce a most moving effect upon the viewer.

Van Eyck excelled in scenes of grandeur, van der Weyden in the depiction of sorrow, and Hans Memling, in expressing grace and tender emotion. The works of Quentin Massys are remarkable for the life that radiates in the faces, the sumptuous garb of the people, and the brilliant yet soft coloring. The influence of these great masters was felt throughout Europe over the next centuries.

The Late Artistic Renaissance in Italy

Three figures dominated the Late Renaissance in Italy: Michelangelo, Leonardo da Vinci, and Raphael.

Michelangelo (1475-1564) worked primarily as a sculptor, but also a painter and an architect. Pope Julius II hired him to build and adorn his tomb. The monumental tomb was never fully completed. The most impressive part of it is the statue of Moses, who is represented as stern and masterful. Pope Julius also asked Michelangelo to decorate the Sistine Chapel ceiling. The ceiling is painted with a power and grandeur that are truly biblical. The Sistine ceiling is considered one of the greatest masterpieces in all art. Later, Pope Leo X hired Michelangelo to work on St. Peter's Basilica in Rome, which he crowned with a magnificent cupola. His powerful imagination expressed itself in titanic creations in all areas of art.

Leonardo da Vinci (1452-1519) was a sculptor, an architect, a painter, and an engineer. His painting of the *Last Supper* (1498) is a drama in oil, in which all the people are expressing their reaction to the words of Christ: "Behold, one of you will betray Me." Among Leonardo's greatest works are the *Annunciation* (1475), the *Mona Lisa* (1503), the *Virgin of the Rocks* (1505), and the *Virgin and Child with St. Ann* (1508).

Raphael (1483-1520) raised classical beauty to its highest perfection. In his short life he was able to produce a phenomenal amount of art. In the apartments, also called stanzas, of the Vatican he painted scenes with both philosophical subjects (*Disputation on the Blessed Sacrament* and *The School of Athens*) and historical subjects (*Heliodorus Expelled from the Temple* and *Attila Halted by St. Leo*). Among the biblical subjects he painted, the best known is the *Transfiguration* (1520). He also painted a series of Madonnas, the

The Disputation on the Blessed Sacrament, by Raphael

earliest of them being tender and candid, the later ones, glorious and
majestic. The most famous are the *Virgin of the Chair* (1514) and the
Sistine Madonna (1513).

Catholic Society During the Renaissance

The fourteenth and fifteenth centuries saw a major decline in
both public and private morality. Nevertheless the faith was still alive.
The number of religious societies increased. There was a widespread
practice of fasting. Generous gifts were given to churches. These periods
also saw the efforts of a few zealous souls to reform the Church. Two of
the most famous were St. Bernardine of Siena and St. Vincent Ferrer.
St. Vincent was a holy Dominican who went about the world preaching
penance and working miracles. Several new religious orders for both

men and women were also started at this time. St. Bridget of Sweden, who rivaled St. Catherine of Siena in urging the popes of Avignon to return to Italy, founded the Order of the Holy Savior.

The new orders could not hope to reach the level of success in Church reforms achieved by Cluny in the eleventh century and the mendicant orders in the thirteenth. However, a movement in the Netherlands was quite successful due to the work of Gerard de Groote. He was born at Deventer in Holland in 1340, and studied at the University of Paris. He was leading a rather worldly life, when a chance meeting with a Carthusian monk led to his embracing the religious life. In 1379, he founded the Sisters of the Common Life, and later the Brothers of the Common Life. After his death a third order planned by him took form: the Canons Regular. Among their number they counted the famous author, Thomas à Kempis, who wrote a very special book.

Thomas à Kempis was born in 1380, and educated by the Brothers of the Common Life at Deventer. He spent his entire life as a monk in the Monastery of the Canons Regular in Holland. In 1418, he wrote a little book called the *Imitation of Christ.* In its beautiful pages we catch a glimpse of the thoughts that were in the minds of holy men and women. The *Imitation of Christ* is considered by many to be the most beautiful book ever penned by the hand of man. Perhaps no book, other than the Bible, has brought more comfort and inspiration to the hearts of men and women from that day until this.

Also during this era, Catholics in every country zealously studied the Bible. This historical fact fully discredits the notion that Martin Luther revived interest in the Bible as a "forgotten book." Many German and French translations of the Bible appeared at this time. The first French Bible was called the Bible of St. Louis and was incredibly successful. Before the Protestant revolt, twenty popular translations of the Bible had appeared in Germany. Many prayer books in local languages were available. Germany alone counted more than one hundred editions of these prayer books.

The Later Renaissance Popes

Pope Julius II (1503-1513), one of Pope Sixtus IV's nephews, was a great statesman and a great soldier. Through a series of clever diplomatic moves, he saved the Papal States and expelled the French from Italy. In 1512, he convoked the Fifth Lateran Council. This ecumenical council, under the leadership of Cardinal Cajetan, established beyond question that the authority of the pope was superior to that of a council.

Pope Leo X (1513-1521), the "Medici Pope," like his predecessor, also created alliances to protect the Papal States. He also was a strong patron of the arts. During his pontificate the Fifth Lateran Council, which Julius II had begun, ended without adopting any measures for the reform of the Church. The last session of this council was held March 16, 1517. The same year Martin Luther nailed his ninety-five theses to the door of the church at Wittenberg.

Review Exercises

1. Who founded the Vatican Library?
2. What was Papal nepotism?
3. Who was Girolamo Savonarola?
4. What was Giotto's masterpiece?
5. Who did Pope John Paul II name as patron of artists?
6. Who were the four outstanding masters of the Northern Renaissance?
7. What book did Thomas a Kempis write?

CHAPTER 18

THE BEGINNING OF THE PROTESTANT REVOLT

Martin Luther disputes with John Eck in Leipzig in 1519.

Causes of the Protestant Revolt

The movement that began early in the sixteenth century and is often wrongly called the Reformation is more correctly called the Protestant Revolt. Many things led to its outbreak. Some of the causes were religious. However, there were other causes that were social, economic, and political. Europe was suffering from many evils during this time. We have seen that many rulers had a hostile attitude towards the papacy. Also, the scandalous behavior of secular and religious leaders aggravated the common people. Renaissance paganism in art and literature had corrupted public morals. Lastly, there was a growing spirit of rebellion against all authority, both civil and religious.

For hundreds of years the popes had valiantly defended the Church's property against civil rulers, petty princes, kings, and emperors. The Church cared for the buildings for public worship at her own expense. She built and supported institutions that cared for the poor, the sick, and orphans. She also ran numerous educational institutions. Over the centuries she became the owner of very extensive property. This aroused the greed of rulers, who looked covetously upon the estates of religious orders, bishops, and the Pope. One can understand why they welcomed a new religion that said that they had a right to seize all this property for themselves.

Greed among rulers, discontent among the working classes, and paganism among the educated Renaissance scholars were the real causes of the Protestant Revolt. Scandals, abuses, and laxity among the clergy were not the primary causes. They were the excuse to destroy the Church, because the Church was the only power that was able to curb the power of the mighty. Only the Church had the power to defend the poor and to Christianize the paganism of the scholars. Only the Church could fix the abuses that had crept into the ranks of the clergy. As we shall see, a revolt looks not to improve but to destroy.

In Germany, the princes had extended their power at the expense of the emperor's authority. The clergy, because they had permitted the morals and manners of secular life to enter their own lives, had lost much of the people's respect and esteem. It was in this setting, so ready to welcome his message of revolt, that Martin Luther appeared.

Martin Luther

Martin Luther was born on November 10, 1483. He was a good student, so after completing his early education, he entered the University of Erfurt in 1501. Luther received his degree four years later and decided to study law as a career. There is nothing to show at this point that he had any sort of religious vocation. In June 1505, during a break from school, he returned to visit his family. The following month as he was walking back to the university, he was caught in a storm that nearly cost him his life. Lightning struck immediately in front of him. Under the influence of fear and terror he vowed that if he lived, he would become a monk.

He carried out his vow against the advice of his friends and father, who knew him well. Luther felt no joy in his vow and later would write

of it with deep sadness and regret. Nevertheless, he had made up his mind and could not be moved. Two weeks after the storm, Luther joined the Augustinian Order at Erfurt. This step proved to be a fatal mistake.

An intelligent and determined man, Luther advanced rapidly in the Order. In 1506, he took his final vows. Two years later he was sent to the University of Wittenburg to teach moral philosophy. In 1512, he became a doctor

Erfurt Cathedral

of theology. However, he was constantly unhappy with his life. Although a priest, he hated confession and never liked to say Mass. His difficulties increased, until finally he sought peace of mind and assurance of eternal salvation in a new false theology.

Luther reached his moment of truth in 1515-1516, when he wrote his "Commentary on the Epistle to the Romans." In it he wrote that man is incapable of doing anything good and is saved solely by faith. God gives faith to the sinful soul, by which it acknowledges itself to be bad.

Wittenberg Palace church doors

The soul then puts its trust in Him, and receives salvation as its reward. The two basic doctrines of Lutheranism are salvation by faith alone and the utter corruption of human nature as the result of original sin. These doctrines created a spiritual refuge for Luther. He no longer needed to struggle with his own personal unworthiness.

Luther Breaks with the Church

A few years earlier, the Archbishop of Mainz had established an indulgence. (An indulgence is the remission in whole or in part of the temporal punishment due to sin.) This indulgence was given to anyone who was in the state of grace who donated money to help rebuild St. Peter's Basilica. This was the excuse that Luther was looking for. He wrote out ninety-five theses attacking the doctrine and practice of indulgences.

He declared that God did not recognize indulgences and that the Church had no treasury of grace from which to dispense them. On October 31, 1517, he nailed these theses to the door of the Wittenberg palace church. Luther lost no time in rallying supporters to his cause. The issue of indulgences was merely an excuse for his break with the Church.

Rome Intervenes

At first, Luther publicly adopted a careful and meek attitude toward the pope. However, on May 9, 1518, Luther wrote a letter to a former teacher that "reform of the Church was impossible." He also wrote that the Church had to be "thoroughly uprooted." This is not the letter of someone who wants to reform the Church but rather a revolutionary who wants to destroy it. On May 30, 1518, Luther sent Pope Leo X (1513-1521) an explanation of his theses on indulgences, together with a humble letter.

The pope then called Luther to Rome. He refused to go but offered to justify his position. At the request of Luther's strongest supporter, the Elector of Saxony, Leo X allowed Luther to appear at Augsburg before a papal tribunal headed by the papal legate, Cardinal Cajetan. Cajetan, who received Luther with great kindness, saw the harmful character of Luther's teaching. He asked Luther to retract his statement that salvation is not effected by the sacraments, but only by faith. Luther agreed to sign a vaguely respectful statement, but refused to recant his errors.

During the night of October 20, Luther secretly left Augsburg. A month later he issued a pamphlet calling for a general council. He was able to take this defiant stand against the pope because the Elector of Saxony was protecting him. The Elector had also forbidden Cajetan to condemn Luther until some university had judged him.

Despite Luther's now public defiance, the Pope again attempted to make Luther recant. He sent another legate to Saxony to speak with the Elector and to bring Luther to terms. At the legate's request, Luther wrote a letter of submission, but refused any formal retraction of his errors.

Soon, Luther set aside all attempts at hedging. When Catholic theologian John Eck drew a friend of Luther's into a public debate, Luther himself appeared to defend his position. In the so-called "Disputation of Leipzig," Luther rejected all authority, including the Church councils. He referred all questions to the Bible, which he said that people could interpret for themselves. Thus he created the principle of private judgment which doomed Protestantism to doctrinal anarchy.

The minutes of Luther's debate with John Eck were sent to the Universities of Paris, Louvain, and Cologne. All three condemned Luther. He angrily replied by issuing another pamphlet that contained all his errors. Rome then condemned Luther's doctrines, including his basic error about the corruption of human nature and salvation by faith alone. Out of Christian charity, the Pope gave Luther sixty days to retract his teachings. Luther responded with a humble letter to the Pope. However, at the same time he published another pamphlet in which he called the Pope "the Antichrist." On January 3, 1521, Pope Leo X finally excommunicated Luther.

Pope Leo X

Imperial Intervention: The Diet of Worms

The Church had done her part to reclaim Luther. It remained for the secular power to intervene. In April 1521, Emperor Charles V summoned Luther to the Diet of Worms. When asked to recant his errors, Luther requested twenty-four hours to prepare his answer. In the meantime he received promises of support from the Elector of Saxony and several German knights. Thus he replied: "I believe neither in the pope nor in the councils. ... I cannot and do not desire to recant anything." Thereupon the Diet issued the Edict of Worms, which declared Luther an outlaw under sentence of death and condemned his heresies. However, the Edict was only worthwhile if it could be enforced. While Charles V did all he could, Luther was still very popular with the German princes and they protected him. In 1523, the Diet of Nuremberg decreed that the execution of the Edict of Worms should be postponed and the examination of the Lutheran question should be left to a general council. This gave the Revolt more time to develop.

The Consequences of Luther's Teachings: The Peasant Wars

Luther had no sooner created his doctrine of private judgment, than people within the Revolt itself began to desert him. At Zwickau, in Saxony, Thomas Munzer, a roving preacher, and Nicholas Storch, a tailor, organized the sect known as the "Anabaptists." These fanatics rejected infant baptism. They violently hated the beliefs and practices not only of Catholics but also all other Christians. They also held the unshakable belief that they alone were the elect of God.

Munzer and Storch went to Wittenberg determined to conquer that stronghold of Lutheranism. They won over to their cause Andreas Carlstadt, who had been an early supporter of Luther's, but who now became one of the leaders of the new even more radical movement. Carlstadt effected a real revolution at Wittenberg. Mass was prohibited, the sacraments were abolished, and statues and paintings in the churches were destroyed. Luther saw that such innovations were opposed to his schemes and that their excesses would endanger the success of his movement. He decided to intervene. He attacked the errors of the Anabaptists so eloquently that they had to leave the city.

Driven from Saxony, Munzer and Carlstadt began to preach their doctrines in Catholic countries. Wherever they went they stirred up the people against the clergy and the nobles. Very soon the throng of angry serfs grew to the alarming number of about 300,000. They plundered monasteries, convents, churches, and castles until the armies of the princes crushed them. The Peasants' War caused frightful devastation to lives and property. Over 300,000 men fell in battle, and more than a thousand convents and castles were burned to the ground. Munzer was finally caught and executed. Carlstadt died of the plague in 1541.

Organization of the Lutheran State Churches: Protestantism

Before long Luther began to call for a state religion. Two princes immediately rallied to his cause: his friend, the Elector of Saxony, and the Landgrave of Hesse. These two took over the control of churches previously held by the bishops. Within a short time the supreme authority over religious matters fell into the hands of civil rulers in almost every principality in northern and central Germany.

In 1529, a Diet was held in Speyer. The Diet prohibited the establishment of state churches where they had not yet been founded. It authorized Catholicism to remain the state religion where it already existed. Immediately the prince "reformers," together with fourteen important cities, protested as heads of the new religion. Their stand accounts for the name "Protestants," which was henceforth attached to all "reformers."

Meanwhile Emperor Charles V, believing that reconciliation was possible, called a Diet at Augsburg. Luther could not appear before the Diet, as he had been banished from the country, so his friend Melanchthon presented a summary of the Protestants' doctrinal views. This summary has since been termed the "Augsburg Confession."

According to Melanchthon, all differences could be traced to certain abuses. Among the abuses he listed were private Masses, clerical celibacy, monastic vows, and the suppression of Communion under both species. After six weeks of deliberation, the Catholic theologians, among them the great John Eck, refused to accept the Confession. Melanchthon seemed willing to make some concessions, but Luther stubbornly refused to yield on any point.

In November 1530, Charles V issued an imperial edict. It commanded the strict enforcement of the Edict of Worms. It instructed that the authority of bishops was to be restored in all places, and

Emperor Charles V

confiscated church property was to be returned to its rightful owners. A month later, in response, the Protestant princes formed the Schmalkaldic League. At first, they formed the League as a defensive alliance against Charles V. However, the members quickly decided that the League would replace the Holy Roman Empire.

Before Charles could deal with the Schmalkaldic League, the greater threat of the Moslems forced him to make peace with the Protestants. The Peace of Nuremberg of 1532 declared that until the next Church council, or at least until the next Diet, the Protestants should not be harmed. Engaged in foreign wars for ten long years, Charles V was unable to deal with the Protestants. This delay furnished Protestantism with another opportunity to expand.

Emperor Charles V and Protestantism

During this time, the Holy Roman Emperor was Charles V. His mother was the daughter of Ferdinand and Isabel of Spain. As a result of that heritage, at the age of sixteen he became King of Spain. His father was a Hapsburg and as a result of that heritage, three years later he became emperor. The greatest emperor since Charlemagne, a true heir of the great kings and queens of Spain, Charles V realized that the vocation of emperor was to defend the Church from the infidel without and the heretic within. For almost his entire adult life he would fight the Protestants in Germany and the Moslems in the East. Almost single-handedly he would try to hold Catholic Europe together.

In April 1521, Luther appeared before Charles at Worms to explain his teachings. Charles had promised him safe passage to and from the meeting. Although his Spanish soldiers wanted to arrest Luther, Charles was a man of his word, so he let him go. Charles understood the danger that Luther posed and the next day he gave his response to his German subjects. No pope or learned theologian could have better expressed the position of the Catholic Church than did the twenty-one year old Emperor:

> "You know that I am born of the most Christian Emperors of the noble German nation, of the Catholic kings of Spain... who were all to the death true sons of the Roman Church, defenders of the Catholic Faith.... **For it is certain that a single monk [Luther] must err if he stands against the opinion of all Christendom. Otherwise Christendom itself would have erred for more than a thousand years.** Therefore I am determined to set my kingdoms and dominions, my friends, my body, my blood, my life, my soul upon it [the defense of the Catholic Faith]."

As Emperor, Charles tried to halt the spread of the Revolt. However, other "Catholic" countries that should have aided him attacked him. Much of Charles' reign was spent fighting King Francis I of France. The first war with France began in 1521 and lasted six years. The third war with Francis began in 1542 after Francis had allied himself with the Moslems against Charles!

Additionally, Charles was almost always fighting with

Charles V at Mühlberg

the Moslem Turks. The Moslems constantly threatened Catholic Europe and the Mediterranean trade. The war against the Moslems was doubly hard to fight as the Protestants in the German government often refused to vote Charles the funds he needed to wage the war. The Protestants saw the Moslems as a good counterweight to the Catholic power.

Finally, in 1544, Charles made peace with the Turks and the French. This enabled him to focus all his attention on the Protestants in Germany. In 1545, the Council of Trent, which Charles had been asking the Pope to call, convened its first session. The Catholic Reformation had begun. In 1546, the year Luther died, Charles declared war on the Schmalkaldic League. His troops defeated the Protestants, driving their troops from southern and western Germany. A second victory, at Mühlberg in 1547, gave Charles control of the cities of northern Germany.

The Catholics and Protestants then entered into peace negotiations. The talks between the parties resulted in a decision to call a diet that would settle the religious question. This diet finally met at Augsburg in February 1555. However, by this time Charles was physically exhausted. He had begun to abdicate the various crowns that he had worn for the past forty years. Thus, it fell to his brother Ferdinand to try to obtain a religious peace at Augsburg.

The Peace of Augsburg was concluded in September 1555. It formally approved the state churches. Lutheran states were explicitly recognized for the first time. The religion of each state was to be chosen by its ruler. Ecclesiastical jurisdiction was suppressed throughout Protestant domains. Protestants were allowed to keep all Church property seized before 1552. Although the Pope never accepted these rules, the Peace of Augsburg became the law of the land in Germany. The Peace of Augsburg temporarily ended the fighting in Germany.

Abdication of Charles V

In 1556, Charles V, old before his time and racked with painful illnesses, turned over Spain and the Netherlands to his son Philip II. His brother Ferdinand succeeded him on the imperial throne. He then withdrew to the monastery at Yuste in Spain, where he died a holy death in 1558. Karl Brandi, Charles V's finest biographer, writes of the noble Emperor: "We may search the annals of history in vain for such another scene, for such another generation of princes such as these of the Hapsburg dynasty, who were ready of their own free will to retire from the scene of their sovereignty...."

Luther's Last Years

On the other hand, Martin Luther's last years were very unhappy. The effects of his teachings upon his disciples were disastrous. He was well aware that his followers used his own teachings to justify their evil lifestyles. In the face of these things,

Luther gave way to despair. He began drinking heavily. However, to the end, he raged against the pope. He constantly referred to the Holy Father as "the Antichrist." In 1546, he died of apoplexy at the age of sixty-three.

Lasting Effects

The effects of Luther's Revolt continue to the present day. It remains unlikely that the wounds of Christendom, caused by the Revolt, can be healed. Since the seventeenth century, not one Western nation has changed its majority religion from Protestant to Catholic or vice versa, or come close to doing so.

Review Exercises

1. What were the real causes of the Protestant Revolt?
2. What Order did Martin Luther join?
3. What evidence do we have that Luther was not a reformer?
4. What is "the principle of private judgment?"
5. Which Pope excommunicated Luther?
6. What was the Edict of Worms of 1521?
7. What was the "Augsburg Confession?"
8. What was the Schmalkaldic League?
9. Who were Charles V's grandparents?
10. Where did Charles V die?

CHAPTER 19

THE PROTESTANT REVOLT SPREADS AND ENGLAND IS LOST TO THE CHURCH

Scenes from the Life of St. John Fisher: St. John Fisher refuses the Oath of Supremacy, St. John Fisher meets St. Thomas More on the way to his execution, and the execution of St. John Fisher

Protestantism in Switzerland

While the Protestant Revolution had its birth in Germany, full religious war came first to Switzerland. The battle for Europe between Catholics and Protestants, once begun, would last for almost 120 years. The man who brought the religious wars to Switzerland was Ulrich Zwingli.

277

Ulrich Zwingli was the youngest son of a government official in Switzerland. In 1504, he was ordained a priest. Later he was assigned to Einsiedeln, the home of the famous Benedictine abbey. News of his eloquence soon reached Zurich, where he was called to take up the duties in the principal church there.

Salvation by faith alone was the core of Martin Luther's doctrinal teaching. Zwingli went a step further. He held that man had no free will and is at the complete mercy of God, Who does both good and evil in him. Zwingli "reformed" himself by marrying. He "reformed" others by abolishing all statues, images, and altars in churches. His preaching led to numerous iconoclastic revolts. At first he tried to stop this revolutionary movement, but later encouraged it. His followers thoroughly plundered the beautiful churches of Zurich.

Zwingli's movement spread rapidly through Switzerland. In 1528, the Zurich government ordered the treasures of the churches to be melted down and the Mass abolished. At Basel, his followers seized the weapons in the armory. Then they forced the government to abolish the Mass. At St. Gall, his supporters ransacked the magnificent abbey church. (Two years later the Abbot began to restore St. Gall's. Today it is considered the most important Baroque building in Switzerland.)

St. Gall's Abbey

Victory of the Catholic Cantons

Seven of the thirteen Swiss cantons stayed faithful to the Catholic Church. Since the votes in the Swiss Diet were cast by cantons, the Catholics held a majority in the national government. However, the Protestants controlled the wealthy cities. With the Catholics in control of the national government and the Protestants controlling the local governments, a conflict seemed inevitable.

However, at this point, many Swiss citizens believed that the cantons could reach a peaceful political resolution despite their religious differences. Zwingli, in his fanaticism, urged a declaration of war. Supported by a secret council devoted to his cause, he allied Zurich and the Protestant cantons with some German Protestants. The Catholic cantons responded by forming an alliance with Catholic Austria. At the Battle of Kappel in 1531, the Catholics attacked a force from Zurich led by Zwingli himself. The Catholic forces won a decisive victory. Several hundred Protestants died in the battle. Zwingli was one of them.

John Calvin Spreads the Revolt

The man who would do the most to spread Luther's revolt was a Frenchman named John Calvin. John Calvin was born in 1509 in France. He attended the University of Paris, where he studied logic. Upon his graduation he went on to study law at Bourges. There he came under the influence of a Lutheran professor and became a heretic. His heretical views caused him to be driven out of France. In 1535, he fled to Basel where he wrote down his ideas and worked out a system of theology in his book, *The Institutes of the Christian Religion*.

Calvin's doctrines were much like Luther's. The major difference had to do with Calvin's belief in Predestination. According to Calvin, God directly created some people to go to Heaven and other people to go to Hell. Nothing that a person does in this life, good or bad, will make a difference. This dogma of absolute predestination, which is both cruel and gratifying (to those who think they are saved), forms the very core of Calvinism.

Calvin had two "sacraments:" Baptism and the Lord's Supper. However, he taught that neither was needed for salvation. He also denied the Real Presence. Calvin's religious service was as cold and barren as Zwingli's in Zurich. No images, ornaments, or holy water were allowed.

Geneva, the Stronghold of Calvinism

Calvin left Basel and traveled to Geneva. There he decided to carry on his work as a preacher and professor of theology. He also determined to organize a new church. In his catechism he set forth the beliefs of this church. Every citizen had to agree to them or be exiled. Growing more and more repressive, Calvin then claimed the right to supervise the private lives of the citizens. This was too much for the people of Geneva, who determined to resist the tyrant. In 1538, they threw him out of Geneva.

Calvin went to Strasburg, where he spent his time studying theology. Three years later, public opinion at Geneva changed, and his followers asked him to return. Upon his arrival he became the dictator of the city. He drew up a sort of religious constitution for the organization of the Geneva Church. By the end of nine years he completely controlled the city. He set up a theocracy that was supposed to be a government of the people directed by God. Calvin enacted a code of laws of unmatched severity. Death was the penalty for idolatry, heresy, blasphemy, and adultery. He required that everyone attend divine services. He harshly punished anyone caught dancing, gambling, or wearing fine clothes. He had spies everywhere, who even forced themselves into people's homes to catechize them. When a Spanish doctor named Michael Servetus opposed him, Calvin burned him at the stake. This caused Calvin to write a book in which he tried to prove that all heretics should be executed. One of his most important actions was to found a school at Geneva.

The Spread of Calvinism

Under Calvin, Geneva soon became the heart of the Protestant Revolt. Thousands of Protestants poured into the city. For their benefit Calvin founded a school for training pastors who would preach his anti-Catholic message. This school soon became the Mecca for all the followers of Calvin. They in turn founded other Protestant academies and later on the Presbyterian universities of Scotland. Calvin himself worked untiringly to spread his doctrines. He took a hand in the religious policies of England, especially during the reign of Edward VI (1547-1553). John Knox, the Scottish "reformer," was one of his ablest disciples. However, Calvin's chief interest was in France. He devoted most of his energy to the success of the Protestant church there.

The English Schism: England is Lost to the Church

When the Protestant Revolt broke out, England's King Henry VIII (1509-1547) showed himself a zealous champion of the Church. He wrote a defense of Catholic doctrine that won for him from Pope Leo X the title of "Defender of the Faith." (Historians now believe St. Thomas More wrote the defense. Despite his actions against the Church in his later years, Henry never accepted Luther's doctrines.)

In those days England was allied with Spain against France. To strengthen this alliance, Henry VIII's father, Henry VII, had married his son Arthur to Catherine of Aragon. Catherine was the daughter of King Ferdinand and Queen Isabel of Spain. However, Arthur died young and unexpectedly. His brother Henry VIII married Catherine to maintain the alliance with Spain. Henry first obtained the papal dispensation required for such a marriage.

After many years of marriage, Catherine and Henry were unable to have a son, although they did have a daughter, Mary. Henry, however, wanted a son who would be King after him and continue his dynasty. Thus, he rejected his wife Catherine. Anne Boleyn, a lady-in-waiting to the Queen, had replaced her in his affections.

King Henry's Divorce

Henry asked the Pope to annul his eighteen-year marriage to the good and noble Catherine. He argued that his marriage was invalid because divine law did not allow him to marry his dead brother's wife. The King also asked Cardinal Wolsey to give him a divorce from Catherine. Wolsey was Lord Chancellor, Henry's most loyal advisor and administrator. He was also the Archbishop of York, the second most important See in England. Once Wolsey would grant the divorce, Henry would marry Anne. Only when the deed was done would Henry ask the pope to approve the marriage. Acting more like the King's puppet than

Catherine of Aragon

a cardinal in the Catholic Church, Wolsey complied with the King's wishes and consented to the divorce.

Pope Clement VII (1523-1534) then assigned Cardinal Campeggio and Wolsey to examine the case, but not to issue a decision. The two cardinals began proceedings in London, May 31, 1529. However, two months later Campeggio adjourned the court until October 1. Meanwhile Pope Clement called the case before his tribunal in Rome, as Catherine had appealed her case directly to him. His action spelled the downfall of Wolsey, who had to admit complete defeat. Wolsey had not been able to give the King the annulment he wanted. Wolsey died just in time to escape being imprisoned by Henry. On his deathbed he wished that he had served God as well as he had served Henry.

Pope Clement VII was a weak pope. The great Catholic historian Warren Carroll writes of Clement VII that he "seemed constitutionally incapable of making a firm stand for anything." Yet, he was the Vicar of Christ. He could not, and would not, annul a marriage that a lawful dispensation had made valid and which eighteen years of married life had consecrated. When the Duke of Norfolk pressured Pope Clement, he encountered a passive resistance by the Pope that could not be shaken. In January 1531, Pope Clement threatened severe penalties against anyone who tried to bring the King's case to an English court. He also warned Henry not to remarry until he had given his decision.

Meanwhile, Catherine of Aragon showed that she was the daughter of the great Queen Isabel of Spain. When pushed by Henry's minions to enter a convent, she replied that marriage was her vocation and that she would defend her marriage to the death. The Queen defended her rights and confidently relied on the protection of her nephew Emperor Charles V.

Thomas Cranmer

Despite the Pope's stern warning that he not remarry, Henry chose not to listen. He continued to work for the divorce. When the Archbishop of Canterbury, William Warham, died, Henry nominated Thomas Cranmer to succeed him. The new Archbishop accepted the Lutheran ideas and was secretly married to the niece of a Protestant. He openly declared himself to be on the King's side in the conflict with the Holy See.

Pope Clement VII

By repeated intrigues, Cranmer paved the way for the divorce. He called the noble Queen Catherine before his tribunal and declared her marriage invalid. He claimed that the Pope did not have the power to grant the dispensation. Five days later Cranmer validated the King's secret marriage to Anne Boleyn. Boleyn was crowned queen at Westminster amid the protests of the people, who still almost all loved Queen Catherine. Upon hearing the news, Clement declared that Henry's divorce and "marriage" were invalid. He excommunicated Henry. However, he added a clause that the excommunication should not take effect immediately.

The Act of Supremacy

After the Pope had issued his decision, the English Parliament passed the Act of Supremacy in 1534. This Act completed the schism by making the King the Supreme Head of the Church of England. The Act transferred all church power to the king. He in turn delegated it to the bishops, whom he alone elected. In addition, every English subject was required to take the Oath of Succession. The Oath recognized the validity of the marriage of Henry and Anne Boleyn, and denied the authority of the pope. Very soon the Treason Laws supplemented these acts by making a traitor of any person who, even by his silence, acknowledged the authority of the pope.

Realizing that Henry would have them killed, the clergy offered little opposition. Royal commissioners went throughout the land to make the clergy take the Oath of Supremacy. Sadly, only one bishop bravely and boldly refused to bend his knee before the adulterous tyrant. This was the seventy-seven year old Bishop of Rochester, St. John Fisher. He was thrown into prison, convicted of high treason, and beheaded in 1535.

Henry VIII condemns St. John Fisher to death for refusing to sign the Oath of Supremacy and divorce.

One eminent layman also refused to set his loyalty to the king above his loyalty to the Vicar of Christ. The layman was Thomas More, the Chancellor of England. When Henry VIII broke with the Church, Sir Thomas More did everything possible to try to bring him to his senses. This brought the King's wrath upon him. He was deprived of his high office and his property. He and his family were forced to live in poverty while he tried to make a living practicing law. In

St. Thomas More

April 1534, Henry had him thrown into prison. Although every attempt was made to force him to take the Oath of Supremacy, he refused. Finally he was beheaded on July 6, 1535. Pope Pius XI canonized Thomas More along with John Fisher in 1935.

Catherine of Aragon died in 1536. Her daughter, Mary Tudor, would be the last hope for a Catholic England. Like her mother and grandmother before her, she was steadfast in her Faith.

The Last Days of Henry VIII

A few Franciscans, the monks of the Abbey of Sion, and the Carthusians of London refused to take the Oath of Supremacy. The resistance offered by these few monasteries gave Henry the excuse to seize all the monasteries. His agent in these thefts was Thomas Cromwell. In 1538, all the English monasteries were suppressed. Their property was given to greedy English nobles. That same year, Pope Paul III (1534-1549) finally excommunicated Henry and released his subjects from their oath of allegiance to him.

In 1536, Henry beheaded Anne Boleyn for adultery and high treason. The following day he married Jane Seymour. She died in October 1537, after having given birth to the future Edward VI. In 1539, for political motives, Thomas Cromwell advised Henry to marry a Lutheran princess, Anne of Cleves. Anne was related to the leader of the Protestant princes of Germany. However, Henry found her unattractive and had the marriage annulled by his bishops in 1540.

Later in 1540, Henry married Catherine Howard. He had Thomas Cromwell beheaded the same day. Two years later, Henry beheaded Catherine for adultery. The following year he married his sixth wife, Catherine Parr, a Protestant. She outlived him. Henry died in 1547. At the funeral, the court orators forbade the people to weep for their monarch. They said that such a good and holy king must surely have gone straight to Heaven.

Introduction of Protestantism to England

Three children survived Henry VIII from his six marriages. Mary, the daughter of Catherine of Aragon, was a staunch Catholic. Henry seemed to have loved her enough at least not to have her beheaded. However, ever since the death of her mother she had lived in constant fear of her life. Anne Boleyn had given Henry a daughter, Elizabeth, whom Catholics could never regard as legitimate because she was born while Catherine still lived. Henry's last child was Jane Seymour's son, Edward. Even Catholics considered Edward legitimate because Catherine had died before Henry's marriage to Jane.

Upon Henry's death, Edward, the oldest male heir, was proclaimed king. However, since he was only ten years old, a regency council ruled in his name. The young Edward VI was raised by Protestant preachers and became a Protestant. During his reign, the English Church moved faster and faster in the direction of out-and-out Protestantism. The leader of the Regent's Council, the Duke of Somerset, was moderate at first, trying not to be too openly heretical. Dogmas that caused the most debate were written so vaguely that a Catholic interpretation was still possible.

Parliament next passed laws forcing the entire kingdom to use a Protestant prayer book. Despite its moderation, the prayer book was unpopular because it clashed with the old traditions and habits. A revolt broke out in the western portion of England, where the people demanded a return to the traditional Catholic Faith. An army of mercenaries hastily recruited by Somerset defeated the Catholics.

The man primarily responsible for the changes in the Church in England during the reign of Edward VI was Thomas Cranmer, the Archbishop of Canterbury. While Cranmer had willing helped Henry with his divorce, his true desire was to make sweeping changes in the Faith in England. Cranmer favored a Protestantism that became more and more radical over time. He replaced the Mass with a service that completely abolished belief in the Real Presence. Altars, vestments, and ornaments were destroyed as idolatry. However, when Edward died in 1553 it appeared that Cranmer's "reforms" were not going to last.

The Catholic Restoration under Mary Tudor

Following Edward's death, Mary Tudor became Queen (1553-1558). Mary's succession to the throne restored the old order, and began to restore Catholicism. Anti-Papal laws were repealed.

Many of the leaders of the revolt returned to the Faith. The pope made their return to the Faith easier when he decreed that laymen would be allowed to keep the Church lands that Henry VIII had given them. Mary removed Cranmer as Archbishop. The pope appointed Cardinal Reginald Pole Archbishop of Canterbury, and gave him the task of reconciling England with Rome.

Queen Mary Tudor

At the beginning of Mary's reign, Protestantism had only just been introduced into England. It had not yet had time to become deeply rooted. The English people still retained much love and respect for the ancient customs and traditions. Therefore a law abolishing the changes made by Edward would have been in order and perhaps enough to set matters right. Everything was proceeding well when Mary, against the advice of Cardinal Pole and her cousin, the Emperor Charles V, decided to persecute the heretics.

The Queen's advisers urged the revival of certain ancient laws that condemned all heretics to be burned at the stake. After making six successive recantations of heresy, none of them sincere,

Cranmer was sentenced to death. Cardinal Pole attempted in vain to counteract the influence of the Queen's advisers. Against his counsel, she had Cranmer, the three bishops appointed by Edward VI, and two hundred and eighty of their supporters, burned at the stake.

Queen Mary then made another decision that she felt was divinely inspired, but which the majority of historians, both Catholic and non-Catholic, feel was a disaster. That was her decision to marry King Philip II of Spain, her second cousin. (Ferdinand and Isabel of Spain were Mary's grandparents and Philip's great-grandparents.) Although almost all historians feel that Mary's marriage to Philip was a great mistake, one of the finest Catholic historians of the twentieth century does not agree. Dr. Warren Carroll in his book *The Cleaving of Christendom* writes:

Philip II of Spain

> This historian firmly believes that Queen Mary's acceptance of Philip II of Spain to be her husband was the best possible decision she could have made under all the circumstances. If only she had been able to conceive a child, it would have changed the whole history of Christendom and the world, very much for the better from the Catholic standpoint.

Dr. Carroll goes on to point out that it was Mary's belief that only Spanish Catholicism was sufficiently pure to rid England of heresy. Mary also believed that she needed Spain to defend her against France, England's traditional enemy, and also against Scotland. Most importantly, Mary fervently believed that she could have a son who would succeed her on the throne of England. Her son, as a Catholic king, would keep England in the Church. Consider the future had England remained in the Church: the colonies England founded would likely have been Catholic. Sadly, for the history of the world and of the Catholic Church, Mary was unable to have a baby.

Queen Mary Tudor died in 1558. She was only forty-two. She named her half sister Elizabeth as her successor, on the condition that Elizabeth would continue to uphold the Catholic faith in England. Sadly, it was not a promise Elizabeth was to keep.

Review Exercises

1. Who was the leader of the Protestant forces in Switzerland?
2. What was the main difference between Calvinism and Lutheranism?
3. Why is there no doubt that Henry VIII's marriage to Catherine of Aragon was valid?
4. Briefly describe the character of Pope Clement VII.
5. Who was Thomas Cranmer?
6. What was the Act of Supremacy?
7. Who was Cardinal Pole?
8. Why did Mary Tudor marry Philip II of Spain?

CHAPTER 20

THE CATHOLIC REFORMATION

St. Ignatius of Loyola

Beginning of Reform in the Church

Even before the Protestant Revolt broke out, devout Catholics all over, both the clergy and the laity, were shocked by the abuses that had crept into the Church. These concerned men and women sought ways to bring about real reform. This true spirit of Catholic reform had begun in the monasteries and religious orders. In many places holy men and women introduced a stricter observance of the rule and founded new orders to meet the needs of the time.

One new order, the Capuchins, began in Italy in 1525. The Capuchins were a new branch of the Franciscan order. They aimed at returning to the rigorous life of St. Francis and his first followers. They practiced severe poverty and devoted themselves to the spiritual welfare of the common people. Like their Franciscan brothers, they were also great preachers. Their exhibition of self-sacrifice and love of God brought comfort and strength to millions, who, without them, might have been lost to the Church.

The Council of Trent

For years everyone in the Church realized that a general council should be held. A council could define the Church teachings that the Protestants had questioned. Some of those who became Lutherans fell into error because they simply did not know any better. A council could also create better discipline and order to abolish the abuses that had arisen. The Emperor Charles V realized that only through a council could the spread of Lutheranism be checked.

Each pope during this time seriously considered calling a council. Most popes wanted and tried to call one. Pope Julius II (1503-1513) convoked the Fifth Lateran Council which lasted from 1512 to 1517. Pope Leo X (1513-1521) continued the council but little was accomplished. Leo's successor, Adrian VI (1522-1523), was a native of Holland and former tutor of Charles V. A stern man, he planned a total reform of the Church's leaders. His intentions were good, but his methods were harsh. His short reign prevented him from carrying out his plans.

Pope Adrian's successor was Clement VII (1523-1534). He also attempted to call a general council. However, as we have seen, Clement had his hands full with Henry VIII. He was also a man who had trouble making decisions. There were other problems that delayed the council for years. The war between Charles V and France and the refusal of the German princes to cooperate postponed the council. There was also the

difficulty of finding a safe, neutral place to hold it. Thus it fell to Clement's successor, Pope Paul III (1534-1549) to launch the endeavor.

In 1545, Pope Paul III finally called the bishops of the world to the little city of Trent. There, in the mountains of northern Italy, they would hold a general council. The Council met, with some breaks, from 1545 to 1563. The Council's main task was to answer the false teachings of the Protestants.

Pope Paul III

The religious basis of the Protestant Revolt was the denial of certain basic teachings of the Catholic Church and the substitution of new doctrines in their place. Therefore it was vital that the Council clearly explain the Church's doctrines in these matters. Lutheranism contained three basic errors the Council had to address. First, the sole rule of faith is the Bible as interpreted by the private judgment of each person. Second, human nature is basically corrupted by original sin. Last, salvation is obtained only by external application of Christ's merits. A person's good works are of no value. The results of these errors were the revolt against the authority of the Church and tradition, the rejection of free will, and the denial of any internal regeneration in the souls of the justified sinner.

The Bible. Luther, in his translation of the Bible, took out certain parts, because they clearly contradicted his new doctrine. The Council of Trent published a list of the books that make up the Bible. It declared that the Latin Bible, known as the Vulgate, is the only standard and authorized text. The Council said that Scripture and Tradition are the two sources of divine revelation. It also said that in matters of faith and morals no one may interpret the Scriptures contrary to the authoritative interpretation of the Church or the unanimous consensus of the Church Fathers.

Salvation. Man is born into this world with original sin upon his soul. How is this sin removed? By mortal sin man loses the state of grace and his right to Heaven. How does he recover the state of grace? In other words, how is a sinner saved? The Council said that original sin, transmitted to us from our first parents, is removed by the merits of Christ applied to each soul by the Sacrament of Baptism. However, a tendency to evil remains. The question of salvation was the most basic point of Lutheran doctrine, which taught that a sinner is saved solely by trust in God, that is, salvation by faith alone. The Council said that we are saved by the saving merits of Christ, which effect an interior regeneration in men and women. The Council went on to say that people can, with the aid of God's grace, assist in their own salvation by doing good works.

The Sacraments. Trent confirmed the traditional Catholic teachings on the Sacraments: their divine institution, nature, minister, and effects. The Council also explained what a person had to do to be able to receive them validly and fruitfully. Since the Protestants had so distorted the teachings on the Mass and the Eucharist, the Council dealt with these doctrines in depth. As regards the Eucharist, the Council clearly defined the doctrine of the Real Presence. It wrote that in the Holy Eucharist the body, blood, soul, and divinity of Jesus Christ are really and truly present. Anyone who denies this, and says that they are there only as a sign or symbol, is **anathema**.

In light of Henry VIII's divorce, the Council also wrote about the Sacrament of Matrimony. The Council affirmed the Church's power to establish impediments to marriage. It also stressed the life-long nature of marriage.

In addition to its doctrinal decrees, the Council of Trent also issued a number of disciplinary rules. It reminded bishops and pastors of the duties of their vocation. Bishops were to live personally in their dioceses. They could be absent only for two or three months each year and never during Advent or Lent. Bishops who ignored this rule were deprived of a portion of their income. If a bishop remained stubborn, his case would be referred to the pope, who could remove the bishop. Bishops were also required to visit all parts of their dioceses at least every two years. The purpose of these visits was to reform the morals of the clergy and laity and to protect Church discipline.

The Council reminded pastors of their duty to teach the catechism and to instruct their people on Sundays. It also reminded monks and nuns about the rules governing their vocations. To suppress abuses that had crept into the monastic life, the Council set the age for taking religious vows at sixteen for boys and twelve for girls.

It was not the purpose of the Council of Trent to set forth a complete statement of the Catholic faith. Its purpose was merely to reaffirm and clarify those doctrines that the Protestants had attacked. However, the Council directed that a catechism should be prepared that would be a summary of Catholic doctrine. This catechism was first published in 1566. From this catechism, many other catechisms have followed.

The doctrinal and disciplinary decrees of the Council of Trent were now in place. It remained to carry out the work that the Council had begun. For this purpose, the Holy Spirit called forth some of the greatest champions the Faith has ever known and raised up a line of saintly popes.

The Greatest Order of the Catholic Reformation: The Jesuits

Of all the new Orders founded in these days of dire need, the most illustrious was the Society of Jesus. Its founder, St. Ignatius, was born of a noble family in Loyola, Spain, in 1491. A few months after the birth of Ignatius, Ferdinand and Isabella captured Granada, the last Moslem stronghold on the Iberian Peninsula. After 770 years, Spain was free from the Moslem invaders. At the age of thirteen Ignatius became a page to King Ferdinand. He received the usual training of a page. This meant little formal schooling, but he did learn to read and write. When Ignatius was old enough, he was knighted and began a career as a Spanish soldier.

While fighting for Spain against the French at the siege of Pamplona, Ignatius was severely wounded in his leg. He returned to Loyola to recover from his wounds. However, his recovery was slow and he was confined to bed for many weeks. His leg had to be set and re-broken three times because it was done incorrectly! He almost died and received the Last Rites more than once. As he lay in his bed recovering, this man, who had never been a student or a great reader, asked for some books to read. There were only two books available. One was *The Life of Christ*, and the other was a collection of the lives of the saints.

A religious vocation is a call from God. It is a call to dedicate one's life to the service of God. There are many vocations and most have no great historical significance, although the spiritual value is inestimable. In moments of historical crisis, however, a vocation may be more, summoning a man or woman to play a role in saving the entire Church. Such was the vocation of St. Paul on the road to Damascus. Such was the vocation that came to Ignatius as he lay reading.

As he read, Ignatius began to realize that many of the saints were remarkable heroes. St. Francis of Assisi and St. Dominic very much impressed him. In 1521, Ignatius decided to give up his career as a soldier and to devote his life to the service of the Church. This was the same year that Martin Luther left the Catholic Church. It cannot be a coincidence that Ignatius was called at this exact historical moment. Although they would never meet in person, these two men would do battle through the centuries.

It took Ignatius some time to decide what form his service to the Church would actually take. He spent many weeks in prayer and in meditation. Then he wrote a book called *Spiritual Exercises*. Next, he made a pilgrimage to the Holy Land, where as a result, he became interested in converting the Moslems.

St. Ignatius of Loyola

On his return to Spain, he determined to improve his education. He realized that if he really was going to help others, he had to become a priest. Although he was thirty-three years old he resumed the study of Latin for two years. Then he then entered the Universities of Alcala and Salamanca where he studied philosophy and theology. Next he set out for the University of Paris, where at the end of seven years he received his master's degree in 1535.

While studying in Paris, Ignatius' holy life attracted the attention of several of his fellow students. There were six devoted companions whom he won to his project. On the feast of the Assumption, 1534, all seven took a vow. They promised to practice perpetual poverty and chastity. They promised to make a pilgrimage to the Holy Land, where they would work to convert the Moslems. If they could not go to the Holy Land, they would place themselves at the call of the pope.

Three years later the seven friends arrived in Venice where they prepared to embark for the Holy Land. Venice was then at war with the Turks, so for a whole year the seven waited in vain. They then went to Vicenza to carry out the second part of their vow. They laid the foundations of the new Society of Jesus (S.J.). Ignatius and two others journeyed on to Rome. There, Pope Paul III received them with great kindness and approved the new order. However, he approved it on the condition that the number of its members be kept to sixty. Three years later, in 1544, he approved it without any conditions.

From the beginning, the Jesuits had three goals. First, they would restore Catholic education in Europe. Second, they would evangelize the newly discovered lands. Third, they would re-convert the Protestants. In their motto the Jesuits had pledged themselves to work *ad majorem Dei gloriam* (to the greater glory of God).

The Jesuits soon began to be used to check the religious revolt. Each Jesuit went through a long training period before his ordination to the priesthood. As a result, they became renowned for their piety, virtue, and learning. Furthermore, the Jesuits, despite being men of outstanding virtue and ability, refused to accept high honors in the Church. A Jesuit would become a bishop or cardinal only when commanded by the pope. It pleased the people to see such devotion to duty without hope of reward. A new respect for the priesthood developed.

Another Jesuit goal was the education of children and young people. To accomplish this goal, the Jesuits opened schools and colleges in many European countries. Jesuit colleges became known as fortresses of the Faith. Jesuit schools and colleges became so famous that even many Protestants sent their sons to be educated by the Jesuits. A Jesuit education was once considered the finest in the world.

The primary goal of the Society was to win back those parts of Europe that had been lost to Protestantism. Despite strong Protestant opposition and even the threat of death, the Jesuits began their work of preaching and teaching the truths of the Faith. They brought the Mass and the Sacraments to people who had been deprived of these instruments of grace for years. They were so successful that much of Europe that had been lost was won back to the Catholic Faith.

One of the most dangerous places in Europe for a priest to evangelize was Elizabethan England. In England, during the reign of Queen Elizabeth I (1559-1603), a priest would be executed if he were found in the kingdom. Nevertheless, some of the English Jesuits returned to their homeland in disguise. Traveling secretly from house to house, they said Mass for a few people at a time. These brave men were able to bring the Sacraments to the English Catholics. Many priests were caught and killed, but still they kept coming and continued to spread the Faith.

The Jesuits Evangelize the Newly Discovered Lands

One of the Jesuit's main goals was to evangelize the newly discovered lands. Jesuits evangelized the native peoples of North and South America (about which we will study in a later chapter). They also traveled to the Far East where they brought the Faith to the peoples of China, Japan, and India. These brave men left on a journey that, for them, took longer than it takes men to travel to the moon. Unlike the astronauts, these men knew they would almost certainly never return to their homelands.

English Jesuit Edmund Campion is hanged.

St. Francis Xavier

Born in Navarre, Spain in 1506, Francis Xavier was a descendant of the Kings of Aragon and Navarre. He became the great Apostle of India and Japan. In March 1540, six months before the final papal recognition of the Jesuit order, one of its seven founders, St. Francis, agreed on just one day's notice to depart for the Far East. On April 7, 1541, he left Portugal for India. On May 6, 1542, he landed at the great Portuguese stronghold of Goa, in India. There he immediately began his missionary work.

Wherever St. Francis went, he converted many to the Church. This was fertile ground for the Church as there were millions to be converted. He cleansed the cities and towns of immorality. As he traveled eastward he won victory after victory for the cause of Christ. On August 15, 1549, he finally reached Japan, where he established a Jesuit province. In Japan he followed his usual practice of translating the basic prayers, the Creed, and the Ten Commandments into Japanese.

After working for more than a year in Japan, Francis returned to India. He planned to journey next into China. He was able to travel as far as Sancian Island off the coast of mainland China. However, the Chinese did not allow foreigners to enter China and he was unable to find anyone brave enough to take him to the Chinese mainland. On November 13, 1552, he wrote his last letter. It indicates that he was determined to enter China. A week later he fell ill. On December 2, 1552,

St. Francis Xavier baptizes an Oriental princess.

the greatest missionary the Church had known since St. Paul died. His body was buried in the earth and covered with lime. After a year he was dug up—totally incorrupt. The following year the body was returned to India, incorrupt. It was buried for five months, but in 1554 it was brought to Goa, still incorrupt. In 1694, one hundred forty-two years after his death, his body was exhumed again and examined by the local bishop and a French Jesuit. He remained incorrupt. However, this evidence of sanctity was not necessary. The world and the Catholic Church already well knew he was a saint. Francis Xavier had been canonized more than seventy years before.

The Jesuits in China

It was for another Jesuit, Father Matteo Ricci, to take up the work of St. Francis Xavier and enter China. Father Ricci was one of the most intelligent men in Europe. He had received a superb education from the great St. Robert Bellarmine, among others. In addition to his theological training, he had been trained in mathematics and astronomy. In 1577, he was ordered to India. He left immediately.

In 1578, a group of Portuguese merchants obtained permission from the Chinese Emperor to live in China. The following year Father Ricci and two companions went with them. He decided that the best way to win the Chinese would be to enter into their lives and adopt their ways and customs, so he devoted himself to the task of becoming a true Chinese. He learned Chinese, the most difficult major language in the world. By 1583, Ricci spoke Chinese well enough to be understood by the local peoples. Over time, he became treated as a member of the Chinese nobility.

In the spring of 1584, Fr. Ricci baptized his first Chinese. In the fall, he published a translation of the Ten Commandments and the catechism of the Council of Trent. He wrote a book in the Chinese language called *A True Account of God*, which had a very high literary value. The Chinese had been a highly civilized nation for many centuries and there were many learned men and scholars among them. They followed the doctrines of Confucius, who, although not a religious leader, was an ethical philosopher. Instead of attacking the teachings of Confucius, which would have set the Chinese against him, Father

Ricci respected them and used them to show that in many things they were like the teachings of Christ. In fact, Fr. Ricci was the one who westernized the Chinese name of Kung Fu-tze to Confucius.

For the next seventeen years Ricci worked diligently to spread the Faith through China. He developed an incredible reputation among the Chinese and counted the Emperor among his friends. By 1605, Ricci's friends in the nobility gave him money to buy a house in the Chinese capital of Beijing. There were over two hundred Catholics in Beijing and more than one thousand nationwide. By 1609, with his health declining, he began to write a history of the Chinese missions. Ricci died on May 11, 1610. The Emperor allowed him to be buried in a cemetery where only the greatest Chinese had been buried.

When Father Ricci died, German Jesuit Adam Schall took his place. Father Schall was a learned mathematician. He attracted the attention of the twelve-year-old Chinese Emperor when he showed that he could calculate the time of solar and lunar eclipses. This was something that the Chinese scholars could not do. As a result, the Emperor made him the director of his astronomy bureau and put him in charge of mathematical studies.

Fr. Mateo Ricci's tomb in Beijing

Over the next few years, Fr. Schall developed a very close relationship with the young emperor. The boy emperor called him "grandpa." He even celebrated his eighteenth birthday at Schall's home. His relationship with the Emperor presented the best chance to convert China to the Faith. The problem was that the Emperor had several wives whom he did not want to give up. While the Church had accepted some of the native Chinese, Japanese, and Indian customs, it could not accept polygamy. Thus, the Emperor, though he may have seen the truth of the Faith, never became a Catholic. Even so, due to Schall's influence, many high-ranking Chinese officials became Catholics. When he died, Chinese everywhere venerated his memory.

The Jesuits in India

The missionaries to India faced an almost impossible task in trying to convert the people. India was a country of many different peoples and languages. In fact, the country had no common language until the nineteenth century when the British forced English upon it. Also, the country had three major religions: Islam, Hinduism, and Buddhism. Those religions were also nothing alike. Islam was vigorous and militant and always seeking converts. Hinduism was passive and peaceful. Buddhism was an offshoot of Hinduism. This meant that the Catholic missionaries had to deal with very different situations depending on whether they were preaching to Moslems or Hindis.

The first European missionaries to India made the mistake of trying to make their converts not only accept the Catholic Faith, but also the social customs of Europe. However, the customs of India and the customs of Europe were nothing alike. India had the "caste system." It had existed for centuries in India. No other country in the world had anything like it. While the European countries had social classes, they were nothing like the Indian system. In the caste system every contact by a person of a higher caste with one of a lower caste, even at a distance, was considered a personal defilement of the person of the higher caste. The highest caste were the Brahmins. They refused to become members of a religion that was contrary to the caste system. As a result, the converts made by St. Francis were all lower caste, mostly laborers and fishermen.

In order to attract the Brahmins to the Faith, an Italian Jesuit named Robert de Nobili decided to adopt the customs of India. When he arrived in India in 1606, he obtained the approval of his bishop to dress as a Brahmin. He also began to live like a Brahmin and follow their dietary customs. In the summer of 1608, a well-known Brahmin came to him to learn more about this intriguing foreigner. This man taught Fr. de Nobili about Hinduism and taught him his language, Sanskrit. By 1609, de Nobili had made about fifty converts. Over the next thirty-five years he worked to convert the Indians, especially the Brahmins. In 1644, age and disability forced de Nobili to leave the mission field. He died in 1656 at the shrine where St. Thomas the Apostle had been martyred more than fifteen hundred years earlier.

Review Exercises

1. Which Pope finally called the Council of Trent?
2. What did the Council of Trent teach about the Bible?
3. What did the Council of Trent teach about the question of Justification?
4. What did the Council teach about the Sacraments?
5. What did the Council teach about the Holy Eucharist?
6. What were the three goals of the Jesuits?
7. Who was known as the great Apostle of India and Japan?
8. Who was Matteo Ricci?
9. Who was Robert de Nobili?

CHAPTER 21

THE GREAT SAINTS OF THE CATHOLIC REFORMATION

St. Charles Borromeo cares for plague victims.

The Great Popes of the Catholic Reformation

The popes of the second half of the sixteenth century did all they could to carry out the reforms of the Council of Trent and to enforce its decrees. Even during the Council, steps were taken in this direction. Pope Paul III (1534–1549) created the Congregation of the Holy Office, or the Inquisition. Its primary purpose was to defend the Catholic faith. It did this by issuing decrees and pointing out heretical statements of doctrine that should be condemned.

The first head of the Holy Office was Cardinal Gian Caraffa. In 1555, Caraffa became Pope Paul IV (1555-1559). One of his acts as pope was to publish a bull notifying princes, bishops, and any one else who had fallen into heresy, that they were all answerable to the Inquisition. Pope Pius IV (1559-1564), who officially closed the Council of Trent, also worked to carry out its decisions. He created a Congregation of Cardinals for the Interpretation of the Decrees of the Council of Trent.

The next two popes focused on reforming individuals, particularly bishops and priests. Pope St. Pius V (1566-1572) was a Dominican. He was very concerned with simony. He said that no one could receive the benefits of an office unless he was invested by Rome. He took every precaution to ensure that only men of the highest character became bishops. Once a bishop was appointed, Pius demanded that he strictly observe the decrees of the Council. He also decreed that those bishops failing to observe the rules would be removed from their Sees within one month. Lastly, he wanted to replace greedy priests with a new generation of holy priests qualified to teach their flocks. Thus, he ordered the clergy to study the Catechism of the Council of Trent.

Pius had a worthy successor in Pope Gregory XIII (1571-1585). Gregory continued to defend the Church against Protestantism. Gregory sent papal representatives, called *nuncios*, to the countries of Europe. The nuncios ensured that decrees of Trent were followed. They also established seminaries and colleges and began re-conversion missions among the Protestants. Pope Gregory wanted each nation to have a college in Rome where young men would be trained for the priesthood. The German and English Colleges were founded during his lifetime. Gregory also reformed the calendar that Julius Caesar had created. A year under Caesar's calendar lasted eleven minutes and fourteen seconds longer than the actual sun year. This resulted in three extra days in 400 years. Gregory fixed this by creating the Leap Year.

In 1585, the Franciscan Order gave the Church a Pope, Sixtus V (1585-1590). Although his reign was not long, he did many wonderful things. As a young man he had joined the Franciscans and became a well-known preacher. Recognizing his abilities, Pope Pius V had made him a Cardinal. As Pope, Sixtus restored order in Rome by taking strong measures against bandit gangs who had been causing trouble. He improved the city of Rome through various public works programs. He built new streets, new squares with beautiful fountains, and a new aqueduct to bring pure water down from the mountains into the city. He finished the dome of St. Peter's, rebuilt the Lateran Palace, the Vatican Library, and enlarged the Vatican itself. Sixtus also continued the work of Trent. He established a printing press to print books to defend the Church and spread the Faith. He also encouraged scholars to take up the defense of the Faith, among whom was the great Jesuit Cardinal, St. Robert Bellarmine.

St. Robert Bellarmine

One of the most important Cardinals of the Catholic Reformation was the great Jesuit theologian Robert Bellarmine. Born in Italy in 1542 to a noble family, his intellectual abilities showed themselves at an early age. His father hoped he would enter politcs. His mother had higher ambitions for him—the Jesuits. In 1560, he entered the Order. At once the Jesuits saw that they had acquired a pearl of great price. They sent him to the finest colleges where he learned theology and philosophy.

In 1569, after years of study, Bellarmine was sent as a professor of theology to Louvain, near Brussels in Belgium. Protestantism had been trying for a long time to gain a foothold in Belgium. At Louvain he quickly gained a reputation both as a professor and as a preacher. His sermons attracted both Catholics and Protestants. He stayed at Louvain for seven years until his health forced him to return to Rome. For the next eleven years he taught theology in Rome. In Rome, he also wrote his most important book, *Disputations on the Controversies of the Christian Faith*. It has been described as the definitive defense of papal authority. This monumental work was the earliest attempt to organize the various controversies of the time. It dealt a tremendous blow to Protestantism throughout Europe.

Pope Clement VIII (1592-1605), who had the highest regard for Bellarmine, ordered him to write a catechism. Clement then ordered that the catechism be used in the papal territories. He expressed his wish that it be used in every country. It was translated into many different languages and met with phenomenal success. When the First Vatican Council took up the question of a universal catechism, it suggested Bellarmine's catechism as a model. In 1599, Clement made Bellarmine a cardinal and three years later made him Archbishop of Capua. He spent the rest of his life defending the Church. In his old age he was allowed to return to his ancestral home in Italy, Montepulciano, as its bishop for four years. Then he retired to the Jesuit college of St. Andrew in Rome. During his retirement, he wrote several short books intended to help ordinary people in their spiritual life. Saint Robert Bellarmine died in Rome in 1621.

St. Charles Borromeo

The bishop most responsible for carrying out the reforms enacted by the Council of Trent was St. Charles Borromeo, a nephew of Pope Pius IV. Although he was the Pope's nephew, he never sought favors or honors. Instead, he devoted himself to the service of the Church. He had a great talent for administration that he used to direct the Diocese of Milan. In Milan he ended abuses and introduced strict discipline. During his uncle's pontificate he acted as the Pope's chief adviser. Charles Borromeo, more than anyone else, brought Council of Trent to a successful conclusion.

In 1565, after the death of his uncle, Charles left Rome and went to Milan, where he spent the rest of his life. He completely reformed his diocese. In this work he had the assistance of several religious orders, including the Jesuits whom he put in charge of Milan's seminary. He himself founded a congregation of secular priests called the Oblates of St. Ambrose. Their chief duties were to visit churches, teach catechism, direct nuns, and especially to have charge

St. Charles Borromeo

of colleges and seminaries. St. Charles felt that founding colleges and seminaries was the best way to reform the clergy. He was an excellent example of just how the Council of Trent intended a diocese to be run.

Moreover, St. Charles' influence did not stop at the borders of his archdiocese. The Council of Trent had suggested that several dioceses be visited and inspected by delegates of the Holy See. St. Charles was appointed as one of these visitors and reformed entire regions. His heroic sanctity was especially evident during the dreadful plague that ravaged the city of Milan in 1576. He turned his palace into a hospital, personally nursed the sick, heard their confessions, and gave them the last rites. The story of his tireless zeal went abroad into all lands, so that at his death in 1584, at the age of forty-six, everyone felt that the Church had lost one of her most faithful servants. When St. Charles died, he had accomplished as much in his short lifetime as any bishop in the history of the Church.

St. Teresa of Avila

During the years following the Council of Trent, holy men and women formed new religious orders. Several of the older religious orders were improved. However, no order was more thoroughly reformed than were the Carmelites. The task of reforming the Carmelites was accomplished by one of the Catholic Church's greatest saints, St. Teresa of Avila. She is one of only three women to be named a Doctor of the Church. (The magnificent St. Catherine of Siena and St. Thérèse of Lisieux are the other two.)

St. Teresa was born in Spain to noble parents in 1515. From early childhood she had a spirit of adventure. When she was a little girl, she and her brother left their home and started out alone for Morocco with the intention of winning the crown of martyrdom at the hands of the Moslems. Of course, their family stopped them before they had gone very far.

At the age of twenty, St. Teresa entered the Carmelite convent of the Incarnation in Avila and became a nun. She lived in the convent for many years dedicating herself to a life of prayer without drawing any particular attention to herself. However, like St. Paul and St. Ignatius, at this moment of crisis God suddenly called her to a higher purpose.

In 1562, Teresa left her convent, where the nuns had become very worldly, and founded a smaller but stricter convent at Avila. Five years later she founded two more reformed Carmelite convents. These Carmelites were called "Discalced" because the nuns did not wear shoes. In many ways Teresa resembled St. Catherine of Siena. She was a real leader with a great talent for organization. She firmly believed that there would not have been a Protestant Revolt if the religious orders had remained true to their ideals. Therefore, she threw herself, body and soul, into founding Carmelite convents where the rule of the community was strictly observed.

In 1568, she helped found the first men's community of the Discalced Carmelites. Among the first monks was St. John of the Cross. Like Teresa, he was also to become a Doctor of the Church. Over the next few years she founded more convents. In 1571, the head of her order put her in charge of the convent of the Incarnation at Avila, where the nuns were personally hostile to her. However, her charm and holiness won the nuns to her, and they accepted her reforms. The convent of the Incarnation still exists today and continues to draw young women to a vocation with the Carmelites. She continued to found and reform convents up to the moment of her death in 1582. By the time she died, she had founded sixteen convents and helped reform many others. Pope Gregory XV canonized her in 1622. In 1970, Pope Paul VI declared her a Doctor of the Church.

St. Teresa of Avila

St. Peter Canisius

St. Peter Canisius was born in 1521, in Holland, which at that time was part of Germany. He entered the Society of Jesus at the age of twenty-one. He worked so successfully for the preservation of the Faith in Germany that he has justly been called the "Second Apostle of Germany." His success was due primarily to the three catechisms he wrote. One was intended for pupils in colleges and universities. The second was published for young children and those adults who had received little of no instruction in the Faith. The third catechism was for the use of children in grade schools.

St. Peter Canisius, because of his catechisms, became known as the "Hammer of Heretics." People living at this time referred to his catechisms as "banners of war, which gleamed in the religious struggles and won the most glorious victories." The catechisms were translated into every European language. They were reprinted in countless editions. There were four hundred editions in Germany alone. Like the Baltimore Catechism, St. Peter's catechisms are in the form of questions and answers. He stresses the points of Catholic doctrine disputed by Protestants by a clear and thorough explanation of the Catholic teaching.

St. Peter spent thirty years in Bavaria and Austria. He worked tirelessly to reform universities and found colleges and seminaries. He spent the last seventeen years of his life in Switzerland, preaching, giving retreats, writing books, and promoting the Catholic reform in every way. He died there in 1597. In 1925, Pope Pius XI canonized him and declared him a Doctor of the Church.

St. Philip Neri

St. Philip Neri showed the world how happiness and holiness can go hand in hand. He was born in Florence in 1515 to a noble

family and received his early
education from Dominican
friars. At the age of eighteen,
his wealthy uncle promised to
make him his heir if he would
enter his business and work
for him. Philip tried it for
two years but found that he
no longer cared for the things
of this world, so he traveled
to Rome where he devoted
himself to a life of study.

Philip had a great love
for the poor. Because of his
great charity he soon became
known as the "Apostle of Rome."

**Chiesa Nuova, the Church in Rome
founded by St. Philip Neri**

Following the advice of his
confessor, he was ordained in 1551. His life was then spent in service to
everyone in Rome. Young men came to him by the hundreds for advice
and direction and he spent hours in the confessional. His house had a
large room that he turned into an oratory, or chapel, where every day a
large number of men came together for spiritual exercises.

Before long, St. Philip found that the demands on his time
and energy were more than one person could handle. He needed other
priests to help him, so, he founded a new kind of religious community
called the Congregation of the Oratory. It is one of the most original
creations of the period. The members live in community, provide
their food at their own expense, are held by no vows, and are free to
quit the Congregation at any time. The various houses of Oratorians
are independent of one another and have no Superior General. All

important decisions are reached by a majority vote of the assembled Congregation. The Oratorians, by their zeal and example in Rome and elsewhere, helped in the work of reform that the Council of Trent started. In 1575, Pope Gregory XIII approved the Congregation. It quickly spread into other countries.

St. Philip Neri died at the end of the day on May 25, 1595. He had spent the day as he normally did: hearing confessions and receiving visitors.

St. Angela Merici and the Ursuline Nuns

In 1535, a saintly woman named Angela Merici founded an order of nuns in Italy known as the Ursulines. Angela was born in 1474, in Italy. She was orphaned at the age of ten along with her younger sister. The two girls were raised by their uncle. Young Angela was very upset when her sister died suddenly without receiving the last rites. Throughout her life she prayed for the repose of the soul of her sister. When she was old enough, she joined the Third Order of St. Francis.

Angela believed that young girls needed a better Catholic education than they were receiving. She decided to dedicate her time to teaching girls in her home, which she had converted into a school. This school was such a success that the leaders of a neighboring city invited her to start a school in their town. She happily accepted this offer. She spent her days teaching and doing works of charity and her nights in prayer.

In 1524, a great affliction befell Angela. She went blind while on a pilgrimage to the Holy Land. While in the Holy Land she had a vision to found a community of women who would devote themselves to the education of children. She recovered her sight and returned to Italy. In 1535, St Angela chose twelve other women and founded the "Company of St Ursula." Though they continued to live in their own homes, they met together at regular times for prayer and spiritual exercises. They devoted their time to the instruction of children and the care of the sick.

The Ursulines received great support from St. Charles Borromeo. He introduced the Order into all of the towns of Italy. Soon they had houses in France and Germany. They were the first Sisters to come to the New World, when they came to Canada in 1636. In 1727, they opened a convent in New Orleans. There they founded the first school taught by nuns within the present boundaries of the United States.

St. Angela Merici died January 27, 1540. She was buried in the Church of St. Afra in Brescia where she had lived almost her entire life. She was dressed in the habit of a Third Order Franciscan. Pope Pius VII canonized her in 1807.

Review Exercises

1. Name at least four popes who worked to implement the reforms of the Council of Trent.
2. What was the most important book that St. Robert Bellarmine wrote?
3. Where was St. Charles Borromeo bishop?
4. Name the three women who are Doctors of the Church.
5. What does "Discalced" mean?
6. Who has been called the "Second Apostle of Germany?"
7. Who was the first Apostle of Germany?
8. Who founded the religious community called the Congregation of the Oratory?
9. What is the main job of the Ursuline nuns?
10. Who founded the Ursuline order?

CHAPTER 22

THE CHURCH IN THE NEW WORLD

Fr. Perez convinces Queen Isabel to give Columbus three ships.

Missionaries in the New World

In 1492, Christopher Columbus sailed west in search of a sea route to India. While he did not find such a route, he did discover the Americas. He took possession of the new land in the name of the King and Queen of Spain. Other Spanish explorers followed. Ponce de Leon came to Florida, Balboa discovered the Pacific Ocean, and Cortes began the conversion of Mexico. Coronado visited the southwestern "United States," and de Soto discovered the Mississippi River. With the explorers came Spanish missionaries: Franciscans, Dominicans, and Jesuits. They came to preach the Gospel to the natives of the New World.

Mexico

In 1521, Cortes conquered Mexico for Spain. Over the next five years, twelve Franciscans arrived. They founded missions, and soon Dominicans and Augustinians joined them. However, the Gospel would not have spread so quickly had it not been for the apparition of our Lady at Guadalupe.

On the morning of December 9, 1531, Juan Diego saw a vision of the Blessed Mother on the slopes of the hill of Tepeyac. She asked him to build her a church on the site. When Juan Diego told his bishop about the vision, the bishop asked him to return to the hill and ask the Lady for a miraculous sign to prove her claim. Juan returned and relayed the bishop's request. Our Lady told Juan to gather flowers from the hilltop, although it was winter and no flowers bloomed. On the hilltop he found roses. He gathered them together and the Blessed Mother herself arranged them in his tilma (cloak). When Juan returned and presented the roses to the bishop, the image of Our Lady had miraculously appeared on his tilma.

In 1754, Pope Benedict XIV declared Our Lady of Guadalupe the patroness of New Spain. She is still recognized as the Patron Saint of all the Americas. In 2002, Pope John Paul II canonized Juan Diego.

News of the apparition quickly spread through Mexico. In the seven years from 1532 through 1538, eight million native Mexicans became Catholics. All through Mexico, the missions prospered. The

Our Lady of Guadalupe Basilica

Church built schools and colleges to educate a native clergy who went out to preach the Faith. Later the Jesuits, who had been laboring in Florida, moved their missionary activity to the northwestern coast of Mexico. There they worked among the native people. For centuries, the Church in Mexico grew steadily. Schools and colleges multiplied. Eventually the entire country became Catholic.

South America

In Peru, Dominicans founded the National University of San Marcos at Lima in 1551. It is the oldest university in the New World. The Jesuits came to Lima in 1568 and established the first printing press in

America. St. Rose, the first native of the Americas to be a canonized, was born in Lima in 1586. She entered a Dominican convent in 1602. During her life as a nun she fasted and did great penances for the salvation of souls. She died on August 24, 1617. Pope Clement X canonized her in 1671.

St. Rose of Lima

In 1586, the Jesuits arrived in Paraguay where they established their famous "Reductions." These were settlements composed entirely of Catholic Indians. They were organized into small states with a spiritual leader as their governor. In the center of all the villages there was a Catholic church. The Jesuits taught the Indians to farm as well as to read and write. They set aside part of the land as the property of God. The whole community farmed this land to protect against famine and to provide food for the sick and the elderly. Sadly, when Portuguese expelled the Jesuits from Paraguay in 1767, the Reductions soon disappeared. Historians are only now rediscovering them.

Missionaries in Florida

The earliest record of missionaries in the territory that is now the United States was an effort by three Dominicans lead by Father Luis Cancer de Barbastro. In 1549, Father Luis and his companions attempted to found a mission near Tampa Bay, Florida. The three priests sailed from

Mexico to Florida. They took along a Native American woman who had converted to the Faith to act as interpreter. However, when they landed in Florida, she betrayed them. The priests were martyred at the hands of the local peoples. Father Luis is known as the proto-martyr of Florida. In 1565, the first permanent settlement and the first parish in the continental United States were founded at St. Augustine, Florida.

Dominicans, Franciscans, and Jesuits all labored in this new field. Jesuits were sent to Florida in 1566 and 1568. They labored as far north as the Rappahannock River in Virginia. There they suffered martyrdom at the hands of the natives. The Franciscans took up the banner and continued their work with equal success. Governor Moore's invasion from Carolina in 1704 brought the work of the missionaries to a premature end. In 1763, when Spain gave Florida to England, the Spanish population withdrew. Catholicism almost disappeared from the area.

French Missionaries

The French were the first to settle in what is now Canada. In 1608, King Henry IV of France asked the Jesuits to preach the Gospel in Canada. Henry had seen how the missionary labors of the Spanish had given Spain a stronghold in the New World. He hoped that the Jesuits would have the same effect in the north.

The Jesuits founded a college at Quebec and began converting the Indians. From Canada missionaries came south into what is now the United States. In 1604, they said Mass in present day Maine. They established a permanent settlement in 1613 near Bar Harbor, Maine. Twenty years later, the Capuchins founded a mission on the Penobscot River. Shortly after, the Jesuits settled on the Kennebec River. These missions lasted until the beginning of the eighteenth century. Sadly, English soldiers from Massachusetts destroyed the missions and murdered the priests.

St. Isaac Jogues

St. Isaac Jogues

In 1642, gallant Father Isaac Jogues met his death at the hands of the Iroquois. The first time the Iroquois took him prisoner they cruelly tortured him. The Satanic nature of the torture is evident in that the Indians burned off the two fingers of his right hand that he used to bless them. Dutch Protestants finally rescued him and he returned to France. He went to Rome, where, in spite of the loss of his fingers, Pope Urban VIII permitted him to say Mass, saying, "It is not fitting that Christ's martyr should not drink Christ's Blood."

Despite his sufferings, Father Jogues was eager to return to Canada. He loved the Indians and had a great desire to convert them. On his return, he visited the Iroquois near Auriesville, close to present-day Albany. He hoped to create peace between them and their long-time enemies the Hurons. Although unsuccessful, he did not give up hope. He tried again. This time the Iroquois took him prisoner, and lured him to a lodge where they murdered him. Over the next three years, the Iroquois killed five other Jesuit missionaries. Pope Pius XI canonized these Jesuit martyrs on June 29, 1930.

Father Marquette

Jesuit Father Jacques Marquette was a missionary and an explorer. He explored the Mississippi River. He preached the Gospel to the Native

Americans living along its shores. He had come to Canada from France in 1666. Seven years later he accompanied the explorer Louis Joliet down the Wisconsin and Mississippi Rivers as far as the Arkansas River. Two years later, he returned to preach to the Illinois Indians and established the Immaculate Conception Mission at Kaskaskia. He died there at the age of 39.

Blessed Kateri Tekakwitha (1656-1680)

Since the Mohawk Indians were allies of the Protestant English, they opposed Catholic missionaries preaching to them. The Mohawks killed many missionaries. Yet it was to the Mohawks that the saintly Kateri Tekakwitha belonged. She is called the "Lily of the Mohawks." Jesuit missionaries instructed her in the Faith. She died at the age of twenty-four after a life of great sanctity. She is the patroness of ecology and the environment.

Blessed Kateri Tekakwitha

CATHOLICISM IN THE ENGLISH COLONIES

The English colonies in North America were founded at a time when the Church was being bitterly persecuted in England. Puritans or Anglicans settled all the English colonies. These included Virginia, the Carolinas, and Georgia. Since they were settled by Protestants, few Catholics were allowed to live in them. The Catholics were left Maryland. The English Catholic nobleman, George Calvert planned it, and his son Cecil Calvert founded it.

Maryland

In 1634, Cecil Calvert, the second Lord Baltimore, established a Catholic colony in Maryland. Jesuit priests came with the first settlers. The first settlement was called St. Mary's. Wherever the settlers established a new settlement, they built a chapel and school. Since they had endured much persecution in England, the Catholics in Maryland tolerated all religions. They also worked successfully to convert the local native tribes.

Later, Protestants at the urging of an enemy of the Baltimore family began to oppress the Catholics. The Protestants sent a number of Jesuits back to England in chains. They deprived many Catholics of their property and banished them from the colony. The situation became so bad that, at the insistence of Lord Baltimore, the Assembly of Maryland in 1649 passed the famous Maryland Toleration Act. This Act guaranteed religious freedom and toleration to everyone.

New York

In 1683, Catholic King James II made Thomas Dongan the governor of the colony of New York. On October 14, 1683 Dongan convoked the first representative assembly in New York. He persuaded the assembly to pass an act decreeing religious liberty for all. When the Jesuits arrived in New York, they established a college in New York City. From there they had a positive influence throughout the colony.

Dongan intended to found a settlement of Irish Catholics in the center of the colony. However, he had to abandon this plan when he was replaced as governor and an anti-Catholic law was enacted in 1689. This law said that any priest caught within New York could be put in prison for life. In addition, any priest who escaped from prison and was recaptured could be hanged. As a result of this law, the Faith in New

York colony began to fade. The few Catholics who continued to live in New York City had to go to Philadelphia for the Sacraments. Even as late as the American War for Independence, New York Catholics needed to go to Philadelphia to receive the Sacraments.

Pennsylvania

In Pennsylvania, the Quakers under William Penn tolerated Catholics. In 1686, Catholics erected a chapel in Philadelphia. In 1730, the Jesuits sent Father Joseph Greaton to that city as the first resident priest. Over the years the Faith grew, and Catholics built St. Joseph's Church in 1733, St. Mary's in 1763, and Holy Trinity in 1768. However, the congregations remained small and consisted mainly of Irish and German immigrants. By 1763, there were about 7,000 Catholics in the English Colonies. They lived mainly in Maryland and Pennsylvania.

The Southwest

The missionaries who came with the Spanish explorer Francisco Coronado in 1514-15 made the first attempts to spread the Faith to the Native Americans in the future Southwestern United States. In the following years Spanish missionaries made more attempts to establish permanent missions in this area. Three Franciscans, who gave New Mexico its name, made one such effort in 1581. Other Franciscans founded the city of Santa Fe about 1608. They built the first parish church there in 1622.

California

The leading figure in the history of the Church in early California is the Spanish Franciscan friar, Father Junipero Serra. Father Serra was born on the Spanish island of Majorca in 1713. At the age of sixteen, he entered the Franciscan Order. Blessed with a brilliant mind, he became a professor of theology and taught at a college in Majorca. Despite his pleasant life at the college, he felt called to the mission field. In 1749, he left Spain and came to Mexico City. However, he stayed there only briefly before he volunteered for the Indian missions. There he spent about nine years teaching and catechizing the native peoples. Recalled to Mexico City, over the next ten years he became famous as an outstanding preacher and missionary.

In 1768, he received the task to which he would dedicate the remainder of his life. Along with fifteen other Franciscans he traveled to California to spread the Gospel and establish missions. In 1769, he founded the mission of San Diego. Then, in quick succession, he founded San Carlos, San Antonio de Padua, San Gabriel, San Luis Obispo, San Francisco, San Juan Capistrano, Santa Clara, and San Buenaventura.

Towards the end of his life Father Serra received papal approval to administer the Sacrament of Confirmation. For the last three years of his life he re-visited all the missions from San Diego to San Francisco, to confirm those who had been baptized. He confirmed about 5,300 people, almost all of whom were Native Americans. He died in 1785 at Mission San Carlos Borromeo where he is buried. Pope John Paul II beatified him in 1988.

Louisiana

Catholics built the first church in Louisiana in 1717 in Robeline. The next year, French settlers, lead by Jean-Baptiste de Bienville, founded the city of New Orleans, and the Capuchins erected a brick church on the site of the present cathedral. In 1727, a group of French Ursuline nuns arrived in New Orleans. They took charge of the Royal Hospital and

Carmel Mission

taught the colony's girls and women. They instructed the African and Native American girls as well as the daughters of the French settlers. Their school remains the oldest continuously operating school in the United States. They also opened the first convent for women in the United States.

In 1762, France gave Louisiana to Spain. The Church continued to grow under Spanish rule. The Church established two new parishes in 1772 and 1787. In 1800, France regained the area. In 1803, the United States bought Louisiana from France.

Illinois and the Northwest Territory

The first missionary activity in Illinois occurred in 1675. That was the year that Fr. Marquette established the Immaculate

Conception mission at Old Kaskaskia. In 1687, Jesuit Father Jacques
Gravier became head of the mission. He worked there for ten years,
enduring incredible hardships. In 1696, he established the Guardian
Angel mission on the site of the present city of Chicago. In 1700, Father
Gravier moved the mission at Old Kaskaskia to the present city of
Kaskaskia. Six years later, the Peoria tribe attacked Father Gravier. He
died two years later from the wounds he received. In 1721, the Jesuits
established a college at Kaskaskia.

When France lost the Northwest Territory to Great Britain in
1763, after the French and Indian War, the British expelled the Jesuits.
French Jesuit Pierre Gibault, known as the Patriot Priest of the West, left
Quebec in 1768 and came to Kaskaskia. There he served the French and
Native American Catholics. He also labored at Vincennes, Mackinac,
Detroit, and Peoria. In 1770, he blessed the first church in St. Louis,
which stood on the site of St. Louis' Old Cathedral.

Father Gibault was a strong supporter of the American War
for Independence. He was in Kaskaskia when an American force
under George Rogers Clark arrived. Father Gibault told Clark that he
supported the American cause but that his first concern was for the
Catholics in the area. Clark assured him that Catholics would have
religious freedom in the new country. It was chiefly Father Gibault's
influence that made it possible for George Rogers Clark to achieve
military victory in the Northwest Territory and secure it for the United
States.

Catholics in the War for Independence

The American War for Independence proved most favorable to
religious freedom. The official proclamation of this freedom in 1789 was
prompted no doubt by the memory of the heroic deeds of the Catholics

in the colonies. Like Father Gibault, the great majority of Catholics sided with the colonists during the War. Many Catholics fought in the Continental army and navy. Catholic generals came from Europe to aid the American cause. On the sea, Catholic Commodore John Barry won for himself the title "Father of the American Navy."

Catholics were involved at the highest levels of government during the War for Independence and during the Constitutional Convention. A Catholic, Charles Carroll, signed the Declaration of Independence. Two Catholics, Thomas Fitzsimons and Daniel Carroll, signed the Constitution. During the War, Thomas Sim Lee, another Catholic, served as governor of Maryland from 1779 to 1783. He also worked closely with many of the Founding Fathers.

Review Exercises

1. What event accounted for the rapid spread of the Faith in Mexico?
2. Who was the first native of the Americas to be canonized?
3. What were the Jesuit "Reductions?"
4. Who is the proto-martyr of Florida?
5. Who is known as the "Lily of the Mohawks?"
6. What family was most influential in founding Maryland?
7. Which of the colonies were tolerant of Catholics?
8. Who was the most important person in the history of the California missions?
9. Why was Father Pierre Gibault known as the Patriot Priest of the West?
10. Name at least three important Catholics who aided America during the War for Independence.

CHAPTER 23

THE CHURCH IN NORTHERN EUROPE DURING THE 16TH AND 17TH CENTURIES

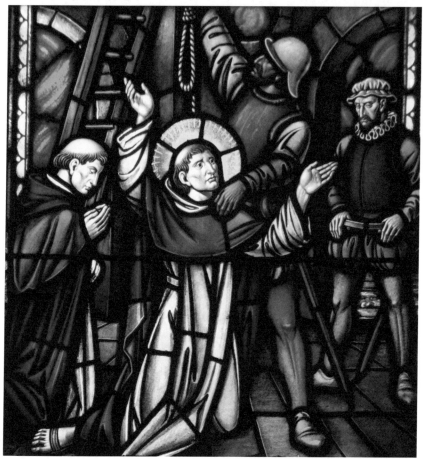

At Gorkum, in Holland, on July 9, 1572, seventeen priests were martyred for the Faith.

England: Anglicanism

In 1559, Elizabeth, Anne Boleyn's daughter, succeeded Mary Tudor as Queen of England. Before her accession to the throne, the new queen had promised her half-sister that she would maintain the Catholic Faith in England. Her brother-in-law, King Philip II of Spain, believed that she was inclined towards Catholicism. Whether she ever intended to keep her promise, she certainly did not. After her accession she embraced Protestantism. The English people, out of loyalty to her, did not object. Parliament passed the Act of Uniformity, which ordered the use of the Book of Common Prayer by all the people. Thus the Protestant religion was restored, as it had existed under Edward VI.

A large group of about 120,000 Catholics remained firmly attached to their faith. The government deposed about four hundred priests and many others resigned. Unlike the days of Henry VIII, all the bishops, but one, objected and were immediately removed from office. To replace the former bishops, the government created an entirely new hierarchy. Elizabeth herself appointed her mother's former chaplain, Matthew Parker, Archbishop of Canterbury. The present Anglican hierarchy descends directly from him. Other bishops were then consecrated. They then invalidly ordained a large number of men to the priesthood, giving no regard to their moral character.

Scotland: Presbyterianism

Meanwhile Queen Elizabeth lived in mortal fear that her Catholic subjects, whose lives had become very difficult under her rule, would transfer their allegiance to the young Catholic princess, Mary Stuart. Mary was the grand-niece of Henry VIII. Her mother had raised Mary in France. She had inherited the throne of Scotland through her father, King James V. At the age of seventeen, through her marriage to King Francis II of France, Mary became ruler of both France and Scotland, England's historical enemies. When Francis died in 1560, she was left an eighteen-year-old widow. She decided to return to Scotland to reclaim her throne. Elizabeth feared that Mary, who had a valid claim to the English throne, especially in the eyes of Catholics who viewed Elizabeth as illegitimate, would seek to win the throne of England.

Elizabeth also feared that Mary, as the widow of a French king, could depend upon the sympathy and support of the French people. In Mary, England's two great rivalries were combined.

When Mary arrived in Scotland in 1561, the religious situation was unstable. During the reign of James V (1524-1542), strong measures had been used to suppress heresy. Patrick Hamilton, a member of the royal family, was executed along with a number of monks who had fallen into heresy. Under the rule of the Regent, Mary Guise, Mary Stuart's mother, the heretics again lifted their heads. They were confident that they could depend upon the Scottish nobles. The nobles coveted the wealth of the Church and desired a victory over the king and the clergy. In May 1546, the Protestants seized Cardinal David Beaton, the Archbishop Primate of Scotland and hanged him from the walls of his own castle.

The leader of the Protestant revolutionaries in Scotland was the preacher, John Knox (1505-1572). Born at Haddington in Scotland, the son of a poor farmer, he had a very checkered career. He was ordained a priest, but after spending time in Germany became a Protestant. In July 1547, he was arrested on a charge of conspiracy in the murder of Cardinal Beaton, whose murder he had gleefully applauded. He was deported to France and condemned to the king's galleys. After serving as a galley slave for two-and-a-half years, Knox was released and went to England. There, he came under the protection of Thomas Cranmer. He preached his brand of Protestantism and even became King Edward VI's chaplain. Forced to leave England during the reign of Mary Tudor, he went to Geneva, where he joined John Calvin. The week after Mary landed in Scotland, Knox gave a violent sermon against her. He declared that he feared one Mass more than ten thousand armed enemies. They met in person the following week.

Mary was an eighteen-year-old princess, beautiful, gentle, and charming. Knox was a forty-seven year old man who had spent two and a half years as a galley slave and survived. He was a bitter, ruthless enemy of the Catholic Church. She had been raised to love the Church. The two could not possibly co-exist.

Meanwhile, Queen Elizabeth's coming to the throne united the resistance of Scottish Protestants by dividing the people into two factions. One group supported the Catholic Church and allied itself with France. The other group supported Protestantism and was backed by England. The Protestant lords formed a powerful league known as the Lords of the Congregation. They were lead by Mary Stuart's traitorous half-brother, James Stuart. Soon the Lords of the Congregation abolished the French garrisons established in Scotland. A parliament made up of followers of John Knox forbade Catholic worship in Scotland. They set up the Presbyterian Church, which was based on the teachings of John Calvin. (The church is called "Presbyterian" because assemblies called presbyteries, rather than bishops, govern it.)

Mary Queen of Scots

Such was the situation when Mary Stuart arrived in Scotland in 1561. Unable to cope with the state of affairs by herself, Mary looked around for support. She chose her Catholic cousin, Henry Stuart, Lord Darnley. She married him in July 1565, after having known him for less than six months. In marrying Lord Darnley, Mary hoped not only to consolidate her power, but also to restore the Catholic religion in Scotland. Sadly, the young Queen married the eighteen year old Darnley, without really getting to know him. He was tall and strikingly handsome. He was also unreliable, greedy, and cowardly.

Soon after the wedding, the ambitious Darnley demanded royal authority. When the Queen refused to yield to his demands, he had her secretary, David Riccio, assassinated right in front of her. Mary, five months pregnant at the time, turned on Darnley and accused him of trying to murder her and their unborn child by inducing a miscarriage, so that he might be the sole ruler. Otherwise, why was the attack made right in front of her? Riccio could have been killed somewhere else. Darnley had no sufficient answer. Three months later Mary gave birth to a son whom she named James. Although he would be baptized a Catholic, he would be taken from his mother at an early age and raised a Protestant.

The Earl of Bothwell then resolved to replace Darnley and take the throne. He murdered Darnley and forced Queen Mary to marry him in a Protestant ceremony. The Lords of the Congregation instantly began the rumor that Mary Stuart had agreed to Lord Darnley's murder in order to marry Bothwell. Their leader, the Earl of Moray, assumed the regency. At the same time he proclaimed Mary and Darnley's son, James VI, King of Scotland. Bothwell fled to Norway where his creditors arrested him. They took him to Denmark where they imprisoned him. He died in prison. The Queen's supporters rose to her defense, but were defeated in battle, and the Queen was also thrown into prison. Eleven months later, in early May 1568, loyal followers helped her escape.

In May 1568, Mary faced the most critical decision of her life. She could return to France where her relatives could protect her, or she could travel to England and try to gain the support of Queen Elizabeth, her cousin whom she had never met. History will probably never be able to explain why she chose to walk into the lion's den. Her family could protect her, though she likely would never have been Queen of Scotland again. Elizabeth, though Mary did not realize it, was her deadliest enemy. Mary fled to England where she sought assistance and asylum with Elizabeth, who promptly cast her into prison. In February 1587, after nineteen years of captivity, Mary was put to death based on false charges.

English Jesuit Alex Briant is martyred, December 2, 1581.

The Survival of Catholicism in England: Seminaries and Missions

In 1570, Pope Pius V excommunicated Queen Elizabeth I. Parliament retaliated with the treason laws, declaring those who obeyed the Pope criminals. At the same time it voted to seize the property of all English Catholics who had fled England and sought refuge across the Channel. Meanwhile the refugees began to organize. John Allen, the former headmaster at St. Mary's College, Oxford, was convinced that the English people had given up the Faith only through force. He felt that preaching would restore them to the Catholic faith. He established a seminary to educate and train English priests at Douay, under the protection of King Philip II of Spain. This college, which moved to Reims as the result of the revolt in Holland, played an important role in the religious and literary history of English Catholics. It trained a number of priests for the English missions, many of whom died for the Faith.

Persecution of the Puritans under King James I

Queen Elizabeth I died in 1603. James VI, the King of Scotland, and Mary Stuart's son, succeeded her. The two kingdoms of England and Scotland were thus brought under one ruler, who took the name of James I (1603-1625). One of the first tasks confronting the new king was the problem of the Puritans. These Protestants called themselves Puritans because their goal was to "purify" Anglican worship of any Catholic remnant. They essentially were strict English Calvinists. Elizabeth had dealt severely with them. She imprisoned or exiled them if they would not accept the Anglican religion.

James was no more willing than Elizabeth had been to deal gently with the Puritans. Unable to obtain satisfaction for the persecutions they had endured under Queen Elizabeth, they allied themselves with Parliament and the nobility against James. The result was another persecution. James had about three hundred Puritan ministers exiled from the kingdom. Among those expelled were the American Pilgrim Fathers.

The Gunpowder Plot

While King of Scotland, James had given assurances of tolerance to the Catholics, to win them to his side. However, as King of England, it was not long before he began persecuting the Church. James felt that Catholicism was dangerous because it claimed the right to guide, judge, and even depose civil rulers. The discontent of English Catholics reached its climax when King James, upset at the number of conversions made by priests who had returned to England, started a persecution. In 1604, he ordered all Jesuits out of the country and imposed more restrictive laws against Catholics. By 1605, it was clear to every Englishman that James would persecute the Church just as vigorously as Elizabeth had.

This was the background for the conspiracy known as the "Gunpowder Plot." The purpose of the conspirators was to place thirty-six barrels of gunpowder in the cellar under the Houses

King James I of England

of Parliament. They intended to blow up the King, his son, and Parliament. Though the plotters were horribly misguided, they were committed Catholics who had lived for forty-five years under terrible persecution. They had no prospect of a future in which the Catholic faith could be openly practiced. Nevertheless, it was an act of pure terrorism. It would brand English Catholics as revolutionaries and murderers. Rather than making the situation better and ending the persecutions, it would make them much, much worse.

The plot was discovered. Its leader, Robert Catesby, and eight of his friends, were condemned to death. Another plotter, Guy Fawkes, who had been chosen to explode the bomb, was caught actually carrying gunpowder into the cellar. Catholicism in England was effectively crippled for the next three hundred years. The Faith would be linked for three centuries to the plot. Every November 5, until the twentieth century, Protestant English men and women celebrated Guy Fawkes Day the way Americans celebrate the Fourth of July.

The Conflict between Anglo-Catholicism and Puritanism

James I was succeed by his son Charles I (1625-1649). He had no feelings against Catholicism. In fact, his wife, whom he loved very much, was a Catholic. However, Parliament became more hostile towards Catholics. They even accused Charles of apostasy for not attacking Catholicism strongly enough. They demanded that, in order to get rid of Catholicism completely, the children of Catholics be raised as Protestants. To clear himself of charges of apostasy, Charles I was

King Charles I, Queen Henrietta Maria, and their children

forced at times to employ harsh measures against Catholics. In general, however, the position of Catholics improved during his reign. Their taxes were reduced and they were allowed to attend Mass in their homes.

At this point the English Puritans allied themselves with the Scottish Presbyterians, who also had grievances against both Charles and his dead father. For several years Charles waged war against the Scots and the English Puritans. Sadly, by January 1647, he had been utterly defeated. In August, a Puritan army lead by Oliver Cromwell occupied London and took control of the government. Oliver Cromwell was now the ruler of England. He had Charles tried and condemned to death. Charles was beheaded January 30, 1649.

Oliver Cromwell

Since the summer of 1647, the Puritan dictator Oliver Cromwell had ruled England. This extraordinary man gradually rose from a country gentleman to become the dictator of the three kingdoms of England, Scotland, and Ireland. Of the same family as Thomas Cromwell, Henry VIII's minister, Oliver became a Puritan at the age of forty. Sadly for the history of the Church, especially the Church in Ireland, he was the greatest military leader of the time. He also had the wealth of England supporting him. He had a deep hatred for two things: Catholicism and the Irish.

In August 1649, Cromwell landed with his army in Ireland for the express purpose of destroying the Catholic Church there. He first attacked the city of Drogheda. He captured the city and slaughtered its 3,500 citizens, including women and children. Sadly, the massacre of Drogheda set the pattern he was to follow throughout the island. For the next two years he swept over Ireland like a demonic plague murdering the Irish.

In 1651 he returned to England to a hero's welcome. For the next seven years he ruled England and defended her from various opponents, notably the Scots. In September 1658, Oliver Cromwell died. He was one of the greatest enemies the Catholic Church had ever known.

England after Cromwell

There has never been a military dictatorship in England, with the exception of Cromwell, and he was a unique man. After his death, the English people wanted to restore the monarchy. Charles II, the son of Charles I, restored official Anglicanism to its original position in England. He tried, without success, to suspend the laws against Catholics. His successor, James II, the last Catholic English monarch, sadly displayed more zeal than good judgment in trying to assert the rights of Catholicism. His attempts to create religious liberty for his people went against the wishes of Parliament. In 1688, Parliament deposed him. He was replaced, not by his Catholic son James, but by his Protestant daughter Mary and her husband William III. The reign of William III and Mary began a period of religious tolerance among the Protestant sects, in which Catholics would eventually be included.

The Church in Ireland

Despite the best efforts of the English, Ireland had never been completely conquered by them. The more the English persecuted them, the more loyal to the Church they became. Heroic priests, educated in seminaries abroad, cared for their spiritual needs. Under Elizabeth I, six bishops and hundreds of the clergy suffered martyrdom. Oliver Cromwell massacred the Irish and destroyed their towns. He drove the Irish into that part of the island that lies west of the River Shannon. All the territory to the east was given to the Protestants.

The last Irish martyr to die was St. Oliver Plunkett (1629-1681). St. Oliver was the Archbishop of Armagh and the Primate of Ireland. Despite the English persecutions, he continued to perform his duties. However, they finally arrested him. The English tried him for treason and falsely convicted him. On July 1, 1681, he was dragged behind a horse to Tyburn. There he was hanged, drawn, and quartered. Pope Paul VI canonized him in 1975.

In 1690, during the reign of William and Mary, the Irish revolted against their English oppressors. Once again the English attempted to wipe out the Irish and destroy the Faith. Catholics were deprived of all religious and civil rights. Children were offered their parents' land if they became Protestants, and were allowed to take possession of it even while their parents were living.

Shrine of St. Oliver Plunkett in Drogheda

Catholics were forbidden to buy land or build schools. The English offered a reward to anyone who revealed a priest's hiding place. They shipped twenty thousand Irish men and women to America as indentured servants.

Despite the massive persecutions, the Irish held staunchly to the Faith. The work of St. Patrick and the early monks had indeed been well done. The Faith was too deeply rooted to be torn, or burned, or gouged out of the hearts of the people. The Irish exiles became the messengers of the Gospel in other lands. As in earlier years, when Irish missionaries had carried the Faith and learning to all the countries of Europe, so now, driven from home by fire and sword, Irish immigrants carried the Faith across the sea to the lands where they found peace and refuge.

Calvinism Spreads to France

Although France was a Catholic country, a number of high-ranking people embraced Calvinism. The real ruler of France at this time was Catherine de Medici (1519-1589), the widow of King Henry II and the mother of a son too young to rule. In 1559, she had become the ruler of France after the accidental death of her husband. Although she was a good Catholic, the Calvinist revolutionaries frightened her. She sought to make peace with them. However, it is in the nature of the revolutionary never to make peace. Thus, Calvinism continued to spread throughout France. In 1561, a Calvinist service was conducted in Paris and attended by more than 6,000 people. On March 1, 1562, the first of six religious wars broke out in France. They were to last for the next thirty-two years.

In 1572, Catherine decided that the only way to end the ten years of religious warfare in France was to marry her daughter Marguerite to Henry of Navarre, a Calvinist prince. On August 18, Catherine had them married, despite Pope Gregory XIII's (1572-1585) refusal to grant a dispensation for the wedding. Great crowds flocked to Paris for the ceremony, among them about two thousand Calvinists. The Calvinist leader in France was Admiral Gaspard Coligny, whom Catherine both feared and hated. On the morning of August 22, she attempted to have him assassinated. She failed. The attempt would trigger even greater violence.

There were thousands of Calvinists still in Paris who had attended the wedding. The situation became increasingly dangerous for everyone. Catherine and her son, King Charles IX, believed that the Calvinists planned to kill them in revenge for the attempt on Coligny's life. Before they could be attacked, they decided to kill Coligny and about thirty of the Calvinist leaders. It was August 23, the eve of St. Bartholomew's Day. While the plan had been to kill only the leaders, the violence soon spread. The Catholic mob, hearing that there was a plan to kill the king and thinking the king had ordered them to attack, killed every Calvinist they could, including women and children. The mob killed more than two thousand people.

After the massacre, Catherine sent word to all the rulers of Europe, including the Pope. She told them that the massacre had been necessary because a plot had been discovered to kill the King. Having no other information, Pope Gregory believed her. He had a solemn hymn of gratitude sung in Rome, not for the death of the Calvinists, but for the safe delivery of the royal family. Nevertheless, the fact of the massacre horrified him. He would only later learn all the facts.

The evil that men do lives after them; the good is often interred with their bones. King Charles IX died in May 1574 of tuberculosis. His brother, Henry III, succeeded him on the throne. He reigned for fifteen years but had no children. In August 1589, he fell victim to an assassin's dagger. As he lay dying, he called his brother-in-law, Henry of Navarre, to his bedside and recognized him as his successor. Henry was born and raised a Calvinist, although he became a Catholic in July 1593. In 1598, he issued the Edict of Nantes, which guaranteed full liberty of conscience and toleration to the Calvinists. Nevertheless, for the next fifteen years of his life Henry was actively and visibly Catholic. Had Henry reverted to Calvinism, France may very well have been lost to the Faith. For now at least, France had been saved for the Church.

Calvinism in Holland

At the time of the Protestant revolt, Holland was the wealthiest country in Europe.   Calvinism did not have much success in Holland during the lifetime of Emperor Charles V, who had been born in Holland. When he abdicated, he placed Holland under the rule of his son, Philip II of Spain. During Philip's reign, the Calvinists spread rumors about Philip, who was born and raised in Spain. Notably, the Calvinists said that he would introduce the Spanish Inquisition into Holland, something Philip had no intention of doing. As a result of the rumors, the populace become fearful and suspicious of Phillip. In August 1566, the people of Holland, under Prince William of Orange, revolted against the lawful rule of King Philip. They declared themselves independent of Philip and Spain. The war with Spain would rage off and on until 1648.

During the first few weeks of the Dutch revolt, mobs of Calvinist revolutionaries swept over Holland. They roamed the land, plundering churches, and persecuting the clergy, monks, and nuns. On August 20, 1566, almost all the religious images and paintings in Antwerp's forty-two churches were destroyed. In Ghent, Brussels, Utrecht, and Amsterdam the Calvinists destroyed thousands of art treasures. Of Holland's major cities, only the churches in Bruges were defended.

Of all the men and women who died for the Faith during the Dutch Revolt, one group deserves special mention. On July 9, 1572, at Gorkum, seventeen priests and two lay brothers were martyred. They were cruelly mutilated and hanged in a shed for refusing to deny the

Real Presence of Our Lord in the Blessed Sacrament and the Supremacy of the Pope. Pius IX canonized them June 29, 1865.

In 1567, Philip II sent an army under the Duke of Alba to suppress the revolt. Sadly, he was not completely successful. Spain succeeded in regaining the ten southern provinces, modern day Belgium, and these returned to the Catholic Faith. The northern seven provinces, modern day Holland (or the Netherlands) remained in the hands of the Calvinists. The Catholic cathedrals in present-day Belgium are beautiful works of art. One of the most stunning is the cathedral in Antwerp, which is filled with paintings by the great artist Peter Paul Rubens. The Protestant cathedrals in the Netherlands resemble nothing so much as giant whitewashed barns, lacking any art or beauty, but which were once treasure houses of Catholic art.

Queen Christina of Sweden

In all of European history, no monarch has ever given up the crown for the Faith—with one exception.

The most aggressively Protestant country in Europe at this time was Sweden. In Sweden simply being a Catholic meant death or exile. (Other countries only imposed these penalties on priests.) Yet it was from Sweden that one of the most amazing conversions in all of history occurred, that of Queen Christina of Sweden.

Christina ascended the throne of Sweden in 1644, at the age of 18. A young woman of extraordinary intellectual gifts, the more she considered the official Lutheranism of Sweden, the less she liked it. She knew that if she became a Catholic, she would either be removed from, or have to abdicate, the throne. She did not flinch from the prospect.

In October 1649, the philosopher Rene Descartes came to Sweden to instruct her. From Descartes she learned that truth was more valuable than a crown. In July 1650, the Portuguese ambassador arrived in Sweden with a Jesuit priest. Christina soon began talking to the priest about the Faith. By the summer of 1652, she had decided to become a Catholic and abdicate. On June 9, 1654, she gave up her throne. That night she traveled in disguise to Antwerp in Catholic Belgium. On Christmas Eve she professed her Catholic Faith, attended Midnight Mass, and received the Holy Eucharist.

She planned to travel to Rome where she would spend the rest of her life. One year later on December 23, Pope Alexander VII received her in Rome. She died in 1689 and is buried in St. Peter's Basilica.

Review Exercises

1. Who was John Knox?
2. What was the Gunpowder Plot?
3. Who was Oliver Cromwell?
4. What did Oliver Cromwell do in Drogheda?
5. Who was the last Catholic monarch of England?
6. Who was Catherine de Medici?
7. What was the Edict of Nantes of 1598?
8. Who lead the Dutch revolt against Spain?
9. What is unique about Queen Christina of Sweden?
10. Where would you go if you wanted to visit the tomb of Queen Christina of Sweden?

CHAPTER 24

THE CATHOLIC REVIVAL OF THE 17ᵀᴴ AND 18ᵀᴴ CENTURIES

St. Vincent de Paul cares for the poor in 17th century France.

The Evangelization of the People: St. Vincent de Paul

As a result of the bitter conflicts waged during the sixteenth century, many old religious practices had disappeared. In the remote

348

country districts, conditions were at their worst. Ignorance of the Faith and lack of care in practicing it were widespread. Among the men and women who dedicated their lives to fixing this situation, St. Vincent de Paul occupies a prominent place.

St. Vincent was born in 1580 to a poor family of shepherds. At a young age, his family realized that he had a great gift so every sacrifice was made to help him to become a priest. He worked his way through college and in 1600, became a priest. At first his life as a priest was not particularly zealous. However, in 1605, Vincent had an incredible ordeal that changed his life forever. While on a sea voyage, Moslem pirates captured Vincent and took him to Tunis where they sold him into slavery. His owner was an apostate Christian. Vincent converted him, and both escaped to France in 1607. He then traveled to Rome where he continued his studies for two years. Upon his return to France, he became chaplain to Queen Margaret of Valois.

In 1613, Count Emmanuel de Gondi, commander of the royal galleys and brother of the Archbishop of Paris, chose Vincent to tutor his son, the future Cardinal de Retz. While engaged in this work, Vincent became acquainted with the Countess de Gondi. Saddened at the sight of the spiritual misery of her tenants, she begged Vincent to preach missions to them and evangelize the poor on the Count's estates. His success in this work gave Vincent the idea of founding an order of priests especially tasked to teach and assist the poor in the country districts. They would go from village to village, and instruct, exhort, and catechize the poor. This is the origin of the Society of the Priests of the Mission. Pope Urban VIII approved the society in 1632. Since the headquarters of the Society was the priory of St. Lazarus in Paris, the members were sometimes called Lazarists. They are now usually called Vincentians.

In seventeenth century France, charitable care of the poor was completely disorganized. St. Vincent knew that there needed to be some organized system to give aid to the poor and the unfortunate. Otherwise, the undeserving might benefit at the expense of the truly needy. Therefore, in 1633, he and St. Louise de Marillac founded the Sisters of Charity. This was a community of women whose purpose was to see that relief was given in a just and orderly way. He himself recruited their members and supervised their training. When St. Vincent de Paul died in 1660, the poor of Paris lost their best friend. Humanity lost one of its greatest saints. Owing to the interest which he aroused for the poor and the sick, many religious orders have since been founded for their care and relief.

St. Francis de Sales

The other giant of the Faith of this period was St. Francis de Sales, the Bishop of Geneva. St. Francis de Sales was born in 1567. He attended a Jesuit college and then studied law at the University of Padua, where he received his degree in 1592. He was about to be appointed to the senate and marry a lovely noblewoman when he declared his intention to become a priest. Although his family objected, he would not be swayed from his decision. In 1593, he was ordained.

From the time of the Protestant Revolt, the See of the Bishop of Geneva had been located at Annecy. As we have seen, the Protestants ruled Geneva. At Annecy, Father de Sales devoted himself to preaching, hearing confessions, and ministering to the people. Risking his life, he journeyed through the entire area, which was under the control of the Calvinists, preaching constantly. By his learning, kindness, and holiness, he converted many.

In 1602, at the age of thirty-five, St. Francis was made Bishop of Geneva. As Bishop he immediately instituted instruction in the catechism for the faithful, both young and old. He crafted wise rules to guide his priests. He visited the parishes scattered through the rugged mountains of his diocese and reformed the religious communities. He heard confessions, gave advice, and preached continually. St. Francis believed that the Church would never prosper unless the laity was directed into paths of holiness. The saintly Bishop of Geneva was instrumental in bringing more than 70,000 Calvinists back to the Church. These fallen away Catholics were drawn to him by his holy virtues and self-sacrifice. To help people to sanctify their souls, St. Francis, in addition to his sermons, wrote two simple little books on the spiritual life.

St. Francis de Sales had a great friend, the widow, St. Jane Frances de Chantal. He was her spiritual adviser. In 1607, they founded the Institute of the Visitation of the Blessed Virgin. This was an order for young girls and widows who, feeling themselves called to

St. Francis de Sales gives the rule for the Visitation Order to St. Jane Frances de Chantal.

the religious life, lacked the strength or inclination for the physical austerities of the great orders. The purpose of this community was to visit the poor and the sick in their homes. Later this community departed from its original purpose and devoted itself to prayer and contemplation.

St. Francis de Sales died in 1622. Pope Alexander VII canonized him in 1665. In 1877, Pope Pius IX proclaimed him a Doctor of the Church.

Devotion to the Sacred Heart

The most important spiritual event in the closing years of the seventeenth century was a further development in the devotion to the Sacred Heart of Jesus. This devotion was not new. St. Bernard, St. Gertrude, and St. Bonaventure had encouraged it during the Middle Ages. The privilege of extending it to the world at large was granted to a Visitation nun, St. Margaret Mary Alacocque. Our Lord appeared to her in 1674. He requested that His Heart, "encircled by a crown of thorns, surrounded by flames, and surmounted by a cross," be honored and its picture exposed. He also asked for a worship of love and penance, to be expressed by Communion on the first Fridays and by the Holy Hour. The Sacred Heart, therefore, demanded public worship. In 1689, Our Lord declared that His Heart wished "to reign in the palace of the king, and be painted on his standards and his arms."

St. Margaret Mary Alacocque worked untiringly to spread this beautiful devotion. Her confessor, the Jesuit priest, St. Claude de la Columbiere, aided her. St. Claude served for a few years as chaplain to the Duchess of York, the future Queen of England. The English imprisoned him during the reign of Charles II. Being a French subject, the English forced Claude to return to France rather than killing him.

He died in 1682. Margaret Mary died in 1690. Pope Benedict XV canonized her in 1920.

Catholic Art and Architecture

During the seventeenth century, Catholic art and architecture began to flourish once more. A new style of art emerged and became popular. It is called "Baroque," and its greatest supporters were the Jesuits. The Church had decided at this time that the arts should communicate religious themes more directly and create an emotional involvement in the viewer. Baroque art had an exuberance and joy about it. Baroque churches were covered in pictures painted in bright and glorious colors. Even the ceiling had paintings on it, oftentimes showing the Ascension or the Assumption. The walls glittered with gold leaf. There were beautifully carved pillars, pulpits, and choir lofts. Everywhere there were paintings of angels and saints. The Baroque was the answer to the iconoclasm of the Calvinists, who destroyed beautiful art and images. Baroque art drew the people into the churches and still does. In a way, the Baroque style seemed to tell the people that in spite of her suffering, the Church had survived, and the Truth she taught had been victorious.

The artist most responsible for Baroque art is Michelangelo Merisi da Caravaggio. (1571-1610). To the art of painting he introduced intense emotion, the dramatic use of lighting, and a realistic naturalism based on close physical observation. From 1600 until his death, he was the most sought after painter in the world. Sadly, he lived a very immoral personal life. This evil lifestyle led to his untimely death. Nevertheless, he influenced a generation of painters who followed him. He is widely regarded as one of the greatest painters in European history.

The greatest painter of the Baroque age and one of the greatest painters in all of art history was Peter Paul Rubens (1577-1640). Rubens numbered the Jesuits among his best clients. Rubens, and his workshop, painted more than two thousand paintings during his lifetime. He was active not only in his native Belgium, but also Italy, Spain, and England. A master of the grandiose, he excelled in painting figures that seem larger than life. His Last Judgment is a gigantic canvas worthy of Michelangelo. Every large museum anywhere in the world has at least a few of his works. His paintings are considered the most valuable of the "Old Masters."

Peter Paul Rubens, *Self-portrait*

In Calvinistic Holland flourished Rembrandt (1606-1669). He is also one of the finest and most inventive painters of all times. By a clever manipulation of light and shadow, he obtained effects that are nothing short of fairy-like. He could depict the serenity of Christ, as in the *Supper at Emmaus"* with just as much ease as the surprise on the face of Belshazzar (Baltasar) and his party guests, as in his *The Feast of Balshazzar.*

Spain was blessed with two incredible Baroque painters: Diego Velazquez (1599-1669) and Bartolomé Esteban Murillo (1618-1682). Velazquez was the court painter for King Philip IV. However, he also did several religious paintings. Among his most notable are *The Coronation of Mary* and the *Adoration of the Magi*. He is counted among the best painters of all time.

Bartolomé Esteban Murillo (1618-1682) was born in Seville, the youngest son in a family of fourteen. In 1642, he traveled to Madrid where he met Velazquez, also a native of Seville. Velazquez welcomed his young compatriot and gave him access to the royal galleries. There, Murillo was able to see great works of art. He lived in Madrid for three years before returning to Seville where he spent the rest of his life. In contrast to Velazquez, Murillo's body of work consists almost entirely of religious paintings. With the exception of a few portraits and some paintings of street urchins and flower girls, he created very few secular pictures. He is most well known for his wonderful Madonnas and is considered the world's foremost painter of the Immaculate Conception. (Devotion to the Immaculate Conception was probably more popular in Spain than in any other European country.) Murillo treated this theme more than twenty times without repeating himself.

In France, Nicholas Poussin (1594-1665) was the leading artist of the seventeenth century. As a young artist he worked in Rome. In 1640, King Louis XIII asked him to be official court painter and he returned to Paris. However, after only two years he returned to Rome where he spent the rest of his life. He created a tremendous number of paintings, many of them religious. Among his most famous religious works are a series of paintings on the Sacraments, *The Holy Family Arrives in Egypt*, and the *Adoration of the Golden Calf*.

The Immaculate Conception of El Escorial, by Murillo

Christian Music

The eighteenth century was the golden age of music. It gave us such illustrious musicians as Johann Sebastian Bach (1685-1750), a Lutheran. During his life he created a tremendous body of work. He is regarded as the greatest composer of the Baroque age. His *St. Matthew Passion* is considered by many to be the finest piece of church music ever written. He is counted the greatest composer ever to have lived. Late in the twentieth century an eminent NASA scientist was asked what message we should send into space. He said that we should send the complete works of Bach, but if we did, we would be bragging.

Another great composer of the time was George Frederick Handel (1685-1759). He was also a Protestant. He composed lengthy pieces, which reproduce many poetical scenes of the Bible: the Israelites in Egypt, Samson, and Joshua. His two great masterpieces are *Judas Machabaeus* and "the Hallelujah" of the *Messiah*. The latter depicts in the most intense music the enthusiasm of the Christians singing the praises of the risen Christ.

Catholic composer Wolfgang Amadeus Mozart (1756-1791) was another of the great classic composers of the time. During his short life he wrote over six hundred pieces of music. He was only thirty-four when he died. His famous *Requiem* Mass is regarded as the high point of German Church music. Written in 1791, it was his last and one of his most popular works.

THE THIRTY YEARS' WAR 1618-1648

The peace that the Protestant and Catholic princes had made in 1555 at Augsburg did not last. In fact it had never really existed at all. From the Peace of Augsburg in 1555, until the outbreak of the Thirty Years War in 1618, Germany was in a constant state of unrest from the

Attack near Dachau in the Thirty Years' War

underlying religious conflict. Although the Catholics, Lutherans, and Calvinists never formally fought a religious war, the sides were so utterly opposed to each other that a full-blown religious war was inevitable. Gradually, what began as a German war developed into a wider conflict that involved many of the other European powers.

The Defenestration of Prague

By the start of the seventeenth century the Holy Roman Empire was a fragmented group of mostly independent states. The position of the emperor had become largely symbolic. However, the emperors did directly rule Austria, Bohemia, and Hungary. For years the Hungarian nobles had been unhappy under Hapsburg rule. Their struggle against the Hapsburgs reached its climax during the last years of the reign of Emperor Rudolph II (1576-1612).

In 1607, the Protestant nobles in Hungary revolted. They forced Rudolph to give the thrones of Hungary and Austria to his brother Matthias. Matthias was willing to grant religious freedom to the Protestants in Hungary and Austria. In 1608, he became King of Hungary.

In 1612, Rudolph died and Matthias became Emperor (1612-1619). However, Matthias had no children. By 1617, it was clear that Matthias, now also King of Bohemia, would die without an heir. Before he died, he wanted to be sure that there would be an orderly transition of the government, so he decided to have his nearest male relative elected to the thrones of Bohemia and Hungary. The relative was his cousin Archduke Ferdinand II of Austria, who was a devout Catholic. This made Ferdinand very unpopular in Protestant Bohemia. The Protestant leaders in Bohemia were afraid that they might lose the religious rights granted to them by Rudolf II. They preferred a Protestant king. Nevertheless, in 1617, the Bohemian nobility duly elected Ferdinand the Crown Prince. Moreover, when Matthias died, they made Ferdinand the King of Bohemia.

In May 1618, Ferdinand sent two Catholic representatives to Prague to administer the government in his absence. Bohemian rebels suddenly seized them and threw them out of the palace window, some fifty feet above the ground. They were miraculously saved when they landed in a pile of horse manure. This event, known as the Defenestration of Prague, started the Thirty Years War. The weakness of both the Emperor Ferdinand and of the Bohemians caused the war to spread to western Germany. Ferdinand had to call on his nephew, King Philip IV of Spain. Philip sent an army to support the Emperor. The Bohemians, desperate for allies against the Emperor, appealed to the German Protestants.

The War Spreads

A Catholic army, under the command of General John Tilly, a devout Catholic over the age of sixty, pacified Upper Austria. At the same time the Emperor's forces pacified Lower Austria. The two armies united and moved north into Bohemia. Tilly decisively defeated the Protestants at the Battle of White Mountain, near Prague, on November 8, 1620. This victory restored the Faith in Bohemia. In Rome, Pope Paul V gave thanks for the victory.

Meanwhile, in France, a sinister figure was moving onto history's stage. Louis XIII (1601-1643) had become King of France in 1610, following his father's assassination. However, the real ruler of France was Cardinal Armand Richelieu (1585-1642). He was a man with no principles. Consecrated a bishop in 1608, he had astonishing personal ambition. Once bishop, he lusted to be Cardinal. In 1622, he obtained the red hat. In August 1624, he became Prime Minister of France. His goal was to make France the greatest power in the world, no matter the cost. To that end, he worked time and again with the

Cardinal Richelieu

Calvinists against fellow Catholics. In the history of the Church, no other churchman worked so diligently against the Church. Sadly, he was almost always successful.

In Rome, Pope Paul V died in 1621. Pope Gregory XV (1621-1623) succeeded him. In his brief pontificate Gregory supported the Catholic armies, the Emperor, and the Jesuits in France. In 1623, Pope Urban VIII (1623-1644) succeeded him. Urban tried to end the Thirty Years War. In spite of his long reign, he was unable to do so.

Denmark Enters the War

Despite the victory at White Mountain, peace did not last long in the Empire. Denmark resumed the war. Danish involvement began when her Lutheran King Christian IV, helped the Lutheran rulers of neighboring Lower Saxony by leading an army against the Imperial forces. Denmark feared that the recent Catholic successes threatened its existence as a Protestant nation. France and England gave Denmark money to aid her war effort.

To fight Denmark and its allies, Emperor Ferdinand II enlisted the military aid of Albrecht von Wallenstein. Wallenstein was a Catholic Bohemian nobleman with a large army. Although he was a Catholic, he was a dedicated astrologer (a practice condemned by the Church). As a result, Ferdinand did not fully trust him. The combined forces of Wallenstein and Tilly forced King Christian to retreat. In 1626, Wallenstein and Tilly each defeated Protestant armies in battle. However, unable to invade and conquer Denmark, Wallenstein decided to make peace. The peace treaty stated that Christian IV could keep control of Denmark but had to abandon his support for the Protestant German states.

Over the next two years the Catholics won more victories and took control of more territory. At this point, the Catholics in Germany convinced Ferdinand to take back the property that had been taken from the Catholic Church since 1555. According to the Peace of Augsburg, this land rightfully belonged to the Catholic Church. Over 500 churches and monasteries were involved. The decree issued by Ferdinand was called the Edict of Restoration. It was remarkably effective. In 1630, six Catholic dioceses were reestablished in Germany along with about two hundred monasteries and convents. The Protestants were furious but helpless. Without outside support there was nothing that they could do.

Sweden Enters the War

Sadly, at this moment in history the greatest general of the age was a Protestant. He was also the king of Sweden, Gustavus Adolphus. Young, determined, and incredibly able, Adolphus had everything he needed to help the German Lutherans, but one thing: money. Sweden was a small, poor country. He needed somebody to pay for the war. Cardinal Richelieu was that person. In January 1631, Catholic France signed an alliance with Protestant Sweden to subsidize their war effort against Catholic Germany. For the next four years, Swedish-led armies drove back the Catholic forces. The Swedes regained much of the territory the Protestants had lost.

In 1631, at the Battle of Breitenfeld, the army of Gustavus Adolphus defeated the Catholic army led by General Tilly. In December 1631, Pope Urban wrote to the King and Queen of France and to Richelieu. He begged them to stop aiding the Swedish and the Protestants in Germany. His letter fell on deaf ears. The next year, the now seventy-three year old Tilly, who commanded his army from his deathbed, met Adolphus in battle for the final time. The Swedish King was victorious. With the steadfast Tilly dead, Ferdinand II had to call again upon the untrustworthy Wallenstein.

Wallenstein and Adolphus clashed in the Battle of Lützen in 1632, one of the most important military turning points in the history of the world. The Swedes prevailed. However, Adolphus was killed while leading a cavalry charge. In 1634, the Protestant forces, lacking Adolphus' military genius, were defeated at the Battle of Nördlingen. The following year the two sides signed a peace treaty at Prague. However, this treaty failed to satisfy the ambitious Richelieu, because it did not weaken Spain or Germany enough. France then openly entered the war. Richelieu declared war on Spain in May 1635, and on the Holy Roman Empire in August 1636.

The Battle of Lützen and the death of Gustavus Adolphus

France in the War and Peace

The first French military efforts met with disaster. The Spanish then counter-attacked, invading French territory. The Hapsburg forces won several victories and even threatened Paris in 1636 before being repulsed back towards the borders of France. Widespread fighting ensued, with neither side gaining an advantage. In 1642, Cardinal Richelieu died. Although he lay in his grave, he had achieved his goal. France was the strongest country in Europe. It was also still Catholic despite all he had done. (Interestingly, Richelieu left most of his estate to St. Vincent de Paul.) A year later, Louis XIII died a holy death in the arms of St. Vincent, leaving his five-year-old son Louis XIV on the throne. His prime minister, Cardinal Jules Mazarin, began working to end the war.

The Peace of Westphalia finally ended the war in 1648. It was an epic moment in the history of the Church. From this moment forward,

Christendom would be permanently divided between Catholic and Protestant. All states that were Protestant in 1624, and all states that were Catholic in 1624, would remain so. Spain, previously the strongest country in Europe, was in decline. Germany was shattered into various small states. France was now the strongest nation in Europe and would remain so for nearly two hundred years.

Galileo

In the midst of this horrible conflict, the Church dealt with an issue that is still used to attack her even after almost four centuries. This is the matter of Galileo. In the early seventeenth century, Galileo had revived the Copernican notion that the earth revolved around the sun. At the time, the controlling theory was that the sun revolved around the earth. This was due to passages in the Bible that referred to the sun staying its course at the prayer of Joshua, and the earth as being ever immovable. Thus, a theory that said that the earth revolved around the sun was considered anti-Biblical and thus heretical.

In 1615, Galileo went to Rome to defend his position before certain members of the Inquisition. One member was Cardinal Robert Bellarmine. The Inquisition held that his system was scientifically false and anti-Scriptural, so he must cease teaching it as fact. They did not say he could not teach it as an hypothesis. In 1616, he agreed. Cardinal Bellarmine, who found Galileo's ideas interesting, even wrote to him encouraging him in his work.

In 1630, Galileo wrote a book called *Dialogue on the Two Great World Systems*. This book supported the idea that the earth revolved around the sun. In the book, Galileo made it clear that he considered the theory as absolutely true, not simply an hypothesis. He also made fun of opposing views. Also in his book he included some anti-Copernican comments that Pope Urban had made. Naturally, this made the Pope furious.

In August 1632, after the Jesuits had publicly criticized the *Dialogue*, Pope Urban set up a commission to examine it. On June 16, 1633, the Inquisition censured Galileo for advocating the view that the sun was the center of the universe as being contrary to Scripture. It forbade him from teaching the idea, even as a theory. It also banned his *Dialogue*. However, the ruling of the committee was disciplinary, not doctrinal. Galileo was convicted of disobedience for breaking his promise in 1616. He was not convicted nor punished for heresy. Neither Pope Urban, nor any other Pope, ever declared or taught as a matter of Faith that Galileo's theory was heretical, although Urban personally felt that it was not scientifically supported.

Review Exercises

1. Who helped St. Vincent de Paul found the Sisters of Charity?
2. Where was St. Francis de Sales bishop?
3. Who helped St. Francis de Sales found the Visitation Order?
4. Who is most responsible for spreading the devotion to the Sacred Heart?
5. Name three influential Baroque artists.
6. What was the Defenestration of Prague?
7. What was the Edict of Restitution?
8. Why was Galileo censured by the Inquisition?
9. Does the Galileo affair disprove papal infalliblity? Why or why not?

CHAPTER 25

THE CHURCH IN THE "AGE OF THE ENLIGHTENMENT"

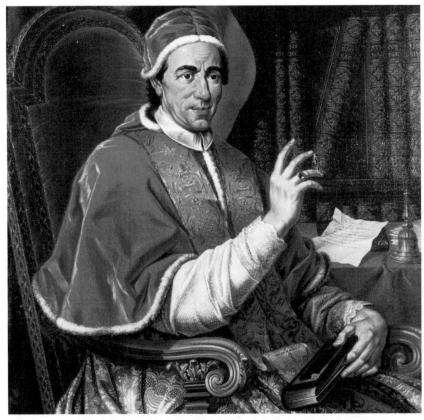

Pope Clement XIV, the Pope who Suppressed the Jesuits

The Rise of Rationalism

The leaders of the Protestant Revolt had taught the principle of "private judgment." This doctrine said that each individual Christian could interpret the Bible, and using their own reason, discover its meaning. This encouraged the boldest kind of religious guesswork. Before long, some people said that their reason told them that the Church was not necessary. They said that the human mind needed no guidance from Divine Grace. This way of thinking is called "Rationalism." During the seventeenth and eighteenth centuries it began to influence many of the leaders of European society. The movement that it started is called "The Enlightenment." The name came from its leaders. They claimed that clouds of superstition had kept the light of truth away from human minds, but now "the pure light of reason" had broken through and chased away the darkness that had been caused by religious faith. In other words, they falsely asserted that the truths of Catholic Church had kept men in darkness but now a new philosophy would enlighten them.

Rationalists refused to accept any authority in intellectual matters. They had no respect for Divine Revelation or the teachings of the Church. They also refused to respect public opinion or the laws of the State unless these agreed with their way of thinking. They had the highest confidence in human nature and its powers. They considered the doctrine of Original Sin absurd. Rationalists held that human beings would be good and find happiness if they were allowed to follow their own inclinations. They whole-heartedly embraced history's second oldest faith: Faith in Man. Sadly, this was a period where there was an overall decline in Catholic fervor and not many saints.

Deism

This new movement had its beginnings in England. There, a new idea of the relationship between God and the world was taught called "Deism." This new system of thought promoted belief in a personal God founded on reason alone, to the exclusion of revelation and authority. According to the Deists, God exists, but He has nothing to do with the world He created. After He made the world, He left it to itself and does not interfere in worldly affairs. God can be compared to a watchmaker, who makes a watch but then leaves it to run on its own.

The Enlightenment in France

Voltaire

The ideas of the Rationalists were the most popular in France. They found a particularly strong following among the upper classes, whose lives had become very worldly. The great apostle of the French Enlightenment was Voltaire (1694-1778). He considered it his mission in life to destroy Christianity and the Catholic Church. His entire personality can be summarized in his favorite phrase, "Ecrasons l'Infame" ("Let us crush the infamous thing," that is, the Church). He ridiculed everything holy. He thought that by laughing at religion, he could destroy it.

There was also in France a small group of writers called "philosophes." They rallied around Voltaire and wrote articles expressing their materialistic and atheistic views on religion and philosophy. They published these in the main organ of French rationalism, the *Encyclopedia*. They regarded religion as a popular superstition. They hated the Church's firm stand in matters of doctrine and its strictness in the field of morality. The principal author of the Encyclopedia was Denis Diderot. His fervent wish was that "the last king might be strangled with the entrails of the last priest." The French Revolution was not far off.

The other influential French thinker of the Enlightenment was Jean Jacques Rousseau. Unlike Voltaire, Rousseau did not rant against Catholicism. However, he proposed many false ideas. He set forth his false doctrines about education and marriage in his novel, *Emile*. In his book, *Confessions,* he mocked morality. As he was an influential writer, this did much to lead public opinion astray and to lower moral standards. Many of the false notions about education that are taught in the world today can be traced back to Rousseau. Lastly, in his "Social Contract" he developed the political principle that the right to govern is derived, not from God, but solely from the people. This principle directly paved the way for the French Revolution. The Archbishop of Paris condemned Rousseau's ideas. He said that they destroyed the foundations of Christianity and taught a moral doctrine contrary to the Gospel.

The Attack on the Jesuits and on the Church

The Enlightenment was more than just a group of men gathered in rooms discussing philosophy. It was an attack on the Church. From their inception the Jesuits had been the Church's front line troops in their war against the Protestant Revolution. Moreover, they had been incredibly effective. The Jesuits, through their schools and missionaries had re-converted tens of thousands and brought them back into the Church. By the beginning of the seventeenth century they were running seven hundred colleges and over three hundred missions. They were also very influential, as Jesuit priests were the confessors to many of the rulers of Europe. If the enemies of the Faith were to be victorious, they needed to destroy the Jesuits. Voltaire once said "once we have destroyed the Jesuits we will have the game in our hands." Surprisingly, with the number of enemies the Jesuits had in France, the first attack launched against them was not in France, but in Portugal.

Portugal

At this time, the Marquis de Pombal governed Portugal. He was the prime minister for the weak King Jose I. Pombal was an enemy of the Church and of the Jesuits. He wanted to see both destroyed. Pombal began his attack by harassing the Jesuits. He forced them to resign as confessors to the King and the royal family. Unable to trump up any charges against them in Portugal, he turned his eyes in the direction of the colonies of Paraguay, where the Jesuits had established their famous reductions. In 1750 Pombal had signed a treaty with Spain. The treaty said that in exchange for the colony of San Sacramento, Portugal would receive the seven districts of Paraguay where the Jesuit reductions were located. Pombal thought the Jesuits had gold mines in the reductions. When the land exchange was completed, the Indians were forced to leave the reductions. They left, but during the harsh journey they rose in revolt and were suppressed. Pombal immediately laid the blame for their aggression at the door of the Jesuits.

On April 1, 1758, Pope Benedict XIV (1740-1758) began an investigation into the charges against the Jesuits. However, he died five weeks later. Meanwhile Pombal worked to destroy the Jesuits' reputation. Yielding to Pombal's insistence, the Archbishop of Lisbon

Pope Clement XIII

forbade the Jesuits to work within his jurisdiction. Before Clement XIII (1758-1769) had become pope on July 6, 1758, Pombal had achieved his goal. In the coming years the Jesuits in Portugal were arrested and imprisoned. In one of history's great ironies, after Pombal had fallen from power and been forsaken by his friends, he ended up dying in the arms of a Jesuit priest.

France

Meanwhile the enemies of the Jesuits in France were only waiting for an opportunity to imitate Pombal's example. It came in May 1761. Father Antoine La Valette was the superior of the Jesuit mission on the Caribbean island of Martinique. The mission there had an extensive commercial enterprise that became insolvent. Lavaliere's creditors at Marseilles demanded that the Jesuits in France reimburse them for their losses. The French Jesuits refused. They pointed out that there was no common ownership and no connection existed between the Jesuits in France and those in Martinique. Their argument was sound. The different houses of the Order were independent of one another. The resources of each house came from foundations established for local and fixed purposes. Nevertheless, the French Jesuits lost their case in the French courts, which held them liable with Father Lavaliere. The French Parliament then used the trial an excuse for a general investigation into the Society as a whole. The result of the investigation was a foregone conclusion. The Parliament declared that the Society of Jesus was illegal in France.

King Louis XV objected to Parliament's decision. For several months he sought to protect the Jesuits. However, on April 1, 1763, the order of Parliament went into effect. The government closed all Jesuit colleges in France. In March 1764, the Jesuits were required to renounce their vows or be banished. The fighting spirit of St. Ignatius Loyola was alive in the hearts of these noble priests—only a handful renounced their vows. In November 1764, King Louis unwillingly signed an edict dissolving the Order throughout French territory.

Spain

Two years later, the most Catholic country in Europe, Spain, struck at the Jesuits. The Jesuit Fathers believed that they had a friend in the devoutly Catholic King Charles III. However, his prime minister, the Count of Aranda, was their bitter enemy. Aranda succeeded in poisoning the King's mind against them by means of the infamous "Jesuit Letters." These letters were an abominable forgery, in which the Jesuits were accused of inciting rebellion against the government in an attempt to overthrow the king. On the night of April 2, 1767, Charles had all the Jesuits in his kingdom, about 6,000, placed under arrest and marched like convicts to the coast. Despite the protests of Pope Clement XIII, the government deported the Jesuits to the Papal States.

Ferdinand IV, the young king of Naples, followed the example of his father, Charles III of Spain. He suppressed the Society in his kingdom. A military escort conducted the Jesuits out of Naples to the Papal States.

Suppression of the Jesuits

Pressure was now brought to bear on Pope Clement XIII (1758-1769) by the kings of Europe who were members of the Bourbon dynasty. These rulers had made a pact to suppress the entire Society of Jesus. These kings and their emissaries harassed and insulted the Pope. They told him that unless he suppressed the Jesuits a great schism would occur. Despite these threats, Clement XIII energetically and gallantly refused to go along with their demands.

Pope Clement XIII died on February 2, 1769, after one of the most heroic pontificates in Church history. There was one question for discussion for the Cardinals in the conclave that met in 1769 to elect his successor. What would the new Pope do with the Jesuits? Although none of the Cardinals specifically promised to suppress the Jesuits, Cardinal Lorenzo Ganganelli made it known that if he were elected, the Bourbon rulers would have a friend on the throne of St. Peter. In May 1768, Ganganelli was elected Pope. He chose the name Clement XIV (1769-1774). It was an interesting choice for a man who hinted that he would suppress the Jesuits. The previous Clement had refused to suppress them. Meanwhile, the Bourbons waited.

In the history of the Papacy unworthy men have become Pope. However, the Chair of St. Peter does something to the soul of a man. The story of Pope Vigilius (537-555), the only anti-Pope to become Pope, is one remarkable example of a man who underwent a complete change of heart. Whatever Cardinal Ganganelli had promised, or seemed to promise to be elected, once he became Pope Clement XIV he took no action against the Jesuits. In fact, the more the kings of Europe pushed him to suppress them, the more strongly he refused. For four years he resisted every sort of pressure that was brought to bear as he negotiated for the life of the Society of Jesus.

Finally, in 1773, Charles III, the King of Spain, threatened to take Spain out of the Church unless Clement suppressed the Jesuits. This threat was pure bluff. The Spain of Ignatius of Loyola, Francis Xavier, and Teresa of Avila would never leave the Church. Spain was still the most Catholic country in Europe. It was the only country where the Protestant revolt had never made any headway. A great Pope might have had the strength to call the bluff, and over the next two hundred and thirty years the Church would be blessed with some of its finest Pontiffs (one Saint, two Blesseds, and one many call "the Great") but Clement was not the measure of these men.

In 1773, Pope Clement XIV issued the Brief of Suppression against the Jesuits, purposely omitting the customary clause *motu proprio* (of our own accord). The brief contained no charges against the Jesuits. It laid no blame on the Society, the personal conduct of its members, or the soundness of their teaching. The pope merely stated that "the Church could not enjoy true and lasting peace so long as the Society remained in existence." Basically, he suppressed the Jesuits for being divisive. The brief was published, and the bishops communicated its contents to the Jesuits of their dioceses.

Empress Catherine II of Russia did not publish the papal suppression in Russia, so the Jesuits in Russia continued to teach in the two colleges they had there. In 1778, Pope Pius VI (1774-1798) approved this situation. The Jesuits continued to recruit members in Russia. Thus the Society was never totally suppressed.

Pope Clement fell ill soon after he issued his decree. He said that he had cut off his right hand. He died on September 22, 1774. Following the issuance of the suppression decree, Voltaire felt he had won a great victory. He declared that in twenty years (1793), the Church would be no more. He was very nearly correct.

New Religious Orders

Fortunately, toward the end of Louis XV's reign, the life of the Church was strengthened by new teaching orders, whose influence was felt throughout the eighteenth century. A canon of the Cathedral of Reims, St. John Baptist de la Salle (1651-1714), was spiritual director of the Sisters of the Holy Child, an order founded for the teaching of poor girls. Later, he conceived the idea of founding an order of men who would render the same service to poor boys. He called the members of his congregation Brothers of the Christian Schools. The Christian Brothers, as we know this community, did glorious work in the cause of popular education. To prepare the members of the Order for a career in teaching, he founded the first teachers' college. He also worked out a system whereby a number of children could be taught in a class at the same time. St. John is rightly regarded as one of the founders of modern education.

St. Alphonsus Liguori (1696-1787) was born near Naples. He founded the Redemptorists (Congregation of the Most Holy Redeemer) to preach the Gospel and give spiritual direction to souls. The Order developed rapidly. When St. Alphonsus was crippled with arthritis and no longer able to carry on the work of preaching in town and country, he began his career as a writer. He was an authority on moral theology. His work on moral theology has gained for him a place among the Doctors of the Church.

St. Alphonsus Ligouri praying before the Blessed Sacrament

Review Exercises

1. What is Rationalism?
2. What is Deism?
3. Who was the great apostle of the French Enlightenment?
4. Who was Pombal?
5. What were the "Jesuit Letters?"
6. Which Pope suppressed the Jesuits?
7. Who founded the Christian Brothers?

CHAPTER 26

THE CHURCH DURING THE FRENCH REVOLUTION

Notre Dame Cathedral—the symbol of French Catholicism for over a thousand years. During the French Revolution it was subjected to terrible blasphemy.

What is a Revolution?

A Revolution is the destruction and uprooting of the basic foundations of human society. Unlike the American War for Independence, which sought to change the government, the French Revolution and the Communist Revolution in Russia in 1917, sought to change society. Changing the government was only a part of their goal. The great enemy of Revolution is the Catholic Church. This is because Revolution puts Man in the place of God. As such, Revolutionaries believe that anything that helps the Revolution to succeed is justified. That is why all Revolutions lead to Terrorism. Once a revolution has begun, unless it is destroyed quickly, a reign of terror is inevitable.

Modern Distortions about the French Revolution

The French Revolution was not inevitable. Modern secular historians teach that the uprising in France was spontaneous and driven by the overwhelming oppression of the people by the king and the nobility. They teach that the Paris prison, the Bastille, was filled with prisoners who were released when the mob stormed the Bastille. In actuality, it held seven prisoners. They claim that Queen Marie Antoinette was an empty-headed girl. As proof they claim that when she was told the people were starving and had no bread she said, "Then let them eat cake." She did not. (Actually it was the wife of Louis XIV, Marie's great-great grandmother who said it.) Marie was a devout Catholic and devoted mother who oppressed no one. As in most things involving the Church and the attacks upon her, her defenders are attacked, and her attackers are applauded. However, the actions of the French Revolutionaries are so heinous, that even those who "defend" them admit, "They went too far."

How the Revolution Began

France in the 1780s was a country with problems, but none so severe as to lead to a revolution. Before the Revolution, France had been at peace for six years. There was no famine or pestilence. Although there was not an overabundance of food, the people had enough to eat. The ideas of the Enlightenment, while somewhat popular amongst the nobility, had not really touched the common people. The common people were not clamoring for a change in religion. Unlike Voltaire and his cronies, they loved the Catholic Church. There was also no political group crying for an overthrow of the government, because there was no systematic oppression of the people. The problems with the government were mainly problems of neglect. Those in power were not doing their jobs very well. When people were oppressed it was more from omission than commission.

Still, France had problems. The Estates General, the national representative body, had not met in almost 175 years before it met in 1789. This shows that the government had lost contact with the people. Reform was needed. However, nothing in France's history can fully explain why its Revolution occurred. The only other event similar to the French Revolution is the Communist Revolution in Russia in 1917. However, in Russia in 1917, there was war, famine, pestilence, and a group calling for revolution.

Calling of the Estates General

By 1789, the French government was running out of money. Moreover, King Louis XVI had exhausted every means of obtaining enough money to run his government. On the advice of his finance minister he convoked the Estates General. Due to the nature of the

The first meeting of the Estates General, May 5, 1789.

French monarchy as shaped by Cardinal Richelieu, the Estates General had not met since 1614.

The Estates General consisted of three groups, or Estates. The First Estate was the entire clergy, which was divided into higher and lower clergy. At the time of Louis XVI, all the bishops of France were from the nobility, the Second Estate. The Third Estate was everyone else: the common people. Of the twelve hundred deputies elected to the Estates General, over half were from the Third Estate.

Each of the estates elected its own deputies. The local assemblies that selected the deputies also drew up *cahiers*, or grievance lists, to accompany the representative to Paris. The cahiers denounced absolute royal power, infringements on personal liberty, and unjust taxation. However, no complaint was made against the monarchy or the Church. The Estates General assembled on May 5, 1789, at the royal Palace at Versailles about twelve miles from Paris.

The National Assembly

Almost at once, the Third Estate began to demand fundamental changes in the government. They proposed to form a single assembly of the three-branch Estates General. The King, the nobles, and most of the clergy opposed this idea. The meetings became noisy debates as the Third Estate lurched from crisis to crisis.

In an attempt to regain control, the King locked the doors to the Hall where the Estates General had been meeting. The deputies of the Third Estate and its allies in the First and Second Estate moved to a nearby tennis court where they continued to meet. In late June 1789, they declared themselves to be a National Assembly. They said that they represented all the people. They swore not to disband until France had a new and written constitution. Although the king had troops to crush the National Assembly, he hesitated. After some of the nobles and clergy joined the Third Estate in the National Assembly, the King consented to its existence.

Storming the Bastille

Meanwhile, revolutionary agitators were active among the people of Paris. The agitators claimed the Bastille was full of innocent prisoners. In reality the Bastille contained only seven prisoners. A mob gathered before it on the morning of July 14. They stormed it and murdered its garrison and the Mayor of Paris. This grisly event marked the "triumph" of the Parisians over the authorities. It has since been celebrated in France as a national holiday.

Suppression of the Church

To the Revolutionaries, their most crucial job was to destroy "the infamous thing," the Catholic Church. In November 1789, the National Assembly seized the property of the Catholic Church. On November 2, the possessions of the Crown and the clergy were sold. In return for the money received from the sale of the stolen property, the state took on the task of supporting the Church and the clergy. They thus became the salaried employees of the state. In the spring of 1790, the monasteries, convents, and other religious houses were suppressed. The government sold their land and other possessions.

The next step was for the clergy to be deprived of their liberty. This was accomplished when the Assembly passed the "Civil Constitution of the Clergy." This document completely reorganized the Church in France. It granted all French citizens the right to elect bishops and pastors regardless of their religious affiliations. The priests of the parish were to have no say in the matter and the pope could not intervene in any way. On August 24, 1790, the Civil Constitution of the Clergy became law.

When Pope Pius VI (1775-1799) was presented with the Civil Constitution of the Clergy, he privately rejected it. This rejection caused the National Assembly to demand that all clergy in France take an oath to support it. In an act worthy of the descendants of Clovis and Clotilda, a substantial majority heroically refused. Only six of the 134 French bishops took the oath. The question of the

Pope Pius VI

oath split the Church of France into two factions. Those who took the oath were known as "jurors." Those who refused to take the oath were known as "non-jurors" (from the Latin, *jurare*, to take an oath).

In March 1791, Pope Pius VI publicly condemned the Civil Constitution of the Clergy. He prohibited priests from taking the oath. Many priests who had taken the oath retracted their promise after the Pope's public condemnation.

In November 1791, all the clergy were obliged to take the oath within eight days. If they declined they would lose their salaries and might be expelled from their parish. King Louis XVI bravely refused to approve these and similar measures. When in the end he lost his crown and his life, it was due in part to this refusal.

The King Becomes a Prisoner

On August 10, 1792, the Revolutionary mob attacked the royal palace. They massacred the King's Swiss guards, who had laid down their weapons at the King's command. The enraged mob killed every man they could find in the palace who had served the King, from noblemen to cooks. The Assembly deposed and imprisoned the King despite promises in the Constitution that he would remain untouched. The election of a new legislative body, the Convention, was ordered. In one stroke the Revolutionaries had ended the Monarchy, the Constitution, and the existing Assembly.

The September Massacres

On September 5, 1792, elections were held for the National Convention. First elected was Maximilien Robespierre, who would be the architect of the Reign of Terror. Next to be elected was Georges-Jacques Danton. Danton emerged as the leader when he was elected Minister of Justice in the new government.

Prior to August 10, 1792, the penalty for failing to take the oath to support the Civil Constitution was the loss of the priest's parish or diocese. This was a severe penalty for most priests whose only source of income was from the parish. However, after August 10, when the King was deposed, the non-jurors were seen as traitors. By August 15, 1792, the new government of France began to arrest them.

On September 2, the martyrdoms began. In less than two hours, one hundred and twenty priests met their deaths. That night, seventy-six more priests perished. For four days the streets of Paris ran red with the blood of the martyrs as thousands died. Many of those killed were priests and nuns, as well as other religious. Some who were killed were only guilty of treating those going to their deaths with kindness.

Toward the end of 1792, the clergy began to leave France. They fled to Spain, Germany, England, the United States, but more especially to the Papal States, where they were warmly welcomed. Many priests, however, remained in France at the risk of their lives. They went about in disguise performing the functions of their sacred ministry.

The Execution of the King

On September 21, 1792, the first regular session of the National Convention met. Three tasks faced the Convention. It needed to decide the fate of the imprisoned king, create a provisional government, and carry on the war France was waging. It cast aside the Constitution of 1791, officially dethroned Louis XVI, and proclaimed France a republic. King Louis XVI was tried and executed on January

Louis XVI distributing alms to the poor of Versailles in the Winter of 1788

21, 1793. This grim event made a profound impression not only in France but also throughout Europe. Queen Marie Antoinette and the King's sister, Elizabeth, soon shared his fate.

The Rising of Europe

Whatever the explanations of later secular historians, those who were then alive knew full well what the execution of King Louis XVI meant. When news of the killing of King Louis reached London, Great Britain immediately broke off diplomatic relations with France. In Parliament, the Prime Minister of Great Britain, William Pitt, recognized that the Revolution would try to destroy England, Europe, and the world. He declared that England stood resolved to fight the French with all that it had.

On February 1, 1793, the Convention declared war on England and the Netherlands. France was now at war with every western European country but Spain. They would address that situation the following month. An alliance developed against France that included Austria, Prussia, the larger German states, Great Britain, and the Netherlands. For a time it seemed that these powers must surely prevail against the Revolutionary government. However, they were not sufficiently united in purpose and policy to pursue a common aim or strategy. Meanwhile, the French instituted a draft to mobilize large conscripted armies. The French armies fought with fanatical fury and turned their enemies back.

The Persecution Continues

In France the persecution intensified. Legislation against the non-jurors was gradually tightened, so as to allow no one to escape. Soon the jurors were also exposed to danger. Another new law condemned to death any person who concealed a priest in his home. The various local officials rigorously enforced these laws.

The victims of the new persecution fell into three classes: the recluses, the deported, and the condemned. The recluses were aged or infirm priests, who were herded together and imprisoned. They were subjected to extreme hardships. Forced to move from one prison to another under brutal conditions, many of them died. One Revolution official came up with the idea of drowning the priests in the Loire River by loading them in boats and sinking them. On the first trip eighty priests lost their lives. One hundred and thirty-seven priests drowned on the second trip.

The "deported" formed a group perhaps even more to be pitied than the recluses. Hundreds of priests were driven in carts to various French ports. As the British fleet kept too close a watch on the ports it was actually impossible to deport these unfortunate priests. Consequently, they were detained in the hold of the ships where they died of hunger or suffocated. Of the 825 priests imprisoned on two ships at the port of Rochefort, 542 perished.

Finally, there were those who suffered outright martyrdom. These included priests who celebrated Mass in secret, as well as men and women who had dared to offer them lodging. It also included nuns who had refused to take the oath. Several of these martyrs have been beatified.

New Revolutionary Forms of Worship

In replacing Catholicism with a new form of worship, the first step was to replace the Gregorian calendar with one created by the Revolution. The new Revolutionary era was to begin September 22, 1792. The date of the creation of the French Republic marked the beginning of the new era and was deemed of greater importance than the birth of Our Lord Jesus Christ. The new week was to be ten days. The tenth day took the place of Sunday.

The creation of the new calendar also marked a new period of attacks against the Church. The Convention declared that Notre Dame Cathedral in Paris, the symbol of French Catholicism for almost a thousand years, was now to be known as the "Temple of the Goddess of Reason." Religious images were removed and the Cathedral was turned into the Temple of Reason. The Convention outlawed the Mass in the Cathedral and replaced it with a blasphemous "Festival of Reason." They crowned this blasphemy by placing a dancing girl in the cathedral to impersonate the new "goddess."

Notre Dame Cathedral

Throughout France, churches, especially the great French cathedrals, suffered similar sacrileges. Most of the churches in Paris were closed. At the end of November the Committee issued orders to close all the Catholic churches in France. Anyone asking to have a church opened would be executed.

The Rising in the Vendee (1793)

The area known as the Vendee is located in western France halfway down the coast around the city of Nantes. The people who live there called it the "Bocage," or the Hedge country. The Vendeans had a strong sense of personal freedom and responsibility. They also had a fervent love for the Catholic Church. More than three-fourths of the priests in the Vendee refused to take the oath to support the Civil Constitution of the Clergy.

In order to fight its enemies, the Revolutionary government had instituted a draft. When the government's conscription decree arrived in the Vendee, the people understood it meant more than the mere horrors of war. It meant fighting for a government that had murdered their King and was doing its best to destroy the Catholic Church. The drawing of lots for the draft was set for March 12, 1793. On March 12, the Catholics of the Vendee rose up against the Revolution. Composed almost entirely of peasants and farmers, these men would form the Catholic and Royal Army. Many wore crosses and images of the Sacred Heart.

Within a week after the uprising had started, the Catholic and Royal Army had freed most of the Vendee and parts of the neighboring areas. At this point the Revolutionary government became aware something was wrong in western France. The Convention decreed that any Frenchman carrying arms against the government would be executed within one day of his capture. On April 6, the Convention created the Committee of Public Safety. This committee worked in secret. It protected the Revolution not only from those actively fighting it, but also from those who might not be supporting it strongly enough. The head of the Committee was Georges-Jacques Danton.

Meanwhile the Vendee magnificently carried foward the Catholic spirit of Clovis and Clotilda. Throughout the month of May they continued to be victorious. By the end of the month, they had taken almost full control of the Vendee. Only the port city of Nantes remained in Revolutionary hands. On June 15, they decided to attack Nantes. This would give them a port from which they could receive supplies from England. On June 29, the Catholic army attacked the strongly defended city of Nantes. Sadly, when their leading general was killed during the attack, it failed. For the next two months the Vendeans fought a defensive action to hold the land that they had taken.

Jacques Cathelineau, one of the leaders of the rising in the Vendee

Robespierre and the Reign of Terror

While Danton was in the country for three weeks, Robespierre took over the Committee of Public Safety. A leader of the radical Parisian mobs, Robespierre removed Danton from the Committee. From that moment on, the Committee became the real government of France. Robespierre became a virtual dictator in a Reign of Terror. Almost two thousand people lost their lives during the Reign.

On October 16, following a two-day show trial, Queen Marie Antoinette was executed. The following day the Catholic and Royal Army suffered a devastating defeat. The Vendee was lost. One hundred thousand refugees from the Vendee fled into northern France away from the army that had defeated them.

While Robespierre had removed him from the Committee of Public Safety, Danton was still well regarded by most of the Revolutionaries. Thus, Robespierre could not move directly against him. However, in January 1794, Robespierre began to have Danton's supporters arrested. That same month the last remains of the Catholic and Royal Army were destroyed. In February and March, Robespierre plotted to arrest Danton. On March 31, he did. Danton was tried and found guilty. In the end he rejected the evil that he had caused. He asked the pardon of God and of men for his part in the Revolution.

From Danton's death on April 5 until the execution of Robespierre on July 28, 1794, thousands were killed throughout France. More people were in jails waiting to be executed. One of the last groups killed before the Terror ended was a group of sixteen Carmelite nuns. They are known as the Martyrs of Compiegne. When brought before the Revolutionaries, they chose to die rather than renounce their Faith. During the half hour it took to guillotine the nuns, they sang hymns. The mob, which normally screamed and shouted during the beheadings, was completely silent. In May 1906, Pope Pius X beatified the Martyrs of Compiegne.

The Terror had finally become too horrifying for anyone to endure. The members of the Convention were constantly in a state of agitation. They feared that at any moment Robespierre might order their deaths. Thus, out of fear for their own lives, Robespierre's colleagues plotted his downfall. On July 26, the conspirators denounced him while he spoke before the Convention. Amid shouts of "Down with the tyrants!" the Convention ordered the arrest of the dictator and his friends. Then they ordered his execution. The death of Robespierre on July 28, 1794, marked the beginning of the end of the Terror. The worst was over for the majority of the French people, but not for her priests.

Review Exercises

1. What is a Revolution?
2. What was "Civil Constitution of the Clergy?"
3. Who were the "non-jurors?"
4. Who were the "recluses," the "deported," and the "condemned?"
5. Why did the people of the Vendee rise against the Revolutionaries?

CHAPTER 27

THE CHURCH DURING THE AGE OF NAPOLEON

Napoleon crowns himself while Pope Pius VII looks on.

The Directory Persecutes the Church

After the fall of Robespierre, the Committee of Public Safety lost its dictatorial powers. The Convention then created a new constitution that placed executive power in a five-man Directory. It ruled from 1795 until 1799. It separated the Catholic Church from the state and proclaimed freedom of worship. However, like the Revolutionary governments before it, the Directory persecuted the Church. The Directory deported a number of priests to French Guiana. Many other priests were tortured and imprisoned at

Rochefort. Some were imprisoned on the islands off the coast where the majority of them died of disease.

The Rise of Napoleon Bonaparte

The Directory faced grave economic problems arising from the war and inflation. France needed conquests, not only to end the war, but also to obtain plunder. Therefore, in 1796, they sent a great army into Italy to defeat the Austrian army and to establish French control of the Italian states. The commander of the army was General Napoleon Bonaparte. Sadly for the world, he may have been history's greatest general.

Napoleon Bonaparte was born in Corsica in 1769. He attended the military academy at Brienne. Upon his graduation, he received a commission in the artillery corps. The French Revolution created an opportunity for the talented and ambitious young man to play a leading role in France. In February 1794, he became a brigadier general. The following year he achieved national fame when he dispersed an attack on the Convention. To reward his action, the Convention gave him command of an army. (In an interesting character note: despite being completely amoral and pragmatic, Napoleon refused to serve against the Vendeans.)

In 1796-1797, Napoleon won many brilliant victories in Italy. As a result, Austria signed a peace treaty with France. The treaty made France dominant in Italy and in Western Europe. Napoleon returned to France a national hero.

Napoleon's next assignment was in Egypt. He proposed to conquer Egypt, which would then be used as a base for an attack on British-controlled India. In May 1798, a French expedition sailed from France with thirty-eight thousand troops. Outside Cairo, at the Battle of the Pyramids, Napoleon won control of Egypt. However, at the Battle of the Nile, the British fleet destroyed the French fleet. This cut off Napoleon's communications with France. It was a crippling blow. Bonaparte's plans to conquer India were dashed. In August 1799, he left his troops in Egypt and returned to France. Meanwhile, France had invaded the Papal States and had taken Pope Pius VI prisoner.

War with the Holy See

Almost from the beginning, Pope Pius VI (1775-1799) had seen that the French Revolution was the mortal enemy of the Papacy and the Catholic Church. The Revolution hated Pius for a number of reasons, not the least of which was because he was the Pope. They hated him because he had rejected the Civil Constitution of the Clergy, encouraged the non-jurors to stand firm in their Faith, and gave shelter to Catholic refugees.

During his campaign in Italy, Napoleon had taken control of large parts of Italy. He also demanded a large sum of money from the Pope. After his victories over Austria, Napoleon forced Pius VI to sign the oppressive Treaty of Tolentino. This treaty greatly increased the amount of money the Holy See had to pay to France. It also stated that French troops would occupy Italy until the Pope paid.

The excuse for the French occupation of Rome was the death of a French general in a riot. French troops entered the city unopposed on February 10, 1798. The French troops disarmed the papal troops, forced their way into the Vatican, and pillaged the Pope's apartments. They plundered the Eternal City and ten days later abducted the eighty-year-old Pope. The French Revolutionaries declared that he would be the last Pope. French troops escorted him to Siena. From there his Holiness went to the Carthusian monastery at Florence. Finally he was taken across the Alps into France in March 1799. The French people of the various border towns came out to greet and warmly welcome him.

Pius VI spent the last months of his life in exile in the citadel of Valence. There, like Our Lord on the Cross, he prayed for the forgiveness of his enemies. He also had three specific prayers in his last months. He prayed that the Faith would be restored to France. He prayed that the Pope would be restored to Rome. Finally, he prayed that peace would be restored to Europe. He died at Valence, August 29, 1799, having then reigned longer than any Pope. The Revolutionaries believed that they had won. However, the enemies of the Church always seem to make one mistake—they forget Christ's promise to a humble fisherman, "...and the Gates of Hell shall not prevail against it."

The Election of Pope Pius VII

Pope Pius VI was concerned that Napoleon might try to take control of the Papacy by forcing the College of Cardinals to elect someone he chose. Thus, Pius VI had ordered that the Conclave that elected his successor had to meet in a place not controlled by Napoleon. The Cardinals met on the island of San Giorgio Maggiore,

Pope Pius VII in 1805

directly opposite the city of Venice. After three months, they elected the humble bishop of Imola, Cardinal Luigi Chiaramonti, a Benedictine. He took the name Pius VII (1800-1823).

Napoleon Becomes Ruler of France

At this point, the conditions in France were perfect for a man of Napoleon's abilities. With the help of his brother Lucien and other politicians, the thirty-year-old Bonaparte seized power. Soldiers drove out protesting members of the legislature. The new government was called the Consulate. It ruled from 1799 until 1804. Napoleon was made First Consul with a ten-year term. He was basically an absolute dictator. From the time he took power in November 1799, until his final defeat fifteen years later, France was almost constantly at war.

In a display of his military brilliance, Napoleon, to the amazement of his enemies, suddenly crossed the Alps into Italy during the spring of 1800. On June 14, 1800, he won a decisive victory over the Austrians at the Battle of Marengo. All of Italy was now under his control. As a result of the battle, Austria had to sign a peace treaty. In 1802, Britain was compelled to make peace with France. Napoleon was now the supreme power in Europe.

The Concordat of 1801

Napoleon Bonaparte accepted the French Revolution's worldview. This means he was no friend to the Catholic Church. Throughout his entire life he was probably an atheist. However, he had a pragmatic view of the Church. He knew the people of France were essentially Catholic. He knew that to gain their obedience and control them, he had to let them have the Faith. However, he wanted to control the Church. Five days after his victory at Marengo,

Napoleon and the Holy See began negotiations that resulted in the Concordat of 1801.

The Concordat did not fully restore the Church in France to its former position. It provided that the Catholic Faith could be freely exercised in France. The Church could worship in public but only as long as it conformed to the rules the government felt were essential for public peace. There was also a section about the nomination of bishops. The First Consul (Napoleon) was to nominate candidates to episcopal Sees and the pope was to confer canonical institution. Bishops and priests had to swear allegiance to the government. In exchange, the government would financially support the clergy. In an act of heroic unselfishness, the Church in France gave up any claim to Church property seized during the Revolution.

War Resumes against Napoleon

Great Britain, among all the European powers, best recognized Napoleon for who he truly was: the inheritor of the French Revolution. They knew there could be no lasting peace with him. All treaties were merely lulls in the struggles between Napoleon and Great Britain. In 1803, the war resumed. By 1805, Austria, Russia, and Sweden had joined Britain to end French mastery of Europe.

To destroy his great enemy, Napoleon had to invade Great Britain. A successful invasion depended on his controlling the English Channel long enough to transport his armies across the Channel in barges. However, the combined French and Spanish fleets could not control the Channel. So, in 1805, Napoleon turned to meet Austrian and Russian armies to the east. He ordered his naval forces into the Mediterranean. In one of history's most decisive battles, the British navy caught Napoleon's naval forces. The British destroyed the combined French and Spanish fleets at Trafalgar off the coast of Spain. The British victory permanently destroyed Bonaparte's naval power and any chance of invasion.

Despite the failure of his forces on the seas, Napoleon remained undefeatable on land. In a dazzling display of his military genius, he crushed a combined Austrian and Russian army at Austerlitz in 1805. This victory alarmed Prussia, who had worked with France since 1795. Prussia now declared war on Napoleon. However, the highly regarded Prussian army received a terrible beating at the Battle of Jena in 1806. Napoleon next turned to the Russians. His defeat of the Russians led not only to a peace treaty but also to an alliance with Russia in 1807.

Napoleon is victorious at the Battle of Austerlitz

The French Empire was now at its zenith. It had carved up Europe with Russia. As long as this alliance lasted, Great Britain could accomplish little. Napoleon then compelled Spain to become his ally. Germany was under his "protection." In 1806, he abolished the Holy Roman Empire. The former Holy Roman Emperor became the Emperor of Austria. Napoleon completely dominated all of continental Europe. All that stood between Napoleon and world domination was the British navy.

The Coronation of the Emperor

In 1802, Napoleon had become First Consul for life with the powers of a king. In 1804, the French people elected him Emperor. To assure the succession of his heirs, Napoleon asked Pius VII to officiate at his coronation. The pope felt it best not to refuse. Pius also hoped that in exchange for this courtesy, he might obtain some concessions from Napoleon.

The coronation ceremony took place on December 2, 1804, in Notre Dame Cathedral. Pope Pius VII began by anointing Napoleon. Although Napoleon had promised the Pope that he would follow the rules of the ceremony, he did not. He ascended the altar steps and astonished the Pope when he took the crown and placed it on his head himself. It was the low point in Pius VII's papacy. Although Pius VII stayed in Paris until the spring, he could not obtain any concessions from Napoleon.

Europe Rises Against Napoleon

During 1808 and 1809, the freedom loving people of Europe rose again to try to overthrow Napoleon's yoke of tyranny. Early in 1808, French troops seized Rome. Napoleon was angry with Pope Pius. The pope refused to abandon his neutral status and join a confederation of Italian princes who supported Napoleon. A few months later the people of Spain revolted against Napoleon's oppression of their country. Great Britain sent an army to aid the Spanish rebels. The French army in Spain was not able to crush the Spanish rebels or dislodge the British army.

In 1809, Austria attacked the French in an attempt to free Germany. Great Britain sent an army to attack the French in Holland. Napoleon again completely defeated these nations. He forced a very harsh treaty on Austria. He seized the Papal States and declared them French territory. For this the Pope excommunicated him. In savage retaliation, Napoleon made the Pope his prisoner.

The Pope as Prisoner of Napoleon

Almost from the start of his reign, Pius VII clashed with Napoleon. Their initial conflict arose from the dissolution of the marriage of Napoleon's brother, Jerome. In 1803, Bishop John Carroll of Baltimore had married Jerome and a wealthy American. However, Napoleon wanted his family to marry European royalty. Since he was unhappy with the marriage, he wanted it annulled. However, there was no canonical reason to dissolve the marriage, so Pope Pius refused to grant an annulment.

The underlying cause of the conflict between the Pope and Napoleon was the issue of control. Napoleon wanted to control the Pope. In the spiritual order he revived the investitures quarrel by interfering in the election of bishops. In the temporal order he renewed the conflict with the Pope by insisting on his authority over Rome.

The issue of rule over the city of Rome caused ever more friction between the Pope and the Emperor. Pius VII refused to comply with the Emperor's demand that he expel all Russian and British subjects from the Papal States. Pius also declined to close the papal ports to British ships. He also rejected the Emperor's demand that the French occupy the papal fortresses. Napoleon retaliated by seizing the Papal States. He did offer Pius VII an annual payment as compensation. At this point, Pius heroically excommunicated Napoleon.

The excommunication was the signal for open warfare. During the night of July 6, 1809, Napoleon arrested Pius VII. His captors gave him two hours to get ready to leave. As they had done with Pope Pius

VI they carried him off into France. He went first to Grenoble, then to Savona on the Riviera, near Genoa.

During his captivity at Savona, Pius VII was strictly guarded. He was allowed no advisers. His captors severely censored all his communications. He

Pope Pius VII as he looked in 1819

was allowed no visitors except in the presence of his jailors. He offered passive resistance by reverting to the role of a simple Benedictine monk. He refused to invest new bishops in France or any of its client states.

By June 1812, Napoleon had lost patience with the humble Pope. Enraged that Pius refused to do his bidding, Napoleon ordered the Pope moved. Pius was transferred to Fontainebleau, just outside of Paris. The journey was made secretly, speedily, and brutally to prevent any popular outcry. On the journey, Pius fell ill and even received the Last Rites. It was this exhausted Pope, sick with fever, whom Napoleon again attempted to cajole.

In his weakened state, Pius agreed to surrender the States of the Church. He also declared that if the Pope failed to confer canonical institution within six months after the imperial nomination of a bishop, the metropolitan was allowed to confer institution without declaring that he acted in the name of the Holy See. These decrees, extorted by force and trick, almost immediately filled Pius with remorse. Pius revoked them.

The Invasion of Russia

From 1809 to 1812, Napoleon's empire appeared invincible. However the forces that would overthrow it were at work. The British navy steadily destroyed all Napoleon's overseas trade. The Spanish who had fought 770 years to expel the Moslems, continued to fight to expel Napoleon. The anger of conquered peoples grew ever greater. Most importantly, France's relations with Russia declined. Finally, Napoleon decided to impose his will on Russia and attack her.

In June 1812, Napoleon led an army of six hundred thousand men, the largest army the world had ever known, into Russia. However, the Russians refused to fight and retreated eastward. As they retreated across the incredible vastness of Russia, they burned and destroyed whatever the invaders could use. Finally the Russians made a stand at Borodino but were defeated. Moscow lay open. However, there was no triumphal entry into Moscow for the French. The Russians had burned the city and deserted it.

Napoleon had no choice but to retreat back to Smolensk where he hoped to find food for his troops. However there were no supplies in Smolensk. The only course was to return to France. Hounded by the brutal Russian winter, where the temperature fell to thirty degrees below zero, and by fierce Russian attacks, the remnants of the once-proud French Army staggered back to Europe with less than one hundred thousand men. All of a sudden Napoleon did not seem so invincible, so Austria declared its neutrality, and Prussia made an alliance with Russia.

Napoleon had suffered a colossal military disaster. Nevertheless, he was not at the end of his resources. He still controlled most of Germany and all of Italy. His armies had finally chased the British out of Spain and into Portugal.

Napoleon's retreat from Russia

Allied Victory

Napoleon gathered a new army to meet the combined armies of Russia, Prussia, and Austria. He fought them at Leipzig in October 1813. Overwhelming defeat forced the French to flee across the Rhine as the Germans rose to hasten the downfall of the tyrant.

The next step was for the allies to invade France. They moved into eastern France, while the British liberated Spain and entered France from the south. Napoleon fought brilliantly to repel the invasion, but the allied armies were too much for him. As they entered Paris, the allies found the French people exhausted from nearly a quarter century of revolution and war. The allies were not vindictive. They brought peace rather than revenge to France.

The allies restored the Bourbon dynasty and ended all revolutionary policies. As Louis XVI's son, Louis XVII, had been killed by the Revolution, Louis XVI's brother returned to rule as Louis XVIII. Peace was made with France, and allied troops went home. Napoleon was exiled to the island of Elba off the coast of Italy.

As defeat loomed on the horizon, Napoleon had proposed yet another treaty to the Pope. This treaty would acknowledge Napoleon as the ruler of Rome and of the former Papal States presently annexed to the French Empire. A healthy Pius VII once again refused. Napoleon was forced to set him free. On May 24, 1814, after five years in captivity, Pius VII re-entered Rome amid universal rejoicing. One of his first acts upon returning to Rome was to restore the Jesuits.

The Battle of Waterloo

Although Napoleon had been exiled to Elba, he had not written "the end" to his part of history. On February 26, 1815, he escaped from Elba less then ten months after he arrived. Two days later he landed on the French mainland. The troops sent to arrest

Wellington is congratulated for his victory at Waterloo.

him became the core of his new army. King Louis XVIII fled as Napoleon approached Paris. The allies formed a new army and met Napoleon in battle at Waterloo on June 18, 1815. After the Allied victory, the commander of the Allied forces, the Duke of Wellington, said that the allies had barely won the battle. He hinted that if Napoleon had had another ten thousand troops he would have won this decisive battle. In May, the Vendee had risen in revolt. Napoleon had sent ten thousand men to suppress the revolt.

This time, the allies exiled Napoleon to an island in the Atlantic Ocean a thousand miles from anywhere: St. Helena. He died on May 5, 1821. Although he had been a lifelong atheist, in his last months he may have found the Faith. Before he died, he made his last confession and received the Last Rites.

Review Exercises

1. During the last months of his life, in addition to praying for his enemies, what three things did Pope Pius VI pray would happen?
2. Why did Napoleon sign the Concordat of 1801?
3. What is the Battle of Trafalgar?
4. Give two reasons why Pius VII agreed to crown Napoleon.
5. Why did Pius VII excommunicate Napoleon?
6. What did Napoleon do once Pius excommunicated him?
7. Which Pope restored the Jesuits?

CHAPTER 28

THE CHURCH IN THE UNITED STATES DURING THE 18ᵀᴴ AND 19ᵀᴴ CENTURIES

St. John Neumann prays for the Catholic immigrants coming to America.

Establishment of the Hierarchy

After the establishment of the United States, the status of American Catholics was an odd one. The United States was a new country. However, her Catholics were under the authority of the Church in London. At the request of the Catholics in the United States, Pope Pius VI appointed Father John Carroll to lead all the Catholics of the former English colonies. In 1789, Pope Pius made John Carroll Bishop of Baltimore. He had authority over all Catholics in the new country. His diocese extended from Georgia to Maine and west all the way to the Mississippi River. At the time there were only about 25,000 Catholics in all of this territory.

Bishop Carroll's main job was to develop a native clergy. With this end in view, he enlisted the aid of the Sulpicians. They founded Mount St. Mary's Seminary at Emmitsburg, near Baltimore, in 1806. The seminary, which still exists, gave many wonderful priests and bishops to the United States. In addition to the Sulpicians, Bishop Carroll also welcomed the Dominicans, the Augustinians, and many others.

In 1791, Bishop Carroll founded a college for young men at Georgetown, on the banks of the Potomac River. When the Pope restored the Jesuits, Bishop Carroll put them in charge of Georgetown College. In 1815, Georgetown was given the rank of a university.

By 1807, the number of Catholics in the United States had grown to about 150,000. There were 70 parishes and 80 churches. The next year Pope Pius VII created the Metropolitan See of Baltimore. There were also Sees in New York City, Philadelphia, Boston, and Bardstown (Kentucky). Later, Bardstown became the Diocese of Louisville. After Louisiana was purchased in 1803, the Diocese of New Orleans, which was formed in 1793, was also added. Archbishop John Carroll died in 1815. By the time of his death, the Catholic Church had planted deep roots in the United States.

For the rest of the nineteenth century, the Church grew quickly in the United States. Three factors account for the rapid growth of the Catholic population during this period. The Church grew naturally as Catholic parents had children. Catholics made converts to the Faith. Finally, the leading reason for growth was the large number of Catholics coming to America from Catholic countries, especially Ireland. The chart below shows Catholic population growth from 1830 to 1900:

1830	360,000	1870	4,600,000
1840	1,000,000	1880	7,000,000
1850	1,700,000	1890	10,000,000
1860	3,000,000	1900	11,700,000

Catholicism Spreads in the Young United States

In 1791, the Sulpicians founded a seminary in Baltimore. One of their first students, and the second priest to be ordained in the United States, was Father Demetrius Augustine Gallitzin. Father Gallitzin was born a Russian prince. He had come to the United States in 1792 to study and travel. However, he discovered that he had a vocation and entered the seminary. In 1795, Bishop Carroll ordained him. After his ordination he made his way westward and settled in the heart of the Allegheny Mountains. For forty-one years, he worked among the people of western Pennsylvania. For his work in spreading the Faith, he is known as the "Apostle of the Alleghenies." He died May 6, 1840.

The first Bishop of Bardstown, Kentucky was Bishop Benedict Joseph Flaget, a Sulpician. When he arrived in Bardstown in 1811 one of his first actions was to found a seminary. The Bishop lived in one little log cabin and the seminarians lived in another. Later, they built a church, a seminary building, and the famous Cathedral of St. Joseph.

In 1817, the Vincentians built two log cabins in Missouri. These simple cabins would become the Kenrick Theological Seminary of St. Louis. Based on the advice of Bishop Flaget, the Diocese of Cincinnati was formed in 1821. It included Ohio and Michigan.

Father Edward Fenwick, a Dominican, became its first Bishop in 1822. In 1841, Father Edward Sorin and six lay Brothers from the Congregation of the Holy Cross came to Northern Indiana. They founded the University of Notre Dame the next year.

While there were Catholic schools for girls in Quebec and New Orleans, the Catholics of the English colonies usually sent their daughters to France or Belgium to receive an education. In 1792, the Poor Clares came from France and opened a convent in Frederick, Maryland. In 1801, they opened an academy for girls at Georgetown. When they returned to France, the school was taken over by the Congregation of the Pious Ladies. This was a religious order for women that had been founded in the United States in 1799.

Anti-Catholic Movements

As a result of immigration, the number of Catholics in the United States increased dramatically during the nineteenth century. In fact, so many came to this country that by 1850, Catholics were the nation's largest single denomination. Many of these immigrants came from Ireland. From 1845 to 1850, Ireland suffered a terrible famine. Many had to leave Ireland or starve to death. The growing number of immigrants stirred up the resentment of some American Protestants. Some of these anti-Catholics started a movement known as "Native Americanism." They considered Catholicism to be a national menace. The Native Americanism movement became a political party called the "Know-Nothing Party." Later in the century this group became involved with the Ku Klux Klan.

In 1843, anti-Catholic mobs destroyed two Catholic churches and a convent in Philadelphia. The following year Boston and New York were threatened with riots. (These three cities had very large Irish Catholic populations.) The Church responded to the threats by calling provincial and plenary councils. These councils strengthened the organization of the Church. They also helped promote conversions in the new American territories in the West and Southwest.

During the Civil War (1861-1865), nuns and priests assisted both the North and the South. These acts of self-sacrifice, especially on the part of nuns who acted as nurses on the battlefields, greatly increased the prestige of the Church. They did much to reduce anti-Catholic bigotry.

Provincial and Plenary Councils

The purpose of provincial and plenary councils, and diocesan synods, is to make rules. These rules govern Church affairs in a particular country or diocese. The first diocesan synod in the United States met in 1791 at Bishop Carroll's house in Baltimore. The first provincial council met in 1829. Between 1837 and 1849, six other provincial councils were held to discuss the various issues facing the Church in the United States.

In 1852, Pope Pius IX gave the American bishops permission to hold a plenary, or national council. It met at Baltimore. Six archbishops and twenty-six bishops attended its sessions. The bishops issued several decrees on the Faith. They professed their allegiance to the Holy Father as the divinely appointed head of the Church. They also declared their belief in the entire Catholic Faith as taught by the popes and the Church councils.

The Second Plenary Council of Baltimore met in 1866. This Council also dealt with issues of the Faith that concerned the young Church. Of special concern to this Council was the heresy of

"Indifferentism." This heresy, which is still strong in America even today, holds that one religion is as good as another. The Council strongly condemned this heresy. It also issued rules governing the Mass and the Sacraments. In addition, it discussed Catholic education. The Council called for a Catholic school to be built in every parish. It also expressed a desire to establish a Catholic University in the United States.

In 1884, the Third Plenary Council of Baltimore met. Its chief concerns were the education of the clergy and the building of parochial schools. The Council appointed a commission to begin work on founding a Catholic university. It decreed that immigrants should be instructed by priests in their own language. It also decreed six holy days of obligation for the United States. The Council appointed a commission to edit a catechism. Finally, the Council asked the Vatican to begin the beatification process for Father Isaac Jogues, Rene Goupil, and Kateri Tekakwitha.

Kateri Tekakwitha learns about the Faith.

Outstanding American Bishops of the Nineteenth Century

Archbishop John Hughes (1797-1864)

John Hughes was the fourth bishop of the diocese of New York. He then became its first Archbishop. Born in Ireland, his family came to America in 1817. As a young man he felt the call to the priesthood, so he went to Mount Saint Mary's College at Emmitsburg where he worked for a year as a gardener before being admitted as a student. In 1826, he was ordained. He was assigned to the Philadelphia diocese where his abilities attracted widespread attention.

In 1842, after the death of Bishop Dubois, Father Hughes became Bishop of New York City. In 1851, on a visit to the Pope, Pius IX personally chose him to be the first Archbishop of New York City. His great zeal for Catholic education inspired him to fight for public support of Catholic schools. Sadly, he soon saw that he could not make non-Catholics realize that Catholics were being treated unjustly. They were being deprived of the right to share in the educational benefits for which they were being taxed. Because of this, he began building Catholic schools in every parish in his diocese.

For many years Bishop Hughes defended the Church against bigotry and intolerance. Many American Protestants believed that a person could not be both a good American and a good Catholic. The "Native Americans" were the leading source of this intolerance. As we have seen, in 1844 this hate group burned two Catholic churches and a convent in Philadelphia. They planned to have a meeting in New York City the following year. Bishop Hughes urged the mayor not to allow the meeting for fear of violence. However, Bishop Hughes also made plans to protect Church property. His fearless attitude prevented the meeting from being held. Later, another group replaced the "Native Americans." This was a political party known as the "Know-Nothing" party. Bishop Hughes fought the "Native Americans" and the "Know-Nothing" party with all his power. Over the years, his great love of the people and his self-sacrificing patriotism won the support of fair-minded Americans. For awhile, at least, the power of anti-Catholic bigotry was broken.

During the Civil War, Archbishop Hughes gave a wonderful example of patriotism. He inspired priests and nuns to go onto the battlefields to care for the sick and wounded and to minister to them in hospitals. He traveled to France and obtained support for the Union. When he died, President Lincoln honored his service to America.

Among his other notable achievements, Archbishop Hughes founded Fordham University. Deeply distressed by the condition of the poor in New York City, he established the Society of St. Vincent de Paul. He also laid the cornerstone for St. Patrick's Cathedral on the Feast of the Assumption, 1858. After the cathedral was completed, his remains were moved there and buried under the sanctuary. The cathedral stands as a fitting monument to this great bishop.

Bishop St. John Neumann (1811-1860)

The Catholic Church in America during the nineteenth century was blessed with many outstanding leaders who led the fledging Church through many rough times. However, of that number, only one member of the hierarchy has achieved that highest of honors, the title Saint. That man is St. John Neumann.

John Nepomucene Neumann was born in Bohemia in 1881. He received his education for the priesthood in his native land.

St. John Neumann worked as a missionary priest in western New York.

Unable to find a parish in Europe where he could serve, he came to America. In 1836, he was ordained in New York City. For four years he worked as a missionary in the western part of New York State. In 1840, he joined the Redemptorist Order, and in March 1852, he became Bishop of Philadelphia. He would govern this diocese with great zeal, wisdom, and love for the rest of his life.

Bishop John Neumann was one of the leading theologian at the first plenary council of Baltimore. He had great personal devotion to Our Blessed Lady. Pope Pius IX invited him to come to Rome at the time that he defined the dogma of the Immaculate Conception. He also had a great devotion to the Blessed Sacrament. He established the Forty Hours Devotion in his diocese. He used every means to enflame the people with a love of their Eucharistic Savior. Bishop Neumann died in 1860. Pope Paul VI canonized him in 1977.

James Cardinal Gibbons (1834-1921)

Another outstanding figure in the American hierarchy was Archbishop James Gibbons of Baltimore. He served as Bishop of Richmond from 1872 to 1877. In 1877, he was made Archbishop of Baltimore. He served in this post until he died in 1921. In 1884, Archbishop Gibbons presided over the Third Council of Baltimore. Two years later, Pope Leo XIII made him a cardinal. He was the second American bishop to become a cardinal. (In 1875, Pope Pius IX had made the archbishop of New York, John McCloskey, a cardinal.)

Cardinal Gibbons was a champion of the rights of labor. The subject of the rights of labor was a matter of great concern. Many Catholics were being exploited by the industrial expansion at the turn of the century. Gibbons felt that the workers had the right to protect themselves. He played a key role in obtaining papal permission for Catholics to join labor unions. Pope Leo XIII's famous Encyclical "Rerum Novarum" (On the Condition of Labor), issued in 1891, completely agreed with the Cardinal's position.

In addition to his other accomplishments, Cardinal Gibbons is among the best-selling Catholic authors of all time. In 1876, he published his best-selling book *The Faith of Our Fathers*. This book is a simple yet strong explanation of Catholic doctrine. It has appealed to Catholics readers since it debuted. The book has been translated into many languages. As of 1980, it was in its 111th printing.

Cardinal Gibbons was an ardent patriot and a personal friend to many national leaders. Presidents Grover Cleveland and William Howard Taft both honored Cardinal Gibbons. President Theodore Roosevelt said Gibbons was the most venerated, respected, and useful citizen in America. The Cardinal died March 24, 1921, at the age of eighty-seven.

AMERICAN SAINTS OF THE NINETEENTH CENTURY

St. Elizabeth Ann Seton (1774-1821)

Elizabeth Ann Seton was born in New York City in 1774 and raised in the Episcopalian Church. When she was nineteen, she married William Seton. God blessed them with five children. When her husband became ill, their doctors told them to go to Italy for its warmer climate. Sadly, in 1803 her husband died. She was left alone to care for their children. While staying in Italy she learned about the Faith and decided to become a Catholic. In 1805, after her return to the United States, Archbishop Carroll received her and her children into the Church despite the opposition of her family and friends, who then abandoned her.

St. Elizabeth Ann Seton

In 1808, Elizabeth Ann Seton and three other women opened a Catholic school for girls in Baltimore. Since the women wished to devote themselves more completely to God, they formed a religious community which they called the Sisters of Charity. Despite the fact that she was still raising her children, Mother Seton was elected the first superior. She spent the rest of her life leading and developing the new order. The Order grew and established new convents around the country. It was dedicated to educating young people and caring for the poor. Mother Seton died in 1821. Pope Paul VI canonized her in 1975. She is the first native-born American citizen to be canonized. She is a patron saint of Catholic schools, especially in the United States. There are several Catholic churches, schools, and even one home study school named in her honor.

St. Rose Duchesne (1769-1852)

St. Rose Phillippine Duchesne was born in Grenoble, France. Along with St. Madeline Sophie Barat, she founded the Society of the Sacred Heart. She had been a Visitation nun, but after the French Revolution suppressed the Visitation Order, she joined Mother Barat to start the Society of the Sacred Heart. In 1818, Rose came to New Orleans to work in the American missions. She founded her main mission at St. Charles, Missouri (the site of her shrine). Six additional missions followed which included schools and orphanages. She had a special concern for Native Americans. She devoted much of her work to their care and education. During her lifetime, Pope Leo XII made note of her accomplishments and blessed her work. Pope John Paul II canonized her in 1988.

St. Mother Theodore Guerin (1798-1856)

Anne-Therese Guerin was born in France in 1798. At the time of her birth, the French Revolution was trying to destroy the Catholic Church in France. The government was closing schools and churches. Consequently, her mother home schooled Anne-Therese. At the age of ten she felt called to a vocation. She wanted to enter a religious community when she was fifteen but could not because she had to care for her sister and her sick mother. In 1825, she was able to join the Sisters of Providence and took the name Sister St. Theodore. She spent her next years teaching and caring for the sick and the poor.

In 1839, the Bishop of Vincennes, Indiana, sent a priest to France to find a religious order that could come to his diocese to teach and to assist with the poor. The bishop knew how valuable such an order could be. He had worked with St. Elizabeth Ann Seton and her Sisters of Charity. In October 1840, Sister Theodore and five other nuns arrived in Vincennes. As head of the new mission she would be called "Mother."

Mother Theodore and her sisters immediately began their missionary activities. From 1840 to 1855 she and her nuns opened several parish schools in Indiana. In 1841, they established a boarding school for girls. This school later became St. Mary of the Woods College. She also established two orphanages in Vincennes. Pope Benedict XVI canonized her in 2006.

St. Frances Xavier Cabrini (1850-1917)

Francesca (Frances) Cabrini was born in Italy in 1850, the youngest of thirteen children. Born two months premature, her health was delicate her entire life. When she was thirteen, she was sent to study with the Daughters of the Sacred Heart. At the age of eighteen she became a teacher. When she tried to become a member of the Daughters of the Sacred Heart, they refused her admission because of her frail health. Instead, she supported her parents until they died and helped the family on their farm. She also taught at a private school. In 1871, she became a public school teacher in a nearby village at the request of her pastor.

In 1877, Frances was finally able to take religious vows. She added Xavier to her name to honor the great missionary, St. Francis Xavier. She became the mother superior of an orphanage. When the orphanage was closed in 1880, she and six other sisters founded the Missionary Sisters of the Sacred Heart of Jesus. Mother Cabrini acted as superior-general of the order until her death. In its first five years the order established seven homes, a free school, and a nursery. The order's success brought Mother Cabrini to the attention of Pope Leo XIII.

Although her lifelong dream was to be a missionary to China like her namesake, in 1889, Pope Leo sent Mother Cabrini to New York City. There, with the permission of Archbishop

Pope Leo XIII sends Mother Cabrini to America

Michael Corrigan, she founded an orphanage. It was the first of sixty-seven institutions she founded across the United States, South America, and Europe. In 1909, Mother Cabrini became an American citizen. She died on December 22, 1917. Pope Pius XII canonized her in 1946. St. Frances Xavier Cabrini is the patron saint of immigrants.

Creation of the Catholic School System in the United States

Early in our country's history, the American people decided that educated citizens were the best way to secure the blessings of liberty. To try to make sure that all the people were educated, the United States set up free government-run schools for all children. Every state has a public school system. Sadly, many of those who were the most active in creating the public school system were influenced by the false ideas of the Enlightenment. As a result, they tried to prevent Christianity from having any influence in the public school system. This attitude was entirely contrary to the spirit of the American settlers and pioneers. The pioneers, whether Catholic or Protestant, did everything they could to provide a religious education to their children.

In addition, even when the public schools were influenced by Christianity, which they were to some extent in the nineteenth century, it was Protestant Christianity. Thus, at best, the public schools were Protestant schools. The Catholic Church has always taught that Catholicism must be in all parts of education. The Church could not allow her children to be educated in schools where there was no place for religion. She also could not allow them in schools that were teaching Protestant Christianity. As a result, Catholics rallied to the support of their bishops and pastors and built schools of their own. It was a tremendous task. Most Catholics were poor and the Catholic schools received no State aid. In addition, as Archbishop Hughes pointed out, they paid taxes to support the public schools.

However, Catholic schools were able to exist only due to the self-sacrifice of the religious orders. Young men joined the teaching orders for men and taught Catholic boys. Orders of nuns, like the Sisters of Charity, grew and multiplied and taught young girls. When immigrants came to this country, nuns and brothers of their own nationality followed them. Since these religious spoke the immigrants' languages, the children of the immigrants could enter into the life of the new world without losing their Faith. Moreover, since these teachers had taken a vow of poverty, they worked in the classroom for only what they needed to live. Their self-sacrifice made the growth of Catholic education in the United States possible.

Review Exercises

1. Who was America's first Bishop?
2. What three factors account for the rapid growth of the Catholic population in the US during the nineteenth century?
3. Who is the only American bishop to be canonized?
4. What is the name of Cardinal Gibbon's best-selling book?
5. Where did Elizabeth Ann Seton learn about the Catholic Faith?
6. What order did Elizabeth Ann Seton found?
7. In what state did Mother Theodore do her work?
8. Of whom is Mother Cabrini the patron saint?
9. Why was the Catholic school system started?

CHAPTER 29

THE CHURCH IN THE 19ᵀᴴ CENTURY (1815 - 1878)

Cologne Cathedral as it appeared in 1880, shortly after it was completed. Cologne Cathedral became a symbol of the Catholic Revival in Germany.

The Catholic Revival

Because of his heroic defiance of Napoleon, Pope Pius VII, and the Catholic Church as a whole, came to be much admired throughout Europe. As a result, there was a great opportunity for a Catholic revival.

Almost immediately upon his return to Rome, the Holy Father began to undo the damage that Napoleon and the Revolution had caused throughout Europe. One of his first acts was to restore the Society of Jesus. Once more the Jesuits worked to spread the Faith. Pope Pius VII also began making agreements, called concordats, with the various European nations to protect the rights of the Church.

France

The first half of the nineteenth century was a period of rebirth for the Church of France. A number of Catholic laymen led by Count Chateaubriand sought to restore Catholicism to its rightful place. They defended the Church against the government, which was continually interfering in her affairs. One of these men, Henry Lacordaire, was a brilliant writer. When the Pope condemned the newspaper where he worked as an editor, he declared that his only desire was to be obedient to the Church. He gave up his career as a journalist and became a Dominican priest.

Another writer who fought for the Church in France was Joseph de Maistre. In his book *On the Pope*, he shows how throughout history it has been the Pope who has been the great champion of Christianity against all its enemies. Other French writers who defended the Church included the priest Robert Lamennais, the historian Rene Montalembert, and the poet Alphonse Lamartine. These men were zealous and had the best intentions; however, they made some serious mistakes. The pope declared that some of their ideas concerning democracy did not agree with the teachings of the Church. They linked the Church with the political and social plans promoted by the Revolution. Lacordaire and Montalembert submitted to the judgment of the Holy See. However, Lamennais remained stubborn and was excommunicated. Sadly, he refused a priest even on his deathbed.

Germany

In Germany the Catholic revival was bound up with the "Romantic Movement." The great German writers, like Goethe and Schiller, had modeled their books on the ancient pagan cultures of Greece and Rome. The writers of the Romantic Movement found the inspiration for their books in the history of Germany during the Middle Ages. These writers discovered how the Catholic Church had enriched the lives of the people during the ages of Faith.

One of the key leaders of the revival was a convert, Joseph von Gorres. This great defender of the Faith converted as a result of his study of German history. Later he founded the monthly magazine, *Katholik*. It became the chief organ of Catholic ideas in Germany.

Stained glass window in Cologne Cathedral dedicated to Joseph von Gorres. The dedication in the shield reads: "Joseph von Gorres. Born at Koblenz on January 25, 1776. Died at Munich on January 29, 1848."

The great centers of the Catholic revival in Germany were Munster, Landshut, Munich, and Cologne. Cologne's famous cathedral symbolized the new goals of art. Beginning in 1804, two Catholic brothers, Sulpiz and Melchior Boisseree, began to buy the treasures of Catholic medieval art that Napoleon had looted. In 1827, the brothers sold their magnificent collection to King Ludwig I of Bavaria. It became part of the "Alte Pinakothek" (The Old Picture Gallery). (This Gallery is in Munich. It is one of the finest art museums in the world.) In 1842, the two brothers also played a large part in having the work on the Cologne Cathedral resumed. The Cathedral was not completed until 1880.

The strength of the reorganized German Catholics was tested in 1838. The issue involved the question of mixed marriages. In 1830, Pope Pius VIII had forbidden any priest to assist at a mixed marriage unless the parties agreed that their children would be raised Catholic. The government insisted that in a mixed marriage, boys should follow the religion of their father, and girls that of their mother. The Archbishop of Cologne publicly defended the Church's position. As a result, he was arrested and thrown into prison. This action incited anger throughout Germany. Public opinion favored the Pope. Joseph von Gorres published a sharp criticism of the government's policies that was widely circulated. The Archbishop's courage and von Gorres' pen finally won a victory for the Catholic position.

Great Britain

There were three outstanding events in the history of Catholicism in Great Britain during the first half of the nineteenth century. The first was Catholic emancipation. The second was the Oxford Movement. The third was the restoration of the Catholic hierarchy.

Catholic Emancipation (Citizenship)

In 1792, a large Catholic convention met in Dublin, Ireland. It forced the Protestant Irish Parliament to make several political concessions. Irish Catholics were given the right to vote, to serve on juries, and to hold certain civil and military offices. However, they still were not allowed to serve in the Houses of Parliament. They also could not hold most of the higher state offices in the British Empire.

In 1801, the Kingdom of Great Britain (England and Scotland) merged with the Kingdom of Ireland. This union created the United Kingdom of Great Britain and Ireland. (Even today Great Britain is officially known as the United Kingdom.) There was now one Parliament for England and Ireland: the Parliament of Great Britain. Representatives of the Irish people could become members of the British Parliament. However, there was an obstacle for Catholics. Members of Parliament were required to take an oath denying the Real Presence and the Mass. Under the leadership of the great Irish patriot Daniel O'Connell, Irish Catholics resolved to fight to be freed from this injustice. They would fight, not through revolutionary violence, but by peaceful methods.

In 1823, Daniel O'Connell founded the Catholic Association. Its purpose was to gain the full rights of citizenship for the Catholics of England and Ireland. Over the next few years the Association became quite large and politically powerful. In 1826, Irish Catholics resolved to oppose any candidate for Parliament who refused to support their emancipation. Two years later, Daniel O'Connell ran for Parliament and was elected by a large majority. His election deeply concerned the British government. They knew that he would not take the anti-Catholic oath. They feared that his refusal would trigger a rebellion by the Irish Catholics.

Consequently, after a period of negotiation, the Act of Catholic Emancipation was enacted in 1829. Catholics could now hold public office or become members of Parliament without having to renounce their faith. In 1830, Daniel O'Connell took his place as a Member of Parliament. He would become one of the most famous orators of the time. Until the end of his life, he fought for the freedom of Ireland. He insisted that the Irish people had the right to govern themselves and not

DANIEL O'CONNELL REFUSING TO TAKE THE OATH OF SUPREMACY.

Contemporary poster showing Daniel O'Connell refusing to take the anti-Catholic oath.

be subject to England. Although he did not succeed in obtaining Irish independence, he kept the desire for freedom alive in the hearts of Irish men and women everywhere.

The Oxford Movement

By the beginning of the nineteenth century, Anglicanism was in a state of exhaustion. State control had paralyzed its spiritual energies. There were a phenomenal number of Anglican theologians who questioned all its dogmas. These theologians seriously threatened the very existence of Anglicanism. These men called themselves the "Broad Church." Their idea of the Church of England was that it should be broad enough to admit anyone who professed the basic dogmas of Christianity.

The "High Church Movement" was started to offset the influence of the Broad Church. Richard Froude, a leading Anglican priest, convinced fellow Anglican priest John Henry Newman of the importance of tradition, and of the necessity of devotion to the saints. He stressed the idea of a Church that was independent of state control and possessed a sound hierarchy. Together they advocated a return to the early Christianity of the Fathers, and a revival of dogma and theology. They basically suggested establishing a Church that would hold a middle position between Catholicism and Protestantism.

Newman set forth the beliefs of the High Church in a series of pamphlets entitled "Tracts for the Times." He addressed such topics as Apostolic succession, the liturgy, and the constitution of the Anglican Church. His tracts created much enthusiasm among clergymen and students. However, the Tractarians, as they were called, were soon accused of Romanism. While Newman conceded that Rome was correct on some points he was still far from being a Catholic. To defend himself, he published a book explaining the doctrines of the Tractarians. It then became clear that Newman advocated a form of Catholic Anglicanism. Unlike Protestantism, it defended the dogmas and the sacramental system of the Catholic Church. However, it rejected her doctrine of Papal infallibility.

During February 1841, in an effort to prevent some of the Tractarians from becoming Catholics, Newman attempted a Catholic interpretation of the doctrines of the Anglican Church. This caused a storm in the Church of England. The heads of Oxford University and the Bishop of Oxford condemned his work. They requested that he retract his statements. Newman refused.

The Anglicans had good reason to be alarmed. Many Anglicans were joining the Catholic Church. In 1842, disturbed in the innermost depths of his soul, craving peace and an opportunity to reflect, Newman withdrew from public life. Along with some of his closest friends he made a deep inquiry into the nature of his religious beliefs. The following year he published a retraction of his most violent attacks on the Catholic Church. In 1844, William Ward, one of Newman's followers, published *The Ideal of a Christian Church*. In this work he proposed the Roman Catholic Church herself as the ideal. In September 1845, Ward became a Catholic. One month later Newman entered the Catholic Church. He left behind him in the Anglican Church all his relatives and his closest friends. On the advice of Monsignor Nicholas Wiseman, he journeyed to Rome and was ordained a Catholic priest. Upon his return to England, he founded an English Congregation of the Oratory of St. Philip Neri at Birmingham in 1847. Thanks to the missionary labors of these English Oratorians, Catholicism in England had a new lease on life.

The English Hierarchy

In 1850, Pope Pius IX restored the Catholic hierarchy in England. That year he made Nicholas Wiseman a Cardinal and the first Archbishop of Westminster. The pope also divided England into a number of Catholic dioceses. Sadly, these actions aroused a storm of anti-Catholic bigotry in Great Britain. During this great hurricane of religious bigotry, Cardinal Wiseman remained perfectly calm. He appealed to the English people's sense of fair play. He mildly reproached the Protestants for their partiality, and sought to dispel their prejudices. The tempest was soon quelled, and all grievances were forgotten. The agitation had one good result: it brought well-known Anglican Henry Edward Manning into the Church. Wiseman, Newman, and Manning all became Cardinals. They were the outstanding churchmen who guided the Catholic Church in England in the nineteenth century.

Troubles in Italy

One of the most difficult problems confronting the popes in the nineteenth century was the question of the temporal power of the papacy. After Napoleon's defeat, the Papal States had been restored to the Holy See. However, the Church had been unable to deal with the hordes of armed

Cardinal Newman

bandits that roamed the countryside. The Church also had to deal with the Carbonari. This was a secret revolutionary society. They sought to rid the country of the influence of the Church and bring about the unification of Italy. As a result, they were always seeking to undermine the Church.

Pope Leo XII (1824-1829) was a strict man. His was a pontificate of extreme severity. He issued orders to prosecute the Carbonari. They were either imprisoned or exiled. However, trouble continued to brew. It was increased by the Revolution of 1830 and a new rebellion that broke out during the **interregnum** that followed the death of Pius VIII (1829-1830), the short-lived successor of Leo XII.

The new pope, Gregory XVI (1831-1846), would have preferred to put down the revolution in Italy without the aid of any foreign power. However, he was unable to do so. Thus he called upon Austria and France for troops. For a while, peace was restored. Then a new enemy appeared: Joseph Mazzini. In 1831 Mazzini founded the "Young Italy" movement. The goal of the movement was to create a united Italian republic by means of a general insurrection. Mazzini believed that a popular uprising would create a unified Italy.

Blessed Pope Pius IX

In 1846, Cardinal Giovanni Mastai-Ferretti was elected pope and took the name Pius IX (1846-1878). He was young, only fifty-four years old, and popular. He was known to be a man of a loving, kindly disposition. He was expected to be a liberal. He immediately took steps to make the government of the Papal States more democratic. He appointed laymen to all the important positions in the government. He announced that from now on, there would be a Parliament in Rome so that the people could have more of a voice in the conduct of the government affairs.

Immediately after his accession, Pius IX was drawn into that great political and national movement which the Italians called *il Risorgimento* (the Resurgence). This movement sought to unify the Italian states into the nation of Italy. At that time there were eight separate provincial governments on the Italian peninsula. This lack of national unity was hard for patriotic Italians to bear. Everywhere there was a desire for union.

Pius IX himself supported the idea of a unified Italy. He was actually planning a confederation of all the Italian states. He would be its president and have a cabinet composed almost exclusively of laymen. However, in 1848, a revolution led by Mazzini broke out in the city of Rome. Count Pellegrino Rossi, the Pope's chief minister, was stabbed to death in broad daylight by one of Mazzini's henchmen. The Swiss guards were disarmed and the Pope himself was imprisoned in

Blessed Pius IX was only 54 years old when he was elected pope.

the Quirinal Palace. With the help of the Spanish ambassador, the Pope fled in disguise to the Kingdom of Naples. Rome was left to the revolutionaries.

In February 1849, an assembly announced the flight of Pius IX. It also proclaimed the Roman Republic under a government headed by Mazzini. From exile, Pius excommunicated all active participants in the government. As usual with a revolution, Mazzini's followers plundered the churches and killed many priests. On Easter Sunday, they desecrated St. Peter's by having a secular victory celebration instead of the Mass.

Pius IX begged the Catholic powers of Europe to come to his aid. In answer to his appeal, French, Spanish, Austrian, and Neapolitan troops arrived in Italy. They besieged the city of Rome.

Realizing that resistance would be futile, Giuseppe Garibaldi, the new leader of the Republican forces, abandoned the Eternal City. In April 1850, Pius returned to Rome. French troops remained in Rome to maintain order and assure the security of the Holy See.

In 1860, the Republican revolution, under the leadership of Garibaldi, gained possession of the kingdom of Naples. They then invaded the Papal States. Garibaldi's forces defeated the papal army in September 1860. The ruthless Republicans then determined to take Rome from the Pope. The government of Sardinia favored this move, because it regarded Rome as the real capital of a united Italy. Events came to a climax in 1870.

In 1870, France and Prussia went to war. As France needed all of its soldiers, the French King recalled his troops from Rome. Immediately the King of Sardinia, Victor Emmanuel II, who had assumed the title of King of Italy, invaded the Papal States. His army, led by Garibaldi, laid siege to Rome. On September 20, 1870, Pius IX, rather than have any bloodshed, surrendered the city and the Papal States. The pope was allowed to retain St. Peter's Basilica and the Vatican Palace. Pius IX refused to accept the terms of the peace treaty. Until the day of his death he remained a voluntary prisoner in the Vatican. It was not until 1929 that the Italian Government and Pope Pius XI signed a peace treaty.

The First Vatican Council

The First Vatican Council opened on December 8, 1869, in St. Peter's Basilica. The definition of the dogma of papal infallibility was the main topic. The bishops were divided into two camps. A large majority favored the dogma. However, a sizeable minority opposed it. Those bishops in the minority were from countries with mixed religious populations, like France and the United States. Strong resistance came from the bishops of Germany. The German bishops opposed a formal definition, not because they doubted the doctrine itself, but because they felt the timing was wrong for a formal definition. They also feared there might be political consequences.

In the first sessions, the Vatican Council defined the teaching of the Church concerning God and Divine Revelation. The council showed that there is no contradiction between reason and revelation. Faith does not destroy reason but raises it up and brings it new light. The Council condemned the principal errors of the day including pantheism, materialism, and atheism. Then the bishops declared that the Pope is infallible when, as the Supreme Shepherd and Teacher of all the Faithful, he proclaims a doctrine of faith or morals by a definitive act. For the Pope is the rock upon which Christ built His Church and promised that the gates of Hell would not prevail against it.

Bismarck and the Kulturkampf

The decree on papal infallibility was the excuse in Germany for a persecution of orthodox Catholics. This persecution was called the Kulturkampf (culture war). The first blows in the culture war involved the group known as the "Old Catholics." These were Catholics who denied papal infallibility. Some of these Old Catholics were professors of theology in the state universities and colleges. The bishops, as guardians of orthodoxy, had forbidden these Old Catholics to teach. When they refused to comply, the bishops had rightly excommunicated them. At this point they should no longer have been allowed to teach Catholic doctrine in any college or university in the country.

However, since these Old Catholics were teaching in state-run institutions, they appealed to the German government. They wanted the government to let them keep their jobs despite their excommunicated status. The head of the German government was its chancellor. During this period the chancellor was Otto von Bismarck. He objected to the bishops' decision and upheld the teachers. The bishops protested in a letter to the Emperor. Bismarck then forbade members of any religious order to teach. Then he banished the Jesuits and the teaching orders presumably allied with them from the Empire.

In 1873, Germany began a systematic persecution of German Catholics. That year the government passed the infamous Falk Laws. These laws sought to transform bishops and priests into state officials. They also tried to bring the seminaries under state control. Any bishop refusing to obey was to be deposed. The German bishops courageously refused to obey. This resulted in a bitter conflict between the Church and Bismarck. In 1874, three bishops were imprisoned. The next year two bishops were deposed. The following year, the Bishop of Munster and the Archbishop of Cologne were exiled. In 1877, the Bishop of Limburg was imprisoned. Exiled bishops continued to administer their dioceses through delegates. In vacant parishes, where Catholic worship was forbidden, priests carried on their sacred ministry in secret.

Bismarck had hoped that the Falk Laws would unite and strengthen Germany. By 1877, it was clear that the Falk Laws were creating discord and weakening the government. Consequently, Bismarck gradually gave up the fight. The government slowly abolished the Falk Laws. By 1886, most of the anti-Catholic laws had been repealed. The last remnants of the Kulturkampf disappeared when all the laws against the Jesuits were abolished during World War I.

Pope Pius IX did not live to see the end of persecution in Germany. He died in 1878, having ruled the Church longer than any pope since St. Peter. Pope John Paul II beatified him in 2000.

The Curé of Ars

It was evening in the little French village of Dardilly and the family of Matthew Vianney was eating dinner. There was a knock on the door and Matthew opened it. A man, after looking around to be sure that no one saw him, entered the home. He had come from a nearby town to bring word that the next night a priest would say Mass in a barn at the edge of the village. The next evening after darkness had fallen, the family quietly left the house. In the barn they found their neighbors gathered with a stranger in their midst. This was the priest who, after hearing their confessions, said Mass. Such were the first religious memories of Jean Marie Vianney who grew up during the French Revolution.

Jean Marie Vianney was born in 1786. His father was a farmer and from early childhood, Jean Marie helped on the family farm. However, on his way to his work in the fields, he always stopped in the church to pray. Even as a young boy Jean Marie wanted to become a priest and win souls to God. In 1806, he entered the seminary. Though he struggled with his studies, especially Latin, he had a strong vocation. He persevered and with the help of his fellow students he finally completed his studies. On August 13, 1815, the Bishop of Grenoble ordained him a priest.

In 1818, Father Vianney was made parish priest of Ars, a poor village not far from Lyons. It was as a simple parish priest in this remote French hamlet that as the "Curé d'Ars" he became known throughout France and the Christian world. It was in the confessional directing souls that he achieved his universal fame. He had not been at Ars long when people began coming to him from other parishes, then from all over France, and finally from other countries. During the last ten years of his life, he spent from sixteen to eighteen hours a day in the confessional. His spiritual direction was characterized by common sense, remarkable insight, and supernatural knowledge. He would sometimes divine sins withheld in an imperfect confession.

Throughout his life he practiced mortification. In order that he could spend so many hours in the confessional, Our Lord gave him a special blessing. For the last forty years of his life, his food and sleep were insufficient, for a normal human, to sustain life. Yet he labored incessantly, with unfailing humility, gentleness, patience, and cheerfulness, until he was more than seventy-three years old.

St. John Vianney, the Curé of Ars

He died on August 4, 1859. Pope Pius XI canonized him in 1925. He is the patron saint of parish priests.

The Miraculous Medal

In 1830, Our Blessed Mother appeared three times to a member of the Daughters of Charity of St. Vincent de Paul. The Sister's name was Catherine Labouré. During the second visit the Blessed Mother displayed herself inside an oval frame. She was standing upon a globe. Dazzling rays of light were coming from rings on her fingers over the globe. She said the rays were symbols of the graces that would be bestowed on all who asked for them. Asked why some of her rings did not shed light, Mary replied, "Those are the graces for which people forget to ask." Around the edge of the oval frame in golden letters appeared the words in French, "O Mary, conceived without sin, pray for us who have recourse to thee." The frame then rotated showing the back. On the back was a circle of twelve stars and a large letter M surmounted by a cross. Underneath the Cross and M, was the Sacred Heart of Jesus crowned with thorns and the Immaculate Heart of Mary pierced with a sword.

Our Lady told Catherine to take these images to her confessor and tell him that they should be put on medals. Our Lady promised great graces to those who wear the medal when blessed. Catherine did as she was asked. After an investigation of two years, her spiritual director obtained the approval of the Archbishop of Paris to produce the medal. The first medals were made on June 30, 1832. With their distribution, the devotion spread rapidly throughout the world. Those who wore the medal felt that they had received great blessings. Soon the medal came to be called the "Miraculous Medal." Pope Pius XII canonized Catherine Labouré in 1947.

St. Bernadette

On February 11, 1858, a fourteen-year-old French girl named Bernadette Soubirous was gathering firewood with her sister on the banks of a little river near Lourdes, France. She happened to glance up at a nearby grotto, where she saw a beautiful lady. The Lady was standing in the grotto surrounded by a heavenly light. She was dressed

Our Lady appears to St. Bernadette

all in white and a white veil covered her head. Around her waist she wore a blue sash. Her hands were folded in prayer and she held a rosary. Startled, Bernadette fell to her knees, took out her own rosary and began to pray. When she came to the last "Glory Be" the Lady disappeared.

Bernadette told her parents and neighbors about the vision. The following Sunday Bernadette came back to the same spot and again she saw the vision. She waited until Thursday before she returned and the same thing happened. This time, the vision told Bernadette to come to the grotto every day for fifteen days. As a reward she promised to make Bernadette happy, not in this world but in the next.

Bernadette soon had a large number of people following her on her daily journey. Some came out of curiosity but others came because they believed they were witnessing a miracle. They did not see the Lady but they could see from the look on Bernadette's face and the manner in which she knelt and prayed, that the Lady was there.

During the ninth visit, the Lady told Bernadette to drink and wash from a nearby spring. However, Bernadette could see no spring. However, she did as she was told by digging in the dirt with her bare hands and then attempting to drink some muddy drops. When she turned to the crowd, her face was smeared with mud and no spring had been revealed. However, in the next few days a spring began to flow from the muddy patch dug by Bernadette. Some devout people followed her example by drinking and washing in the water, which was soon reported to have healing properties.

During the thirteenth apparition Bernadette told her family that the Lady had said to tell the priests to build a chapel at the grotto. Accompanied by two of her aunts, Bernadette duly went to the parish priest with the request. He told Bernadette that the Lady must identify herself. On her next visit Bernadette asked the Lady her name, but the Lady only smiled and said nothing. At last, on March 25, the Feast of the Annunciation, the Lady answered Bernadette's question. "I am the Immaculate Conception," she said. Four years earlier on December 8, 1854, Pope Pius IX had defined the Dogma of the Immaculate Conception: that, alone of all human beings who have ever lived (save for Jesus, Adam, and Eve), Mary, by a singular grace and privilege, was conceived without the stain of original sin. Bernadette's parents, teachers, and priests all later testified that she had never heard the words "immaculate conception" from them.

For a while the Bishop hesitated to build the chapel as Our Lady requested, because he wanted to be sure that the vision was real. Miracles were happening. People who drank from the spring and washed themselves with its water were cured of various sicknesses. These miracles convinced the Bishop that it was indeed the Blessed Mother who had spoken to Bernadette. He began construction of the chapel. Today a magnificent basilica, hospital, and shrine have been built. Every year millions of pilgrims travel to Lourdes seeking physical and spiritual healing.

Disliking the attention she was attracting, Bernadette went to the boarding school run by the Sisters of Charity, where she finally learned to read and write. In 1866, at the age of 22, she joined the Sisters of Charity and moved into their motherhouse at Nevers. She spent the rest of her brief life there, working in the infirmary and as a sacristan, creating beautiful embroidery for altar cloths and vestments. She later contracted tuberculosis. She died of her illness at the age of 35 on April 16, 1879. Pope Pius XI canonized her on December 8, 1933. The promise of Our Lady was fulfilled. Bernadette's happiness did not come in this world but in the next. She is the patron saint of the sick and the family.

Review Exercises

1. Who were some of the leaders of the Catholic Revival in France?
2. Where were the great centers of the Catholic Revival in Germany?
3. Who led the Catholic emancipation movement in nineteenth century Great Britain?
4. Who was the leader of the Oxford movement?
5. Name three English cardinals during the nineteenth century.
6. Which pope restored the Catholic hierarchy in England?
7. What was the most significant accomplishment of the First Vatican Council?
8. What were the "Falk Laws" in Germany?
9. With what Sacrament is the Curé of Ars most closely associated?
10. What is the Dogma of the Immaculate Conception?

THE CHURCH IN THE
TURN OF THE CENTURY (1878 - 1922)

Pope St. Pius X distributes First Holy Communion. The pope taught that young children had a right to receive the Blessed Sacrament as soon as they reached the age of reason, about seven years old.

The Election of Pope Leo XIII

When Pope Pius IX died, Cardinal Vincenzo Pecci succeeded him. He chose to be called Leo XIII (1878-1903). Leo XIII was one of the greatest popes ever to sit on the throne of St. Peter. His pontificate was particularly brilliant, as it followed the loss of the temporal prestige of the papacy during the reign of Pius IX. At his election, Leo was sixty-eight years old and in poor health. Thus, no one expected him to live very long. However, in the providence of God, he ruled the Church for twenty-five years. A born leader, he endeared himself to Catholics and non-Catholics alike. For a quarter of a century, he proved himself on every occasion to be a talented diplomat, a polished scholar, a deep thinker, a friend of the working classes, and, most importantly, a holy man.

Leo XIII as Diplomat

Throughout his reign, Leo XIII proved that he was a brilliant statesman and diplomat. Early in his papacy he became involved in the troubles of the Church in Germany. Talks between Germany and the Holy See resulted in improved relations and the gradual abolishment of the Falk Laws. In the early 1880s, the French government passed some anti-clerical laws. Pope Leo wrote to the bishops of France. He urged them to try to work with the French government. He followed this letter with another in which he insisted that the right to govern is not linked with any one form of government. In Italy, he energetically opposed the measures adopted by that government to suppress papal power and influence.

Through his diplomatic skills, Pope Leo won the respect of many nations. Even non-Catholic rulers visited him and paid him their respects. Though he had no temporal power and never left the Vatican, his influence in world affairs was as great as that of any other pope.

443

Rerum Novarum

In 1891, Pope Leo XIII issued his encyclical, *Rerum Novarum* (On the Condition of the Working Classes). This is one of the greatest pronouncements ever made on the subject of Labor. It attracted universal attention. Leo wrote that there must not be strife among the classes. The working classes must not endeavor to ruin the capitalists. In response to a growing faction who believed otherwise, Leo wrote "private property is a natural right of man." However, Leo also recognized that there was a balance. He was careful to point out that property involves certain obligations. Consequently, employers must pay their workers a decent wage. They must never work them beyond their capacity nor employ them in work unsuited to their age or gender. He also said employers must ensure that their workers have time for their religious duties. The encyclical was received with great enthusiasm and translated into all major languages. It was seen as an approval of the Church's past work and a guide for her future.

Leo XIII on Education

In addition to his other concerns, Leo XIII was also interested in advancing science and education. In 1879, he wrote an encyclical that created new interest in the writings and the philosophy of St. Thomas Aquinas. He encouraged scholars to study St. Thomas' writings more deeply. He hoped that they could use Thomas's ideas to solve modern problems. Later he proclaimed St. Thomas patron of Catholic colleges and universities. In 1883, Pope Leo opened the Vatican archives to scholars and students.

Leo XIII and the Missions

Towards the end of the nineteenth century, the nations of Europe turned their eyes toward Asia and Africa. The Europeans needed raw materials for their factories and food for their people. They thought that areas of Asia and Africa would make good colonies and could provide these raw materials. Leo XIII became the champion of the native peoples in these colonies. He opposed an attempt to enslave the native peoples. Most importantly, he sent missionaries along with the colonists to preach Catholicism to the pagans. During his papacy, zeal for the missions became worldwide. Religious orders

Pope Leo XIII

prepared priests and nuns for the mission fields and the laity made generous financial contributions to help spread the Faith.

The Election of Pope St. Pius X

Pope Leo XIII died in 1903. The conclave that followed elected Joseph Sarto, the Archbishop of Venice, as pope. He chose to be called Pius X (1903-1914). He was a holy man with all the characteristics of a simple parish priest. All his life he had loved the poor and labored among them. The motto that he took at the beginning of his pontificate, "To restore all things in Christ," was the key to the whole program of his reign. Pius X was first and last a great shepherd of souls. His long career as a parish priest had prepared him for this special task.

Pius X and the Holy Eucharist

In 1905, Pope Pius X issued a landmark decree that significantly changed the practice of the Church regarding the reception of the Eucharist. The pope now invited the faithful to receive Holy Communion as often as possible. Too many Catholics had the mistaken idea that they were not good enough to receive daily. Pius reminded them that it is Our Lord's desire that the Holy Eucharist become our Daily Bread. Christ invites sinners as well as saints to eat His Flesh and drink His Blood. The graces people receive from the frequent reception of the Eucharist will strengthen them. These graces will help them to conquer temptation and lead holy lives.

Another mistaken idea about the Eucharist was that a child had to be an adolescent to receive the Eucharist. Children had to wait until they were over twelve years old before they received for the first time. Pius X taught that young children had a right to receive Holy Communion as soon as they attained the age of reason, about seven years old. Children simply had to know that Our Lord is really and truly present in the Eucharist. He wanted young children to be united with Christ before their souls had been tainted by sin.

Pius X on Church Music and Canon Law

Also in 1905, Pope Pius ordered a reform of Church music. His love for the Eucharist and the Mass caused the Pope to order that Gregorian Chant be used in the Mass. Church music had become very worldly. Many of the Masses and hymns were not fit for the Church. The pope wanted the simple beauty of the Church's own music to be restored. He felt that when the people heard and sang the Chant their spirits would be raised to higher things and they would not be distracted in their worship.

Pius X was zealous to spread Catholic learning. In 1909, he founded a school in Rome called the Biblical Institute. This school was dedicated to the study of the Sacred Scripture. Pius X also issued a number of excellent disciplinary decrees. He redrafted the laws of the Church. He arranged them in a more orderly fashion and adapted them to the needs of his day. He appointed a commission to study the code of Canon Law. The New Code would not actually appear until the reign of Benedict XV (1914-1922).

The Condemnation of Modernism

One of the outstanding achievements of Pius X was the detection and swift condemnation of the errors of Modernism, which he called the "synthesis of all errors." There were those who thought that the Church could make more progress in the world if only she would bring her teachings into conformity with popular ideas. They wanted the Church to be "modern." However, the Modernists strayed from the Truth. It was not long before they were teaching heretical doctrines concerning God, Our Lord, and the Bible. Unfortunately several prominent Catholic priests, especially in France, England, and Italy, defended Modernism. Pius X sensed the danger and took a firm stand.

Pius X condemned Modernism as containing three fundamental errors. Firstly, it taught that supernatural truths could not be known with certainty by human reason. Secondly, it taught that Scripture and Tradition do not contain revelations from God. They are merely the feelings and inner experiences of extremely religious people. Finally, Modernists taught that Jesus Christ had not instituted the Church, her dogmas, and moral standards. Rather, her dogmas and morality are the result of a gradual evolution. As such they can change. Over time, the Church will be forced to change her dogmas and moral standards. This third part of the heresy of Modernism is perhaps the most dangerous position of the Modernists. It is still common today among some Catholics who believe that the Church will change her most basic moral teachings.

In 1907, Pius X wrote the great encyclical *Pascendi* against Modernism. He hoped to bring the Modernist priests to their senses and to remind the world of the Church's true teachings. He also published a syllabus of Modernist errors. This document contained a list of sixty-five propositions, the majority of which restated the errors of the Modernists. The remedies were clear. The Holy Father insisted that priests be given sound

Pope St. Pius X

training in the seminaries and be thoroughly grounded in **Scholastic** philosophy and theology. He also ordered that all priests take an oath not to teach Modernist theories.

Pius X and the Church in France

The leaders of the French government that had been created in 1870 hated the Church and persecuted her relentlessly. During their reigns, Pius IX and Leo XIII had protested against the treatment of priests and religious in France. In 1875, the government started a violent persecution against the Church. Catholic universities were not allowed to grant degrees. Priests were forced to serve in the army. Children were compelled to attend schools where religious instruction was forbidden. Despite the persecution, Pope Leo XIII had been very patient with the Eldest Daughter of the Church. Leo XIII encouraged Catholics to try to be loyal to the government. As a result, the French government toned down its anti-Catholic activities for a while.

In 1901, however, the vicious attacks on the Church resumed. The French government set aside all the agreements it had made with the Church. The government passed the infamous "Associations Law." This law decreed that all religious associations had to disband. The government refused to allow any religious order to exist in France without special permission and drove out all but a very few of them. In 1902 and 1903, almost six thousand Catholic schools were closed. A little later eighty-one orders of nuns were forced to disband. The nuns had to leave their convents. They either had to work in secular society or were exiled.

Finally, in 1905, the government passed a law completely separating the Church and the State. From now on, there was to be no government support for any Church activity. Church property was taken over by the State. Bishops were put out of their residences. Seminaries became public buildings.

Pius X protested against the actions of the French government and condemned the Separation Law. In spite of all the harm that had been done, particularly to the children of France who were deprived of a Catholic education, the Church in France grew spiritually. Priests became closer to their parishioners. Since the faithful had to support the Church themselves, their love for the Church began to deepen. Prior to the Separation Law, the French government could become involved in the appointment of bishops. Henceforth this was not the case. Now the bishops could give their full allegiance to the Pope and not worry about the State.

Pope Benedict XV and World War I

In August 1914, Austria declared war on Serbia. Pius X pleaded with the Emperor, Franz Joseph, not to take this step. However, the Emperor, a good and holy Catholic, had seen his wife and nephew murdered by Serbian anarchists. The Emperor did not listen to the Pope and within a few months all of Europe was at war. The pope was an old man in failing health. The horrible spectacle of war was too much for him to bear. He died on August 20, 1914. Forty years later, Pope Pius XII declared him a saint. It was the first canonization of a pope since 1712.

In September, Cardinal Della Chiesa, the Archbishop of Bologna, was elected pope. He took the name Benedict XV (1914-1922). In his first year as pope, he appealed three times to the rulers of the warring nations, pleading with them to end the bloody conflict. On August 1, 1917, he sent a note to the warring powers suggesting terms of a just peace. Had the rulers of Europe listened to his plea, the lives of more than a million men would have been spared.

Pope Benedict XV

All during the war Pope Benedict's influence increased. In 1914, England appointed an ambassador to the Vatican. In 1916, Holland appointed a representative for the first time since the days of Luther. In 1917, the German government revoked the law against the Jesuits. In 1918, Portugal resumed diplomatic relations after a break of many years. After the French elections of 1919, the Catholics were so strong in the government that religious freedom was restored and relations with the Holy See resumed. The Prince of Wales, the English Prime Minister, and the President of the United States all visited Benedict XV. All over the world the Faithful, in answer to the Holy Father's call, prayed for peace.

Pope Benedict not only tried to end the war, but also was concerned for its victims. He encouraged charitable organizations of every kind in their task of easing the suffering and famine that are a result of war. He created one of the first agencies to locate prisoners of war and soldiers who were missing. He worked for the exchange of the more seriously wounded prisoners. He condemned the cutting off of food supplies from the starving people of Central Europe. He begged the faithful in neutral countries, especially in the United States before it entered the war, to contribute money to him. Catholics responded to his plea and he was able to raise millions of dollars. He used the money to feed starving people and care for needy children everywhere. He was the great benefactor to people in all places, regardless of their nationality or their religion.

Everyone admired the care with which the Holy Father, who had children on both sides of the conflict, observed the strictest neutrality. He preserved his neutrality when he invited the warring nations to end the universal carnage. He blamed only in a general way the crimes committed against justice. After the war, the League of Nations acknowledged its gratitude to him for his generous work. At the close of the war, he published his famous Peace Encyclical. This letter did more than all other agencies combined to break down the barriers of hatred between the nations. Pope Benedict XV died January 22, 1922.

Review Exercises

1. What was the subject of the encyclical, *Rerum Novarum*?
2. What did Pope Leo XIII write about private property?
3. What was the motto of Pope Pius X?
4. What two major changes did Pius X make regarding Holy Communion?
5. Name the three fundamental errors Pius X condemned Modernism as containing.
6. In addition to trying to end World War I, Pope Benedict XV also did many other things to alleviate the suffering the War caused. Name at least three things Benedict did to alleviate suffering.

CHAPTER 31

THE CHURCH FACES THE
GREAT THREATS OF THE 20ᵀᴴ CENTURY:
NAZISM AND COMMUNISM

The Valley of the Fallen and the Basilica of the Holy Cross in El Escorial, Spain. The memorial is dedicated to the Spaniards who died during the Spanish Civil War.

Pius XI and Universal Peace

Following the death of Pope Benedict XV, the Sacred College elected Cardinal Achille Ratti to the Holy See. He chose to be called Pius XI (1922-1939). The new Pope had become a priest at the age of twenty-two. Throughout his life he was an accomplished scholar but always a humble priest. Due to his excellent education he was made director of the Ambrosian Library at Milan and head of the Vatican Library. After World War I, he served as papal nuncio to Poland. In

453

1921, Benedict XV made him cardinal archbishop of Milan. Like his predecessor, the new Pope was deeply concerned with the problem of universal peace. Much of his time would be spent working for peace. Sadly, he would die on the eve of history's most terrible war.

Social Teachings

Pius XI issued his first encyclical in December 1922. It was called *On the Peace of Christ*. It dealt with his goal of Christianizing a world that was becoming more and more secular. It also started the "Catholic Action" movement. The idea behind Catholic Action was to involve the laity in an organization, supervised by the bishops, which would actively spread Catholic values and political ideas. Pius XI also approved associations of young Catholic industrial workers who wanted to

Pope Pius XI

Christianize the workforce. These groups would also provide a Catholic alternative to Communist and socialist trade unions.

Pius XI's 1930 encyclical, *Casti Connubii* (On Christian Marriage) dealt with marriage and the family. He showed how Christian marriage and the family are the foundation for any good society. He taught that parents have the power and the right to educate their children. This power comes from the sacramental graces of Matrimony.

One of Pius XI's most important encyclicals on modern society was *Quadragesimo Anno* (On Reconstruction of the Social Order). In it, Pius XI argued for a reconstruction of economic and political life based on religious values. Issued in 1931, *Quadragesimo Anno* was written to mark "forty years" since Pope Leo XIII's landmark encyclical *Rerum Novarum*. It restated that encyclical's warnings against both socialism and unrestrained capitalism. Both are enemies of human freedom and dignity. Pius XI pictured an economy based on co-operation and unity between worker and employer.

The Soviet Union

Like his predecessor, Pius XI sought to ease physical suffering. He wanted to help the starving people of the Soviet Union. However, he did not want to support the Communist government. Therefore, he insisted that Catholic priests accompany all shipments of food to the Soviet Union. He entered into talks with the Soviet government and succeeded in helping many of the needy. Papal diplomats also asked the Soviets to stop the religious persecution in their country. The Holy See requested the return of all confiscated Church property. The Vatican even offered to buy back a number of precious works of art. The papacy, however, did not reckon with the bad faith of the Communists, who insisted that religion and material welfare were incompatible. They flooded the country with indecent, blasphemous, and atheistic materials and newspapers. Sadly, as is almost always the case with Communists, the talks failed to bear fruit.

Italy

The forces of King Victor Emmanuel II had seized most of the Papal States in 1860, when the modern unified Italian state was founded. The rest of the Papal States, including Rome, were taken in 1870. Since then, the Papacy and the Italian government had had an uneasy relationship. The popes had refused to recognize Italy's seizure of the Papal States. They had chosen to live as voluntary prisoners in the Vatican. For its part, Italy's government had policies that were anti-clerical. Pius XI aimed to end the long breach between the papacy and the Italian government. He hoped to gain recognition once more of the sovereign independence of the Holy See. These aims led to one of his most notable achievements. In 1929, the Pope and the Italian government signed the Lateran Treaty.

In the Lateran Treaty the Holy See acknowledged the unity of the Kingdom of Italy, with Rome as its capital. The Italian government recognized the independence of the Holy See and its supreme authority over Vatican City. The Treaty marked the end of the separation of Church and State in Italy. The Treaty made Catholicism the state religion. It required that the Catholic Faith be taught in all primary and secondary schools. Catholic organizations received full recognition. Catholic marriages were legalized. All clerics and religious were removed from the jurisdiction of the civil courts.

Unfortunately, the Vatican's relationship with the Italian government deteriorated severely in the following years. At this time an evil man named Benito Mussolini led Italy. His tyrannical ambitions began to impinge more and more on the freedom of the Church. In 1931, he disbanded the Catholic youth groups in Italy. He wanted his Fascist youth groups to be the only ones. As a consequence, Pius issued an encyclical. He criticized Mussolini's idea of a totalitarian state and his treatment of the Church. Relations with Italy continued to worsen throughout the rest of Pius XI's pontificate.

The signing of the Lateran Treaty. Benito Mussolini is seated in the middle.

Mexico and the Cristero Rebellion

During the reign of Pius XI, the Mexican government subjected the Catholic Church to extreme persecutions. Over 5,000 priests, bishops, and religious were killed. Venustiano Carranza, who was president from 1917 to 1920, and Alvaro Obregon, who ruled from 1920 to 1924, were both Communists. They both viciously persecuted the Church. Carranza exiled the Mexican bishops. In 1917 he helped create the Constitution of Queretaro. This thoroughly anti-Catholic document almost destroyed the Church in Mexico.

Obregon's successor was another Communist, Elias Calles. He ruled from 1924 to 1928. Calles was one of the greatest enemies the Church has ever known. He began his presidency by launching a vigorous attack on the Church. His first step was to expel all foreign-born priests. Once he was rid of them, he proceeded to enforce a part of the Constitution that limited the number of priests according to the population of each state. The governors of the Mexican states enforced Calles' orders with a brutal efficiency. In the Mexican state of Michoacan, where 523 priests had formerly served the people, the government allowed only fifty priests. In the state of Oaxaca thirty priests were allowed. In Tabasco only five priests remained and the state forced them to marry. In 1926, the government issued a decree forbidding priests to teach in the schools. Schools were prohibited from possessing chapels. Another government decree threatened foreign priests and Catholic teachers with death or exile. The government also threatened anyone who spoke out against its actions and policies with death or exile.

Rather than yielding to these outrageous policies, the bishops of Mexico suspended all church services. The bishops believed that a country that had been saved from the darkness of the Aztecs would not fall to the Communists. They put their faith in Our Lady of Guadalupe and the Catholics of Mexico. Beginning on July 31, 1926, all forms of public worship were discontinued throughout the nation. The faithful could still visit their parish churches and pray, but no priests ministered to their needs. Then the bishops and a number of priests went into voluntary exile. Other priests remained to exercise their sacred functions at the risk of their lives.

The Catholics of Mexico displayed great courage throughout this cruel persecution. Frequently the leaders of a community would gather the people in the parish church. There, they would all recite the prayers of the Mass and teach the catechism to their children. The Catholic political party, which had been torn by divisions and strife, set aside its differences. They organized a political response. Calles retaliated with further bloody persecutions. Men and women from every rank of society were put to death.

In 1926, with the persecutions at their height, the Catholics of Mexico fought back. Following some small attacks, full-scale fighting broke out in January 1927. The Catholics called themselves "Cristeros" because they were fighting for Christ. The Cristero Rebellion had begun.

Most of the world looked on but refused to be moved by the bloodshed. However, Pius XI, backed by the American bishops, protested against the actions of the Mexican government. He praised the Catholics of Mexico for their courage and heroism. In 1929, as the Cristeros were winning the war, the United States intervened and negotiated an end to the war. However, Calles was a Communist and a totally dishonorable man. He did not abide by the terms of the peace treaty. He resumed the persecutions. In the years that followed, he murdered about six thousand Cristeros. In 1932, Pius XI again condemned the Mexican government. The persecution continued until 1940, when Manuel Ávila Camacho, a Catholic, became President. He finally returned the Mexican churches to the Catholic Church.

The damage done to the Church in Mexico by Calles and his Communist allies was devastating. In 1926, there had been about 4,500 Mexican priests serving the Mexican people. By 1934, over 90% of them had suffered some form of persecution. Over 4,100 Mexican priests had left, been forced out, or been murdered. The government licensed only 334 priests to serve fifteen million people. By 1935, seventeen of Mexico's thirty-one states had no priests at all.

Spain: The Spanish Civil War (1936-1939)

One of the most significant events to occur during the reign of Pius XI was the Spanish Civil War. Many secular historians feel that the wrong side won: the Nationalist (Catholic) side. They point out that the leader of the Nationalist forces, Francisco Franco, received

General Francisco Franco

aid from Nazi Germany. This is quite true. However, they almost never mention the thousands of Catholic priests and nuns whom the other side, the Republican (Communist) forces, murdered. Though Franco took German military aid during the Civil War, he did not help Germany during World War II. Franco refused Hitler's demands in 1940, the year of Hitler's greatest power, that Spain assist him. Spain remained neutral during World War II. The Republican forces also received foreign military aid. Most of it came from the Soviet Union. Also, many Communists came from all over the world, including the United States, to fight on the Republican side.

The government that came to power in Spain in the beginning of 1931, while called "Republican," was, in fact, Communist to its core. Like all Communist governments it was extremely anti-Catholic. The government secularized education and prohibited the teaching of the Faith in the schools. The government closed many Catholic schools throughout Spain and some were even destroyed. The Communists expelled the Jesuits from Spain.

In May 1931, the Archbishop of Toledo, the leader of the Church in Spain, wrote a pastoral letter. He urged Spanish Catholics to obey and respect the new government. However, he also wrote that he thought that the establishment of a republic was not good for Spain. The letter became the excuse for government attacks on churches throughout the country. They were burned and looted. In June, after he returned to Spain from a meeting in Rome with Pius XI, the government had the Archbishop arrested and deported.

In 1932, Pius XI protested against these actions. He urged the Catholics in Spain to fight against these injustices with all legal means. In 1933, he issued an encyclical in which he complained about the government's seizure of all Church buildings, seminaries, monasteries, and the residences of priests and bishops. They were now the property of the Spanish State. The Church had to pay rent and taxes in order to use them. The government also seized religious vestments, liturgical instruments, statues, pictures, and other objects necessary for worship.

Throughout the spring of 1936, the persecution in Spain grew even worse. On May 1, thousands of Communists paraded down Madrid's main street carrying pictures of Lenin and Stalin. Three days later a number of churches in Madrid were attacked, as were several religious. A Communist mob killed three nuns. From May until July, there were more murders and attacks on priests and nuns. Churches were regularly bombed and destroyed.

The Spanish Civil War began on July 18, 1936. That morning, General Francisco Franco sent out a radio broadcast explaining his reasons for taking up arms against the Spanish government. Catholics supported Franco and his Nationalist forces. The war lasted three years. During the war, the Communists destroyed thousands of churches and murdered thousands of Spanish clergy.

Over 1,100 years earlier, Pelayo had stood in his mountain cave surrounded by Moslems. He refused to surrender or to leave. Now that spirit awaken in Spain's priests and bishops. Aware of the dangers, all of Spain's bishops decided to remain in their dioceses. The Bishop of Cuenca summed up the feelings of his fellow bishops: "I cannot go, here alone is my responsibility, whatever may happen."

By August 1936, the Nationalist forces had mobilized and begun to reclaim Spain from the Communists. For the next three years Heaven and Hell battled for the soul of Spain. In Communist controlled areas, priests and religious continued to suffer martyrdom. Slowly the Catholic forces lead by Franco began to conquer Spain. Most of Spain

Spanish Communists shooting at a statue of the Sacred Heart—July 8, 1936.

fell quickly to Franco. Sadly, Madrid held out for two and a half years before falling.

At the end of December 1936, General Franco, now recognized as the head of the Nationalist government signed a concordat with the Church. In it he promised full freedom for the Church. He promised to work closely with the Church and bring Spanish laws into conformity with Church doctrine. During the thirty-six years that he governed Spain after the Civil War, he strove to keep his agreement.

The total number of Catholic priests and religious martyred in Republican territory during the Spanish Civil War was 6,832. It is the greatest clerical bloodletting in the history of the Catholic Church. It exceeds the number of victims martyred by the French Revolution and the Communist Revolution in Russia. Almost twelve percent of the religious in Spain were martyred. Most of the murders occurred during the first six months of the war. In a 1937 letter, the Spanish bishops estimated that of the 42,000 churches and chapels in Spain, 20,000 had been destroyed. In Barcelona, a Communist stronghold, only ten churches in the entire diocese escaped undamaged.

Germany

Pius XI tried to sign concordats with any country willing to do so. He felt that written treaties were the best way to protect the Church's rights. In January 1933, Nazi leader Adolf Hitler became Chancellor of Germany. When he asked for a concordat, Pius XI agreed. The treaty with Germany guaranteed freedom for the Church, for Catholic organizations, and for Catholic youth groups. It also promised the Church the right to teach religion in the schools. However, Hitler, like Mussolini, was a man of great ambition and great evil. Relations with Germany began to deteriorate very quickly. They soon became quite serious.

In 1937, Pius issued the encyclical *Mit Brennender Sorge* (On the Church and the German Reich). (The title is literally "With burning sorrow.") Unlike most encyclicals, which are written in Latin, this was written in German. The pope wrote in response to the increasing Nazi hostility towards Christianity. He condemned the Nazi ideology of racism and totalitarianism. He also condemned Nazi violations of the 1933 concordat. Since the Nazis would not allow any anti-Nazi material into Germany, copies of the encyclical had to be smuggled into the country. A group of brave motorcyclists secretly distributed them. On Palm Sunday it was read from the pulpit of every Catholic church. It was the first official denunciation of Nazism made by any major organization. The Nazis became even angrier with the Church. They persecuted the Church even more.

Many German Catholics who took part in the secret printing and distribution of the encyclical were discovered and went to jail and concentration camps. Sadly, the Western democracies remained silent. For the rest of his Papacy, Pope Pius XI continued to denounce the Nazis and Hitler's racist policies. In the late 1930s, when Mussolini began imitating Hitler's anti-Jewish laws, Pius condemned them as well. Pope Pius XI died February 10, 1939. The world was on the brink of another World War. The next pontiff would need to be a great diplomat if he were to survive. The conclave of 1939 would choose just such a man.

The Election of Pope Pius XII

Pius XI was succeeded by his Secretary of State, Cardinal Eugenio Pacelli. Upon his election Cardinal Pacelli chose to be called Pius XII (1939-1958) in honor of his friend, Pius XI. An accomplished diplomat, Cardinal Pacelli would continue Pius XI's struggle against the Nazis. He would do so as a virtual prisoner in the Vatican during World War II. After the War, he would face the even greater evil of Communism.

Before becoming Pope, Eugenio Pacelli had one of the most illustrious careers of any man to wear the Fisherman's Ring. Born in 1876, to a noble Italian family, he decided as a young boy that he wanted to be a priest. Ordained in 1899, his first assignment was at

Chiesa Nuova in Rome, where he had served as an altar boy. An extremely bright and able priest, he advanced rapidly in the Church. He became involved in the codification of canon law and then entered the Papal diplomatic service. During World War I, he maintained the Vatican's registry of prisoners of war. In 1915, he traveled to Vienna to assist the apostolic nuncio in his negotiations with Austria. In 1917, Pope Benedict XV made him an archbishop and sent him as papal nuncio

Pope Pius XII

to Germany. In Munich, Archbishop Pacelli conveyed to the German government the papal peace plan to end the War. Sadly, the plan was rejected. The War continued for another year.

In post-war Germany, Archbishop Pacelli worked primarily to improve relations between Church and State. He also worked on diplomatic arrangements between the Vatican and the Soviet Union. He negotiated food shipments to the Soviet Union, which was vigorously persecuting the Church. He met with the Soviets in the hopes of reducing the persecution. However, the Communists would not agree.

In December 1929, Pope Pius XI made Archbishop Pacelli a Cardinal. In February 1930, the Pope appointed him Secretary of State. As Secretary of State, he signed concordats with a number of countries. He also made many diplomatic visits throughout Europe as well as North and South America. In 1936, he visited the United States and met with President Franklin Roosevelt. In December 1939, Roosevelt appointed an envoy to the Vatican. The appointment re-established diplomatic relations that had been broken since 1870. The 1933 concordat with Germany was the most important of Cardinal Pacelli's treaties. Like Pius XI, he hoped the treaty would strengthen the Church's legal position. Following the Nazis' continual violation of the treaty, Cardinal Pacelli was very involved in writing *Mit Brennender Sorge*.

Pius XII and World War II

Pius XII's pontificate began on the eve of World War II. During the war, he adopted a policy of neutrality similar to the one that Pope Benedict XV had followed during World War I. He also employed many of the same policies that Benedict XV had during the First World War. In 1939, Pius XII turned the Vatican into a distribution center for aid that came to him from around the world. He created an information office for prisoners of war and refugees that operated from 1939 until 1947.

Despite being surrounded by his enemies, Pope Pius spoke out against atrocities. In his first encyclical in October 1939, he condemned the invasion of Poland by the Nazis and the Soviet Communists. In a December 1939 speech at the Vatican, Pius condemned the Soviet Union's attack on Finland. In January 1940, in a radio broadcast, he condemned the murder of over 15,000 Polish civilians. For these stands against the Nazis and Communists, even the secular media praised his courage. *Time* magazine credited Pius XII and the Catholic Church for "fighting totalitarianism more knowingly, devoutly, and authoritatively, and for a longer time, than any other organized power." *The New York Times* newspaper also praised him for opposing Nazi anti-Semitism and aggression.

Time Magazine cover of August 16, 1943

In 1943, Hitler made plans to arrest Pius and the cardinals of the Roman Curia. The pope told leading bishops that if the Nazis seized him that his resignation would take immediate effect. The Holy See would move to neutral Portugal where the College of Cardinals would elect a new pope. However, the plan never came to fruition. As the war approached its end in 1945, Pius urged the Allied leaders to be lenient in their treatment of the defeated nations. He hoped to prevent what he perceived to be the mistakes made at the end of World War I.

Pius XII and the Jews

Throughout the war the Church worked to help the Jews who were the victims of such violent Nazi persecution. Under Pius' leadership, the Church helped thousands of Jews escape the Nazis. It has been estimated that the Church saved hundreds of thousands of Jews from death. Many Jews publicly thanked the pope for his help. In September 1945, the general secretary of the World Jewish Council presented an award to the pope "in recognition of the work of the Holy See in rescuing Jews from Fascist and Nazi persecutions." After the war, in the fall of 1945, Harry Greenstein from Baltimore, a close friend of Chief Rabbi Herzog of Jerusalem, told Pius how grateful Jews were for all he had done for them. "My only regret," the pope replied, "is not to have been able to save a greater number of Jews." Most telling of the help Pius provided is the conversion of the chief rabbi of Rome, Israel Zolli. On February 13, 1945, Rabbi Zolli was baptized a Catholic. He chose as his Christian name "Eugenio" in gratitude to the Pope who had done so much for the Jews during the war. His wife was baptized along with him. One year later his daughter also became a Catholic.

Pius XII and China

Relations between Pius XII and China began hopefully. For centuries the people of China had difficulty becoming Catholic. This was because the Church did not recognize the Chinese custom of honoring dead relatives. For the Chinese this was an ancient ritual, but to the Church it was a superstition in conflict with Church teachings. Within a month of becoming Pope, Pius changed the policy of the Church. He declared that the so-called "Chinese Rites" were not superstition and did not violate Church teachings. Within a few years the Church in China began to flourish like never before.

In 1943, the government of China established diplomatic relations with the Vatican. Three years later, Pius created the first Chinese cardinal and established a local Chinese hierarchy. By 1949, the Church seemed to be well on her way to making significant conversions in China. However, in 1949, the Communists, under Mao Zedong, came to power. As all Communists have done, he persecuted the Church. By the early 1950s, the Catholic Church in China had almost been eliminated. By 1953, many Chinese and foreign bishops and priests had been arrested and thrown into prison where many died. In 1957, the government established the Chinese Patriotic Catholic Association. This is the state-run "church." By 1958, when all the Catholic bishops had been arrested, killed, or exiled, the Communists installed Patriotic bishops in their Sees. In his final encyclical, Pius protested the persecutions in China. He blessed and comforted those who remained faithful to the true Church.

Pius XII and the Soviet Union

From the beginning of the Soviet Union in 1917, the Communist government had been hostile to the Catholic Church. Catholic institutions had been dissolved. The Communists had stolen Church property. Pope Benedict XV and Pope Pius XI had both condemned Communism. Despite the protests, the Communists were determined to destroy religion in the Soviet Union and in any other countries that they conquered.

Following World War II, Soviet leader Joseph Stalin had Catholic priests arrested and thrown in prison. By 1946, the Church in the Soviet Union had almost ceased to exist. After Stalin's death in 1953, Pope Pius tried to talk to the new government. He hoped that the Church could again spread into the Soviet Union. For the remainder of his Papacy, Pius continued to work for the persecuted Catholics in the Soviet Union.

The Dogma of the Assumption

Throughout his life, Eugenio Pacelli had a great devotion to the Blessed Mother. On November 1 1950, Pope Pius XII, speaking *ex cathedra* defined the dogma of the Assumption. He infallibly declared that the "Immaculate Mother of God, having completed the course of her earthly life, was assumed body and soul into heavenly glory." In this dogmatic statement, the phrase "having completed the course of her earthly life," leaves open the question of whether Our Blessed Lady died before her Assumption, or, whether she was assumed without death. Both possibilities are allowed. Mary's Assumption was a divine gift to Mary as Mother of God.

The End of Pius XII's Papacy

The final years of Pius XII's reign began in late 1954. He suffered with a long illness, during which he considered resigning. He died on October 9, 1958.

Review Exercises

1. What did the Pope teach in *Casti Connubi*?
2. What was the Cristero Rebellion?
3. Why did Pius XI sign concordats?
4. What were some important gains the Church made as a result of the Lateran Treaty?
5. What is some evidence that Pius XII helped the Jews during WWII?
6. What is the Chinese Patriotic Catholic Association?
7. What is the Dogma of the Assumption?

CHAPTER 32

THE CHURCH AT THE END
OF THE THIRD MILLENNIUM (1958-2005)

Stained Glass window from Southwark Cathedral (London, England) showing Pope John Paul II administering the Sacrament of Anointing of the Sick in 1982.

Blessed Pope John XXIII

Angelo Roncalli was born in Italy on November 25, 1881. In 1904, he was ordained a priest. Pope Pius XI made him a bishop in 1925. Ten years later, the Pope named him Apostolic Delegate to Turkey and Greece. During World War II, as Apostolic Delegate, he helped thousands of Jews escape from the Nazis. In 1944, after the liberation of France, Pope Pius XII sent him as Apostolic Nuncio to France. In 1953, Pius XII made him a Cardinal. Following the death of Pope Pius XII in 1958, Roncalli was elected Pope. He chose the name John XXIII (1958-1963).

Blessed Pope John XXIII

Calling an ecumenical council was the most important act of John XXIII's pontificate. The Second Vatican Council began in October 1962. John XXIII would not live to see its conclusion. He also issued the encyclical *Pacem in Terris* (Peace on Earth) in April 1963. In it he taught that conflicts should be settled by negotiations, not force of arms. This was an important message, especially in an age of nuclear weapons. The pope also stressed the need for all governments to respect individual human rights.

Pope John XXIII died on June 3, 1963. On September 3, 2000, Pope John Paul II declared him "Blessed." Following his beatification, his body was moved from its original burial place below St Peter's. It was placed below an altar in the basilica where it is displayed for veneration.

Election of Pope Paul VI

Giovanni Battista Montini was born in Italy on September 26, 1897. Educated by the Jesuits, he entered the seminary in 1916. In May 1920, he was ordained a priest. From 1922 to 1954, he worked in the Vatican's State Department. There, he was considered one of Pope Pius XII's closest and most influential colleagues. During World War II, Montini worked closely with Pius XII. He helped the Pope answer the thousands of letters he received from all over the world asking for understanding, prayers, and material help. At the Pope's request, he created an information office for prisoners of war and refugees. He also helped to create the Pontifical Assistance Commission. This commission aided large numbers of Romans and refugees with food and shelter, and other material assistance. Montini helped to provide protection to hundreds of Allied soldiers who had escaped from prison camps. He also aided with the effort to save the Jews.

In 1954, Pius XII made Montini Archbishop of Milan. As Archbishop, he used new methods to reach the people of his diocese. His goal was to re-introduce the Faith to a city that had lost its Faith. The Archbishop recognized that Western Europe had become mission territory. In 1958, Pope John XXIII created him Cardinal. Following the Pope's death, the Sacred College elected Cardinal Montini to the Papacy. He chose the name Paul VI (1963-1978) to indicate a renewed worldwide mission to spread the Gospel. One of his first acts as pope was to re-opened Vatican Council II, which had closed with the death of John XXIII.

Vatican Council II

Six days after his election, Pope Paul announced that he would continue Vatican II. The pope re-opened the Council on September 29, 1963. He said he wanted the Council to work to better explain the Catholic Faith. Thus, he asked the Council Fathers not to repeat or create new dogmatic definitions but to explain the Church's teaching in simple terms. He also wanted the Council to address Church reforms, as well as take steps to help unify Christians. In its second session, the Council discussed the Church and the Mass, as well as promoting greater understanding with other religions.

Paul VI opened the third session of the Council on September 14, 1964. He told the Council that he thought that the Dogmatic Constitution on the Church (Lumen Gentium) was the most important document that it had produced. This document, issued in November 1964, dealt with almost every aspect of the Church. It called upon all Christians to become more holy. Its final section formally declared that the Blessed Mother "is acknowledged and honored as being truly the Mother of God and Mother of the Redeemer." As the Mother of Our Lord, she is also Mother of the Church. The Council concluded on December 8, 1965, the Feast of the Immaculate Conception.

Marian Devotion

Pope Paul's decision to declare Mary to be the Mother of the Church did not come as a surprise to those who knew him. Throughout his life, Pope Paul VI had a strong devotion to the Blessed Mother. He often spoke at Marian congresses and loved to visit Marian shrines. As Pope, he attempted to travel to Poland on a Marian pilgrimage, but the Communist government would not allow it. During his Papacy, he issued three Marian encyclicals.

In his first encyclical he called Mary the ideal of Christian perfection. He regarded devotion to her as of supreme importance in living the life of the Gospel. His encyclical, *On Prayers During May*, focused on the Blessed Mother, to whom the month of May is traditionally dedicated as the Mother of God. Paul VI wrote that Mary is rightly to be regarded as the way by which people are led to Christ. "The person who encounters Mary cannot help but encounter Christ likewise." He went on to

Pope Paul VI

write that God has appointed Mary to be "the most generous steward of His merciful gifts." In another encyclical he encouraged devotion to the Rosary.

The New Mass

During Pius XII's reign, the Vatican relaxed the rules on the use of Latin in the Mass. The Church allowed local languages to be used during baptisms, funerals, and other events. The Second Vatican Council then ordered a general revision of the Mass. In April 1969, Paul VI approved the "new Order of the Mass" (Novus Ordo). The Novus Ordo Mass had many significant changes to the old Mass. Some prayers were removed and others introduced. The pope's approval also included permission to use local languages instead of Latin. Not everyone welcomed these changes. Not everyone was happy

with what appeared to be the sudden ban on the centuries-old Mass
to which they were accustomed and which they had all grown up
attending. Also, many Modernists began to experiment with the new
Mass. Some churches replaced Gregorian Chant with pop and folk
music. Guitars replaced organs. Some churches made changes to their
sanctuaries, which some people viewed as sacrilege.

Humanae Vitae

In 1968, the world was closer to a worldwide Revolution
than ever before in history. Terrorist organizations sprang up all over
the world. All over the world there were revolts against established
governments. From Berkeley, California to Paris, France, students
were revolting in the name of "freedom." It was the same freedom that
the Revolutionaries had promised in France in 1789, and in Spain in
1936. It was the same freedom that the serpent had promised Eve in
the Garden. It was freedom from the Church and morality. In 1968,
as the world tottered on the brink, Pope Paul VI issued the most
controversial encyclical of the twentieth century: *Humanae Vitae* (On
Human Life). He condemned artificial birth control. He would spend
the remaining ten years of his Papacy on the Cross as Catholics and
non-Catholics alike decried his decision and howled with rage at him.
However, the world stepped back from oblivion for a little while at
least.

Pope Paul VI issued the encyclical *Humanae Vitae* on July 25,
1968. He explicitly reaffirmed the Catholic Church's long-standing
teaching regarding marriage and birth control. The views of Paul
VI reflected the teachings of all his predecessors. Despite enormous
pressure, especially from Western Europe and the United States, he
never changed his position.

To Paul VI and to all popes, a marriage is more than simply the union of a man and woman. It is a union of the man and the woman with a loving God. In marriage, these two people create a new person materially, while God completes the creation by adding the soul. For this reason, Paul VI writes in the first sentence of *Humanae Vitae*, "the transmission of human life is a most serious role in which married people collaborate freely and responsibly with God the Creator." This partnership with God does not allow for arbitrary human decisions, which may frustrate God's design or contradict the Author of life. Paul VI goes on to reaffirm the earlier teachings of the Church when he writes that the purpose of marriage is the procreation and education of children.

The international reaction to Humane Vitae was mixed. Most of Western Europe with the exceptions of Italy, Spain, Portugal, and Poland reacted negatively to it. The South American nations also mostly supported the Pope. The Patriarch of Constantinople fully supported the Pope. While the negative reaction in Western Europe and the United States concerned the Pope, it did not surprise him. He expected the reaction to be a temporary one. Sadly, he was wrong. Despite the fact that for the rest of his Papacy he would suffer constant verbal attacks for *Humanae Vitae*, he was a man of great courage. On its tenth anniversary, he reconfirmed his teaching. Pope John Paul II, in the face of even greater opposition, later reaffirmed and expanded upon *Humanae Vitae* in his 1995 encyclical *Evangelium Vitae* (The Gospel of Life).

Orthodox Churches

During the 1960's Paul VI met with the leaders of the Eastern Orthodox churches. He was the first pope in centuries to do so. His meeting with the Patriarch of Constantinople led to the withdrawal of the excommunications of the Great Schism of 1054. This was a major step towards restoring communion between Rome and Constantinople. The meetings also produced the Catholic-Orthodox Joint declaration of 1965. While the declaration did not end the schism, it did show a desire for a closer relationship between the two churches. In May 1973, the Coptic Patriarch of Alexandria met with Paul VI. Following the meetings the two prelates issued a joint declaration and Creed. The joint Creed showed that there are now few theological differences between the Coptic and the Catholic Church.

Final Months and Death

On August 6, 1978, less than two weeks after his re-affirmation of Humane Vitae, Pope Paul VI died. His confessor, a Jesuit priest who heard the Pope's weekly confession, said of him that "if Paul VI was not a saint when he was elected Pope, he became one during his pontificate. I was able to witness not only with what energy and dedication he toiled for Christ and the Church but also and above all, how much he suffered for Christ and the Church."

John Paul I

Following Pope Paul's death, Pope John Paul I, who reigned for only thirty-three days, succeeded him. He explained that he chose the name to honor to his two immediate predecessors. John XXIII had made him a bishop and Paul VI had made him a cardinal.

Pope John Paul II (1978-2005)

On October 16, 1978, Karol Jozef Cardinal Wojtyla (KARR-ol YOO-zef voy-TIH-wah) became the new Pope. Only fifty-eight years old, he was the youngest pope elected since the fifty-four-year old Pope Pius

IX in 1846. Young, and in excellent health, John Paul II would govern the Church for almost twenty-seven years. His was the third-longest reign in Church history. Only St. Peter and Blessed Pius IX served longer. Pope John Paul II was one of the most influential leaders of the twentieth century. Perhaps his greatest success was helping to end soviet-style Communism in his native Poland and eventually all

Pope John Paul II

of Eastern Europe. As part of his universal call to holiness, he nearly doubled the number of Saints and Blesseds. He beatified 1,340 people and canonized 483 others.

The Path to the Priesthood

Karol Jozef Wojtyla was born on May 18, 1920, in Wadowice, Poland. In his youth he served as an altar boy and enjoyed playing sports, especially soccer. He would remain physically active throughout his life. He grew up in a unique time in Polish history. The years from 1920, following the defeat of the Soviet army, to 1939, the Nazi invasion, were the only time since 1772 that Poland was a free country. (It would not be free again until 1989.) Thus, Karol grew up in a free country, but with an understanding of how fragile that freedom was. Though he would visit almost 130 countries, his heart never left Poland.

In the summer of 1938, after graduating at the top of his high school class, Karol moved to Krakow. There he enrolled at the Jagiellonian University. His studies came to an abrupt end in 1939 when the Nazis invaded Poland and closed the University. To escape the Nazis, who were killing Poles or putting them into concentration camps, Karol fled with thousands of others to the east. However, the Soviet Union had invaded eastern Poland and they were forced to return to Krakow. To avoid deportation by the Nazis, Karol worked in a chemical plant that the Nazis needed. He also secretly resumed his studies.

In October 1942, increasingly aware of his calling to the priesthood, Karol went to the Archbishop of Krakow. He told the Archbishop that he wanted to be a priest. For the next two years, he secretly attended seminary courses run by the Archbishop.

On August 6, 1944, the Nazis rounded up all the able-bodied men and boys in Krakow. The Nazis wanted to avoid an uprising in Krakow like the one that had occurred in Warsaw. Karol narrowly escaped by hiding in his uncle's basement. The Nazis arrested more than eight thousand men and boys, but Karol escaped to the Archbishop's Palace. He spent the rest of the war there hiding, disguised as a priest. On January 17, 1945, in the face of the advancing Soviet army, the Nazis fled the city. The murder of so many priests by the Nazis showed Karol the true meaning of the priesthood. In 1945, the Poles exchanged one evil tyrant for another. Communists from the Soviet Union replaced Nazis from Germany as the occupiers of Poland.

In 1946, the Archbishop of Krakow ordained Karol Wojtyla. He chose to say his first Mass in Wawel cathedral's crypt church where Poland's monarchs and national heroes were buried. He went to Rome to study theology for two years. Upon his return to Poland in the summer of 1948, he was assigned to the village of Niegowic, fifteen miles from Krakow. In March 1949, the bishop transferred him to Saint Florian parish in Krakow.

During the next decade Fr. Wojtyla taught theology and ethics at the Jagiellonian University and then at the Catholic University of Lublin. He also wrote a series of articles in Krakow's Catholic newspaper dealing with current church issues. He also wrote original literary works. In addition, he became the spiritual advisor to a group of young adults with whom he went camping and kayaking. Despite the Communist rule prohibiting it, they also celebrated Mass in the open.

Bishop and Cardinal

Church leaders had taken note of Wojtyla's ability to run a dynamic pastorate despite Communist restrictions. Thus, in 1958, Pope Pius XII appointed him Auxiliary Bishop of Krakow. At the age of thirty-eight, he was the youngest bishop in Poland and one of the youngest in the world. Beginning in October 1962, Bishop Wojtyla took part in Vatican Council II. He so distinguished himself that in December 1963, Pope Paul VI appointed him Archbishop of Krakow. In June 1967, Paul VI made Archbishop Wojtyla a member of the College of Cardinals. That same year, he helped the Pope to write *Humanae Vitae.*

As Cardinal Archbishop of Krakow, Wojtyla worked closely with Cardinal Stefan Wyszynski (Vi-shin-skee). Wyszynski was the Archbishop of Warsaw and the leader of the Church in Poland. Wyszynski was a national Polish hero and staunch anti-Communist. He had been arrested and put in prison by the Communists from 1953 until 1956. So great was Cardinal Wojtyla's love and respect for Cardinal Wyszynski that after his election as pope, as the cardinals came to kneel before the Holy Father to take their vows and kiss his ring, John Paul II stood up as Cardinal Wyszynski began to kneel down. He stopped him from kissing his ring—and hugged him.

Cardinal Stefan Wyszynski

John Paul II and Communism

John Paul II's second trip as pope was to Poland in June 1979. Wherever he went in Poland ecstatic crowds constantly surrounded him. He declared to his country's men and women that their Catholic faith dictated their right to be free. His visit lifted up the whole nation's spirit and sparked the formation of the Solidarity movement in 1980. On future trips to Poland, he gave support to the organization. This movement eventually brought freedom and human rights to Poland. Lech Walesa, the founder of the Solidarity movement, credited John Paul II with giving Poles the courage to rise up. Walesa said that the pope started a chain of events that led to the fall of Communism. Walesa explained that before John Paul II's pontificate nobody knew how to get rid of Communism. With the Pope's encouragement they were able to change their country.

In the next ten years Pope John Paul traveled to dozens of nations. Wherever he went he reinforced his message of religious freedom, national independence, and human rights. The process that he had begun in Poland would finally lead to the end of the Soviet Union's domination of Eastern Europe in 1989. John Paul II was the spiritual inspiration behind its downfall. He was the catalyst for peaceful change in Poland, which spread like wildfire through Soviet-controlled Europe. However, the Communists did not give up without a fight.

On May 13, 1981, as he entered St. Peter's Square to address an audience, a Turkish gunman shot and nearly killed John Paul. The pope was rushed to the hospital. He underwent five hours of surgery to treat his wounds. Before being operated on he told his doctors not to remove his Brown Scapular. Later, he said that Our Lady of Fatima kept him alive during this attempt on his life. The evidence indicates that the Soviet Union was behind the attack. They were retaliating for the Pope's support of Solidarity.

Social Teachings

John Paul's theology mirrored that of his predecessors. He had been involved in writing *Humanae Vitae* and as pope continued to defend the right to life. In his encyclical, *Evangelium Vitae*, he explicitly re-asserted Catholic moral teachings against murder, euthanasia, and abortion. He also taught about the dignity of women and the importance of the family for the future of mankind.

The Pope and Young People

Throughout his priesthood John Paul II had always had a special relationship with Catholic young people. Before he became Pope, he used to camp, hike, and kayak with young people. The education of future priests was particularly important to him. He made many visits to the seminaries in Rome. In 1984, he established

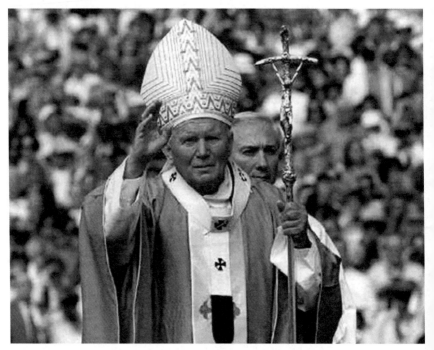

Pope John Paul II blessing the crowd.

World Youth Day. His goal was to bring young Catholics from all over the world together to celebrate the Faith. Millions of young Catholics from around the world attended the World Youth Days during his pontificate.

Eastern Orthodox Churches

Healing the divisions between the Catholic and Eastern Orthodox churches was one of Pope John Paul II's major goals. He worked diligently to end a break that had begun in 1054. In a 1988 Apostolic Letter, he wrote that the Church has two lungs and that it will never breathe easily until it uses both of them. In May 1999, he visited Romania at the invitation of the Patriarch of the Romanian Orthodox Church. This was the first time a pope had visited a predominantly Eastern Orthodox country since the Great Schism. In June 2001, the Pope visited the Ukraine, another heavily Orthodox area. He came at the invitation of the bishops of the Ukrainian Greek Catholic Church and the Catholic bishops of the Ukraine. The pope told the leaders of the Ukrainian Church that ending the Great Schism was one of his fondest desires. That same year he visited Greece where he met with the head of the Greek Orthodox Church. At the meeting, the Pope issued a public apology for the 1204 sacking of Constantinople. This terrible act remained a source of strife even after almost eight hundred years. Later, the two leaders said the Our Father together. This broke an Orthodox rule against praying with Catholics.

Beatification of John Paul "the Great"

Beginning in the early 1990s, the always-healthy Pope was slowed by Parkinson's Disease. Nevertheless, he continued to travel and speak to huge crowds. He said that his visible suffering was a part of his ministry. On April 2, 2005, John Paul II spoke his final words to his aides in Polish, "Let me go to the house of the Father." He died a few hours later.

Almost immediately after his death much of the laity began to refer to him as "John Paul the Great" and call for his canonization. There is no official process for declaring a pope "Great." The title is "granted" through popular and continued usage. In his first address upon becoming Pope, Pope Benedict XVI, spoke of him as "the great Pope John Paul II." Benedict also referred to Pope John Paul II as "the Great" in his homily at John Paul's funeral Mass. Since the funeral Pope Benedict XVI has continued to refer to John Paul II as "the Great." Inspired by calls of "Make him a Saint Now!" from the millions gathered during the funeral, Benedict XVI decided to waive the normal five-year waiting period before the beatification process can begin.

The Election of Pope Benedict XVI

On April 19, 2005, Cardinal Joseph Ratzinger was elected Pope after one of history's fastest Conclaves. He chose to be called Benedict XVI. He chose the name to honor Pope Benedict XV, whom he called "that courageous prophet of peace," and St. Benedict, the co-patron of Europe. Born in 1927 in Bavaria Germany, he was ordained a priest in June 1951. Starting in 1957, Ratzinger began a long and distinguished career teaching dogma and theology in several German universities. He also wrote a number of books about theology. His work attracted the attention of Pope Paul VI, who made him Archbishop of Munich in 1977. Three months later, the Pope made him a cardinal.

Pope Benedict XVI

In 1981, Pope John Paul II made Cardinal Ratzinger head of the Congregation for the Doctrine of the Faith. He was in charge of promoting and safeguarding Catholic doctrine around the world. In this role, he was to make sure that no one in the Church was teaching heresy. The pope and the Cardinal had been friends since 1977. They shared similar backgrounds. Both had lived under oppressive regimes. They held similar views on the Faith. Cardinal Ratzinger would be the Pope's closest advisor until John Paul II's death.

During the first years of his papacy, Benedict XVI has continued many of the policies of his friend John Paul II. He has emphasized the need for the West to return to its fundamental Christian values. He feels that the people of the West have lost their way. He has said that we live at a time when people do not feel the need for God or Our Lord. Everyone feels that they can make it on his or her own. Thus, he has called for a spiritual renewal.

Review Exercises

1. Who called the Second Vatican Council?
2. What did *Humanae Vitae* teach?
3. What does the Church teach are the purposes of marriage?
4. What three popes have had the longest reigns?
5. Which Pope canonized the most Saints?
6. What is the Solidarity movement?
7. Who was Cardinal Stefan Wyszynski?
8. Why did the Pope establish World Youth Day?
9. What did the Pope mean when he said that the Church has two lungs and that it will never breathe easily until it uses both of them?
10. What is the job of the Congregation for the Doctrine of the Faith?

LIST OF POPES

A note on the number of popes: One of the most consistent attacks on the Faith is that Catholics do not even know how many Pope there have been. Our Protestant brethren usually launch this attack. Have there been 266 popes or 265, or some other number entirely? The Church has an official list of the popes. However, due to death and politics there have been issues regarding the *numbering* of the popes. Let us look at two examples.

In 752, Pope Stephen II died after his election but before his consecration as pope. This may or may not result in a problem with the numbering of popes named Stephen. However, his successor, not thinking about Protestants one thousand years later, also decided to be called Stephen. Thus, some lists of popes include the elected, but not consecrated, Stephen, while others do not. The following list does not include him, nor does the official list.

In the first half of the eleventh century, Benedict IX was pope on three separate occasions. Thus he is listed three times, although one of his reigns was very brief, and at the end of the previous reign. For this reason some lists do not acknowledge the "break" in his Papacy and only list him twice. The Church considers him to be the 146th, 148th, and 151st popes. Thus, at the writing of this book, the current pope, Benedict XVI, is the 265th pope.

While the Church's official list of popes does not included antipopes, for historical purposes they are included in the following list.

LIST OF POPES
(Antipopes are printed in italics.)

1.	Peter	32-67	37.	Damasus I	366-384
2.	Linus	67-76		*Ursinus*	366-367
3.	Cletus	76-88	38.	Siricius	384-399
4.	Clement I	88-97	39.	Anastasius I	399-401
5.	Evaristus	97-105	40.	Innocent I	402-417
6.	Alexander I	105-115	41.	Zosimus	417-418
7.	Sixtus I	115-125	42.	Boniface I	418-422
8.	Telesphorus	125-136		*Eulalius*	418-419
9.	Hyginus	136-140	43	Celestine I	422-432
10.	Pius I	140-155	44.	Sixtus III	432-440
11.	Anicetus	155-166	45.	Leo I the Great	440-461
12.	Soter	166-175	46.	Hilary	461-468
13.	Eleutherius	175-189	47.	Simplicius	468-483
14.	Victor I	189-199	48.	Felix II (III)	483-492
15.	Zephyrinus	199-217	49.	Gelasius I	492-496
16.	Callistus I	217-222	50.	Anastasius II	496-498
	Hippolytus	217-235	51.	Symmachus	498-514
17.	Urban I	222-230		*Lawrence*	498-507
18.	Pontian	230-235	52.	Hormisdas	514-523
19.	Anterus	235-236	53.	John I	523-526
20.	Fabian	236-250	54.	Felix III (IV)	526-530
21.	Cornelius	251-253	55.	Boniface II	530-532
	Novatian	251-258		*Dioscorus*	530
22.	Lucius I	253-254	56.	John II	533-535
23.	Stephen I	254-257	S7.	Agapetus I	535-536
24.	Sixtus II	257-258	58.	Silverius	536-538
25.	Dionysius	259-268		*Vigilius*	537-538
26.	Felix I	269-274	59.	Vigilius	538-555
27.	Eutychian	275-283	60.	Pelagius I	556-561
28.	Caius	283-296	61.	John III	561-574
29.	Marcellinus	296-304	62.	Benedict I	575-579
30.	Marcellus	307-309	63.	Pelagius II	579-590
31.	Eusebius	310	64.	Gregory I the Great	590-604
32.	Miltiades	311-314	65.	Sabinian	604-606
33.	Sylvester I	314-335	66.	Boniface III	607
34.	Marcus	336	67.	Boniface IV	608-615
35.	Julius I	337-352	68.	Adeodatus I	615-618
36.	Liberius	352-366	69.	Boniface V	619-625
	Felix II	355-357	70.	Honorius I	625-638

71.	Severinus	640		107.	Adrian II	867-872
72.	John IV	640-642		108.	John VIII	872-882
73.	Theodore I	642-649		109.	Marinus I	882-884
74.	Martin I	649-655		110.	Adrian III	884-885
		(resigned)		111.	Stephen V	885-891
75.	Eugenius I	655-657		112.	Formosus	891-896
76.	Vitalian	657-672		113.	Boniface VI	896
77.	Adeodatus II	672-676		114.	Stephen VI	896-897
78.	Donus	676-678		115.	Romanus	897
79.	Agatho	678-681		116.	Theodore II	897
80.	Leo II	682-683		117.	John IX	898-900
81.	Benedict II	684-685		118.	Benedict IV	900-903
82.	John V	685-686		119.	Leo V	903
83.	Conon	686-687			*Christopher*	903-904
	Theodore	687		120.	Sergius III	904-911
	Paschal	687-692		121.	Anastasius III	911-913
84.	Sergius	687-701		122.	Lando	913-914
85.	John VI	701-705		123.	John X	914-928
86.	John VII	705-707		124.	Leo VI	928
87.	Sisinnius	708		125.	Stephen VII	929-931
88.	Constantine	708-715		126.	John XI	931-935
89.	Gregory II	715-731		127.	Leo VII	936-939
90.	Gregory III	731-741		128.	Stephen VIII	939-942
91.	Zachary	741-752		129.	Marinus II	942-946
92.	Stephen II	752-757		130.	Agapitus II	946-955
93.	Paul I	757-767		131.	John XII	955-964
	Constantine II	767-768		132.	Benedict V	964
	Philip	768				(resigned)
94.	Stephen III	768-772		133.	Leo VIII	964-965
96.	Adrian I	772-795		134.	John XIII	965-972
97.	Leo III	795-816		135.	Benedict VI	973-974
98.	Stephen IV	816-817			*Boniface VII*	974; 984-
99.	Paschal I	817-824				985
100.	Eugene II	824-827		136.	Benedict VII	974-983
101.	Valentine	827		137.	John XIV	983-984
102.	Gregory IV	827-844		138.	John XV	985-996
	John	844		139.	Gregory V	996-999
103.	Sergius II	844-847			*John XVI*	997-998
104.	Leo IV	847-855		140.	Sylvester II	999-1003
105.	Benedict III	855-858		141.	John XVII	1003
	Anastasius	855		142.	John XXIII	1003-1009
106.	Nicholas I the Great	858-867		143.	Sergius IV	1009-1012

144.	Benedict VIII	1012-1024
	Gregory	1012
145.	John XIX	1024-1032
146.	Benedict IX	1032-1045

(resigned) (Benedict appears three times as pope because he was twice deposed and restored.)

147.	Sylvester III	1045
148.	Benedict IX	1045
149.	Gregory VI	1045-1046 (resigned)
150.	Clement II	1046-1047
151.	Benedict IX	1047-1048
152.	Damasus II	1048
153.	Leo IX	1049-1054
154.	Victor II	1055-1057
155.	Stephen IX	1057-1058
	Benedict X	1058
156.	Nicholas II	1059-1061
157.	Alexander II	1061-1073
	Honorius II	1061-1072
158.	Gregory VII	1073-1085
	Clement III	1084-1100
159.	Victor III	1086-1087
160.	Urban II	1088-1099
161.	Paschal II	1099-1118
	Theodoric	1100-1102
	Albert	1102
	Sylvester IV	1105-1111
162.	Gelasius II	1118-1119
	Gregory VIII	1118-1121
163.	Callistus II	1119-1124
164.	Honorius II	1124-1130
	Celestine II	1124
165.	Innocent II	1130-1143
	Anacletus II	1130-1138
	Victor IV	1138
166.	Celestine II	1143-1144
167.	Lucius II	1144-1145
168.	Eugene III	1145-1153
169.	Anastasius IV	1153-1154
170.	Adrian IV	1154-1159
171.	Alexander III	1159-1181
	Victor IV	1159-1164
	Paschal III	1164-1168
	Callistus III	1168-1175
	Innocent III	1179-1181
172.	Lucius III	1181-1185
173.	Urban III	1185-1187
174.	Gregory VIII	1187
175.	Clement III	1187-1191
176.	Celestine III	1191-1198
177.	Innocent III	1198-1216
178.	Honorius III	1216-1227
179.	Gregory IX	1227-1241
180.	Celestine IV	1241
181.	Innocent IV	1243-1254
182.	Alexander IV	1254-1261
183.	Urban IV	1261-1264
184.	Clement IV	1265-1268
185.	Gregory X	1271-1276
186.	Innocent V	1276
187.	Adrian V	1276
188.	John XXI	1276-1277
189.	Nicholas III	1277-1280
190.	Martin IV	1281-1285
191.	Honorius IV	1285-1287
192.	Nicholas IV	1288-1292
193.	Celestine V	1294
194.	Boniface VIII	1294-1303
195.	Benedict XI	1303-1304
196.	Clement V	1305-1314
197.	John XXII	1316-1334
	Nicholas V	1328-1330
198.	Benedict XII	1334-1342
199.	Clement VI	1342-1352
200.	Innocent VI	1352-1362
201.	Urban V	1362-1370
202.	Gregory XI	1370-1378
203.	Urban VI	1378-1389
	Clement VII	1378-1394
204.	Boniface IX	1389-1404
	Benedict XIII	1394-1424
205.	Innocent VII	1404-1406
296.	Gregory XII	1406-1415

	Alexander V	1409-1410	235.	Gregory XV	1621-1623
	John XXIII	1410-1415	236.	Urban VIII	1623-1644
207.	Martin V	1417-1431	237.	Innocent X	1644-1655
	Clement VIII	1424-1429	238.	Alexander VII	1655-1667
	Benedict XIV	1424	239.	Clement IX	1667-1669
208.	Eugene IV	1431-1447	240.	Clement X	1670-1676
	Felix V	1439-1449	241.	Innocent XI	1676-1689
209.	Nicholas V	1447-1455	242.	Alexander VIII	1689-1691
210.	Callistus III	1455-1458	243.	Innocent XII	1691-1700
211.	Pius II	1458-1464	244.	Clement XI	1700-1721
212.	Paul II	1464-1471	245.	Innocent XIII	1721-1724
213.	Sixtus IV	1471-1484	246.	Benedict XIII	1724-1730
214.	Innocent VIII	1484-1492	247.	Clement XII	1730-1740
215.	Alexander VI	1492-1503	248.	Benedict XIV	1740-1758
216.	Pius III	1503	249.	Clement XIII	1758-1769
217.	Julius II	1503-1513	250.	Clement XIV	1769-1774
218.	Leo X	1513-1521	251.	Pius VI	1775-1799
219.	Adrian VI	1522-1523	252.	Pius VII	1800-1823
220.	Clement VII	1523-1534	253.	Leo XII	1823-1829
221.	Paul III	1534-1549	254.	Pius VIII	1829-1830
222.	Julius III	1550-1555	255.	Gregory XVI	1831-1846
223.	Marcellus	1555	256.	Pius IX	1846-1878
224.	Paul IV	1555-1559	257.	Leo XIII	1878-1903
225.	Pius IV	1559-1565	258.	Pius X	1903-1914
226.	Pius V	1566-1572	259.	Benedict XV	1914-1922
227.	Gregory XIII	1572-1585	260.	Pius XI	1922-1939
228.	Sixtus V	1585-1590	261.	Pius XII	1939-1958
229.	Urban VII	1590	262.	John XXIII	1958-1963
230.	Gregory XIV	1590-1591	263.	Paul VI	1963-1978
231.	Innocent IX	1591	264.	John Paul I	1978
232.	Clement VIII	1592-1605	265.	John Paul II	1978-2005
233.	Leo XI	1605	266.	Benedict XVI	2005-
234.	Paul V	1605-1621			

GLOSSARY

A.D. – Anno Domini, Latin term for "in the year of Our Lord," which counts the year of Christ's birth as Year One.

Albigensian heresy – a false teaching that flourished in the 12th and 13th centuries. It held that there were two opposing creators, one good and the other evil, that created the spiritual and material worlds. The Albigensians believed that all things of the world were evil, and all things of the spirit were good. Therefore, they believed that Christ did not have a real human body or that He is God. They did not believe in the resurrection of the body and rejected the sacraments.

Act of Supremacy - law of England's King Henry VIII that declared that the King, not the Pope, was the supreme head of the Catholic Church in England. The Act of Supremacy caused the final break with Rome. It was the beginning of the Anglican religion.

Acts of the Martyrs – Reports of the trials and deaths of the early Christian martyrs. These include official documents from the trials, eyewitness accounts, and writings from a later date.

Altar stone – a stone inserted into an altar that contains the relics of the saints. One relic must be a martyr's.

Anathema – Greek term signifying excommunication

Antichrist – Christ's chief enemy. The antichrist will lead vast numbers of people away from the Christian faith. The Antichrist will precede Our Lord's Second Coming at the end of the world.

Antipope – one who claims to be pope in opposition to the lawfully elected Pope

Apologists – early Church writers who defended the doctrines of the Church against the attacks of the pagans. They explained Catholic teachings. They showed that the arguments against the Church were false and unreasonable.

Apostate – one who completely leaves the faith of Christ to profess a non-Christian religion or none at all.

Apostolic Fathers – Writers of the first and second centuries. These writers personally knew the Apostles or their immediate successors. Others were so influenced by the Apostles that their writings are considered faithful echoes of the Apostles' teaching.

Arian heresy – the false teaching of Arius, a priest of Alexandria. He taught that God the Son was not equal to God the Father. He taught that Christ was not true God, but merely a creature more perfect than other creatures. St. Athanasius and the Council of Nicaea condemned Arianism in 325.

Ascetic – one who practices strict self-denial as a means of spiritual discipline and growth.

Assumption, Dogma of – the taking up into Heaven of the body and soul of the Blessed Mother. In 1950, Pope Pius XII declared this belief to be a dogma. This means it must be believed. Though this dogma was declared in 1950, the Church, from the time of the Apostles, believed in Our Lady's Assumption.

Augsburg Confession – document demanded by Emperor Charles V of the Lutherans which explained their teachings. It was delivered at the Diet of Augsburg in 1530.

Babylonian Captivity – the years from 1305 to 1370. During this period seven popes, from Clement V to Gregory VII, governed the Church from Avignon, France, instead of Rome. The name comes from the fact that the ancient Israelites were taken to Babylon. They were held captive there for seventy years, about the same time that the popes were in France.

Basilica – a title of honor given to certain churches. These churches have special historical or spiritual importance. Many are shrines and sites of pilgrimages. There are four major basilicas, all in Rome. There are about 1,600 minor basilicas around the world. As of the end of 2009 there are 66 basilicas in the United States.

B.C. – "Before Christ." The calendar method of counting years prior to the birth of Christ. 1 A.D. is preceded by 1 B.C.

Bull, Papal – a solemn and important form of papal letter.

Calvinism – the false belief system of John Calvin. It states that God absolutely predestines some to everlasting life and others to damnation. This untrue teaching contradicts the doctrine of free will.

Canon – a member of a body of clerics who live in community according to a rule of life. The canon's duty is to assist the bishop in the tasks of his office.

Canon law – the body of rules, laws, and decrees made by Church authorities for the government of the Church and its members.

Catechumen – a non-baptized adult who is taking classes to learn about the Faith so they can be baptized and received into the Church.

Chivalry – the system of medieval knighthood, with its religious, moral, and social code of honor. In return for a vow to fight virtuously in defense of the Faith, as well as of the weak and defenseless, the Church provided a ritual for the blessing and making of a knight.

Civil Constitution of the Clergy – law passed during the French Revolution. It made the Catholic Church subject to the State. It required the clergy to take an oath to the revolutionary government. It took away the rights of the clergy, abolished many dioceses, and seized and desecrated Church property. Priests and bishops who would not sign it were imprisoned.

Communism - A philosophy of life that is completely opposed to the Faith in almost every way. Communism teaches that there is no God and no afterlife. It teaches that there are no unchanging moral laws. It rejects freedom for individuals. People are simply the tools of the state. Under Communism people are told what to believe, where to go to school, where to work, etc. Communism was the worst evil to afflict the world in the 20th century. By the end of the 20th century, more Christians were martyred under Communism than at any other time in history. The popes have repeatedly condemned Communism.

Concordat – a treaty between the Holy See (the Vatican) and a secular nation.

Crusades – A series of wars whose goal was to deliver the Holy Land from the control of the Moslems. The Crusades were fought from 1095-1270.

Defenestration – to throw a person or thing out of a window.

Deism – the false belief that admits there is a Creator but rejects the notion that He is involved with His creatures. The example of a watchmaker, who constructs and winds his watch then forgets it, is the best way to describe the idea.

Diet – general assembly of the imperial princes of the Holy Roman Empire.

Dogma – a truth revealed by God and taught by the Church that must be believed.

Enlightenment – 18th century intellectual movement in Western Europe. It emphasized science and reason over religion and divine truths. It claimed that "superstition," that is, religion, especially Catholicism, had kept the light of truth away from human minds. However, now "the pure light of reason" had broken through and chased away the darkness that had been caused by religious faith. As a result men were "enlightened."

Ex cathedra – Latin term meaning "from the chair." It signifies the authoritative teaching and definitions given by the Pope. It is the term that is used when a pope speaks infallibly on a matter of faith or morals that is to be held as true by the all members of the Church.

Fatalism – the false teaching, which says that all events are fated to happen, so that human beings have no control of their lives. It is opposed to the doctrine of Free Will.

Feudalism – the legal and social society that existed in medieval Europe. Vassals held land from lords in exchange for military service.

Humanism – a movement of the 14-16th centuries. It sought to base all art and learning on the cultures of ancient Greece and Rome.

Hypothesis – an undeveloped or not fully worked out idea that is made in order to draw out and test its logical consequences; theory.

Iconoclasm – the heresy that teaches that it is unlawful to venerate holy images.

interregnum – Latin term meaning, "between the reigns." It is used to describe the time between the death of the reigning Pope and the election of the new Pope.

Islam – the false religion founded by Mohammed. It contains a mix of elements from the Jewish religion as well as those from the heretical Monophysites.

legate – a representative of the Pope who has a degree of his authority. For example, a papal nuncio.

Metropolitan – a bishop of a region whose position is superior to the bishops who are under him.

Modernism – heresy. Pope St. Pius X said it was the combination of all errors. Modernism questions the authenticity of the Scriptures and attacks the Sacraments. It reduces dogmas to personal opinions and rebels against the authority and disciplines of the Church.

Monophysite heresy – false teaching that believes there is only one nature in Christ. It denied His humanity.

Neophyte – converts who have received Baptism, but are new to the Faith.

Nepotism – From the Italian *nipote*, meaning nephew. The undue exercise of influence in favor of relatives, originating with popes who put their nephews in positions of importance.

Nestorian heresy – the false teaching of Nestorius, the patriarch of Constantinople. In 428 he said that no human being could be the mother of God. He developed the heresy by saying that Christ's humanity was only a "garment" which God put on.

Papal Primacy – the supreme and universal power, right, and authority of the Pope to govern and rule the Church. The primacy of Peter and the popes as his successors is chiefly proven by passages in the New Testament. See: Mt 16:15-19; Mk 3:16; Lk 22:31-2; Jn 1:42; Jn 21:15-17; Acts 2:14; 3:12, 4:8;Mk 16:7; I Cor 15:5; Gal 2:7; Acts 14:7-11, etc.

Patriarch – In the Eastern Church, a bishop who is over the authority of Metropolitans. In the West, the Pope is the only patriarch.

Pelagianism – 5th century heresy. It rejects original sin. It teaches Baptism is not necessary for removing original sin. It also teaches that supernatural grace is not necessary for salvation.

Philosopher – Someone who loves wisdom. A person who seeks to understand and explain the principles of existence and reality.

Photian schism – the breakaway of the Eastern Church after the appointment by the Byzantine Emperor Michael III of Photius as Patriarch of Constantinople in 857.

Primacy of honor – St. Peter's (and his successors) superiority over the other Apostles in terms of the respect and honor due him as their senior, which Christ conferred upon him (Mt 16:18).

Primacy of jurisdiction – the Pope's power to command, based on the authority that Christ conferred on Peter and his successors (Mt 16:18; Jn 21:16-21).

regent – one who takes the place of a ruler in governing a kingdom. A regent is appointed if the ruler is absent, disabled, or too young to rule.

Renaissance – rebirth. The change in the intellectual and moral outlook of Western Europe. It began in Italy in the 14th century and lasted until the 17th century. During this time the appreciation for the culture and lifestyle of the ancient Pagan cultures of Greece and Rome influenced art and architecture. Eventually it effected the morals of Christian society.

Rigorist – one who is very strict, or rigid, in following or applying a certain principle or practice.

Schism – a separation from the Church by refusal to recognize the authority of the Pope or refusal to be united to the members of the Church subject to him.

Scholasticism – the philosophy that flourished during the Middle Ages. It was based on the teaching methods of Aristotle and perfected by St. Thomas Aquinas. Aquinas drew from the teachings of the Church Fathers. He combined them orderly and concisely into a question and answer teaching method.

Sect – St. Paul and St. Peter in their Epistles, use the term to denote divisions in the Church (i.e., "quarrels, divisions, and sects" (Galatians 5:20). The Catholic Church cannot be considered a sect.

See – derived from the Latin word for "seat." Another word for the bishop's diocese.

Simony – the deliberate and sinful buying or selling of spiritual things, e.g. blessings.

synod – a Church council. Ecumenical, plenary, national, provincial, and diocesan councils are all synods.

INDEX

Mary Stuart (Queen of Scotland), 332-336.

Mary Tudor (Queen of England), 286, 288-291.

Maryland (colony), 324-326, 330.

Masaccio, 256.

Mecca, 110-111.

Melanchthon, Philip, 271.

Mendicant Orders, 214-215, 228, 261.

Merovingian dynasty, 113-114.

Methodius, St. (See also Cyril), 145-148.

Mexico, 319-320, 326-327, 457-459.

Michael III (emperor), 138, 146.

Michael Cerularius, 141-142.

Michelangelo, 259, 353-354.

Mieszko, Conversion of, 148-149.

Military Orders (see knights)

Miraculous Medal, 437-438.

Modernism, 447-449, 497.

Mohammed, 110-113, 496.

Monica, St., 73-74.

Monte Cassino, 92-94, 186, 230.

Moravians, Conversion of, 145-146.

More, St. Thomas, 277, 281, 286.

Muhlberg (battle), 273-274.

Muhldorf (battle), 241.

Munzer, Thomas, 269.

Murillo, Bartolome, 355-356.

Mussolini, 456-457, 463, 464.

Nantes, Edict of, 344.

Napoleon Bonaparte, 392-405.

Nazism, 460, 463-468.

Nepotism, 254, 497.

Nero, 21.

Nestorius and Nestorian Heresy, 75-76, 497.

Netherlands, 109, 261, 275, 346, 385.

Neumann, St. John (bishop of Philadelphia), 413-414.

New Mexico, 326.

Newman, John Henry (Cardinal), 428-430.

Nicene Creed, 57, 59, 65, 137.

Nobili, Father Robert de, 306.

Norbert, St., 191.

Norway, 144-145.

O'Connell, Daniel, 426-427.

Orders, Religious (See the individual Order's name)

Origen, 40, 44-45.

Original sin, Doctrine of, 54, 294-295, 367.

Ostrogoths, 83, 85, 87.

Otto I, the Great (German emperor), 169-171.

Otto II (German emperor), 172.

Otto III (German emperor), 172-173.

Oxford movement, 425, 427-429.

Palestine: Judaism in, 2; Moslem conquest of, 112.

Palladius (bishop), 94, 97-98.

Papal States, 430-433, 455-456.

Paraguay, 321-370.

Patrick, St., 94-100.

Paul, St. (Apostle), 2, 4, 9-16.

Peasants' War, 269-270.

Vikings (See also Danes), 101, 144, 152, 160, 169.

Visigoths, 83-85, 91, 112, 116.

Visitation Order (nuns), 351, 417.

Vladimir (Russian King), 152-154.

Voltaire, 368-370, 375.

Vulgate Bible, 72, 295.

Western Schism, 236-251.

Wilfrid, St., 106-109.

William of Orange, 345.

Willibald, St., 125-126.

Willibrord, St., 109, 120, 122.

Wiseman (cardinal), 429.

Wolsey (cardinal), 282-283.

World War I, 450-452.

World War II, 466-468.

Worms: Concordat of, 187; Diet of, 269-271;Edict of, 269-271.

Wyclif, John, 248-249.

Zwingli, Ulrich, 277-280.

ANSWER KEY

CHAPTER 1

1. Christ's Resurrection and the Descent of the Holy Spirit on Pentecost are the two great events that explain the success of the early Church.
2. He was one of the first seven deacons in the early Church
3. He baptized the Ethiopian.
4. The sin of buying or selling of spiritual things.
5. The story of Peter's vision and how he baptized Cornelius.
6. Jerusalem
7. The Council said that new Christians did not need to follow Jewish rituals and the Jewish law.
8. He preached to the City Council but only a few Athenians converted.
9. Ephesus was the home of the pagan temple of Diana, a pilgrimage site for pagans. The silversmiths in Ephesus made a great deal of money selling idols, particularly images of Diana and her temple. Christianity caused the silversmiths to lose business so they rioted and created such disorder that St. Paul had to leave.
10. St. John

CHAPTER 2

1. Peter was crucified upside down.
2. Paul was beheaded.
3. Because it was a religion that admired suffering and humility.
4. She was condemned to be suffocated by steam in her bathroom but she was miraculously saved. Then she was killed with the sword.

5. Someone who denies the Faith. The Church received the apostates back, but imposed severe punishments upon them. Many were forced to do penance until the end of their lives.
6. He was a deacon. He was roasted to death.
7. Nero, Domitian, Marcus Nerva, Trajan, Antoninus Pius, Marcus Aurelius, Septimius Severus, Maximinus, Decius, Valerian, Diocletian, Galerius, and Maximinus Daia. (need 5)
8. As the Good Shepherd.
9. The early Church said Mass on altars under which lay the bodies of the martyrs.
10. Relics of the saints and at least one martyr.

CHAPTER 3

1. Some of the Roman converts who heard Peter preach in Jerusalem at Pentecost may have brought Christianity to Rome. Roman soldiers in the Holy Land may have spread knowledge of the Faith when they returned to Rome. St. Peter may have visited Rome during the reign of Claudius between 41 and 44.
2. The Apostolic Fathers are authors who wrote toward the end of the first and the beginning of the second century. Some of them personally knew the Apostles or their immediate successors. Others lived so close to the time of the Apostles that we are certain to find in their words a faithful echo of the Apostle's teaching.
3. Partly to honor the miracle of the Resurrection which occurred on Sunday, and partly to show the Jewish

converts and the Roman pagans that the Jewish law did not bind Christians.

4. Primacy of honor would have conferred upon one Apostle merely superiority over the others in terms of the respect and honor due to him as their senior. Primacy of jurisdiction made him the head of the Church with supreme authority over all the other Apostles.

5. 1. The Church in Rome, the See of St. Peter, had first place among all the Churches. 2. St. Paul's Epistle to the Romans sets forth the most important truths relating to the Church and its Founder. The fact that he sent this important Epistle to the Romans, who, at the time, formed a very small community, argues strongly that he considered the Roman Church to be the head of all Christian Churches. 3. During the lifetime of St. John the Apostle, Pope Clement I intervened as arbiter in a quarrel that had arisen at Corinth. The Christians of Corinth did not regard the action of St. Clement as an intrusion.

6. An apologist is someone who defends the Catholic faith.

7. Lyons, in France

8. The Hexapla was a six-fold Bible. It contained in parallel columns six different translations of the Old Testament.

9. Tertullian wrote that the Church could not absolve Christians who had fallen into mortal sin.

10. The Edict of Milan imperial edict which granted religious tolerance to Christians.

CHAPTER 4

1. 1. The divine assistance that Christ promised to His Church. 2. The zeal of its missionaries and the saintly lives of its first converts. 3. The nature of Christianity which appealed to everyone. It maintained a definite set of beliefs. It championed virtues which appealed to the masses. It proposed a moral code loftier than any ever held. 4. The condition of the pagan world at the time which was in need of moral reform. Christianity offered the highest moral ideals. It offered a concept of a new social order. 5. The organization of the Roman Empire which allowed the travel of the early missionaries. Everyone in the Empire also understood them as everyone spoke Latin. 6. The unity of the Church's organization.

2. 1. The persistent opposition of the Roman emperors and other Roman authorities. 2. Christianity's attitude to other religions. Because Christians were intolerant of other creeds, that they were hated and despised. 3. Its Founder had suffered the humiliation of crucifixion. 4. The protection it afforded slaves. 5. The Christians' refusal to pay divine honors to the person of the emperor. 6. The false accusations circulated against it by the pagans.

3. The Arian heresy claimed that Jesus Christ was not God but only a man.

4. That Jesus Christ is True God, God from God, Light from Light, True God from True God, begotten, not made, of the same substance as the Father.

5. Emperor Constantius called the Council at Milan for the purpose of admitting the Arians into the Church.

6. St. Basil of Caesarea, St. Gregory of Nyssa, and St. Gregory of Nazianzus.

7. Gratian

CHAPTER 5

1. Constantinople
2. The Vulgate
3. North Africa
4. St. Ambrose
5. Hippo, in northern Africa
6. *The Confessions*
7. The sack of Rome
8. St. Anthony of Egypt and St. Paul of Thebes

9. A. A Metropolitan bishop is one whose position was superior to the others. B. In the East a number of provinces with their Metropolitans were placed under the authority of a "Patriarch."
10. One, the Pope.

CHAPTER 6

1. Emperor Valens
2. The Catholic episcopate and aristocracy represented the Roman Empire that the Vandals hated and the Vandals were fanatical Arians.
3. Pope St. Leo the Great
4. She was the first of the barbarian nations to become Catholic.
5. Obedience, patience, and charity
6. Armargh
7. St. Finian was the man most responsible in bringing about the great explosion of Irish monasticism.
8. Luxeuil
9. King Ethelbert of Kent
10. Canterbury

CHAPTER 7

1. An island monastery founded by St. Columba's monks
2. The date to celebrate Easter
3. Switzerland
4. St. Kilian
5. St. Willibrord
6. Mohammed
7. Fatalism
8. Mohammed's flight from Mecca to Medina
9. The Moslems defeated the Spanish and began their conquest of Spain.
10. 1. Excommunicated any master who killed his slave without the permission of the courts. 2. Proclaimed the lawfulness of the marriages of slaves. 3. Ensured that Christian slaves did not go to pagan masters.

CHAPTER 8

1. Pope Gregory III

2. It stopped the Moslem advanced into France and into the rest of Europe.
3. Fulda
4. St. Boniface
5. Twenty-two towns reconquered from the Lombards
6. He was elected under duress.
7. Pope Leo III
8. He was the head of the palace school at Aachen.

CHAPTER 9

1. It opposes the veneration of images.
2. Images, paintings, and sculptures were destroyed.
3. Breaking from the Church by refusing to recognize the authority of the pope.
4. After years of unrest between the Patriarchs of Constantinople and the Popes, Pope St. Leo IX ordered Patriarch Michael Cerularius to be obedient to papal authority. The pope sent Cardinal Humbert to Constantinople with orders to depose the patriarch if he persisted in his revolt. Humbert and Cerularius were unable to come to an agreement. Humbert excommunicated Cerularius and Cerularius excommunicated the Pope.
5. That the Holy Spirit did not proceed from the Father and the Son.
6. The Patriarch of Constantinople

CHAPTER 10

1. Ansgar was a Frankish monk determined to win the Vikings to Christ. He first preached the Faith in Denmark, and baptized its king. He returned to Germany and was appointed Archbishop of Hamburg. He went to Rome where Pope Gregory IV named him papal legate for the northern lands. He preached the Gospel in Sweden, where he established Gosbert as bishop. Since the missionaries did not receive the Frankish protection their work met

with a disastrous setback. The Vikings unexpectedly sacked Hamburg, destroying all the church's treasures and books. The Swedes killed bishop Gosbert.

2. He persuaded Leif Erikson to introduce Catholicism into Greenland.

3. They are the Apostles of the Slavs

4. St. Adalbert was martyred by the pagans of Prussia, to whom he had gone as a missionary. The King of Poland, Boleslav, purchased the saint's body from the Prussians and placed it in a tomb in the Church of the Blessed Virgin Mary at Gniezno, in Poland. This act pleased Otto III because St. Adalbert had been Otto's confessor when he came to the throne. The saint had deepened and strengthened Otto's Faith. When Otto made a pilgrimage to Gniezno to pray at the saint's shrine. With Papal permission, he established four new Polish dioceses under a metropolitan at Gniezno. This placed them outside German domination. He also he granted Poland political independence.

5. Bishop of Krakow martyred by Boleslav II.

6. Vladimir

7. When Boris was baptized, as was the practice of the time, he ordered that all his subjects also receive baptism. Two years later he sent an embassy to Rome asking Pope St. Nicholas I to send him a bishop and some priests.

8. When the great Hungarian military leader Geza converted to Catholicism

9. Esztergom

CHAPTER 11

1. A hierarchal system of protection

2. Feudalism was unfriendly to the Church. Kings claimed the right to give the bishop his power and authority by handing him the crosier, the symbol of his authority. They expected the bishop to take the oath of fealty and to present

them with a sum of money. This would make the bishop the king's vassal. The bishop would be under the king's authority, not only in civil matters, but in the spiritual government of his diocese. The payment of the money upon the bishop's appointment was another terrible problem. For the most part, kings were not interested in who was appointed bishop as long as he had enough money. Too often the office went to the highest bidder rather than the best man.

3. Pope Stephen V

4. In 961, Pope John XII appealed to King Otto of Germany for aid against the Roman aristocracy and the Lombards. Otto defeated the Lombards, assumed the crown of Italy, and triumphantly entered the city of Rome. As a gesture of gratitude for his services, John XII crowned him emperor.

5. Gregory V

6. Benedict XVI (as of the publication of this book)

7. Henry had received his early education at the monastery of Hildesheim. Later St. Wolfgang had taught Henry. Having been raised with a solidly Catholic background, Henry was a much more devout Catholic than his predecessors.

CHAPTER 12

1. St. Odo, St. Odilo, and St. Hugh

2. In honor of his friend and teacher, Pope Gregory VI

3. Lay investiture

4. Henry took off his shoes and dressed as a penitent. For three days he knelt barefoot in the snow outside the gates of the castle asking the Pope to forgive him.

5. The Romans felt that he was responsible for the Norman's sack of the city.

6. Pope Gregory VII

7. St. Bruno

8. St. Robert

Chapter 13

1. 1. The "Truce of God," which forbade fighting on Fridays, Saturdays, and Sundays, and during Advent and Lent. 2. She convinced the knights that it was cowardly to attack those who were weak and defenseless. 3. Chivalry
2. The ideals and principles according to which the true knight should live.
3. To deliver Jerusalem, the Holy Land, and the tomb of the Savior from the power of the Moslems.
4. The capture of Jerusalem and Antioch.
5. Urban II
6. Innocent III
7. Because they were warrior monks
8. The Knights of St. John of Jerusalem, the Knights Templars, and the Teutonic Knights.
9. By an outbreak of the plague in the army
10. 1. They kept the Turks from attacking Europe. 2. The ideals of the knights were uplifted and their lives ennobled. 3. The West became better acquainted with the East. 4. Explorers set out to discover better trade routes, and as a result of this, America was discovered.

Chapter 14

1. The Ghibelline was the emperor's supporter. The Guelph was the pope's supporter.
2. Frederick II
3. King John insisted on appointing his own choice as Archbishop of Canterbury despite the fact that the Pope had appointed Cardinal Stephen Langton.
4. The story of King Philip and his marriage to the Danish princess.
5. They rejected the humanity of Christ and the goodness of marriage and children. They encouraged suicide. It choked the joy out of living and made existence appear like a bad dream.

6. The Edict of Faith was an edict of the Inquisition addressed to the faithful and commanded them to denounce all heretics under pain of excommunication. The Edict of Grace was an edict of the Inquisition addressed to the heretics themselves. It summoned them to appear before the inquisitor.
7. St. Dominic
8. The Franciscans
9. For not leading a Crusade
10. Rudolf of Hapsburg

Chapter 15

1. The meetings of the Cardinals and the Pope.
2. The feast of Corpus Christi was established in Liege, Belgium, in 1246, as a result of revelations made to St. Juliana.
3. St. Anselm
4. Salerno for medicine, Bologna for law, and Paris for theology.
5. *The Summa Theologica*

Chapter 16

1. Philip wanted to tax the Church without Papal approval.
2. Historians have likened these seventy years to the Babylonian Captivity of the Jews. The popes resided at Avignon for about as long as the Jews were captives in Babylon.
3. Clement V
4. Third Order Dominican
5. Gregory XI
6. Because the Pope had not approved it.
7. His representatives had to convoke the council of Constance and authorize all its future acts.
8. Predestination
9. He refused to recant his errors so was burned as an obstinate heretic.

Chapter 17

1. Pope Nicholas V
2. The practice of putting papal relatives

513

into important positions in the Church in order to protect the papacy from its political enemies.

3. A Dominican friar from Florence. Savonarola was a very stern and holy man, who achieved extraordinary success as a preacher. His sermons reconverted the entire city of Florence, which had given itself over to the vices of the new culture. Pope Alexander VI attempted to silence him. Savonarola complied with the order to be silent but after obtaining permission to resume his preaching, violently denounced the corruption in the Church. He was again forbidden to preach, but this time refused to obey. As a result he was excommunicated, but continued to denounce the Pope. The government of Florence arrested him, tried him, condemned him for heresy (of which he was not guilty though schismatic), and burned him at the stake.

4. The fresco cycle which decorates the Scrovegni Chapel in Padua, commonly called the Arena Chapel.

5. Beato Angelico

6. Jan van Eyck, Roger van der Weyden, Hans Memling, and Quentin Massys

7. *Imitation of Christ*

CHAPTER 18

1. Greed among princes, discontent among the oppressed laboring classes, and paganism among the educated Renaissance scholars were the real causes of the Protestant Revolt. Scandals, abuses, and laxity among the clergy were not the primary causes.

2. Augustinian

3. As early as May 9, 1518, Luther wrote to a former teacher that he felt that "reform of the Church was impossible" and that the Church had to be "thoroughly uprooted." This is not the letter of someone who wants to reform the Church but rather a revolutionary

who wants to destroy it.

4. Luther's teaching that each person could interpret the bible according to his own judgment.

5. Pope Leo X

6. The Edict of German Diet which declared Luther an outlaw under sentence of death and condemned his heresies.

7. The summary of the of the Protestants' doctrinal views that Luther's friend Melanchthon presented at the Diet of Augsburg.

8. They formed the League as a defensive alliance against Charles V, however, the members quickly intended for the League to replace the Holy Roman Empire as a political entity. Protestantism was thus becoming more and more a political party, in which the civil ruler was the dominant factor.

9. Ferdinand and Isabel of Spain

10. The monastery at Yuste in Spain

CHAPTER 19

1. Ulrich Zwingli

2. The main difference had to do with Calvin's teaching concerning Predestination. According to Calvin, God directly created some people to go to heaven and other people to go to hell. Nothing that a person does in this life, good or bad, will make any difference. This dogma of absolute predestination constitutes the very essence of Calvinism.

3. The pope himself had granted a dispensation for them to marry.

4. He was a weak Pope. He "seemed constitutionally incapable of making a firm stand for anything."

5. Henry VIII's choice to be Archbishop of Canterbury, he supported Henry's divorce from Catherine of Aragon.

6. The Act of Supremacy completed the schism by making the King of England the Supreme Head of the Church

of England. The Act transferred all ecclesiastical power to the king. He in turn delegated it to the bishops, who were elected solely by him.

7. The Archbishop of Canterbury under Queen Mary Tudor

8. 1. Mary believed that only Spanish orthodoxy was sufficiently untainted to rid England of heresy. 2. Mary also believed that she needed the power of Spain to defend her against France and Scotland. 3. Mary believed that she could have a son who would succeed her on the throne of England, and, as a Catholic monarch, would keep England in the Church.

CHAPTER 20

1. Paul III

2. Luther, in his translation of the Bible, omitted certain parts, because they contained obvious contradictions of his new doctrine. The Council of Trent published a list of the books that make up the Bible. It declared that the Latin Bible, known as the Vulgate, is the only standard and authorized text. With regard to Scripture and Tradition, the Council defined that they are the two sources of divine revelation. On the question of private interpretation, it said that in matters of faith and morals no one may interpret the Scriptures contrary to the authoritative interpretation of the Church or the unanimous consensus of the Church Fathers.

3. The Council defined that original sin, transmitted to us from our first parents, is removed by the merits of Christ applied to each soul by the Sacrament of Baptism. However, a tendency to evil remains. The question of justification was the most fundamental point of Lutheran doctrine, which taught that a sinner is saved solely by trust in God, that is, justification by faith alone.

The Council said that we are justified by the saving merits of Christ, which effect an interior regeneration in men and women, and that people can, with the aid of God's grace, further their salvation by good works.

4. The Council reaffirmed the traditional Catholic doctrine of the Sacraments: their divine institution, nature, minister, and effects. The council also explained the personal dispositions required to receive them validly and fruitfully.

5. With regard to the Real Presence, the council wrote that anyone who denies that in the Sacrament of the Holy Eucharist that the body, blood, soul, and divinity of Jesus Christ are truly, really, and substantially contained, but maintains that they are there only as a sign or figure or virtually, is anathema.

6. 1. Restore Catholic education in Europe. 2. Evangelize the newly discovered lands. 3. Re-convert the Protestants. In their motto the Jesuits had pledged themselves to work ad majorem Dei gloriam (to the greater glory of God).

7. St. Francis Xavier

8. A Jesuit missionary in China

9. A Jesuit missionary in India

CHAPTER 21

1. 1. Pope Paul III 2. Pope Paul IV 3. Pope Pius IV 4. Pope St. Pius V 5. Pope Gregory XIII 6. Pope Sixtus V

2. *Disputations on the Controversies of the Christian Faith*

3. Milan

4. Catherine of Siena, Teresa of Avila, and Therese of Lisieux

5. It refers to the religious who did not wear shoes

6. St. Peter Canisius

7. St. Boniface

8. St. Philip Neri

9. Teaching

10. Angela Merici

CHAPTER 22

1. The appearance of Our Lady of Guadalupe
2. St. Rose of Lima
3. These were settlements composed entirely of Catholic Indians organized into small states with a spiritual leader as their governor. In the center of these villages was the church. The Jesuits taught the Indians to farm as well as to read and write. They set aside part of the land as the property of God. The whole community cultivated this land in order to provide against famine and to allow for the feeding of the sick and the aged.
4. Father Luis Cancer de Barbastro
5. Blessed Kateri Tekakwitha
6. Calvert
7. Maryland and Pennsylvania
8. Fr. Junipero Serra
9. It was chiefly Father Gibault's influence that made it possible for George Rogers Clark to achieve military victory in the Northwest Territory and secure it for the United States.
10. 1. John Barry 2. Charles Carroll 3. Thomas Fitzsimons 3. Daniel Carroll 4. Thomas Sim Lee

CHAPTER 23

1. The leader of the Protestant revolutionaries in Scotland
2. An attempt by some Catholics to blow up King James I and Parliament
3. Anti-Catholic dictator who ruled England, Scotland, and Ireland
4. He captured it and slaughtered its 3,500 citizens, including women and children.
5. James II
6. The ruler of France
7. An edict which guaranteed full liberty of conscience and toleration to the French Calvinists
8. William of Orange

9. She is the only European monarch who gave up her throne for the Faith
10. St. Peter's Basilica in Rome

CHAPTER 24

1. St. Louise de Marillac
2. Geneva, Switzerland
3. St. Jane Frances de Chantal
4. St. Margaret Mary Alacocque
5. 1. Michelangelo Merisi da Caravaggio 2. Peter Paul Rubens 3. Rembrandt 4. Diego Velazquez 5. Bartolomé Esteban Murillo 6. Nicholas Poussin. (need 3)
6. In May 1618, Emperor Ferdinand sent two Catholic representatives to Prague to administer the government in his absence. Bohemian rebels seized them and threw them out of the palace window, some fifty feet above the ground. They were miraculous saved when they landed in a pile of horse manure. It started the Thirty Years War.
7. An imperial edict which restored the Catholic Church properties taken since 1555, which, according to the Peace of Augsburg, were rightfully the possessions of the Catholic Church.
8. The Inquisition censured Galileo for advocating the sun-centered view of the universe as being contrary to Scripture. The ruling of the committee was disciplinary, not doctrinal. He was convicted not of heresy but of disobedience to his promise of 1616.
9. It does not disprove papal infallibility. Neither Pope Urban, nor any other Pope, ever declared or taught as a matter of Faith that Galileo's theory was heretical. Urban personally felt that it was not scientifically supported.

CHAPTER 25

1. Rationalism is the idea that the Church is not necessary, and that the human mind needed no guidance from Divine Grace. That human reason alone is enough.

2. According to the Deists, God exists but He has nothing to do with the world He created. After He made the world, He left it to itself and does not interfere in worldly affairs. God can be compared to a watchmaker, who makes a watch but then leaves it to run on its own.
3. Voltaire
4. The prime minister of Portugal and a great enemy of the Jesuits
5. These were forged letters, made by the prime minister of Spain, in which the Jesuits were accused of fomenting rebellion against the government in an attempt to overthrow the king. The prime minister wanted to suppress the Jesuits.
6. Pope Clement XIV
7. St. John Baptiste de la Salle

CHAPTER 26

1. A Revolution is the fundamental overturning and uprooting of the foundations of human society. The great enemy of Revolution is the Catholic Church, because Revolution puts Man in the place of God.
2. This document completely reorganized the Church in France. It granted all French citizens the right to elect bishops and pastors regardless of their religious affiliations. The priests were to have no say in the matter and the pope could not intervene in any way.
3. Those priests who would not take the oath to support the Civil Constitution of the Clergy.
4. The recluses were aged or infirm priests, who were herded together and imprisoned. The "deported" were priests who were driven in carts to various French ports. They were not actually deported because the British fleet kept too close a watch on the ports so they were detained in the hold of the ships where they died of hunger or suffocated. The condemned were those

who suffered outright martyrdom.
5. They refused to fight for a government that had murdered their King and was doing its best to destroy the Catholic Church.

CHAPTER 27

1. He prayed that the Faith would be restored in France; that the Pope would be restored to Rome; and that peace would be restored to Europe.
2. He hoped to use it to control the Church in France.
3. A decisive naval battle in which the British navy defeated the combined navies of France and Spain. The British victory permanently destroyed Bonaparte's naval power and any hope of invasion of Great Britain.
4. Pius VII felt that he could not refuse Napoleon and he hoped that he might gain some concessions from Napoleon.
5. Napoleon annexed the Papal States.
6. Napoleon imprisoned the Pope.
7. Pius VII

CHAPTER 28

1. John Carroll
2. a. The Church grew naturally as children were born to Catholic parents. b. Catholics made converts to the Faith. c. There were a large number of Catholics coming to America from Catholic countries.
3. John Neumann
4. *The Faith of Our Fathers*
5. Italy
6. Sisters of Charity
7. Indiana
8. Immigrants
9. So that parents could send their children to schools where the Catholic Faith was taught.

CHAPTER 29

1. Count Chateaubriand, Henry Lacordaire, Joseph de Maistre, Robert

Lamennais, Rene Montalembert, Alphonse Lamartine
2. Munster, Landshut, Munich, and Cologne
3. Daniel O'Connell
4. John Henry Newman
5. Wiseman, Newman, and Manning
6. Pius IX
7. Solemnly defining papal infallibility
8. These laws sought to transform bishops and priests into state officials and to bring the seminaries under state control.
9. Penance
10. That alone of all human beings who have ever lived, except for Jesus, Adam, and Eve, Mary was conceived without the stain of original sin.

CHAPTER 30

1. Just labor practices and duties.
2. That it is a natural right of man.
3. To restore all things in Christ.
4. People could receive more frequently and children could now receive.
5. a. It taught that supernatural truths could not be known with certainty by human reason. b. It taught that Scripture and Tradition do not contain revelations from God, but merely depict the feelings and inner experiences of extremely religious people. c. It taught that Jesus Christ had not instituted Church, her dogmas, and moral standards. Rather her dogmas and morality are the result of a gradual evolution and they can change and the Church will be forced to change to other standards over time.
6. a. He encouraged charitable organizations of every kind in their task of easing the suffering and famine. b. He created a bureau of communication for prisoners of war to assist in locating those who had disappeared. c. He was able to bring about the exchange of the more seriously wounded prisoners.

d. He condemned the cutting off of food supplies from the starving people of Central Europe. e. He begged the faithful in neutral countries to give him money which he used to feed the starving people of Europe and care for needy children everywhere. (need three)

CHAPTER 31

1. Pius XI showed how Christian marriage and the family are the foundations for any good society. He taught that parents have the power and the right to educate their children. This power comes from the sacramental graces of Matrimony.
2. The rebellion of the Catholics against the Communist government in Mexico
3. He felt that written treaties were the best way to protect the Church's rights.
4. The Italian government recognized the independence of the Holy See and its supreme authority over Vatican City. The Treaty marked the end of the separation of Church and State in Italy. The Treaty made Catholicism the state religion. It required that the Catholic Faith be taught in all primary and secondary schools. Catholic organizations received full recognition. Catholic marriages were legalized. All clerics and religious were removed from the jurisdiction of the civil courts.
5. a. In September 1945, the general secretary of the World Jewish Council presented an award to the pope "in recognition of the work of the Holy See in rescuing Jews from Fascist and Nazi persecutions." b. In the fall of 1945, Harry Greenstein from Baltimore, a close friend of Chief Rabbi Herzog of Jerusalem, told Pius how grateful Jews were for all he had done for them. c. On February 13, 1945, the chief rabbi of Rome, Israel Zolli was baptized a Catholic and chose as his Christian name "Eugenio" in gratitude to the

Pope who had done so much for the Jews during the War. His wife and daughter also became Catholics.

6. It is the Communist-controlled Chinese "Catholic" church.

7. That the "Immaculate Mother of God, having completed the course of her earthly life, was assumed body and soul into heavenly glory." In this dogmatic statement, the phrase "having completed the course of her earthly life," leaves open the question of whether Our Blessed Lady died before her Assumption, or, whether she was assumed without death. Both possibilities are allowed. Mary's Assumption was a divine gift to Mary as Mother of God.

CHAPTER 32

1. Pope John XXIII
2. It forbids artificial birth control.
3. The procreation and education of children.
4. St. Peter, Blessed Pius IX, and John Paul II
5. John Paul II
6. This movement eventually brought freedom and human rights to Poland.
7. A Polish Cardinal who fought Communism. He was a good friend of Pope John Paul II.
8. To bring young Catholics from all over the world together to celebrate the Faith.
9. That the Western (Roman) Church and the Eastern Orthodox Churches need to become one church again.
10. To promote and safeguard Catholic doctrine throughout the world.